Organization Theory

Organization Theory
STRUCTURES, SYSTEMS, AND ENVIRONMENTS

WILLIAM M. EVAN
University of Pennsylvania

A WILEY-INTERSCIENCE PUBLICATION

JOHN WILEY & SONS, New York • London • Sydney • Toronto

Library of Congress Cataloging in Publication Data:

Evan, William M.
  Organization theory.

  "A Wiley-Interscience publication."
  Includes bibliographical references and indexes.
    1. Organization. 2. Social role. 3. Organiza-
tional change. 1. Title.

HM131.E9   301.18′32   76-22742
ISBN 0-471-01512-1

Printed in the United States of America

10 9 8 7 6 5 4 3 2

For SARAH

Preface

Even without the benefit of a futurologist's crystal ball, it is safe to predict that organization theory will continue to be a burgeoning field in the 1980s and, very likely, even in the year 2000. The reasons for this are not hard to discern. The problems of designing and managing large, complex organizations in the private as well as in the public sector are baffling, pervasive, and urgent. And the intellectual challenge of modeling diverse organizations is so considerable that it will continue to attract the interest of members of a variety of disciplines to this field.

How, for example, does one justify various types and degrees of hierarchical differentiation in light of increasing claims for participation in decision making and for a greater degree of equality? How does one reconcile the demand for organizational effectiveness with what Barnard calls "organizational efficiency," that is, with the capacity to satisfy the personal expectations of members sufficient to induce their participation?[1] How does one construct general measures of organizational performance essential for both comparative research on organizations and "organizational audits"? How does one measure the impact of different types of environments on an organization, and vice versa? These are but a few of the critical problems that will continue to challenge future generations of organization theorists as well as organization practitioners charged with the responsibility of managing the affairs of business, governmental, educational, religious, and other kinds of organizations.

During the past 15 years, in the course of conducting organizational

---

[1] Chester I. Barnard, *The Functions of the Executive* (Cambridge, Mass.: Harvard University Press), pp. 56 ff, 92 ff, 240.

research, I have written several dozen articles, some theoretical and some empirical. Sixteen of these articles are collected in this volume because they revolve around a threefold theme of hierarchical structures, systemic interrelations, and environmental effects.

Hierarchy is a virtually universal mechanism for achieving coordination and control in organizations. In the chapters in Part I, I examine the theoretical assumptions underlying hierarchical designs, some problems of measuring hierarchy, the functional prerequisities for transforming administrative organizations into voluntary organizations, and the consequences of hierarchy for work alienation, organizational commitment, and organizational effectiveness.

The pervasiveness of hierarchical designs in organizations generates role strains as well as conflicts among members. In Part II, I consider problems of role strain in relation to various structural properties of organizations and the tendency of members of react in a conformist manner to the expectations of superiors. The differential distribution of authority and power in organizations tends to give rise to conflicts between superiors and subordinates. In Chapter 7 I develop the concept of "organizational constitutionalism" and present some evidence of a trend toward the constitutionalization of organizations that may have the effect of reducing role strains and resolving some hierarchically induced conflicts. If the problems associated with "organizational lag"—that is, a discrepancy in the rate at which new technical and administrative ideas are implemented in an organization—are to be solved, programs of planned change guided by an experimental perspective will be required.[2]

The chapters in Part III seek to model the complex boundary relations among organizations. The mechanism of hierarchical differentiation, indispensable as it appears to be in managing the internal relations of organizations, is of no avail when organizations interact with other organizations in their environment. Instead, mechanisms of exchange, coalition formation, competition, conflict, and the like are called into play.[3] In Chapter 9 an organization is conceptualized as a system engaged in various exchanges and interactions with other organizations in its environment. These patterned linkages constitute an "interorganizational system" and affect the inputs, internal structures, processes, and the outputs of the focal organization. The "organization-set" model is applied in Chapter 10 to the problems of defining, measuring, and changing "organizational climate". And in Chapter 11 the model is reformulated and applied in an analysis of the regulatory impact of federal administrative agencies.

[2] William M. Evan, "Editor's Postscript," in William M. Evan, ed., *Organizational Experiments* (New York: Harper and Row, 1971), p. 263.
[3] See William M. Evan, ed., *Interorganizational Relations: Selected Readings* (London: Penguin Books, 1976).

Since interorganizational linkages do not exhaust the influences of the environment on any given organizational system, it is necessary to go beyond this type of environmental impact to what I call in Part IV "transorganizational environments." The legal system of any modern society consists, on the one hand, of a complex of norms embodied in statutes, judicial decisions, and administrative actions, and on the other hand, of specialized personnel and agencies performing executive, legislative, adjudicative, and enforcement functions. The functioning of the "public legal system" engenders the development of homologous "private legal systems" within the population of private organizations in a society. The interaction of public and private legal systems, as I point out in Chapter 12, results in mutual changes and in significant effects on the society as a whole. This is particularly the case as regards the functioning of a multitude of administrative agencies in the nation-state. In Chapter 13 I try to build a bridge between administrative law and organization theory which, hopefully, will prove beneficial to both fields.

More inclusive than the legal system is the culture of the society at large, namely, the corpus of norms and values that impinge on the behavior of members of any organizational system as well as on the texture of its interorganizational relations (see Chapter 15). Multinational corporations operating in different cultural contexts (see Chapter 14) have become increasingly sensitive to the potential impact of the culture of a host country on organizational effectiveness.

Another type of environmental effect has its source in the social structure, that is, in the network of social relationships of a society (see Chapter 16). Every member of an organization, by virtue of his simultaneous participation in various institutional spheres of a society (namely, familial, economic, educational, religious, political, etc.) has a "status-set."[4] Mapping the status-sets of different categories of members of an organization, particularly the occupants of boundary roles and major decision-making roles, is but one way of ascertaining social-structural effects. Membership in an international professional association, a type of organization analyzed in Chapter 14, is an example of an attribute of a status-set that transcends societal boundaries and that can serve as an important channel of information for an organizational system.

Underlying the 16 chapters in this book is a systems-theoretic model of organizations that may be summarized in a concentric circle diagram shown in the accompanying figure. The innermost circle represents an organizational system, the design of which may vary along many dimensions, especially as regards types and degrees of hierarchical differentiation of its role structure. Surrounding this system is an interorganizational system that consists of a com-

---

[4] Robert K. Merton, *Social Theory and Social Structure,* rev. ed. (Glencoe, Ill.: The Free Press, 1957), pp. 380–84.

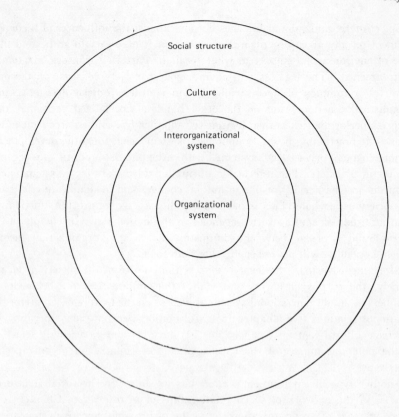

plex of organizations with which the focal organization has sustained relations. Impinging on the interorganizational system as well as on the organizational system is the culture of the society as a whole. The outermost circle, the social structure of the society, in turn affects the culture, the interorganizational system as well as the organizational system.

Operationalizing and measuring the dimensions of each of the circles in this model and then measuring their relationships to organizational effectiveness[5] will surely challenge the ingenuity of organizational researchers for years to come. If the present volume contributes to this ongoing intellectual adventure, it will have served its purpose.

WILLIAM M. EVAN

Swarthmore, Pennsylvania
December 1975

[5] William M. Evan, "Organization Theory and Organizational Effectiveness," *Organization and Administrative Science* 7 (1976): 15–28.

Acknowledgments

I wish to thank the publishers listed below for permission to reprint the following papers:

Chapter 1   "Indices of the Hierarchical Structure of Industrial Organizations," *Management Science* 9 (April 1963): 468–77.

Chapter 2   "Some Functional Prerequisites for a Voluntary Industrial Organization" ("Les conditions fonctionnelles d'existence d'organizations industrielles voluntaires"), *Sociologie du Travail* 5 (Juillet-Septembre, 1963): 237–46.

Chapter 3   "Hierarchy, Alienation, Commitment, and Organizational Effectiveness," *Human Relations,* 1976 (in press)

Chapter 4   "Role Strain and the Norm of Reciprocity in Research Organizations," *American Journal of Sociology* 68 (November 1962): 346–54.

Chapter 5   "Organization Man and Due Process of Law," *American Sociological Review* 26 (August 1961): 540–47.

Chapter 6   "Superior-Subordinate Conflict in Research Organizations," *Administrative Science Quarterly* **10** (June 1965): 52–64.

Chapter 7   "Power, Conflict, and Constitutionalism in Organizations," *Social Science Information* **14** (1975): 53–80.

Chapter 8   "Organizational Lag," *Human Organization* **25** (Spring 1966): 51–53.

Chapter 9   "The Organization-Set: Toward a Theory of Inter-Organizational Relations," in James D. Thompson, ed., *Approaches to Organizational Design* (Pittsburgh: University of Pittsburgh Press, 1966), pp. 175–90.

Chapter 10   "A Systems Model of Organizational Climate," in Renato Tagiuri and George H. Litwin, eds., *Organizational Climate: Explorations of a Concept* (Boston, Mass.: Division of Research, Graduate School of Business Administration, Harvard University), pp. 107–24.

Chapter 11   "An Organization-Set Model of Interorganizational Relations," in M. F. Tuite, M. Radnor, and R. K. Chisholm, eds., *Interorganizational Decision-Making* (Chicago: Aldine Publishing, 1972), pp. 181–200.

Chapter 12   "Public and Private Legal Systems," in William M. Evan, ed., *Law and Sociology* (New York: The Free Press of Glencoe, 1962), pp. 165–84.

Chapter 13   "Administrative Law and Organization Theory," *Journal of Legal Education* **29** (in press).

Chapter 14   "Multinational Corporations and International Professional Associations," *Human Relations* **27** (1974): 587–625.

Chapter 15   "Culture and Organizational Systems," *Organization and Administrative Sciences* **5** (1975): 1–16.

Chapter 16   "Social Structure and Organizational Systems," *Organization and Administrative Sciences* **7** (in press).

W. M. E.

Contents

Organization Theory

PART ONE

Hierarchical Structures

The pyramid as a model of organizations has long captured the imagination of managers as well as theorists of organizations. Whether the metaphor harks back to the early history of armies, empires, or organized religion is still unclear. However, it is evident that the imagery of a pyramidal organization is so widespread that organizational hierarchy tends to be regarded as inevitable. Some would even consider it an iron law—no less coercive than Michels' "iron law of oligarchy"—which, if violated, results in severe penalties to the organization in question. In a recent study comparing the perceptions of control in a sample of enterprises in five different countries (Italy, Austria, Yugoslavia, the Israeli Kibbutz, and the United States), the authors conclude that "authority and influence are . . . inevitably hierarchical in the work organization, egalitarian ideology notwithstanding."[1]

The three chapters in Part I are concerned with three principal questions: How can organizational hierarchy be conceptualized and measured? What are the causes and consequences of organizational hierarchy? Under what conditions is the degree of organizational hierarchy reduced? In Chapter I three dimensions of the hierarchy of industrial organizations are identified: hierarchy of skills, hierarchy of authority, and hierarchy of rewards. In addition, several hypotheses are formulated concerning the causes and consequences of organizational hierarchy. In Chapter 2 two models of organization are distin-

1

guished: the administrative organization, Weber's ideal-typical bureaucracy which is hierarchical in structure; and the voluntary association, a collegial type of organization relatively unhierarchical in structure. Social scientists have repeatedly noted the tendency for voluntary associations to be transformed into administrative organizations. What about the reverse transformation? What are the necessary preconditions for administrative organizations to be transformed into voluntary organizations? In Chapter 2 six hypothetical preconditions are advanced: (1) the extension of the ideology of egalitarianism from the political to the economic institutional sphere; (2) the reduction of the range of occupational differentiation as a result of technological developments; (3) the growth of "informal organization" encroaching on managerial decision-making prerogatives; (4) the professionalization of management; (5) the professionalization of labor; and (6) the objectification of authority. Whether these particular prerequisites are valid—and some may not be—is not as important as the underlying question: Under what conditions is the degree of organizational hierarchy diminished?

In Chapter 3 a sequel to Chapter 1, which I wrote over a decade later, I introduce a fourth dimension of organizational hierarchy: hierarchy in the distribution of organizational information. Also included in this chapter is a causal model interrelating organizational hierarchy with three other variables: work alienation, organizational commitment, and organizational effectiveness. By measuring the degree of hierarchical differentiation in organizations, it is possible to test the widely held assumption that organizational hierarchy promotes organizational effectiveness, that is, that the two variables are positively related.

The problems of organizational hierarchy are bound to concern managers as well as organization theorists for many years to come—in capitalist and socialist countries alike.[2] New models are being formulated to counteract some of the dysfunctions of organizational hierarchy. For example, Ackoff's model of a "circular organization" is "intended to maximize opportunities for relevant participation by its members, to maximize the extent to which the organization serves the purposes of its members, and, by so doing, better serves its own purposes."[3] The ongoing industrial democracy experiments in Western Europe and the "self-management" systems of Yugoslavia and other countries may be interpreted as groping efforts to diminish the degree of organizational hierarchy.

NOTES

1. Arnold Tanenbaum, Bogdan Kavčič, Menachem Rosner, Mino Vianello and Georg Wieser, *Hierarchy in Organizations* (San Francisco: Jossey-Bass, 1974), p. 209.

2. Cf. Daniel Bell, *The Coming of Post-Industrial Society* (New York: Basic Books, 1973), p. 80.

3. Russell L. Ackoff, *Redesigning the Future* (New York: Wiley-Interscience, 1974), pp. 50–53.

CHAPTER 1

Indices of the Hierarchical Structure of Industrial Organizations

Is there an "iron law of organizational hierarchy"? A postulate common to both organization theory and to the structural-functional theory of social stratification is that hierarchical organization is functionally necessary. An alternative formulation of this postulate—which is probably more heuristic—is that different degrees of hierarchical organization have different consequences for total and partial social systems. Unlike the functional-necessity postulate, which takes hierarchy as a "given" and as a universal "iron law," the modified postulate directs attention to the problem of empirically establishing what degree of variation in fact exists in the hierarchical structure of organizations.[1]

In order to inquire into this question—say, in industrial organization as one type of formal organization—it is, of course, necessary to have measures of hierarchical structure. If, with the aid of such measures, organizations are found to exhibit considerable variation in the degree of hierarchy—as seems likely—it would make possible a study of (1) the causes and organizational

This is a revised version of a paper presented at the Fourth World Congress of Sociology in Stresa, Italy, September 1959.

consequences of the degree of hierarchy; (2) the direction and degree of change of this structural property of industrial organizations; and (3) the degree of hierarchy among different types of organizations and in different societies. The purpose of this chapter is to develop and document some indices of the hierarchical structure of industrial organizations that might facilitate this line of inquiry.

SOME INDICES OF HIERARCHICAL STRUCTURE

Of central importance to organization theory and to theories of social stratification is the problem of differential allocation of tasks, rewards, and authority. How tasks are allocated affects goal attainment; how rewards are allocated affects motivation of personnel and commitment to organizational goals; and how authority is allocated affects integration, coordination, and communication in an organization. For our purpose we will consider nine possible indicators of these three structural dimensions: two for the hierarchy of skills, one for the hierarchy of rewards, and six for the hierarchy of authority. This skewed distribution of indicators reflects, in part, the relative complexity of the three structural dimensions. Where possible, these indicators will be illustrated with comparative data drawn from the literature of industrial sociology.

HIERARCHY OF SKILLS

Perhaps the most critical structural variable in terms of its organizational consequences is the hierarchy of skills. The measurement of skill presents various complexities. One possible measure that is deceptively simple is the length of time spent in relatively formal training—in-plant and/or out-plant—of the manual and nonmanual occupations comprising a factory. In the limiting case an organization has a set of specialized tasks all equivalent in degree of skill or a single homogeneous task performed by all personnel. This type of division of labor would represent a zero degree of hierarchical differentiation of skills.

Several possible shapes of skill distributions of the work force of factories may be identified: for example, a normal curve, a negatively skewed distribution, a positively skewed distribution, a multimodal curve, a U-curve, and a rectangular distribution. In the absence of empirical investigation and pertinent theoretical propositions, the organizational consequences of these and other possible distributions are not apparent. We may conjecture, though, that a rectangular distribution probably signifies a relatively low degree of skill differentiation. The skill classes—as measured, for example, by training time—in the case of a rectangular distribution have an equal proportion of employees; or the ratios of the relative frequencies in adjacent skill classes is 1 : 1. The degree of deviation from such a distribution might prove to be a measure of the degree of hierarchical differentiation of skills.

Another indicator of this dimension of hierarchy is the spread of the percentage distribution of skill or training-time levels. The interquartile range or the difference in the number of skill or training-time levels between the upper 5 percent and the lower 5 percent of the distribution—which may be more appropriate for the problem at hand—would yield a measure of the hierarchy of skills in a single industrial organization or a sample of industrial organizations.

HIERARCHY OF REWARDS

The second structural variable, the hierarchy of rewards, has been traditionally accorded more weight than the hierarchy of skills. Inequality of rewards is a recurrent source of industrial conflict—which is not to say that equality of rewards does not give rise to conflict.[2] The most readily quantifiable measure of the hierarchy of rewards in a factory is, of course, a comparison of the salaries and wages received by people in different statuses. This measure has the disadvantage of omitting fringe benefits and a great variety of perquisites which, in the case of executives, may amount to more than the base salary. Two simple ratios, nevertheless, crudely register the degree of inequality of rewards: the ratio of maximum-minimum earnings or range of earnings in a factory that is, the ratio of the salary of the general manager or president of a factory to the average wage of a worker in the lowest skill category; and the salary ratios of adjacent statuses such as foremen/workers and supervisors/foremen.

Unfortunately, data on earnings of the gamut of occupational categories of a factory have rarely been reported in the literature.[3] In the British Glacier Metals Company the maximum-minimum earning ratio is 20 : 1.[4] In two Yugoslav factories—a textile mill and an electrical motor plant—that I visited in 1959, the maximum-minimum earning ratios were 4 : 1 and 6 : 1, respectively. About Japanese factories in general, we are told that the "difference between managers' and workers' wages as paid in cash is not large"; and in a Japanese metal-processing firm the ratio of earnings of "average staff employees" to "average laborers" is 1.15 : 1.[5]

Given access to wage and salary data—preferably data including the value of prequisites and fringe benefits—for a sample of factories, Lorenz curves could be drawn showing the relationships between the relative size of an occupational or status category and its share of the total earnings. The area between the Lorenz curve and the 45 degree line of equality would provide a measure of the degree of hierarchy of rewards in a factory.

HIERARCHY OF AUTHORITY

The third hierarchical dimension, the structure of authority, is multifaceted. It consists of a body of institutionalized statuses and decision-making rights that range from those vested in top management to those vested in foremen and non-supervisory rank-and-file employees. Because of the inherent complexity of the structure of authority, the six indicators to be presented, although quantitative in character, are crude and imprecise.

The first of these indicators is the "span of control"—a well-known managerial concept.[6] Since the span of control may vary from echelon to echelon, different measures might be obtained such as the ratio of foremen/workers, supervisors/foremen, or division managers/department managers.[7] In a comparison of an American and a German steel plant—virtually identical in size, product, and work force—Harbison and his colleagues found a 1:15 foreman/worker span of control in the American steel plant as compared with a 1:50 ratio in the German counterpart—certainly an impressive difference.[8] The Du Pont Company has even a higher foreman/worker ratio of 1:10 and a supervisor/engineer ratio of 1:7.[9]

The second indicator of authority is simply the number of levels of authority, from top management to workers. How many levels of authority are engaged in making, interpreting, or implementing various decisions? In the Du Pont Company, which has 90,000 employees, there are said to be 13 echelons; in a Japanese radio-communication equipment plant employing about 3,000 persons, there are nine levels; and in the Endicott plant of IBM with a work force of over 7,000, there are four levels.[10] It is doubtful whether the number of echelons is merely a function of organization size, although how much it is related to size obviously awaits research.[11]

A third indicator of authority is Melman's ratio of administration to production, which unlike the span of control takes the entire organization as a unit of analysis instead of a subunit.[12] The administrative component of this ratio includes staff and line as well as their supportive personnel, such as clerical employees. In the automobile industry, for example, the variation in this ratio is considerable. It ranges from 1:3 in the Ford Motor Company, 1:4 in Firm X in Britain, 1:5 in Renault, 1:6 in the Standard Motor Company in England, to 1:10 in Volkswagen.[13]

A fourth indicator of the hierarchy of authority is what Elliott Jaques has called the "time-span of discretion," which he defines as the maximum length of time an employee is authorized to make decisions on his own initiative that commit a given amount of the resources of the organization.[14] What is the ratio of maximum-minimum time-span of discretion from the manager of a factory to the worker in the lowest skill category? Is it larger or smaller than 10 years/one hour, as Jaques found in the Glacier Metals Company in England? This ratio might also be obtained for adjacent statuses, such as foremen and workers, foremen and supervisors, or departmental managers and the general manager.[15]

The fifth indicator of the hierarchy of authority is the degree of centralization in decision making. At what level of authority are certain classes of decisions made? For example, policy making with regard to labor relations may be centralized at the top managerial levels or it may be decentralized at the middle and junior management levels; or the authority to purchase capital equipment or to grant salary increases may be centralized or decentralized. By definition, the degree of decentralization is greater the lower the managerial level at which a given class of decisions is made.[16] In the few empirical studies of this facet of authority, the one by Baker and France of 135 American companies found a highly centralized pattern of decision making about labor relations policies.[17]

The sixth and final indicator of the hierarchy of authority is the degree of limitation on the rights of management to make decisions. One mechanism for limiting authority in the legal system is the complex of norms called "procedural due process of law." These are procedural safeguards incorporated in the judicial institutions of legal systems that ensure a fair and impartial trial, thus limiting the decision-making authority of the courts. Such norms as the right to notice of hearing, the right to confront witnesses and to cross-examine them, and the right to introduce evidence on one's behalf have partially and gradually diffused from the sphere of legal institutions to the sphere of economic institutions. In industrial organizations they have been institutionalized in the form of a grievance procedure with arbitration as the final stage of conflict resolution.[18] Manual workers employed under a labor-management collective bargaining agreement have been granted the right to appeal the decisions of their superiors through the grievance machinery.

An indicator of this aspect of the hierarchy of authority is the number of echelons for which procedural due process of law has been institutionalized. If it is confined to the lowest echelon, namely, to manual workers, it obviously represents a lower degree of limitation of executive authority than if it encompasses more than one echelon, namely, clerical workers, technical personnel, foremen, supervisors, and junior and middle managers.[19]

One of the few discussions of this aspect of authority in the literature of industrial sociology is found in Jaques' study of the Glacier Metals Company.[20] In that company all employees have the right of appeal to successive stages of executive authority and eventually to the chief executive. And even decisions of the chief executive are subject to appeal to an outside independent tribunal. The latter provision is of critical importance, for otherwise the appeals system augments the authority of higher management over lower management. Jaques does not present data about the functioning of this system of appeals other than to observe that the channels for appeals are often used and that "the appeals system has removed the fears of gross injustice which are so common in industry."[21]

EMPIRICAL APPLICATION OF STRUCTURAL INDICES

Some or all of these measures of hierarchical structure can be used, with differing degrees of difficulty, in an empirical study of a sample of industrial organizations. Their use would make possible the answering of as yet unanswered questions about the structure of industrial organizations.

INDEX CONSTRUCTION

Three indices, each measuring a different aspect of hierarchy, or possibly one composite index—in the unlikely event that the three dimensions of hierarchy are independently related—could be constructed, using such measurement techniques as Guttman scaling, latent structure, or some simple weighting scheme. If the reward hierarchy were indexed by a single indicator, it would of course not pose a problem of index construction. However, the multiple indicators of skill hierarchy and of authority hierarchy would pose a problem. An index of authority might be constructed in one of several ways. For example, one procedure would be to test whether the six indicators form a cumulative pattern approximating the Guttman scale model.

Of special interest would be the profiles of a sample of industrial organizations on the three structural indices. The relative position of the organizations on the three indices would provide information as to the degree of hierarchical consistency. Some organizations in the sample may have consistently high or consistently low scores on the three indices, whereas others may have a combination of high and low scores. Ordering a sample of organizations according to the degree of hierarchical consistency is analogous conceptually and procedurally to ordering individuals according to the degree of status consistency.[22] Thus hierarchical consistency is an additional dimension of the hierarchical structure of factories. It raises new problems for inquiry, for example, do industrial organizations with hierarchically inconsistent profiles—such as high relative position with respect to the skill hierarchy and low relative position with respect to the authority and reward hierarchies—tend to move toward consistency. If so, through what processes does this occur?

ANALYSIS OF STRUCTURAL CHANGE

With the aid of three indices or a single composite index it would be possible to study such problems as the direction and degree of change in hierarchical structure over time. This, of course, would entail gathering data for at least two time periods for each of the industrial organizations in a sample. In short, this would require a "panel" study of a sample of factories.[23] Short of such longitudinal research, some inferences regarding change in the hierarchical structure may nevertheless be drawn from a cross-sectional study. For example, if the indicators of the authority hierarchy were to form a Guttman scale, a rank order correlation of the authority scores by age of factories might be tentatively interpreted as representing different stages in the evolution of the structure of authority.[24] For some of the indicators of hierarchy, especially the authority dimension, no secular trends may be found. Instead, cyclical trends may be observed, for example, from centralization of decision making to decentralization and thence to recentralization.

ANALYSIS OF CAUSES AND CONSEQUENCES OF HIERARCHICAL STRUCTURE

The degree of hierarchical structure can be treated as a dependent or as an independent variable. If it is treated as a dependent variable, the following factors might be explored as possible sources of variation in the degree of hierarchical structure: size of organization, age of organization, degree of mechanization, product diversity, degree of competition or monopoly of the industry from which the sample of factories is drawn, type of ownership (i.e., corporate, nationalized, cooperative, individual, partnership, family enterprise, etc.), level of industrialization of the country in which the factories are located, degree of cooperation in labor-management relations, and the degree of emphasis on equality as a cultural value.

If the hierarchical structure is treated as an independent variable, the following consequences of variation in degree of organizational hierarchy might be considered: level of productivity; rate of profit; rate of growth of organizational norms; growth of diverse types of organizational norms; degree of commitment to organizational goals or degree of organizational loyalty; level of morale as measured, for example, by labor turnover, absenteeism, accident rates; and rate of social interaction between and within the status categories of an organization.

With a set of such hypothesized causes and consequences of variation in the degree of organizational hierarchy, it is possible to develop empirically testable hypotheses, particularly of the types Lazarsfeld calls "conditional relations" and "contextual propositions."[25]

Let us consider two illustrative hypotheses. First, the degree of organizational hierarchy is negatively correlated with productivity when labor-management relations are fraught with a high level of conflict, but this correlation is zero or positive when the level of labor-management conflict is low. Second, the degree of organizational hierarchy is negatively correlated with productivity in oligopolistic or monopolistic industries, but this correlation is zero or positive in competitive industries. In these two illustrations the unit of analysis is the organization, and the effect of the degree of organizational hierarchy depends on the structural context of the organizations in question. Moreover, a variable other than degree of hierarchical structure acts as the qualifying variable: In the case of the first hypothesis it is the degree of conflict in labor-management relations; in the second hypothesis it is the degree of competition within the industry. Let us now consider an hypothesis in which the hierarchical structure is the qualifying variable and the other two variables do not characterize organizations but individuals in the organizations. For example, if length of employment in an organization and commitment to its goals are positively related, it may be conjectured that as the degree of hierarchical structure increases this relationship diminishes.

All three propositions thus far presented involve conditional relations, that is, they specify the conditions under which a relationship between two variables exists. We turn now to a contextual proposition in which at least one of the three variables in question pertains to both individuals and organizations. Hierarchical consistency, as we have seen, is a measure of an organization's relative position on the three structural indices. Correspondingly, status consistency measures the relative position of an individual on the hierarchies of skills, rewards, and authority.[26] If we hypothesize that commitment to the organizational goals decreases as the degree of status consistency decreases—and some empirical research makes this a plausible hypothesis—does a decrease in hierarchical consistency intensify or diminish this positive relationship?[27]

COMPARATIVE STUDY OF HIERARCHICAL STRUCTURE

A major qualifying variable affecting the impact of organizational hierarchy is the social and cultural structure of the society in which the organizations in question are embedded. We have already alluded to the possible differential effect on the degree of organizational hierarchy of the level of industrialization of a society and of the degree of emphasis on equality as a cultural value. This suggests the need for cross-national research, quite apart from the general importance of developing uniformities in sociology that transcend a particular society or culture. In addition, the paucity of relevant data in various countries, as we noted in our preliminary review, makes such cross-national research desirable.

Through the cooperation of interested sociologists in different countries, comparable studies could be designed and conducted of the hierarchical dimension of industrial organizations and conceivably of other types of formal organizations, too, such as universities, hospitals, and the like. Such an inquiry might be organized along lines similar to the survey of teachers' attitudes in seven

Western European countries conducted in 1953 under the direction of the Organization for Comparative Social Research.[28]

Another form of comparative research would be cross-organizational in character, that is, comparisons of the hierarchical structures of different kinds of organization (e.g., industrial, educational, military, etc.) More feasible, if not always more significant, than either type of field study are laboratory experiments simulating the hierarchical status relations in factories. Generalizations yielded by such experiments might help to refine those stemming from field studies.[29]

SUMMARY AND CONCLUSION

To recapitulate the rationale and substance of this chapter: We modified the functional-necessity postulate of hierarchy underlying both organization theory and the structural-functional theory of social stratification with the assertion that different degrees of hierarchical organization have different consequences for total and partial social systems. This led us to inquire into the problem of measuring the degree of hierarchical structure of industrial organizations. Three central dimensions of organizational structure were selected: the hierarchy of skills, the hierarchy of rewards, and the hierarchy of authority. For each dimension an attempt was made to develop and document one or more indicators. The question of the empirical application of the indicators of the hierarchical dimensions in turn led us to consider some problems of index construction, analysis of structural change, analysis of causes and consequences of variation in degree of organizational hierarchy, and of comparative research, whether cross-national, cross-organizational, or experimental in character.

The explicit or implicit acceptance of an "iron law of hierarchy" is premature in view of the dearth of evidence on the structure of organizations.[30] In the absence of systematic inquiry, many critical questions remain unanswered, such as whether the advance of industrialism inevitably leads to an increase in organizational hierarchy or whether there are counterforces at work tending to reduce the degree of hierarchy. The significance of this question obviously transcends national boundaries. Comparative research on the degree of hierarchical structure of industrial organizations would add to our practical and theoretical knowledge of organizations as well as of systems of social stratification.

NOTES

1. For a discussion of the span and shape of systems of social stratification, see Bernard Barber, *Social Stratification* (New York: Harcourt, Brace and Co., 1957), pp. 87–93. See also a

related discussion of the degree of social stratification of groups or organizations in Robert K. Merton, *Social Theory and Social Structure,* rev. ed. (Glencoe, Ill.: The Free Press, 1957), p. 315.

2. See Elliott Jaques, *Measurement of Responsibility* (Cambridge, Mass.: Harvard University Press, 1956); S. M. Lipset and Martin Trow, "Reference Group Theory and Trade Union Wage Policy," in Mirra Komarovsky, ed., *Common Frontiers of the Social Sciences* (Glencoe, Ill.: The Free Press, 1957), pp. 381–411.

3. For an approximation to adequate reporting of earnings of different occupational categories, see, for example, W. H. Scott *et al., Technical Change and Industrial Relations* (Liverpool: Liverpool University Press, 1956), pp. 195–96, 297–98.

4. Computed from data in Jaques, *Measurement of Responsibility,* p. 53.

5. James G. Abegglen, *The Japanese Factory* (Glencoe, Ill.: The Free Press, 1958), pp. 62–63. The ratio is computed from data presented on p. 52.

6. See, for example, V. A. Graicunas, "Relationship in Organization," in Luther Gulick and L. Urwick, eds., *Papers on the Science of Administration* (New York: Institute of Public Administration, 1937), pp. 183–187; J. L. Meij, "Human Relations and Fundamental Principles of Management," in E. M. Hugh-Jones, ed., *Human Relations and Modern Management* (Amsterdam: North-Holland Publishing Co., 1958), pp. 2–17; Waino Suojanen, "The Span of Control—Fact or Fable," *Advanced Management* 20 (November 1955): 5–13; Lyndall T. Urwick, "The Span of Control—Some Facts About the Fables," *Advanced Management* 21 (November 1956): 1–11.

7. See Mason Haire, "Biological Models and Empirical Histories of the Growth of Organizations," in Mason Haire, ed., *Modern Organization Theory* (New York: John Wiley & Sons, 1959), pp. 293–97.

8. Frederick II. Harbison, Ernest Köchling, Frank H. Cassell, and Heinrich Reubmann, "Steel Management on Two Continents," *Management Science* 2 (October 1955): 34.

9. Personal communication from an official of Du Pont.

10. *This Is Du Pont* (Wilmington, Del.: 1958), pp. 8, 29; John B. Knox, *The Sociology of Industrial Relations* (New York: Random House, 1955), p. 178; Abegglen, *Japanese Factory,* p. 81; F. L. W. Richardson, Jr. and Charles R. Walker, *Human Relations in an Expanding Company* (New Haven, Conn.: Yale University Labor and Management Center, 1948), pp. 14–15.

11. For an incisive analysis of the relation between size, shape, and function of an organization, see Mason Haire, "Biological Models and Empirical Histories," pp. 272–306.

12. Seymour Melman, *Dynamic Factors in Industrial Productivity* (Oxford: Basil Blackwell, 1956), pp. 69–94. For a critical evaluation of Melman's A/P ratio, see George E. Delehanty, *An Analysis of the Changing Proportion of Nonproductive Workers in U. S. Manufacturing Industries,* Massachusetts Institute of Technology: Unpublished Doctoral Dissertation, 1962, pp. 83–98.

13. Seymour Melman, *Decision Making and Productivity* (Oxford: Basil Blackwell, 1958): Ford Motor Company, p. 175; Firm X in Britain, p. 128; Standard Motor Company, p. 128; Volkswagen, p. 199; Alan Touraine, *L'Evolution du travail ouvrier aux Usines Renault* (Paris: Centre National de la Recherche Scientifique, 1955), p. 165.

14. Jaques, *op. cit.,* p. 23.

15. For related data regarding the frequency of contacts between the general manager and departmental managers, see Scott *et al., Technical Change and Industrial Relations,* pp. 98–99.

16. Ernest Dale, "Centralization versus Decentralization," *Advanced Management* 21 (June 1955): 11.

17. Helen Baker and Robert R. France, *Centralization and Decentralization in Industrial Relations* (Princeton, N. J.: Princeton University Industrial Relations Section, 1954), pp. 195, 201.

18. See, for example, Joseph Lazar, *Due Process on the Railroads* (Los Angeles: University of California, Institute of Industrial Relations, 1953); William M. Evan, "Power, Bargaining, and Law: A Preliminary Analysis of Labor Arbitration Cases," *Social Problems* 7 (Summer 1959): 5–16.

19. Cf. William M. Evan, "Organization Man and Due Process of Law," *American Sociological Review* 26 (August 1961): 540–47; and "Due Process of Law in Military and Industrial Organizations," *Administrative Science Quarterly* 7 (September 1962): 187–207.

20. Elliott Jaques, *The Changing Culture of a Factory* (London: Tavistock Publications, Ltd., 1951), pp. 53, 61–62, 325–26.

21. *Ibid.*, p. 63. For some data on the appeals system at Glacier Metals Company, see Wilfred Brown, *Exploration in Management* (New York: John Wiley & Sons, 1961), pp. 250–73.

22. "Status consistency" refers to the degree of consistency or inconsistency in the scores or rankings of an individual on some dimensions of one or more of his statuses. See, for example, George C. Homans, *Sentiments and Activities: Essays in Social Science* (New York: The Free Press, 1962), pp. 91–102; Gerhard E. Lenski, "Status Crystallization: A Non-Vertical Dimension of Social Status," *American Sociological Review* 19 (August 1954): 405–13; Irwin W. Goffman, "Status consistency and Preference for Change in Power Distribution," *American Sociological Review* 22 (June 1957): 275–81.

23. For the importance of studying the developmental dimension of organizations, see Peter M. Blau, "Formal Organization: Dimensions of Analysis," *American Journal of Sociology* 67 (July 1957): 67–69.

24. For two recent applications of Guttman scaling involving a developmental interpretation, see Stanley Udy, Jr., "'Bureaucratic' Elements in Organizations: Some Research Findings," *American Sociological Review* 23 (August 1958): 415–18; Linton C. Freeman and Robert F. Winch, "Societal Complexity: The Empirical Test of a Typology of Societies," *American Journal of Sociology* 62 (March 1957): 461–66.

25. Paul F. Lazarsfeld, "Problems in Methodology," in Robert K. Merton, Leonard Broom, and Leonard S. Cottrell, Jr., eds., *Sociology Today: Problems and Prospects* (New York: Basic Books, 1959), pp. 67–73.

26. It should be noted that the indicators of the authority dimension comprising a measure of "status consistency" would necessarily differ in some respects from those comprising a measure of "hierarchical consistency." In particular, only three of the six indicators of authority could be transformed into a measure of "status consistency," namely, number of levels of authority, span of control, and time-span of discretion.

27. See Goffman, "Status Consistency and Preference for Change."

28. See, for example, S. Rokkan, "An Experiment in Cross-National Research Cooperation: The Organization for Comparative Social Research," *International Social Science Bulletin* 7 (No. 4, 1955): 645–52; also "Cross-National Research: A Case Study," *Journal of Social Issues* 10, no. 4 (1954).

29. See, for example, Harold Guetzkow and Anne E. Bowes, "The Development of Organizations in a Laboratory," *Management Science* 3 (July 1957): 380–402; William M. Evan and Morris Zelditch, Jr., "A Laboratory Experiment on Bureaucratic Authority,"

American Sociological Review 26 (December 1961): 883–93; Morris Zelditch, Jr. and William M. Evan, "Simulated Bureaucracies: A Methodological Analysis," in Harold Guetzkow, ed., *Simulation in Social Science: Readings* (Englewood Cliffs, N. J.: Prentice-Hall, 1962), pp. 48–60.

30. Kenneth E. Boulding, *The Organizational Revolution* (New York: Harper and Bros., 1953), p. 79. See also Julie Meyer, "Hierarchy and Stratification of the Shop," *Social Research* 14 (June 1947): 169–90.

CHAPTER 2

Some Functional Prerequisites for a Voluntary Industrial Organization

A principal emphasis of functionalism in sociology, as in other social sciences, has been on "requisites" or necessary conditions for the persistence of an ongoing social system. Logically and empirically this approach to functionalism is defective. As Merton has pointed out, it tends to be tautological in attributing a necessary function to that which exists, and static in its preoccupation with the "survival" of a social system.[1]

An alternative mode of functional analysis is concerned with the "functional needs for determinate types of change" by examining pressures, contradictions, and tendencies in an ongoing social system.[2] This mode of inquiry might be called—following, in part, Levy's usage—functional "prerequisite" as distinct from functional "requisite" analysis.[3] The relationship between these two modes of functional analysis remains to be explored. Whether, for example, prerequisites are merely "functional alternatives" to requisites or whether they represent entirely new functions is a problem that transcends the scope of this

This is a revised version of a paper presented at the annual meeting of the American Sociological Association in Washington, August 1957.

chapter. The purpose of this chapter is to inquire into some functional pre-requisites for the transformation of industrial organizations from their present administrative structure into a potential voluntary structure.

FUNCTIONAL REQUISITE ANALYSIS OF FORMAL ORGANIZATIONS

In the study of formal organization, whether in the industrial management or in the Weberian tradition, functional requisite analysis is fairly common. To be sure, all formal organizations have such functional requirements as recruiting personnel, securing financial resources, and establishing normative justifica-tions for organizational decisions. However, the types of functional require-ments alleged to be true of all formal organizations are cast in the form of prescriptive "principles": for example, Fayol's "unity of command" and "unity of direction"; Hamilton's "span of control"; and Mooney and Reiley's "scalar" and "functional" principles of organizations.[4] In setting forth prescriptive prin-ciples of organizations, these and other students of this tradition tend to generalize their experiences and reflections to all formal organizations.[5] Likewise some students of Weber apply his model of bureaucracy to all large, complex organizations, taking his characteristics of a bureaucratic organization as requirements *by definition* for efficiency.[6]

Important as is the effort to generalize about all formal organizations, the type of universal generalizations referred to, however, neglects an important distinction among types of formal organization, a distinction that Weber himself called attention to, namely, the difference between a formal organiza-tion that is administrative or bureaucratic in structure and one that we might call voluntary in structure.[7]

TWO MODELS OF ORGANIZATION

These types of organization are polar ends of a scale of bureaucratization. An administrative organization for present purposes may be defined as one in which control is formally hierarchical and coordination is achieved through the exercise of formal authority based on scalar status or authority of office.[8] A voluntary organization, ideal-typically, is one in which control is not hierarchical but collegial and consensual in nature, and authority is based on functional status or authority of knowledge.[9]

In an ideal-typical voluntary industrial organization, the bulk of the occupa-tions are professional, in the process of professionalization or near-professional in character. Coordination of such occupations is achieved principally through the delineation of spheres of competence and jurisdiction. Obviously, such a pat-tern of interoccupational relations does not guarantee organizational harmony, for conflicts over spheres of competence and jurisdiction persist. However, the chances of authoritarian control coming to the fore are considerably reduced because claims for superordination are neutralized by the norms of self-government of professional or professionalizing occupations. Prototypical cases of such an organization are a university faculty and a medical clinic. The professional mode of organization, exemplified in these types of organization, radically departs in its authority structure from Weber's model of a bureaucratic organization.[10] As Parsons has incisively observed:

. . . Professional services are often, indeed increasingly, carried out in complex organizations rather than by independent individuals. There is , however, considerable evidence that when this is the case there are strong tendencies for them to develop a different sort of structure from that characteristic of the administrative hierarchy which Weber has, in most respects, classically described in his discussions of bureaucracy. Instead of a rigid hierarchy of status and authority there tends to be what is roughly, in formal status, a "company of equals," and equalization of status which ignores the inevitable gradation of distinction and achievement to be found in any considerable group of technically competent persons. . . . It is probable that Weber's neglect to analyze professional authority is associated with a tendency to overemphasize the coercive aspect of authority and hierarchy in human relations, in general, important as it is in particular cases.[11]

The general distinction between a voluntary association and an administrative organization has been made previously, although not in the terms just presented.[12] In fact, sociologists ever since the writings of Michels have been impressed with the tendency for voluntary associations to be transformed into administrative organizations.[13] So profound has Michels' influence been that an exception to his iron law of oligarchy was the occasion for an outstanding study of the International Typographical Union by Lipset, Trow, and Coleman.[14]

What of the reverse of this trend, that is, the transformation of an administrative organization into a voluntary organization? Leaving aside the polemical literature on industrial democracy, sociologists, with rare exceptions, have not attended to this question.[15] However, by raising the question of the prerequisites for a voluntary industrial organization we may discover a considerable degree of diversity of types of industrial organization and pressures and counterpressures for social change.

SIX PREREQUISITES FOR THE TRANSFORMATION OF INDUSTRIAL ORGANIZATIONS

The six prerequisites to be discussed were identified principally with the aid of the model of a voluntary association. They will not be examined as observable trends but rather as hypothesized necessary conditions for a structural change in industrial organization. They are in order of mention: (1) the extension of the ideology of egalitarianism from the political to the economic institutional sphere; (2) the reduction of the range of occupational skills due to technological advances; (3) the growth of informal organization that encroaches on managerial decision-making prerogatives; (4) the professionalization of management; (5) the professionalization of labor; (6) the objectification of authority.

THE EXTENSION OF THE IDEOLOGY OF EGALITARIANISM

A cultural prerequisite is the extension of the ideology of egalitarianism in Western societies from the political to the economic institutional sphere. In spite of the interrelatedness of these two institutional spheres, the dominant value underlying the functioning of one is not the same as that of the other. Formal equality before the law and formal democracy are characteristic of political institutions whereas formal inequality and formal authoritarian control are predominant in the economic sphere. A closer integration of the two institutional spheres would mean the emergence of norms of economic citizenship paralleling the institutionalization of norms of political citizenship.[16] In the absence of such a measure of integration, role discontinuities and alienation from work are engendered. Citizenship status in the world of politics is in marked contrast to the alien status, so to speak, occupied by a large proportion of employees in their occupational relationships. The growth of trade unionism and its doctrines, such as the "right to a job," exert pressure for integration of these two institutional spheres.[17] Through the grievance machinery established in collective bargaining agreements, trade unions have in effect transplanted the norms of procedural due process of law from the legal system to the industrial organizations, so much so that this doctrine has tended to diffuse to some nonunionized employees in industry.[18]

REDUCTION OF THE RANGE OF OCCUPATIONAL SKILLS

Unlike the first prerequisite, which deals with a factor external to industrial organization, the second focuses on an internal organizational prerequisite. Technological change in industry is pervasive, rapid, planned, and unplanned. In the past, technological change in industry has been associated with simplification and standardization of operations as much as with occupational specialization. This pattern need not necessarily continue in the future, for technical complexities of production may require further specialization which may, however, be accompanied by the elimination, of some standardized procedures. Thus it may be possible to "engineer out" low skilled jobs of manual workers as well as some jobs currently performed by junior and middle managers.[19] A reduction in the range of occupational skills could conceivably be accompanied by a reduction in reward differentials and social distance among occupational statuses.

GROWTH OF INFORMAL ORGANIZATION

The discrepancy in dominant values beteeen the political and economic institutional spheres, as well as the ubiquitous occupational threat posed by technological change, generates a wide assortment of informal relationships at all levels in the hierarchy of the industrial organization. Only those types of informal relationships that encroach upon the official decision-making system of an organization are considered here. Such unofficial practices as job rotation and restriction of output augment the security, autonomy, and work satisfaction of employees. This reservoir of norms of informal organization is a source of new official norms regulating the relations between labor and management. Such norms tend to increase the rights of employees vis-à-vis management. Although the content of this type of informal organization is constantly changing, its existence and growth may be an impetus for the transformation of industrial organization.

THE PROFESSIONALIZATION OF MANAGEMENT

The increasing employment of professionally trained personnel in industrial organizations is but one meaning of the term "professionalization of management." A second and related meaning is the increasing recruitment of salaried managers in contrast to the entrepreneur in the era prior to corporate organizations. Both of these meanings are relevant for the sense in which we shall use the term.

If the professional role *minimally* requires an abstract body of knowledge and skills and a collectivity orientation designed to protect the client and to safeguard the autonomy of the profession, then these characteristics suggest some of the requirements of the professionalization of the complex of occupations called "management."[20] The decision-making processes of management of industrial organizations would have to be given a scientific foundation. If and when this occurs, a much greater degree of functionalization and decentralization of management than presently exists would be necessary.[21] Training skills for scientific managers would require, among other things, a knowledge of procedures for resolving incompatible demands made by the different status groups comprising management's role-set, namely, employees, investors, consumers, government officials and so on. The articulation of these conflict-resolving procedures and principles would comprise the code of ethics of the professionalized occupations of management. Moreover, management's technical *coordination* function would have to be separated from its *control* function, not unlike the separation of ownership and control that has occurred with the rise of business corporations. Such a separation of traditionally integrated functions requires the development of processes of decision making based in part on the allocation of authority according to spheres of competence and in part on the consent of those affected by decision, rather than on authoritarian procedures and on the engineering of consent. An integral part of this coordinative function, which would serve to legitimize its authority, is the mediation of conflicting jurisdictional claims. The application of the concept of due process of law by management in the settling of disputes, which inevitably arise among members of different occupations, would give it a quasi-judicial function, thus adding to the legitimacy of management occupations.

PROFESSIONALIZATION OF LABOR

Similarly, if labor is to move in the direction of a quasi-profession or a profession—and Foote contends that this process is under way—it would undergo a change in its functions and in its relationships to management and the public.[22] With routinized work largely eliminated as automation progresses, the task of operating and maintaining complex equipment would require an order of knowledge, skills, and judgment akin to that of highly trained technicians and engineers.[23] An increase in authority and responsibility would flow from this change in functions, which in turn would require a transformation in the concept and function of supervision in industry. Such changes would require that trade unions become more similar in their non-economic functions to professional societies, that is, in advancing occupational skills and knowledge and in improving services to the public.

OBJECTIFICATION OF AUTHORITY

With the professionalization of labor and management occupations, a paradoxical change occurs in their respective positions of authority: To the extent that management is professionalized, it loses its hegemony; and to the extent that labor is professionalized, it gains in authority. The source of authority thereby shifts from a scalar to a functional type. Authority of technical knowledge rather than authority of office is institutionalized, which in effect means the merging of line and staff organization. Expert or functional authority is exercised except where policy questions arise that depend largely on value judgments rather than on technical knowledge, in which case it gives way to consensual or democratic authority. As the personnel of industrial organizations shifts increasingly in the direction of professional or quasi-professional occupations, the authority system—based primarily on technical knowledge and the impartial adjudication of conflicts over incompatible values—becomes more objective and rational.

The foregoing six functional prerequisites are necessary, although perhaps not sufficient, conditions for the transformation of industrial organizations in the direction of a voluntary structure. Some factors, such as type of ownership, have been omitted from consideration because they are deemed neither necessary nor sufficient conditions for a voluntary industrial organization.

RESEARCH IMPLICATIONS

What is the empirical import of this organizational analysis? In the first place, the six prerequisites require investigation to ascertain whether in fact they are trends and what their consequences are for the organizational structure of industry. Of special importance in this connection are studies of industrial organizations which would examine the impact of varying degrees of automated technology on organizational structure. Second, this analysis may provide a framework for research on industrial and nonindustrial organizations. For instance it follows from this analysis that it is of critical importance to study the authority structure of industrial research organizations that have a much higher ratio of professional/nonprofessional personnel than manufacturing organizations. Is the industrial research organization with a high ratio of professional/ nonprofessional employees closer to the type case of a voluntary industrial organization than the manufacturing organization with a low ratio? Third, to test the relationship between such organizational variables as the degree of equality of occupational skills and the type of authority relations, it is necessary to supplement comparative organizational field studies with laboratory and field experiments. For example, a laboratory experiment with several groups interrelated in the performance of a task, some equal and some unequal in skills, would lend itself to a study of the effect of this variable on the type of authority relations that obtain. Are the authority relations in groups with equal skills more autonomous and functional than those in groups with unequal skills? If so, this would give some weight to the hypothesis that the professionalization of labor and management are prerequisites for a voluntary industrial organization. Along with such laboratory experiments (which in reality are studies in formal organization rather than in small groups), field experiments on the structure of authority similar to the experiment by Morse and Reimer, are greatly needed, although the practical difficulties are formidable.[24]

Laboratory and field experiments also serve a specially strategic function with regard to the analysis of functional prerequisites. Whereas the study of functional requisites involves observing existing institutions, functional prerequisites may be studied not only speculatively and theoretically but also with the aid of experimental procedures, whether in the laboratory or in the field. Organizational analogues can be created in the laboratory for testing the effect of novel and alternative social structures. These in turn can be further tested in limited real-life settings within organizations.

By undertaking organizational studies in a functional *prerequisite* rather than in a functional *requisite* framework, industrial sociologists will not only advance our knowledge of the dynamics of industrial organizations but also contribute to the study of social changes in general.

NOTES

1. Robert K. Merton, *Social Theory and Social Structure,* rev. ed. (Glencoe, Ill.: The Free Press, 1957), pp. 52, 122.

2. Robert K. Merton, "Discussion of Parsons' Position of Sociological Theory," *American Sociological Review* 13(1949): 167.

3. Marion J. Levy, Jr., *The Structure of Society* (Princeton: Princeton University Press, 1952), pp. 43–45, 71–76.

4. Henri Fayol, *General and Industrial Management,* trans. Constance Storrs (New York: Pitman Publishing Corp., 1949), pp. 24–26; Ian Hamilton, *The Soul and Body of an Army* (London: Edward Arnold and Co., 1921), pp. 229–30. See also V. A. Graicunas, "Relationship in Organization," in Luther Gulick and L. Urwick, eds., *Papers on the Science of Administration* (New York: Institute of Public Administration, 1937), pp. 183–87; James D. Mooney and Alan C. Reiley, *Onward Industry* (New York: Harper, 1931), Chs. 4 and 5.

5. Mooney and Reiley, *Onward Industry,* pp. ix, 18, 341: "Our approach to the subject of industry through other forms of human association has been rendered necessary by our primary thesis, that there are certain basic and fundamental principles of organization. As such, these principles must be universal and invariable wherever human organization appears." Also Fayol, *General and Industrial Management,* pp. xv., xxi; Chester I. Barnard, *The Functions of the Executive* (Cambridge: Harvard University Press, 1938), pp. 6–7.

6. Max Weber has encouraged this general adaptation of his ideal type by such remarks as, "This type of organization [bureaucratic] is in principle applicable with equal facility to a wide variety of different fields. It may be applied in profit-making business or in charitable organizations, or in any number of other types of private enterprises serving ideal or material ends. It is equally applicable to political and to religious organizations. With varying degrees of approximation to a pure type, its historical existence can be demonstrated in all these fields." *The Theory of Social and Economic Organization,* trans. A. M. Henderson and Talcott Parsons (New York: Oxford University Press, 1947), pp. 334.

7. Cf. Weber, *Theory of Social and Economic Organization,* pp. 151–52, for a discussion of "voluntary" and "compulsory" associations.

8. See Chester I. Barnard, "Functions and Pathology of Status Systems in Formal Organizations," in William F. Whyte, ed., *Industry and Society* (New York: McGraw-Hill Book Co., 1946), p. 49.

9. *Ibid.,* p. 48; William M. Evan and Morris Zelditch, Jr., "A Laboratory Experiment on Bureaucratic Authority," *American Sociological Review* 26 (December 1961): 883–93.

10. Cf. Roy. G. Francis and Robert C. Stone, *Service and Procedure in Bureaucracy* (Minneapolis: University of Minnesota Press, 1956), pp. 153–67; Walter I. Wardwell, "Social Integration, Bureaucratization, and the Professions," *Social Forces* 33(1955): 356–59.

11. Weber, *Theory of Economic and Social Organization,* "Introduction," pp. 59–60, n. 4: also Talcott Parsons, "Suggestions for a Sociological Approach to the Theory of Organizations—II," *Administrative Science Quarterly* 1(1956): 236–37. For a related discussion, see Alvin W. Gouldner, *Patterns of Industrial Bureaucracy* (Glencoe, Ill.: The Free Press, 1954), pp. 22–24.

12. See, for example, Wilbert E. Moore, "Management and Union Organizations: An Analytical Comparison," in Conrad M. Arensberg et al., *Research in Industrial Human Relations* (New York: Harper and Bros., 1957), pp. 119–30; Chester I. Barnard, *Organization and Management* (Cambridge: Harvard University Press, 1948), pp. 150–60; Robert Bierstedt, "The Problem of Authority," in Morroe Berger, Theodore Able, and Charles H. Page, eds., *Freedom and Control in Modern Society* (New York: D. Van Nostrand Company, 1954), pp. 78–79; Peter M. Blau, *Bureaucracy in Modern Society* (New York: Random House, 1956), pp. 22–23, 105–13. For a closely related analysis, see William M. Evan "Dimensions of Participation in Voluntary Associations," *Social Forces* 35 (December 1957): 48–53.

13. See, for example, Bernard Barber, "Participation and Mass Apathy in Associations," in Alvin W. Gouldner, ed., *Studies in Leadership* (New York: Harper, 1950), pp. 477–504; Philip Selznick, "The Iron Law of Bureaucracy," *Modern Review* 7 (January, 1950): 157–65; F. Stuart Chapin, "Formalization Observed in Ten Voluntary Associations: Concepts, Morphology, Process," *Social Forces* 33(1955); 306–9; Peter M. Blau, *Bureaucracy in Modern Society,* p. 117.

14. Seymour M. Lipset, Martin A. Trow, and James S. Coleman, *Union Democracy* (Glencoe, Ill.: The Free Press, 1956).

15. See, for example, G. D. H. Cole, *Self-Government in Industry,* (London: G. Bell and Sons, 1917). Sydney and Beatrice Webb, *Industrial Democracy,* rev. ed. (London: Longmans, Green, 1920), pp. 807–50; Jerome Dowd, "Industrial Democracy," *American Journal of Sociology* 26(1920): 581–84; Harold L. Wilensky, "Human Relations in the Workplace: An Appraisal of Some Recent Research," in Conrad M. Arensberg et al., *Research in Industrial Human Relations,* pp. 25–54. "Under what conditions is a process of bureaucratization slowed or reversed?" p. 37.

16. For a penetrating analysis of the development of the concept of citizenship, see T. H. Marshall, *Citizenship and Social Class* (Cambridge: Cambridge University Press, 1950), pp. 1–85.

17. Cf. Soloman Barkin, "Labor Unions and Workers' Rights in Jobs," in Arthur Kornhauser, Robert Dubin, and Arthur M. Ross, eds., *Industrial Conflict* (New York: McGraw-Hill Book Co., 1954), pp. 121–31.

18. For a discussion of the norms of procedural due process of law as they pertain to industrial organizations, see William M. Evan, "Organization Man and Due Process of Law," *American Sociological Review* 26 (August 1961): 540–47; "Due Process of Law in Military and Industrial Organizations," *Administrative Science Quarterly* 7 (September 1962): 187–208. See also Howard M. Vollmer, *Employee Rights and the Employment Relationship* (Berkeley: University of California Press, 1960), pp. 85–140.

19. See, for example, Georges Friedmann, *Industrial Society: The Emergence of Human Problems of Automation* (Glencoe, Ill.: The Free Press, 1955), pp. 186–87, 218; Adam Abruzzi, *Work, Workers and Work Measurement* (New York: Columbia University Press, 1956), pp. 296 ff.; Russell L. Ackoff, "Automatic Management: A Forecast and Its Educational Implications," *Management Science* 2 (1955): 55–60; John Diebold, *Automation: The Advent of the Automatic Factory* (New York: Van Nostrand, 1952), pp. 163–65; Donald N.

Michael, *Cybernation: The Silent Conquest* (Santa Barbara, Cal.: Center for the Study of Democratic Institutions, 1962), pp. 18–20.

20. As employed here, the phrase "professionalization of management" refers to a structural change, that is, a change in the status and role of management and not merely in its ideology. This distinction is frequently obscured in the mounting literature on the subject. See, for example, Lawrence A. Appley, "Management and the American Future," *General Management Series,* no. 169, (New York: American Management Association, 1954), pp. 3–20; Crawford H. Greenwalt, "The Management Profession," *Advanced Management* 20(1955): 5–7; Howard R. Bowen, "Business Management: A Profession?" *Annals* 297 (January 1955): 112–17; Ralph J. Cordiner, *New Frontiers for Professional Managers* (New York: McGraw-Hill Book Co., 1956). For analyses of changes in the ideology of American management, see Reinhard Bendix, *Work and Authority in Industry* (New York: John Wiley & Sons, 1956), Ch. 5; Sigmund Diamond, *The Reputation of the American Businessman* (Cambridge: Harvard University Press, 1955); Francis X. Sutton *et al., The American Business Creed* (Cambridge: Harvard University Press, 1956).

21. Cf. Frederick W. Taylor's discussion of "functional management" in *Shop Management* (New York: Harper and Bros., 1911), pp. 99 ff; P. Sargant Florence, *The Logic of British and American Industry* (London: Routledge and Keegan Paul, 1953), pp. 154–57; John Lee, "The Pros and Cons of Functionalization," in Gulick and Urwick, *Papers on the Science of Administration* pp. 173–79.

22. Nelson N. Foote, "The Professionalization of Labor in Detroit," *American Journal of Sociology* 58(1953): 371–80.

23. Howard M. Vollmer and Donald L. Mills, "Nuclear Technology and the Professionalization of Labor," *American Journal of Sociology* 67 (May 1962): 690–96.

24. Cf. Nicholas J. Demerath and John W. Thibaut, "Small Groups and Administrative Organizations," *Administrative Science Quarterly* 1 (1956): 139–54; Morris Zelditch, Jr. and William M. Evan, "Simulated Bureaucracies: A Methodological Analysis" in Harold Guetzkow, ed., *Simulation in Social Science* (Englewood Cliffs, N. J.: Prentice-Hall, 1962), pp. 48–60; Nancy C. Morse and Everett Reimer, "The Experimental Change of a Major Organizational Variable," *Journal of Abnormal and Social Psychology* 52(1956): 120–29.

CHAPTER 3

Hierarchy, Alienation, Commitment, and Organizational Effectiveness

O rganizational hierarchy is regarded as an indispensable principle not only by executives but also by researchers in the field of organization theory. To most managers, whether in capitalist or socialist countries, the principle of hierarchical structure commends itself as a rational mechanism for ensuring the coordination of diverse functions, the implementation of policies, and the achievement of organizational objectives. A cogent case for the managerial perspective on hierarchy was made by Sir Bernard Miller, the chairman of the John Lewis partnership, a successful profit-sharing company in England:

It is a fact of life that only a tiny minority of people are able enough to manage large-scale affairs and strong minded enough to take decisions that subordinate short-term and sectional interests to the long-term needs of the whole. If the business is to succeed and to continue, the power to settle policy and to take executive decisions at the highest level must be concentrated in the hands of a few people: it cannot be widely shared in industry any more than it can in our political government.[1]

This is a revised version of a paper prepared for the First International Sociological Conference on Participation and Self-Management, Dubrovnik, Yugoslavia, December 1972.

As regards social science researchers on organizations, Weber's model of a monocratic bureaucracy with its hierarchical structure of offices has had a profound impact on their theory construction as well as their research. In addition, Michels' compelling formulation of the "iron law of oligarchy" in organizations, ostensibly concerned with promoting democracy, seems to have won wide acceptance among sociologists.[2] If the "iron law of oligarchy" holds in organizations devoted to advancing democracy, is it not true, *a fortiori,* in organizations concerned with the mundane objective of making a product or rendering a service?

Evidently, executives as well as social scientists assume that hierarchy is a stubborn fact of organizational life and that it is functionally necessary for attaining organizational goals. Otherwise put, they tend to conceive of organizational hierarchy as either a *constant* or as an *imperative,* rather than as a *variable* or as a *constraint.*

DIMENSIONS OF HIERARCHY

In a paper presented at the Fourth World Congress of Sociology in Stresa in 1959 (see Chapter 1), I concluded:

The explicit or implicit acceptance of an "iron law of hierarchy" is premature in view of the dearth of evidence on the structure of organizations. In the absence of systematic inquiry, many critical questions remain unanswered, such as whether the advance of industrialism inevitably leads to an increase in organizational hierarchy, or whether there are counterforces at work tending to reduce the degree of hierarchy. The significance of this question obviously transcends national boundaries.[3]

In the intervening years there has been a burgeoning of research in various countries on organizational structure and behavior. However, with comparatively few exceptions, such as some of the work of Tannenbaum and his colleagues, Morse and Reimer, and the Bavelas-type experiments on communication nets, there has not been any direct, systematic, let alone cumulative, tests of the proposition that there is a positive relationship between the degree of organizational hierarchy and the degree of organizational effectiveness.[4]

Two kindred organizational principles, having almost the canonized status of organizational hierarchy, are the so-called "size-effect" and the "technological imperative," both of which have been the object of an appreciable amount of research in recent years.[5] As organizations increase in size, do they become more or less hierarchical? Obviously the answer depends on how hierarchy is defined and measured. As organizational technology increases in complexity, do organizations become more or less hierarchical? Again the answer depends on how organizational technology is defined.

Underlying these questions is the hypothesis that size and technological complexity are both positively related to organizational hierarchy. The answers to these questions and a test of the proposition that organizational hierarchy is positively related to organizational effectiveness would clearly have significant implications for organization theory as well as for organization design, and, more specifically, for the theories and practices of industrial democracy. Before considering some old and new dilemmas of industrial democracy from the vantage point of organizational hierarchy, I will recapitulate the conceptualization and operationalization of organizational hierarchy that I developed in Chapter 1.

Organizational hierarchy involves at least three modes of unequal allocation of resources: (1) inequality of skills and knowledge, (2) inequality of reward, and (3) inequality of authority. The heterogeneity of tasks performed in an organization presupposes the availability of personnel possessing the requisite skills and knowledge. Since types of skills and bodies of knowledge vary greatly—one deceptively simple measure of skill differentiation is the length of time required in relatively formal training to perform a task—there is a tendency for occupational differentiation in an organization and in society at large to be viewed in a rank order of prestige and social worth. "In the limiting case, an organization has a set of specialized tasks all equivalent in degree of skill or a single homogeneous task performed by all personnel. This type of division of labor would represent a zero degree of hierarchical differentiation of skills."[6] The actual distribution of skills among the employees of an organization may take various shapes—for example, a normal curve, a negatively or positively skewed distribution, a multimodal curve, a U-curve, and so on.

The second dimension of inequality, the hierarchy of rewards, has received more attention than the hierarchy of skills. If we ignore the variety of non-monetary rewards associated with employment (such as vacations, health insurance, pensions, and various perquisites), the wages and salaries received by employees can be readily measured. Ideally, Lorenz curves can be drawn showing the relationship between the relative size of an occupational category and its share of the total earnings in an organization, thus providing a precise measure of the degree of hierarchy of rewards.[7] In the absence of data on the distribution of earnings of all employees in an organization or for a sample of organizations, two simple ratios crudely measure the degree of inequality of rewards: the ratio of maximum-minimum earnings in an organization, e.g., the salary of the president or general manager compared to the average wage of workers in the lowest-skill category and the earning ratios of adjacent organizational statuses such as foreman/worker and supervisor/foreman.[8]

The third dimension of inequality, the hierarchy of authority, is more complex and multifaceted than the first two. It consists of a body of institutionalized rights and privileges of a legislative, executive, and adjudicative nature associated with various statuses of an organization. Six indicators of the hierarchy of authority are considered: (1) span of control; (2) Melman's ratio of administrative to production personnel, which takes the entire organization as a unit of analysis instead of a subunit, as in the case of the span of control; (3) number of echelons in the administrative structure; (4) Jaques' time-span of discretion; (5) degree of centralization of decision making; and (6) degree of limitation on the rights of management to make adjudicative decisions as reflected in the number of echelons for which procedural due process has been institutionalized.[9]

Thus, the concept of organizational hierarchy, as I used it in the earlier chapter, is three-dimensional in nature. Each of the three dimensions of hierarchy is by definition a linear function of hierarchy. In the decade since the publication of the original article on which Chapter 1 is based, the field of information technology has emerged, and a multitude of applications of this technology has been made in various types of organizations—manufacturing, service, and so on. An extensive body of information concerning the operations of an organization, as regards its technical as well as its administrative functions, is now potentially available with the help of computer technology.[10] Access to the body of organizational information can, on the one hand, be severely restricted to one or more levels of management or, on the other hand, be made available to all employees of an organization, managerial as well as rank and file. In the former case it could be used for the purpose of centralizing the decision-making processes, whereas in the latter case it could serve as a decentralizing mechanism. The number of authority echelons in an organization or the proportion of employees in all occupational categories of an organization that have access to the principal administrative and technical bodies of information would provide a measure of the degree of hierarchy in the distribution of organizational information. This measure I now conceive as the fourth dimension of organizational hierarchy.

AN ALTERNATIVE HYPOTHESIS

With the aid of the four-dimensional concept of hierarchy, it is now possible to formulate an alternative hypothesis as to the consequences of organizational hierarchy. Instead of the prevailing and largely untested hypothesis that hierarchical structure is positively related to organizational effectiveness, I would entertain the counter hypothesis, namely, that hierarchical structure is negatively related to organizational effectiveness. The rationale for this hypothesis is as follows: In all likelihood, there is a tendency for the pattern of hierarchical differentiation in an organization to be consistent across the four dimensions, that is, hierarchical consistency in organizational profiles tends to occur just as individuals tend to exhibit status consistency with respect to the social stratification system of a society.[11] This is not to deny, of course, that some organizations will have hierarchically inconsistent profiles, just as some individuals have status-inconsistent profiles. In the event of hierarchical consistency in the organizational profile, it is reasonable to hypothesize that employees who are uniformly low on the continua of skills, rewards, authority, and information distribution will experience work alienation—in particular, a sense of powerlessness and self-estrangement from their work role.[12] As the degree of work alienation increases, commitment to the organization and the collective goals decreases, as reflected in the rates of absenteeism, turnover, accidents, work errors, and the like. Cumulatively, work alienation and the concomitant decline in organizational commitment can in turn be expected to have dysfunctional consequences for organizational effectiveness.

The alternative hypothesis being advanced is not *ad hoc* in nature; rather, it is linked to a set of hypotheses interrelating hierarchy, work alienation, organizational commitment, and organizational effectiveness. In particular, the set of hypotheses, given the usual *ceteris paribus* condition, is as follows:

1. Organizational hierarchy is positively related to work alienation.
2. Work alienation is negatively related to organizational commitment.
3. Organizational hierarchy is negatively related to organizational commitment.
4. Organizational commitment is positively related to organizational effectiveness.
5. Work alienation is negatively related to organizational effectiveness.
6. Organizational hierarchy is negatively related to organizational effectiveness.

Diagrammatically, the hypothesized relationships are shown in Figure 3.1. Clearly, this set of interrelated hypotheses can be conceived as a causal model

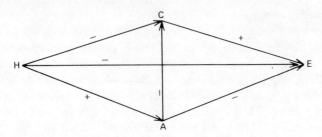

Fig. 3.1 Hypothesized relationships among hierarchy (H), work alienation (A), organizational commitment (C), and organizational effectiveness (E).

that could be tested with the help of path analysis, given a suitable data set on a sample of organizations.

Is there any evidence from empirical research for the plausibility of these hypotheses? Relevant empirical findings, such as they are, are sparse and inconsistent. Several studies will be cited to illustrate the level of support for some of the hypothesized relationships.

Morse and Reimer, in a field experiment with clerical workers in an industrial organization in which they manipulated the degree of centralization of decision making, found that productivity increased to a greater extent in the hierarchically controlled program as compared with the autonomy program.[13] Commenting on the unpredicted result, Trist observes that "the character of the task produced a constant work flow so that only by having less workers could productivity be increased—a result easier to achieve in a more hierarchically controlled group."[14] On the other hand, Van Gils, in a field experiment with several clerical centers of the Netherlands Post Office Cheques and Payment Service, in which he modified the design of the job as well as the social organization of work, found that productivity increased appreciably.[15] Experimental changes increased the level of skill and authority of employees and, in effect, simultaneously decreased work alienation by "increasing the variety of the work" and by "promoting knowledge of interconnected aspects of the work."[16] Leavitt and others who have conducted laboratory experiments on communication networks have found that highly centralized networks have a higher level of productivity than those with a low degree of centralization.[17] Whether this finding is independent of the degree of complexity of the task— and hence of skill differentiation—was not ascertained. Smith and Tannenbaum, on the other hand, in their comparative study of perceived influence on decision making in several different types of organizations, using the control graph technique, observed in some of their voluntary associations that the lower the degree of hierarchical differentiation with respect to influence on decision making, the higher the organizational effectiveness.[18] Similarly, Melman in a comparative study in Israel of six privately owned, hierarchical firms with six Kibbutz, nonhierarchical firms found that the latter were significantly higher in effectiveness.[19]

Of the various studies of work alienation that have been conducted in the past decade in the United States, two have yielded a relationship between hierarchy of authority and work alienation. In a study of professionals in 16 social welfare organizations, Aiken and Hage found that work alienation was higher in those organizations in which there was a high degree of centralization in decision making.[20] Likewise, in a study of scientists and engineers in a large aerospace company, Miller observed that employees working for "directive" supervisors had a higher degree of work alienation than those working for "participatory" or laissez faire supervisors.[21]

It is indeed noteworthy that in none of the empirical studies using the concept of organizational hierarchy were all four dimensions of hierarchy employed. Moreover, in virtually all the studies only the hierarchy of authority is the focus of attention. Curiously enough, this is also the case with the various theories and programs of industrial democracy.

ORGANIZATIONAL HIERARCHY AND INDUSTRIAL DEMOCRACY

Whatever the terminology, whether worker participation, joint consultation, works' councils, workers' councils, workers' control, or workers' self-management, there appears to be a primary concern with modifying the hierarchy of authority. And the principal mechanism employed—whether in Britain, the Netherlands, West Germany, Norway, Yugoslavia, or elsewhere—has been an indirect or representational system of participation involving the election of workers to one or more policy-making bodies of the entire enterprise or a subunit thereof.[22]

In the expanding literature on industrial democracy, there appears to be an increasing realization that prevailing concepts as to the mechanisms for achieving disalienation are not effective. The abolition of private property by means of nationalization of industry or by state ownership in socialist countries has not in itself eliminated the various forms of work alienation such as powerlessness, self-estrangement, normlessness, meaninglessness, and isolation.[23] Nor has a variety of schemes for representational participation on the part of workers contributed to disalienation.

In the Netherlands, Mulder observes that managers on works' councils dominate the proceedings, not only in the frequency of their participation but also in the frequency with which their proposals are accepted.[24] Emery and Thorsrud find that the representation of workers on boards of directors of companies in Norway did not contribute noticeably to the goals of democratization.[25] On the question of the effectiveness of the representation system, they note, tellingly, that:

(a) There is little evidence of active communication and feedback between the workers and their representative. This, in itself, makes suspect the effectiveness of representation, particularly since the representatives are not responsible, over long periods, to party or program.

(b) Nine out of the twelve representatives interviewed make some reference to having to take a board or company view of some matters, particularly production.[26]

Kolaja, in a case study of a workers' council in a textile factory in Poland in 1957, concluded that "it did not function well."[27]

The workers did not identify themselves with the plant and its major function as did the management people. . . . The fact that the factory was state property, i.e., the property of all, did not abolish the differentiation between the managerial group, on the one hand, and the labor group, on the other. Workers still felt that "they" were trying to take advantage of them, depriving them of part of their deserved earnings. Therefore, it is legitimate to conclude that if the means of production become collective property, this does not necessarily result in an individual person's identification with the plant. The ownership by "all" is too diffuse to constitute a stimulus to develop individual ownership identification with the common property.[28]

In Yugoslavia, the findings of several studies point in a similar direction. Unskilled workers tend to be underrepresented on workers' councils; the frequency of participation of managers on the workers' councils is significantly higher than that of workers, particularly as regards the number of suggestions that are accepted.[29] Under the circumstances, the findings by Županov and Tannenbaum in their control-graph study in Yugoslavia that the workers should have more control than they do, and managers less control, seem quite understandable.[30] And in another control-graph study in four Yugoslav industrial organizations, Kavčič, Rus, and Tannenbaum concluded that:

. . . the possible social-psychological effects of indirect or representational participation are limited. Many of the daily events for workers, including the frustrating aspects of technology and bureaucratic administration, are not very much changed by the fact that some members of the organization participate in monthly council meetings. Workers may be too far removed from the actual deliberations of the council to develop the sense of involvement that participation in such deliberations might engender. The workers' daily routine and relationships with supervisors and co-workers may continue unchanged, even though the council makes decisions that affect organizational policy.[31]

But by far the most surprising finding to emerge from a study of workers' councils in Yugoslavia is that by Obradovič. He notes that:

. . . participants in self-management are *more* alienated than nonparticipants. Possibly for these workers the direct experience with self-management has been so frustrating that their sense of alienation has become even greater.[32]

SHOP-FLOOR DEMOCRACY

Several rather important inferences can be drawn from the recent research on industrial democracy. First, representational participation fails to represent the needs and aspirations of the worker constituents; moreover, in light of Michels' thesis of the "iron law of oligarchy" we would expect a process of progressive estrangement to occur between workers and their representatives on workers' councils, possibly due to a tendency for worker representatives to internalize the perspectives of the managers on the council.[33] Second, since managers participating in workers' councils, have on the whole more technical knowledge pertaining to managerial decisions than workers, there is a tendency for the power of managers to increase rather than decrease as a result of the functioning of workers' councils.[34] All of which leads one researcher in the Netherlands to conclude that the works' council is an "hierarchical form of participation in management. Real democracy within the firm requires different ways."[35] Third, several researchers have also concluded that if there are to be any important advances in democratizing the workplace, it will not be by means of indirect forms of participation through a representational system at a strategic policy level of the firm but rather through a direct form of participation at the operating level, that is, at the work site or on the shop floor.[36]

Insofar as industrial democracy means more than extended negotiations and consultations, there is a need for the transfer of some real managerial power to the employees. It is difficult indeed to see how this sharing can be started at the top, at board level. If democratic participation is to become a reality, it seems inevitable that it must be started at a level where a large proportion of employees are *both able and willing to participate.*"[37]

One of the most intriguing examples of shop-floor democracy is Melman's description of the gang system in the Standard Motor Company in Britain. Groups of workers, some very small and some as large as 3,000, autonomously organized their tasks and supervised themselves, sharing in the group bonus as a result of increased productivity.[38] A vivid account of the gang system was published in 1972 by Rayton, himself a worker in an aircraft factory in Coventry.

We worked out between us how many men we would want and the boss agreed. We elected a ganger and a deputy ganger to take charge on night shifts. We sorted out men, openly, to do the work they were best fitted for. We made mistakes, but they were immediately corrected. We reckoned up the various prices of jobs and proved theoretically that we could increase our earnings. We had all the benches and other contraptions moved to suit our way of working. Some of the firm's officials objected that we were "infringing their rights" and the management proper insisted that *they* would appoint the ganger. We said, "No! He would then be a boss and we are not having a boss. He is *our* man responsible to us, and we, individually and collectively will be responsible for all the work done by the gang!" It wasn't put quite so explicitly as I have just written, but that was what was meant, and the managers being good chaps (we knew them personally) accepted it. This, insisting on ourselves appointing the ganger, turned out to be the key to success. The "contract" (written, as is the Common

Law kind of contract) was not between the firm and the ganger, but between the firm and the gang as an entity. In our case "Gang No. 3." Gangers could come and go, but Gang 3 went on. We knew of course that in a serious situation the management could abolish Gang 3—but why should they? They wanted us. Wanted the work. We had endless discussions the first few weeks. We kept watch on the ganger to see that "our money" was being properly "banked" with the wages office. The ganger kept watch on us to see that each of us was earning his keep and a bit over. We watched each other. And then, eventually, finding that everything was working out well we gave up worrying and concentrated on work.

The position was that the ganger kept track of work and money and left discipline and other details to us. He was just one member of a democratic team. He saw to it that the gang was supplied with tools, materials, and information derived from design office memos and blueprints. Clever men helped others decipher difficult drawings, not so clever men were content to do the drudge work. *No* distinction was made on degrees of skill—that was a waste of time. Divisive. All this was tacitly understood. Management also tacitly understood, and no written rules were made. Consequently there were no "orthodoxies," everything being left as fluid as possible. In this way all kinds of initiatives came from the shop floor, and these, added to brilliant design, planning and organization pushed the firm into the lead in aircraft production. Every week men joined us and were accepted at once as equals. Only the ganger and his deputy worried about money; the rest were free to concentrate on their work which was a great relief to men previously tormented by individual piecework. But it still was piecework, still gave men the urge to earn more, and earn it by brains and skill rather than by being driven. Decisions were made at gang meetings (in meal breaks) and the ganger was obliged, as in Parliament, to answer questions. He could also, in return, publicly castigate men who were at fault. Naturally he was the best man on the gang for all this, which was why the men picked him. Men working together almost always "sense" the man they want as leader. And they could also sack him, at a gang meeting.[39]

By developing the gang system, the workers in the Coventry aircraft factory succeeded in modifying their hierarchical profile with respect to all four dimensions. By "having all the benches and other contraptions moved to suit our way of working," the workers redesigned their job and, in the process, reduced skill and knowledge differentials. By means of a group piecework administered by the ganger, the workers increased their earnings and simultaneously reduced reward differentials in the factory. Authority differentials were also reduced by virtue of the fact that workers elected their own foreman, called the "ganger," who "kept track of work and money and left discipline and other details to us. . . . Decisions were made at gang meetings (in meal breaks) and the ganger was obliged, as in Parliament, to answer questions." The workers also had the right to fire their ganger at a gang meeting. Finally, the gang system also had the effect of reducing differentials in organizational information. The ganger "saw to it that the gang was supplied with tools, materials and information derived from design office memos and blueprints." And the workers, in turn, ascertained at gang meetings whether the money "was being properly 'banked' with the wages office."

The phenomena of shop-floor democracy have stimulated interest not only in England but also in the Netherlands, Norway, Sweden and elsewhere.[40] Field experiments and action research programs, guided by the sociotechnical system framework and kindred open systems models, are under way in various countries.[41] It is reasonable to expect that some of these studies will yield increasing evidence pertaining to our hypothesized relationships—such as a negative relationship between hierarchy and organizational effectiveness and a positive relationship between hierarchy and work alienation.[42] Such research promises to redirect theory and research on industrial democracy. Whether it will contribute to our understanding of the problems of transforming hierarchical organizations in the direction of nonhierarchical and voluntary modes of organization remains to be seen.[43]

Direct participation at the shop-floor level, as a strategy for counteracting worker alienation and increasing organizational effectiveness, poses the problem of generalizing the pattern to all categories of employees at all levels of an organization. One approach to this unsolved problem is to conceptualize direct participation as involving a process of *destratification* with respect to all four dimensions of hierarchy.

THE DESTRATIFICATION-RATIONALIZATION HYPOTHESIS

By organizational destratification, I mean redesigning jobs to decrease knowledge and skill differentials, redesigning systems of compensation to decrease reward differentials, redesigning decision making to decrease authority differentials, and redesigning the distribution of organizational information to decrease information differentials among different categories of employees. However, if an effort in the direction of destratification in the service of disalienation is to succeed, it must reckon with the imperious, environmental demands for organizational effectiveness imposed on any firm, whether in a market economy, a planned economy, or a social-ownership society. Another impetus for organizational effectiveness is that it is a prerequisite for increasing the rewards of all constituents of the enterprise. To ensure increasing effectiveness the secular trend for rationalization of industrial enterprises must be taken into account. The process of rationalization—that is, the increasing application of techniques based on science and technology—may, however, be incompatible with the process of destratification, thus posing a dilemma as to how to increase the level of both processes in an organization—destratification as well as rationalization—in order to realize the twin values of simultaneously decreasing work alienation and increasing organizational effectiveness.

An analysis of some facets of rationalization may suggest a possible solution to the dilemma of increasing rationalization as well as increasing destratification, thus avoiding a trade-off situation. Two dimensions of rationalization may be considered: (1) technological progress, and (2) an increase in the use of control mechanisms to ensure predictable and efficient task performance. In developing or employing new technology, jobs can, in principle, be designed so as to upgrade rather than downgrade the occupational skills and knowledge required to perform the various tasks in an organization. By choosing to upgrade skill levels, occupational differentials can be reduced, thereby justifying a reduction in reward, authority, and organizational information differentials. As for control mechanisms to ensure predictable and efficient task performance, there is always a choice between personal versus impersonal control mechanisms. The use of impersonal control mechanisms by means of the formalization of rules and the standardization of procedures reduces the potential for arbitrary and capricious exercise of authority by superiors, particularly if there are adequate due-process safeguards for all employees in an organization.[44]

In short, these considerations suggest a destratification-rationalization hypothesis: As the positive slope of the relationship between these two clusters of variables increases, organizational effectiveness increases and work alienation decreases. Admittedly, organization theory and organization practice, whether or not guided by research on industrial democracy, do not yet throw much light on how to achieve the underlying values of organizational destratification and organizational rationalization.

NEED FOR AN EXPERIMENTAL PERSPECTIVE

At this juncture several predictions of a theoretical and research nature may be in order. Organizations undergoing the joint transformation processes of destratification and rationalization would not necessarily enjoy consensus as regards goal formation and decision making. Instead of the common conception of a unity of interests in the firm, on the part of many organizational researchers in capitalist as well as socialist countries, a diversity of interests is a theoretically more defensible premise. Occupational differentiation within the firm unavoidably gives rise to different perceptions of organizational reality and in turn results in heterogeneous interests emerging and affecting or seeking to affect the decision-making processes. If the firm is to become progressively destratified and rationalized, the diversity of interests requires articulation. To overcome "pluralistic ignorance" and the fear of opposition to organizational policies, the formation of organized coalitions accompanied by the institutionalization of dissent are necessary.[45] The firm as a social system thus

becomes polycentric and polyarchical in nature.[46] To resolve the inevitable conflicts among the various coalitions internal and external to the firm, requires a
process of bargaining, assuming that an autocratic mode of decision making is
incompatible with the model of an industrial enterprise seeking to become more
egalitarian as well as more effective.[47]

Significant progress in research on industrial democracy will probably
require a systematic effort to conduct organizational experiments, whether in
the laboratory or in the field, on the consequences of varying degrees of organizational hierarchy for alienation, commitment, and organizational effectiveness.[48] To undertake field experiments that test the relative efficacy of alternative strategies for democratizing the workplace presupposes an appreciation of
what Campbell calls an "ideology of experimentation."

We must be able to advocate without that excess of commitment that blinds us to reality
testing. . . . Administrators must advocate the importance of the problem rather than the
importance of the answer. They must advocate experimental sequences of reforms,
rather than one certain cure-all, advocating Reform A with Alternative B available to
try next should an honest evaluation of A prove it worthless or harmful.[49]

Although Campbell's prescription to administrators seems highly persuasive,
the fact that relatively few administrators in any present or past society—
except for those associated with the Norwegian Industrial Democracy Project
and cognate studies in other countries—have behaved in accordance with the
"ideology of experimentation" suggests that there are vested interests impeding
the implementation of this principle.[50] This predicament has led Campbell to
speculate on the methodological problems and characteristics of an "experimenting society".

The experimenting society will be one which will vigorously try out proposed solutions
to recurrent problems, which will make hard-headed and multi-dimensional evaluations
of the outcomes, and which will move on to try other alternatives when evaluation
shows one reform to have been ineffective or harmful. We do not have such a society
today. While all societies are engaged in trying out innovative reforms, none is yet
organized to adequately evaluate the outcomes. Programs are instead continued or dis-
continued on inadequate or other grounds. This is due in part to the inertia of social
organizations, in part to political predicaments which oppose evaluation, and in part to
the fact that the methodology of evaluation is still inadequate.[51]

Since organizations are subsystems of a larger society, a prerequisite for fully
implementing an experimental strategy with respect to industrial democracy
may very well be the transformation of the environing society in accordance
with a model of "an experimenting society".

CONCLUSION

Although the four-variable model of organizations developed in this chapter and the empirical studies reviewed deal exclusively with industrial organizations—with the exception of one study pertaining to a voluntary association—there is no intrinsic reason why this model is not generalizable to all nonindustrial organizations as well. Clearly, some types of organization, such as administrative agencies and the military, may on the whole be more hierarchical in structure than most industrial organizations. On the other hand, some types of organizations, particularly those consisting predominantly of professional and technical occupations such as research laboratories, colleges and universities, hospitals, professional associations, and scientific societies, may on the whole be less hierarchical than most industrial organizations. Whether the hypothesized relationships among the four variables in the model would differ depending on the type of organizational context only comparative empirical research could ascertain. A *comparative* test, however, of the six propositions generated by the model would have to take into account a cultural parameter as well as a methodological fact of life in organizational research.

By a cultural parameter, I refer to the distinctive norms and values embedded in the societal environment(s) that impinge on any organization. Thus, for any organization or class of organizations the salient norms and values may be rooted in one or more institutional spheres in society, whether the economy, the political system, the family, law, religion, or education. Thus far, virtually no cross-national or cross-cultural study of organizations has succeeded in conceptualizing and operationalizing the cultural parameters affecting the validity of any proposition in organization theory.[52] Any test of the model advanced in this paper would have to face up to this problem.

Equally problematic is what I referred to as the methodological fact of life in organizational research. In the case of many organizational variables, such as hierarchy, alienation, and commitment, there are many thorny problems of measurement. Although notable progress has been made owing largely to the Aston studies, the problem of standardization of organizational measures persists.[53] Price has made an important contribution to the field by compiling some measures of organizational variables.[54]

When the variable of organizational effectiveness—the dependent variable in our model—is considered, the problem is even more accute. In the first place, there is a dearth of empirical studies in which organizational effectiveness is explicitly and systematically measured. Price's inventory of propositions on organizational effectiveness rests largely on an exegesis of 50 studies but does not succeed in operationalizing a general measure of organizational effectiveness applicable to all types of organizations.[55] Secondly, virtually no empirical studies have undertaken to measure organizational effectiveness in different types of organizations, that is, in a cross-organizational comparison. Thus, any effort to test the model in this chapter, whether within a framework of one class of organizations, cross-organizationally, or cross-culturally, would have to come to grips with the basic problem of measuring organizational effectiveness.[56]

NOTES

1. Bernard Miller, "Foreword," in Allan Flanders, Ruth Pomeranz, and Joan Woodward, *Experiment in Industrial Democracy* (London: Faber and Faber, 1968), p. 17.

2. Robert Michels, *Political Parties*, trans. Eden and Cedar Paul (Glencoe, Ill.: The Free Press, 1949); and J. David Edelstein, "An Organizational Theory of Union Democracy," *American Sociological Review* 32 (April 1967): 19.

3. William M. Evan, "Indices of the Hierarchical Structure of Industrial Organizations," *Management Science* 9 (April 1963): 477.

4. Arnold S. Tannenbaum, *Control in Organizations* (New York: McGraw-Hill Book Co., 1968); Clagett G. Smith and Arnold S. Tannenbaum, "Organizational Control Structure: A Comparative Analysis," *Human Relations* 16 (Fall 1963): 289–316; Nancy C. Morse and Everett Reimer, "The Experimental Change of a Major Organizational Variable," *Journal of Abnormal and Social Psychology* 52 (January 1956): 120–29; A. Bavelas, "Communication Patterns in Task-Oriented Groups," *Journal of Acoustical Society of America* 22 (1950): 725–30; H. J. Leavitt, "Some Effects of Certain Communication Patterns on Group Performance," *Journal of Abnormal and Social Psychology* 46 (January 1951): 38–50; M. E. Shaw, "Some Effects of Problem Complexity Upon Problem Solution Efficiency in Different Communication Nets," *Journal of Experimental Psychology* 48 (September 1954): 211–17; Harold Guetzkow and H. A. Simon, "The Impact of Certain Communication Nets upon Organization and Performance in Task-Oriented Groups," *Management Science* 1 (April-July, 1955): 233–50.

5. Geoffrey K. Ingham, *Organizational Size, Orientation to Work and Industrial Behavior* (Cambridge, University of Cambridge, 1968); David J. Hickson, D. S. Pugh, and Diana C. Pheysey, "Operations Technology and Organization Structure: An Empirical Reappraisal," *Administrative Science Quarterly* 14 (September 1969): 378–97; Peter M. Blau, "Interdependence and Hierarchy in Organizations," *Social Science Research* 1 (April 1972): 1–24; Peter M. Blau, "A Formal Theory of Differentiation in Organizations," *American Sociological Review* 35 (April 1970): 201–18; Marshall W. Meyer, "Size and Structure of Organizations: A Causal Analysis," *American Sociological Review* 37 (August 1972): 434–40; Louis R. Pondy, "Effects of Size, Complexity, and Ownership on Administrative Intensity," *Administrative Science Quarterly* 14 (March 1969): 47–60; William A. Rushing, "The Effects of Industry, Size and Division of Labor on Administration," *Administrative Science Quarterly* 12 (September 1967): 273–95; Joan Woodward, *Industrial Organization: Theory and Practice* (London: Oxford University Press, 1965).

6. Evan, "Indices of the Hierarchical Structure," p. 469.

7. *Ibid*; Thomas L. Whisler, Harold Meyer, Bernard H. Baum, and Peter F. Sorensen, Jr., "Centralization of Organizational Control: An Empirical Study of Its Meaning and Measurement," *Journal of Business* 40 (January 1967): 10–26.

8. Evan, "Indices of the Hierarchical Structure," pp. 469, 470.

9. Ibid., pp. 470–473.

10. William M. Evan, "Organizational Lag," *Human Organization* 25 (Spring 1966): 51–53.

11. Evan, "Indices of the Hierarchical Structure," p. 473.

12. Melvin Seeman, "On the Meaning of Alienation," *American Sociological Review* 24 (December 1959): 783–91; Robert Blauner, *Alienation and Freedom* (Chicago: University of Chicago Press, 1964).

13. Morse and Reimer, "Experimental Change of a Major Organizational Variable."

14. Eric Trist, "The Professional Facilitation of Planned Change in Organizations," in Victor H. Vroom and Edward L. Deci, eds., *Management and Motivation* (London: Penguin Books, 1970), p. 353.

15. M. R. Van Gils, "Job Design Within the Organization," in P. H. Van Gorkum et al., *Industrial Democracy in the Netherlands* (The Hague: J. A. Boom en Zoon, Meppel Publishers, 1969), pp. 94–95.

16. *Ibid.*, p. 86.

17. Leavitt, "Some Effects of Certain Communication Patterns"; Guetzkow and Simon, "Impact of Certain Communication Nets"; Shaw, "Some Effects of Problem Complexity"; and A. M. Cohen, "Changing Small-group Communication Networks," *Administrative Science Quarterly* 6 (March 1962): 443–62.

18. Smith and Tannenbaum, "Organizational Control Structure."

19. Seymour Melman, "Industrial Efficiency Under Managerial vs. Cooperative Decision Making," *Review of Radical Political Economics* 2 (Spring 1970): 9–34.

20. Michael Aiken and Jerald Hage, "Organizational Alienation: A Comparative Analysis," *American Sociological Review* 31 (August 1966): 502–6.

21. George A. Miller, "Professionals in Bureaucracy: Alienation Among Industrial Scientists and Engineers," *American Sociological Review* 32 (October 1967): 762–64.

22. C. J. Lammers, "Power and Participation in Decision-Making in Formal Organizations," *American Journal of Sociology* 73 (September 1967): 209–16.

23. George Fischer, "Sociology," in George Fischer, ed., *Science and Ideology in Soviet Society* (New York: Atherton Press, 1967), pp. 38–45.

24. Mauk Mulder, "Power Equalization Through Participation," *Administrative Science Quarterly* 16 (March 1971): 33.

25. F. E. Emery and Einar Thorsrud, *Form and Content in Industrial Democracy* (London: Tavistock Publications, 1969), pp. 24–25.

26. *Ibid.*, pp. 24–25.

27. Jiri Kolaja, *A Polish Factory* (Lexington, Ky.: University of Kentucky Press, 1960), p. 134.

28. *Ibid.*, p. 135.

29. Jiri Kolaja, *Workers' Councils: The Yugoslav Experience* (New York: Frederick A. Praeger, 1966), pp. 16–17, 20–21; Josip Obradović, John R. P. French, Jr., and Willard L. Rodgers, "Workers' Councils in Yugoslavia," *Human Relations* 23, no. 5 (1970): 470.

30. Josip Županov and Arnold S. Tannenbaum, "The Distribution of Control in Some Yugoslav Industrial Organizations as Perceived by Members," in Arnold S. Tannenbaum, *Control in Organizations* (New York: McGraw-Hill Book Co., 1968), pp. 91–112.

31. Bogdan Kavčič, Veljko Rus, and Arnold S. Tannenbaum, "Control, Participation and Effectiveness in Four Yugoslav Industrial Organizations," *Administrative Science Quarterly* 16 (March 1971): 84.

32. Josip Obradović, "Participation and Work Attitudes in Yugoslavia," *Industrial Relations* 23, no. 5 (1970): 165.

33. P. H. Van Gorkum, "Industrial Democracy at the Level of the Enterprise," in P. H. Van Gorkum et al., *Industrial Democracy in the Netherlands* (The Hague: J. A. Boom en Zoon, Meppel Publishers, 1969), p. 19; Emery and Thorsrud, *Form and Content in Industrial Democracy,* p. 25.

34. Mulder, "Power Equalization Through Participation," p. 34; Mauk Mulder and Henk Wilke, "Participation and Power Equalization," *Organizational Behavior and Human Performance* 5 (September 1970): 446.

35. P. J. D. Drenth, "The Works' Councils in The Netherlands," in P. H. Van Gorkum et al., *Industrial Democracy in the Netherlands* (The Hague: J. A. Boom en Zoon, Meppel Publishers, 1969), p. 39.

36. Mulder, "Power Equalization Through Participation"; Van Gils, "Job Design Within the Organization," pp. 96–97; Emery and Thorsrud, *Form and Content in Industrial Democracy,* p. 86.

37. Emery and Thorsrud, *Form and Content in Industrial Democracy,* p. 86.

38. Seymour Melman, *Decision-Making and Productivity* (Oxford: Basil Blackwell, 1958), pp. 12, 14, 34–36.

39. Dwight Rayton, *Shop Floor Democracy in Action* (London: Russell, 1972), pp. 8–9.

40. Van Gils, "Job Design Within the Organization"; Emery and Thorsrud, *Form and Content in Industrial Democracy.*

41. F. E. Emery and E. L. Trist, "Socio-Technical Systems," in C. West Churchman and M. Verhulst, eds., *Management Science: Models and Techniques,* vol. II (Oxford: Pergamon Press, 1960), pp. 173–191; Louis E. Davis and Eric L. Trist, "Improving the Quality of Work Life: Experience of the Socio-Technical Approach," a background paper commissioned by HEW for a report on *Work in America* (1972) (Offset); Eric Trist, "A Socio-Technical Critique of Scientific Management," in D. O. Edge and J. N. Wolfe, *Meaning and Control* (London: Tavistock, 1973); F. E. Emergy and Einar Thorsrud, *Democracy at Work: The Report of the Norwegian Industrial Democracy Program* (Canberra: The Australian National University, 1976) (offset); William H. McWhinney and James Eldon, "A Reticular Society: New Institutions for a Post-Industrial Democracy," a paper presented at The Center for the Study of Democratic Institutions, Santa Barbara, Cal., 1972 (mimeo).

42. Trist, "A Socio-Technical Critique," p. 110.

43. William M. Evan, "Les conditions functionnelles d'existence d'organisations industrielles volontaires," *Sociologie du travail* 5 (Juillet-Septembre, 1963): 236–46. See Chapter 2 in this volume.

44. William A. Rushing, "Organization Size, Rules, and Surveillance," *Journal of Experimental Social Psychology* 2 (February 1966): 11–26; and "Organizational Rules and Surveillance: Propositions in Comparative Organizational Analysis," *Administrative Science Quarterly* 10 (March 1966): 423–43; Evan, "Indices of the Hierarchical Structure," pp. 472–73.

45. Daniel Katz and Robert L. Kahn, *The Social Psychology of Organizations* (New York: John Wiley & Sons, 1966), pp. 53–54; Seymour Lipset, Martin Trow, and James Coleman, *Union Democracy* (Glencoe, Ill.: The Free Press, 1956), pp. 413–18.

46. Tannenbaum, *Control in Organizations,* 32, 53–54.

47. Richard M. Cyert and James G. March, *A Behavioral Theory of the Firm* (Englewood Cliffs, N.J.: Prentice-Hall, 1963).

48. William M. Evan, ed., *Organizational Experiments* (New York: Harper and Row, 1971).

49. Donald T. Campbell, "Reforms as Experiments," *American Psychologist* 24 (April 1969): 409–29.

50. Emery and Thorsrud, *Democracy at Work.*

51. Donald T. Campbell, *Methods for the Experimenting Society* (Department of Psychology, Northwestern University, 1973) (mimeo).

52. William M. Evan, "Culture and Organizational Systems," *Organization and Administrative Sciences* 5 (Winter 1975): 1–16.

53. D. S. Pugh, D. J. Hickson, C. R. Hinings, and C. Turner, "Dimensions of Organization Structure," *Administrative Science Quarterly* 13 (1968): 33–47; "The Context of Organization Structures," *Administrative Science Quarterly* 14 (1969): 94–114; Harry C. Triandis, "Notes on the Design of Organizations," in James D. Thompson, ed., *Approaches to Organizational Design* (Pittsburgh: University of Pittsburgh Press, 1966).

54. James L. Price, *Handbook of Organizational Measurement* (Lexington, Mass.: D. C. Heath, 1972).

55. James L. Price, *Organizational Effectiveness: An Inventory of Propositions* (Homewood, Ill.: Richard D. Irwin, 1968).

56. William M. Evan, "Organization Theory and Organizational Effectiveness: An Exploratory Analysis," *Organization and Administrative Sciences* (1976).

PART TWO

Role Strain
and Structural Change

O rganizations designed according to principles of hierarchy, as we have seen in the chapters in Part I, coordinate the behavior of their members by means of specified goals, rules, and roles. The incumbents of the various managerial roles have the authority to exercise control over their subordinates in the interest of complying with organizational policies and accomplishing officially-formulated objectives. As a result, inequalities of power are created, accompanied by other inequalities such as in rewards, prestige, and information. Not surprisingly and unintentionally, such inequalities encourage the emergence of conflicts regarding goals, rules, tasks, and the like among the members occupying the various hierarchically-ordered roles. Another consequence of the hierarchical system of controls—not unrelated to the emergence of conflicts—is the widespread occurrence of "role strain," which has been defined as the "felt difficulty in fulfilling role obligations."[1]

In Chapter 4, I explore the role strains of chemists in three different departments (basic research, applied research, and development) of an industrial research laboratory in relation to the allegedly universal "norm of reciprocity."[2] Another type of role strain problem, that of junior and middle executives who tend to develop an ideology of the "organization man," is analyzed in Chapter 5. At least two interrelated structural sources of this ideology are identified: (1) the unstructured tasks of junior and middle executives are conducive to the use by superiors of subjective criteria of performance appraisal; and (2) an authority system devoid of mechanisms to ensure "procedural due process of law" tends to prevail. In Chapter 6, the effects of the presence or absence of due process norms on the occurrence of superior-subordinate conflicts are compared in a government and in an industrial research laboratory.

The exercise of power often arbitrary in organizations and the prevalence of inter-role conflicts are further analyzed in Chapter 7, which I wrote for a symposium on Hirschman's seminal book *Exit, Voice and Loyalty*.[3] To clarify the relationship between power and conflict and the conditions under which organizational members have recourse to the options of "exit" or "voice," I introduce three structural concepts: due process norms, organizational citizenship, and fiduciary management. In turn, these concepts are combined into a composite concept for the design of organizations, namely, "organizational constitutionalism." Each of the components of constitutionalism, I hypothesize, constitutes a point on an evolutionary scale, with due process norms at the lower end of the scale, organizational citizenship at the midpoint, and fiduciary management at the higher end of the scale. To illustrate the applicability of the concept of organizational constitutionalism, I analyze three types of organizations: religious, military, and academic, which vary in the degree to which they have institutionalized the components of constitutionalism.

In the final chapter of Part II, a basic problem in the structural changes of organizations is considered, namely, the relative rate of innovations of a technical vs. an administrative nature. A discrepancy in the rate of technical as compared with administrative innovations is what I designate as "organizational lag." How to minimize organizational lag is a challenging problem to the practitioners of the art of management as well as to organization theorists. Progress in minimizing organizational lag will, in turn, contribute to a reduction of both inter-role conflicts and role strains.

NOTES

1. William J. Goode, "A Theory of Role Strain," *American Sociological Review* 25 (August 1960): 483.
2. Alvin W. Gouldner, "The Norm of Reciprocity," *American Sociological Review* 25 (April 1969): 161–78.
3. Albert O. Hirschman, *Exit, Voice and Loyalty* (Cambridge, Mass.: Harvard University Press, 1970).

CHAPTER 4

Role Strain and the Norm of Reciprocity

In any formal organization, the goals as reflected in the system of functional differentiation result in a distinctive pattern of role differentiation. In turn, role differentiation, whether viewed hierarchically or horizontally, leads to what Mannheim has called "perspectivistic thinking," namely, incumbency in a particular status induces a corresponding set of perceptions, attitudes, and values.[1] In an organization, as in a society as a whole, status occupants tend to develop a commitment to subunit goals and tasks—a commitment that may be dysfunctional from the viewpoint of total organizational goals. In other words, "perspectivistic thinking" may interfere with the coordination of effort toward the accomplishment of total organizational goals, thus generating organizational pressures to ensure adequate levels of performance.

The purpose of this chapter is to inquire into the differential distribution of such pressures in a research organization and their relation to role strains. It should be emphasized that the focus of this chapter is on the ideas that emerged in the course of research rather than on the specific findings. The data to be presented are admittedly fragmentary. Their chief value, as we shall see, is not as evidence for the testing of hypotheses, but as a point of departure for what may prove to be a fruitful way of exploring the relationship between role strain and the norm of reciprocity in research organizations.

This is a revised version of a paper read at the annual meeting of the American Association for the Advancement of Science, New York City, December, 1960.

ORGANIZATIONAL PRESSURES

The research on which this chapter is based was conducted in a relatively small industrial chemical research organization that is part of a large chemical company. Three structural components of this research organization will be the focus of our attention: a basic research department, an applied research department, and a development department.[2] These three units may be conceived as constituting points on a continuum of distance from the primary organizational goal, with the development unit being closest to the organizational goal and the basic research unit being farthest from it. The primary goal of the research organization is presumably to assist the manufacturing divisions of the parent corporation in producing chemical products at a profit. Accordingly, we expected that organizational pressures—which may be defined as efforts on the part of management to ensure a level of performance consonant with organizational requirements—would be higher the more proximate the unit's position is to the organizational goal, that is, highest on the development unit, next highest on the applied research unit, and lowest on the basic research unit.

Organizational pressures may take various forms (such as determining the duration of projects, setting deadlines for projects, or allocating of research funds). The first of two crude indicators of organizational pressures available to us is the proportion of projects in a department initiated and sponsored by the manfacturing divisions as compared with the research organization itself. Sponsorship of projects by manufacturing divisions may engender greater pressures to produce a "useful" result in a given time than does sponsorship by the research organization itself. As shown in Table 4.1, the development unit, in contrast to the basic research unit, is engaged almost exclusively in work initiated and sponsored by the manufacturing divisions of the parent corporation, whereas the basic unit devotes one-half of its project time to studies initiated and sponsored by the research organization itself; the applied research department—at least in this particular organization—has virtually the same proportion of its projects as the basic research unit sponsored by the research organization.

The second indicator of organizational pressure is the mean number of projects per chemist per unit of time. Admittedly, projects differ in degree of complexity and amount of time required for completion. Bearing this qualification in mind, the development department again appears to be subject to a greater degree of organizational pressure than either of the other departments: the mean number of projects per chemist in 1958 was 1.7 for the development department, 1.5 for the applied research department, and 1.3 for the basic research department. In short, my expectation that organizational pressures would be differentially distributed in the three functionally distinct departments appears to be borne out.

Table 4.1   Projects Sponsored by Manufacturing Divisions and the Research Organization, by Department, 1958[a]

Department and Source of Sponsorship	No.	Percentage
Basic research:		
Research organization	12	50
Management divisions	12	50
Applied research:		
Research organization	23	48
Management divisions	25	52
Development:		
Research organization	9	15
Management divisions	51	85

[a] *Source:*   Administrative records of the research organization.

ROLE STRAINS

Role strain, according to Goode, is the "felt difficulty in fulfilling role obligations."[3] As in the case of organizational pressures, role strains may also take various forms. For example, some types of role-set[4] relations may entail conflicting obligations; and inconsistent rank orderings on various dimensions of a role, such as autonomy, prestige, rewards—that is, "status incongruency"— may engender tension.

I shall focus only on those role strains that have their source in organizational pressures, my hypothesis being that there is a positive and linear relationship between organizational pressures and role strains. The first of two measures of role strain consists of conventional morale indicators, such as absenteeism, turnover, and accident rate. The distribution of role strain, as measured by these indicators, for the three departments is shown in Table 4.2. The applied research unit is consistently higher in its rates of accidents, absenteeism, lateness, and labor turnover than the other two units, the basic research and development units being approximately equal on the morale measure of role strain. Thus, my prediction of a linear relationship between organizational pressure and role strain as measured by these indicators was not confirmed; the actual relationship appears to be roughly curvilinear—using the terms "linear" and "curvilinear" very loosely since my data are not metrical and we have a "sample" of one of the three types of departments.

When we turn to the second measure of role strain—the degree of discrepancy between a scientist's actual research project and his ideal research

Table 4.2   Morale Indicators, by Department, 1958[a]

| | Mean Number | | |
Morale Indicator	Basic Research (N = 18)	Applied Research (N = 31)	Development (N = 35)
Accidents	0.06	0.23	0.14
Absences (days)	4.33	6.53	6.17
Punctuality:			
Late arrivals	14.44	19.68	15.03
Early departures	2.05	9.06	1.77
Turnover (dismissals and resignations)	0.06	0.45	0.26

[a] *Source:*   Administrative records of the research organization.

project—the data become even more fragmentary: we are dealing here with only 15 chemists divided into three subgroups, one for each department. Each chemist was asked to give a technical description of the major research project on which he was currently working and a technical description of his ideal research project, assuming no organizational limitations on time and money. The pairs of statements of actual and ideal research projects were compared and rated independently by three judges, all of whom hold doctorates in chemistry and have several years of research experience. The ratings were in terms of what is considered basic research in chemistry and were scored in one of three ways: Whether the actual project and the ideal project are the same or equal in such terms; whether the actual project is closer than the ideal project to basic research; or whether the ideal project is closer than the actual project to basic research. I assumed that either of the two forms of divergence between actual and ideal research would indicate role strain.

The statements of nine chemists were rated as congruent; those of the remaining six were rated as incongruent—from which we infer that the latter are subject to the task-dimension of role strain. The cases of role strain distributed themselves with the mode at the department of applied research—one case (out of three) in basic research, four cases (out of seven) in applied research, and one case (out of four) in development. Given the small sample sizes, we may merely suggest that a higher proportion of chemists in the applied research department have role strain than do those in either basic research or development.

A possible interpretation of the role strain of the chemist in the applied research department is that he may subjectively experience a greater amount of relative deprivation compared to members of the basic research and development departments. On the one hand, since his training is roughly comparable to that of the chemists in the basic research department, he may wish to pursue problems more deeply than he does. On the other hand, although he is expected to obtain results of potential value to the company, his work is not as close to the goal of the organization as is that of the chemist in the development department; nor does he generally learn of the use to which his results are put by the manufacturing divisions. Hence, he may feel deprived both of the opportunity of engaging in basic research as well as of the gratification of contributing directly and visibly to the accomplishment of the mission of the organization.

We may also liken the position of the applied researcher in the industrial research organization to that of a foreman in a production organization: Both occupy an intermediate position that has conflicting or ambiguous expectations and orientations. The foreman, as the lowest man on the managerial ladder, hardly feels part of the management; nor does he feel part of the group of workers. Analogously, the applied researcher feels that he is not part of either the basic research or the development group.[5]

The frequent inadequacies of existing theory and the difficulties of applying it to the solution of novel and practical problems suggest that the task of the applied researcher is fraught with more ambiguity than the tasks of those engaged in either basic research or development. If inquiry establishes that applied researchers—in general and not only in this particular research organization—perceive greater ambiguity in their task than either basic researchers or those engaged in development work, this would throw some light on the finding of greater role strain among this group of chemists.

THE NORM OF RECIPROCITY

The two possible interpretations set forth above of the finding that applied chemists exhibit more role strain than either basic research or development chemists may be formulated in terms of the "norm of reciprocity" cogently analyzed by Gouldner.[6] For the applied researcher the norm of reciprocity as it pertains to his relationship with his employer may be more salient than for either the basic research or the development chemist.

All institutionalized role relationships, whether employer-employee, husband-wife, parent-child, teacher-student, and so on, are grounded in a set of mutual expectations. As part of conforming with one another's normative expectations, the role partners share in common a moral norm of reciprocity. This norm obliges Ego to give benefits to Alter from whom he has received benefits.

Hobbes includes reciprocity as one of his "laws of nature."[7] And according to Westermarck, reciprocity is a universal norm. "To requite a benefit, or to be grateful to him who bestows it, is probably everywhere, at least under certain circumstances, regarded as a duty."[8] There is obviously no need to view reciprocity as an instinct. Rather, it may be viewed as a tendency generated by the common social and cultural attributes of all human role relationships. To the extent that this norm is internalized by members of a society in all their role relationships, it is obviously an important mechanism of social stability. This, however, does not preclude the possibility that the norm of reciprocity may under some conditions have dysfunctions in some role relationships, which possibility Gouldner recognized but did not examine in his analysis.[9]

In the case of the scientist engaged in basic research in industrial organizations the goals of the role partners may be *perceived* as divergent even if in actuality they are not. The scientist, focused on contributing to scientific knowledge per se, becomes cognizant of the fact that this does not contribute— at least not always in the immediate or foreseeable future—to the principal goal of the company, which is profit. Accordingly, he may feel that he is not "earning his keep." To counterbalance this disquieting feeling, the basic researcher may seek refuge in his status as a member of a scientific community with its norms of contributing to the body of scientific knowledge. In addition, to reduce his dissonance, accentuated by his awareness that he is in effect not conforming to the moral norm of reciprocity, he is impelled to "adjust" his research to increase the chances of a "useful end result" emerging, thereby reciprocating the benefits bestowed on him by his employer.

This process of adjusting one's research interests to ensure compliance with the norm of reciprocity may prove more difficult for the applied research chemist than for the basic research chemist. The former may not be more socialized into the value of providing his employer with a service than the latter, yet his work is supposed to show more promise of a "payoff." In view of the nature of his training he may have a degree of identification with the scientific community comparable to that of the basic researcher; hence, the norm of reciprocity confronts him with a conflict of loyalties to competing reference groups: the scientific community versus the employer or employing organization. The chemist engaged in development work probably experiences no such difficulties in his role performance. His task is explicitly structured to promote the employer's interests, and hence he is not likely to perceive the norm of reciprocity as imposing any burden on him. The different responses to the norm of reciprocity appear to be a function of the type of role a scientist performs vis-à-vis his employer.

ALTERNATIVE ROLE MODELS

Sociologists studying research organizations tend to conceptualize the position of the scientist as a "professional" whose goals and values are in conflict with those of his status as a "bureaucratic employee."[10] This, however, implies that the scientist has a professional-client relationship with his employer, which is not true of the scientist interested in basic research, although it may be true of the engineer and of the scientist engaged in applied research and development. For, by definition, a professional is one who provides a service based on established knowledge to someone—namely, a client—who requests his specialized service. However, the scientist interested solely in creating new knowledge, who is employed by an industrial research organization, is in fact not performing the role of a "professional" vis-à-vis the impersonal client, the organization. Only if he abdicates his scientific role of discovering new knowledge and seeks to *apply* existing scientific knowledge to the solution of the organization's problems is he acting as a professional with reference to his employer, the client. In all probability, a substantial porportion of scientists employed in industry are engaged in activities that might be characterized as applied research and hence are actually providing a professional service to their client. An even higher proportion of scientists are probably engaged in development work and perform a role akin to that of an "employee" vis-à-vis an "employer" in that they are "assigned" projects with detailed specifications as to the end product desired, and have no autonomy with respect to the research process. And only a relatively small proportion of scientists are conducting basic research in industry.[11]

Neither the employer-employee relationship nor the professional-client relationship appears to be a functional role model for the basic research scientist employed in industry. Since the number of such scientists in industry is increasing as the size of basic research budgets grows from year to year, a clarification of this role relationship is of practical as well as theoretical significance.

An alternative role model for the basic researcher in industry is that of the "patron-artist" relationship. This model, as we will see, seems more functional than either that of the employer-employee relationship or that of the professional-client relationship.

The ideal-typical patron-artist relationship is one in which the patron affords the artist the freedom to pursue, in his own manner, his artistic impulses. The conception of "an autonomous, non-utilitarian art enjoyable in itself" or "art for art's sake"—already familiar to the Greeks but forgotten in the Middle Ages—was rediscovered in the Renaissance.[12] To be sure, patrons in the Renaissance and thereafter have tried to influence the work of the artist—against the latter's wishes—in a variety of ways. Since the Renaissance, patrons have tended to deviate in at least two directions from the ideal-typical patron-artist relationship: They have assumed either the status of an employer vis-à-vis the artist or that of a client, so to speak. In both cases these forms of deviation from the ideal type impair the autonomy of the artist. In the status of an employer, the patron feels that he has the right to specify precisely the end product of the work of the artist by virtue of his formal or informal contractual relationship. He believes that he is entitled to dictate not only what the employee should do but how he should do it. Indeed, in the pre-Renaissance period, artists had a status comparable to employees; in fact, they were commonly called "artisans" rather than "artists." And their work was closely regulated by the dictates of the Church and the guilds.[13]

In the status of a client, the patron throws himself, as it were, on the mercy of the artist in the hope that the artist, in the capacity of a competent professional, will provide him with the best possible service. He trusts that the artist can discover what he, the client, really wishes and needs. In this type of relationship the artist also has to relinquish his own independent artistic judgments and impulses on behalf of the aesthetic needs—as he divines them—of the client.

Clearly, the ideal-typical patron-artist relationship, in contrast to the employer-employee and client-professional relationships, fits the requirements of the basic researcher in industry. In all likelihood, many industrial research organizations accord scientists the status of professional vis-à-vis a client; some persist in assigning them the status of an employee vis-à-vis an employer; a few are experimenting with a new role relationship that we may interpret as being, in effect, modeled after the kind of patron-artist relationship I have discussed— a role relationship in which the basic research scientist, like the artist, is granted the right by his patron, the industrial organization, to pursue his research in accordance with his own scientific interests and standards.

In some large industrial laboratories all three analytically distinguishable work relationships may be found. The employer-employee relationship may apply not only to manual and clerical employees but also to engineers and scientists engaged in development work; the professional-client relationship may apply to legal and medical personnel as well as to applied researchers; and the patron-scientist relationship may apply to those engaged in basic research.

The status-sequences of scientists employed in industrial research organizations may entail movement from basic research to applied research and thence to development, or from the role of a scientist to a professional and thence to an employee. The frequency of different status sequences of scientists in industrial research organizations is, of course, an empirical question. Barring movement out of research into administrative work, a one-step sequence from basic research to applied research or from applied research to development is probably more common than a two-step sequence from basic research to applied research and from applied research to development. Some virtuosos may resolve their role strains and conform to the norm of reciprocity by alternating in their performance of the roles of scientist, professional, and employee.

Each of these three ideal-typical work relationships is presumably governed by a distinctive and dominant norm: In the employer-employee relationship, the norm of obedience to a superior is fundamental; in the client-professional relationship, it is the norm of service to a client; and in the patron-patronee relationship, the governing norm is that of autonomy for the patronee to pursue his work as he sees fit. The norms underlying each of these role models stand in a different relationship to the norm of reciprocity: The norm of obedience in the employer-employee relationship is compatible with the norm of reciprocity; the norm of service to a cleient in the client-professional relationship intensifies the bindingness of the norm of reciprocity, as our findings on the applied research chemist suggest; and the norm of autonomy in the patron-patronee relationship is incompatible with the norm of reciprocity. The incompatibility between the norm of autonomy and the norm of reciprocity points to a condition under which the alleged universal norm of reciprocity may prove dysfunctional.

A plausible hypothesis may be advanced that the norm of reciprocity in the industrial employer-scientist relationship functions as a mechanism for diverting research energies from basic research to applied research. If this hypothesis is confirmed, it would point to a built-in pressure for the erosion of basic research in industry. Since the amount of basic research conducted in industry is now relatively small, but growing because of technological requirements and developments, the pressure on the basic research scientist stemming from the norm of reciprocity may become increasingly problematic and dysfunctional for science as well as industry.[14]

SCOPE OF THE PROBLEM OF ROLE STRAIN

The problem of role strains of the scientist and of the potential dysfunctions of the norm of reciprocity is very likely not confined to the industrial research context. In other institutional contexts, academic and government, similar problems may arise. The university scientist who applies for a grant to a public or private foundation may "custom tailer" his project to what he takes to be the practical or applied interests of his prospective grantor or patron. After receiving the grant, he may feel an obligation to express his gratitude to the foundation by focusing on the applied rather than on the theoretical aspects of his research, although the latter may in fact be of more interest to him. In a series of conferences on interdisciplinary team research in social science, it was observed:

Often the researcher fears that the person or organization making the grant will be annoyed that he is not working on the problem as set forth in the application for funds. . . . It was agreed that the grantor has a right to know what is going on in the research and to exercise a modicum of control over it. . . . And when an investigator begins a search for funds, he gives up some of his freedom.[15]

In a study of research in an academic setting, Bennis found that a university research group financed on a year-to-year basis by a private foundation was market-oriented, whereas another research group with a four-year contract was task-oriented. As one member of the former research group put it:

The main problem here is doing research and justifying ourselves to the foundation. The thing that's annoyed me the most is that we spend so much time looking at our navel without doing anything—except justifying our existence.[16]

Similarly, government scientists, supported by taxpayers and answerable yearly to Congress when it makes its appropriations, may feel that they should justify their existence by producing something of practical value. Moreover, the specific missions of the parent agencies of government laboratories, whether it be in the field of health, defense, agriculture, or whatever, may tend to restrict the selection of research problems.[17]

Judging from an unpublished report by an official of a government-granting agency on the state of a particular field of science in Europe, this problem is by no means unknown there.

The scientist in Europe builds his academic career by dedicating himself early to an established institute or institute director. He works his way through the ranks, always at the service of the director. He cultivates the friendship of other institute directors, thereby hoping to establish himself in the good graces of those who will pass upon his application for promotion and tenure.

This suggests a guildlike, master-journeyman relationship that requires the scientist to express his fealty to the institute director. In this feudal atmosphere we would also expect to observe instances of wholly extraneous considerations brought to bear on the selection and conduct of research. The scientist is here enmeshed in a social system in which the norm of reciprocity is crucial to his continuing role as a scientist.

CONCLUSION

There are some signs of progress toward the institutionalization of the role model of the patron-artist for the employer-scientist and the grantor-scientist relationship. For example, the National Science Foundation is by federal mandate interested in the advancement of basic research. Unlike other federal agencies concerned with the promotion of science, this foundation has no specific mission other than the advancement of basic research. Recognition of the need for freedom to pursue research without interference is also expressed in the Public Health Service, as evidenced by the following statement of two of its officials that the investigator "must also be free in the use of the funds granted to change his research as desired, to permit follow-up of any new and promising leads. Public Health Service research grant policy does permit this sort of freedom and encourages the investigator to use the research funds for the most important research purposes he determines."[18] Both of these public foundations have recently begun to award relatively long-term research grants.[19] Similarly, some private foundations, such as the Alfred P. Sloan Foundation, have initiated a program of flexible grants to promising scientists without regard to the merits of the projects to be undertaken.[20]

A small though increasing number of industrial organizations are evidently experimenting with programs of basic research—that is, with acting as a patron to the scientist. To be sure, only the larger and financially more secure corporations can afford such a venture, since the return on such an investment is uncertain and remote in time.

The further institutionalization of the role model of the patron-artist for the employer-scientist and the grantor-scientist relationship would probably reduce organizational pressures on the scientist and in turn reduce his role strains. As progress is made toward a social redefinition of the role relationship of the scientist to his employer or grantor, the potentially dysfunctional consequences for basic research, due to particular social structures, will diminish. The crystallization of the new patron-artist role model would probably throw in relief the old role model of professional-client, thereby possibly facilitating the socialization of the applied researcher who, in discharging his "professional" obligations to his client, would thus experience less role strain.

NOTES

1. Cf. Karl Mannheim, *Ideology and Utopia,* trans. Louis Wirth and Edward Shils (London: Routledge & Kegan Paul, 1936), pp. 51, 91–96, 239, 244.

2. The terms used here refer to the following definitions:

   Basic research—Includes original investigations for the advancement of scientific knowledge that do not have specific commercial objectives, although such investigations may be in fields of present or potential interest to the reporting company.

   Applied research—Includes investigations directed to the discovery of new scientific knowledge that have specific commercial objectives with respect to products or processes.

   Development—Includes technical activities of a nonroutine nature concerned with translating research findings or other scientific knowledge into products or processes. Development does not include routine technical services to customers or other items excluded from the above definition of research and development (National Science Foundation, *Funds for Research and Development in Industry 1957* [Washington, D.C.: Government Printing Office, 1960], p. viii).

3. William J. Goode, "A Theory of Role Strain," *American Sociological Review* 25 (August 1960): 483.

4. Cf. Robert K. Merton, "The Role-Set: Problems in Sociological Theory," *British Journal of Sociology* 8 (June 1957): 106–20.

5. Cf. Burleigh B. Gardner and William F. Whyte, "The Man in the Middle: Position and Problems of the Foremen," *Applied Anthropology* 4 (Spring 1945): 1–28; Fritz J. Roethlisberger, "The Foreman: Master and Victim of Double Talk," *Harvard Business Review* 23 (Spring 1945): 283–98; Donald E. Wray, "Marginal Men of Industry: The Foreman," *American Journal of Sociology* 54 (January 1949): 298–301.

6. Alvin W. Gouldner, "The Norm of Reciprocity," *American Sociological Review* 25 (April 1960): 161–78.

7. Thomas Hobbes, *Leviathan,* Parts 1 and 2 (New York: Liberal Arts Press, 1958), p. 125.

8. Quoted in Gouldner, "The Norm of Reciprocity," p. 171.

9. *Ibid.,* p. 177.

10. See, for example, Simon Marcson, *The American Scientist in Industry* (Princeton, N.J.: Industrial Relations Section, Princeton University, 1960); David N. Solomon, "Professional Persons in Bureaucratic Organizations," in *Symposium on Preventive and Social Psychiatry, 15–17 April, 1957* (Washington, D.C.: Government Printing Office, 1957), pp. 253–66; and the special issue on the administration of research in *Administrative Science Quarterly,* vol. I (December 1956).

11. These imprecise statements are due to the absence of data on the distribution by function of the 149,000 scientists employed in industry. They are inferred from some data on the allocation of funds in industry to basic research (3 percent), applied research (21 percent), and development (75 percent); and from some very gross information on the functions performed by scientists grouped together with engineers. For the source with respect to allocation of funds see National Science Foundation, *Funds for Research and Development in Industry 1957* (Washington, D.C.: Government Printing Office, 1960), p. ix; for the source regarding functions performed by scientists and engineers see National Science Foundation, *Scientific and Technical Personnel in American Industry* (Washington, D.C.: Government Printing Office, 1960), p. 11.

12. Arnold Hauser, "*The Social History of Art,* vol. II (New York: Vintage Books, 1959, p. 74.

13. *Ibid.,* pp. 51–84. See also Germain Bazin, *A History of Art* (Boston: Houghton Mifflin, 1959), p. 198.

14. For data on the percentage increase in funds of basic research in industry during 1953–1958 see National Science Foundation, "Funds for Research and Development Performance in American Industry, 1958," *Review of Data on Research and Development,* No. 20 (Washington, D.C.: Government Printing Office, 1960).

15. Margaret Luszki, *Interdisciplinary Team Research Methods and Problems* (New York: New York University Press, 1958), pp. 283–84.

16. Warren G. Bennis, "The Effect on Academic Goods of Their Market," *American Journal of Sociology* 62 (July 1956): 30.

17. Cf. Allen V. Astin, "Basic Research in Government Laboratories," in Dael Wolfle, ed., *Symposium on Basic Research* (Washington, D.C.: American Association for the Advancement of Science, 1959), pp. 154–55.

18. Quoted in Alan C. Ronkin, "The Administrative Process of Contract and Grant Research," *Administrative Science Quarterly* 1 (December 1956): 292.

19. Small wonder that the Public Health Service and the National Science Foundation have a highly prestigious standing among scientists. In an unpublished survey on attitudes toward sources of research funds, a nonrandom sample of 89 prominent scientists were asked to rate

the desirability of six sources of funds, assuming that all of them are willing to provide the desired support in the same amount and according to their present policies, as these are understood by the respondents. The resulting rank order was as follows: (1) National Science Foundation, (2) National Institutes of Health, (3) Rockefeller Foundation, (4) funds from your own institution, (5) American Cancer Society, (6) Atomic Energy Commission.

20. Cf. Warren Weaver's Preface to Wolfle, ed., *Symposium on Basic Research,* pp. xi–xii.

CHAPTER 5

Organization Man and Due Process of Law

Increasing usage of the term "organization man" among laymen or of its technical equivalents among social scientists, suggests that Whyte has identified a significant phenomenon in large organizations.[1] Although he asserts that the phenomenon conveyed by this term is observable in industrial, educational, governmental, and other types of organizations, his point of departure is the industrial organization; and the status of "organization man" that appears to concern him primarily is that of the junior or middle executive.

Unlike the ubiquitous entrepreneur of the nineteenth century whose ideology was rooted in the Protestant Ethic, the ideology of the equally ubiquitous corporate manager of the twentieth century, according to Whyte, is founded on the Social Ethic.[2] Whereas the entrepreneur was an individualist and an innovator, the organization man is a conformist, socialized into the values of organizational loyalty, teamwork, and the avoidance of independent opinions or original ideas. By Social Ethic Whyte means "that contemporary body of thought which makes morally legitimate the pressures of society against the individual. Its major propositions are three: a belief in the group as the source of creativity; a belief in 'belongingness' as the ultimate need of the individual; and

This is a revised version of a paper read at the annual meeting of the Eastern Sociological Society, Boston, Massachusetts, April, 1960.

a belief in the application of science to achieve the belongingness."[3] This ethic or ideology of the organization man, as we will refer to it, "rationalizes the organization's demands for fealty and gives those who offer it wholeheartedly a sense of dedication in doing so—*in extremis,* you might say, it converts what would seem in other times a bill of no rights into a restatement of individualism."[4]

The contrast Whyte draws between the Protestant Ethic and the Social Ethic is not unlike Riesman's distinction between "inner-directed" and "other-directed" character structure.[5] It is also related to the analyses by Bendix and Sutton of the entrepreneurial versus the managerial ideology.[6] The historic warrant for the assertion advanced by Whyte and others about the transition from the Protestant to the Social Ethic is a question that transcends the scope of this chapter. Nor will we be concerned with appraising the evidence for the currency of the ideology of the organization man among junior and middle executives.[7] Rather, our purpose is to analyze some social-structural sources and consequences of this ideology.

A CRITICISM OF WHYTE'S THESIS

Whyte, like Weber, deplores the trend toward the bureaucratization of society and the restrictions this imposes on the individual. Unlike Weber, however, Whyte advocates a deliberate course of action that he urges on the organization man. While disclaiming that his book is a plea for nonconformity, he nevertheless exhorts the organization man to resist the pressures of the organization even if it means the loss of his job.[8]

Although he repeatedly acknowledges that the organization is the creation of man and can be changed by man, he virtually never criticizes the architecture, so to speak, of the organization; nor does he address any proposals for reform to the "architects" of the organization, but rather to the individual organization man.[9] As he puts it, "The fault is not in organization, in short; it is in our worship of it. . . . To say that the incubus lies in organization itself would be partially correct, but it would also be somewhat futile."[10] Obviously, it need not be "futile" if the structure of the organization can be redesigned so as to counteract the ideology of the organization man.

Whyte's effort to eliminate the evils of the ideology of the organization man by exhorting him to fight the organization is misplaced. Assuming that the ideology of the organization man is as pervasive a phenomenon in industrial and other types of organizations as Whyte claims, a logically prior question is one pertaining to the social-structural sources of this ideology.

STRUCTURAL SOURCES OF THE IDEOLOGY
OF THE ORGANIZATION MAN

The growth of the ideology of the organization man may be viewed in part as a product of the historical transformation of the structure of industrial management. With the progress of industrialism, owner-managers have been steadily replaced by salaried managers.[11] Instead of relying largely on inheritance and wealth as a mode of recruitment, as was the case when owner-managers or entrepreneurs dominated industry, corporate managers are typically nonowners who are recruited, presumably, because of their managerial ability and skills.

The work of management, however, is not presently founded on a distinct, recognizable and transmissible body of knowledge and skills. This means, among other things, that managerial performance cannot be objectively evaluated. In this respect management differs from virtually all other occupations in an industrial organization. Whereas manual occupations involve a body of well-defined skills that readily lend themselves to appraisal, this is not true of the management occupation. Professional occupations in an industrial organization, such as engineers and scientists, may be viewed as occupying an intermediate position—on an hypothetical scale of objective-subjective criteria of performance appraisal—between the occupations of manual workers and management. Both the high order of complexity of the body of knowledge and skills of a profession and the difficulty of evaluating the end product complicate the process of performance appraisal. In contrast, the relatively low order of complexity of the knowledge and skills required of a manual occupation facilitates an objective evaluation of the end product.

In the absence of objective criteria for evaluating the performance of junior and middle management, subjective criteria tend to predominate, such as degree of loyalty to the objectives of the organization.[12] The value placed on organizational loyalty is due both to the lack of professionalization of management and to the need for a principle to ensure the recruitment of trustworthy managers who will participate in critical decision making or in the execution of decisions, in spite of their owning a small amount of stocks or none at all in the enterprise. As a student of business administration puts it:

There is little knowledge as to the particular abilities which are required for a manager to act successfully in a specific situation. Even where certain abilities have been ascertained as desirable, it is seldom that they can be expressed in terms which are quantifiable. They are seldom established on the basis of what the man can do; rather they are usually expressed in terms of what he *is*, e.g., sincere, capable, loyal, patient, trained, experienced, etc. These attributes are difficult to relate to later performance, however measured.[13]

Another consequence of the absence of objective and rational criteria is the tendency for a system of sponsorship or patronage to develop. Organization men are motivated to become the protégés of superordinates in the hope that they will sponsor them for promotion to a higher level. A system of sponsorship, however, is fraught with insecurity. Problems develop when a sponsor loses his position of authority because of organizational changes, retirement, resignation, and the like, or when a protégé is dropped by a sponsor.[14]

In short, one of the major sources of the ideology of the organization man lies in the structure of the management occupation in industrial organizations.

A second and closely related source of the ideology of the organization man is the nature of the hierarchical structure of corporate management. The immediate superior of the junior or middle manager has the authority to issue various types of orders as well as to appraise his subordinate's performance and recommend negative or positive sanctions. Thus, in effect, he is in a position to determine his subordinate's fate in the organization, with the latter having no protection against arbitrary and capricious authority.[15] In the event of a conflict between a junior or middle executive and his superior, there is no institutionalized procedure for impartially adjudicating the dispute. In the absence of an impersonal procedure that a set of norms provides for resolving conflicts, the superior may exercise power or personal influence instead of legitimate authority. This is in sharp contrast with the case of a manual worker vis-à-vis a foreman in an organization in which there is a collective bargaining agreement between management and a trade union. Given such an agreement, a multistep grievance procedure culminating in arbitration is provided for resolving conflicts between the manual worker and his superior. This procedure, in effect, limits the authority of the worker's superordinate by providing the worker with a court of appeals, so to speak. The established right to appeal a governmental decision adversely affecting one's interests and the right to a fair and impartial hearing are important procedural components of the constitutional guarantees of due process of law.[16]

By comparison with the unionized manual worker, whose occupational rights are protected by the grievance machinery provided by the collective bargaining agreement, the junior or middle manager is at a distinct disadvantage: Lacking the right of appeal, he is at the mercy of the decisions of his immediate superior who, in his decisions regarding his subordinates, may function simultaneously as judge, jury, and prosecutor.[17] From this perspective the organization man appears to be a member of a "new proletariat" in present-day American industry. He does not have the protection of an outside occupational organization, as unionized employees do; nor does he have a code of professional ethics to govern his relationships with his superordinates, his peers, and his subordinates; nor does he have the protection of colleague control, as professionals do, to counteract hierarchical control. Since the nature of his work makes objective evaluation of performance difficult, and since he lacks the right of appeal, he is, therefore, highly motivated to fulfill his superior's expectations—even at the expense of his own ideas and wishes—in order to ensure a positive appraisal and the associated rewards. However, to fullfill his superior's expectations, which are often ambiguous, he learns to avoid any actions he suspects might displease his superior. Such actions may range from joining or not joining the Masons to the choice of style of clothing.[18] The organization man's process of adapting himself to the expectations and behavior patterns of his superior and of relinquishing, if necessary, his own preferences and judgments may be likened to the conformity patterns experimentally observed by Sherif and Asch. Subjects faced with an ambiguous and unstructured situation—as in the case of the auto-kinetic effect—tend to adjust their statements of perceptions to one another; and some subjects faced with an unambiguous and structured situation relinquish their true statement of perceptions of reality in favor of a false statement of perceptions made by others.[19]

In brief, the ideology of the organization man has at least two interrelated sources: occupational and organizational. Occupationally, the amorphous character of managerial work encourages the use of subjective criteria for evaluating performance, including a pattern of sponsorship or patronage and a concern for the organizational loyalty of subordinates. Organizationally, in the absence of norms of procedural due process of law, such as the right to appeal the decision of a superordinate, junior and middle managers are encouraged to become conformists, developing an over-sensitivity to the expectations of superordinates in order to ensure positive appraisal and corresponding rewards. Otherwise put, the ideology of organization man is an adaptation to certain normless elements in the work situation of junior and middle managers.

SOME CONSEQUENCES OF THE IDEOLOGY
OF THE ORGANIZATION MAN

The consequences of the ideology of the organization man are presumably—in the absence of systematic data—largely dysfunctional from the viewpoint of the individual executive as well as from the viewpoint of the industrial organization and society at large. Several illustrative and hypothetical dysfunctions will be considered.

From the standpoint of the individual executive as well as the organization, the ideology tends to inhibit original and creative effort that, by definition, departs from prevailing practices, and hence runs the risk of not being approved by a superordinate. Accordingly, the industrial organization must increasingly rely on staff specialists for new ideas rather than on line management. This entails a loss to the organization of a potential source of valuable innovations—which is not to gainsay the advantages of having staff specialists concern themselves principally with problems of innovation.

Another consequence of this ideology for the individual as well as for the organization is the paradoxical combination of high job immobility with high job insecurity. By definition, the organization man's loyalty induces him to devote his entire career to his organization. He has a "local" rather than a "cosmopolitan" orientation; in other words, his reference group is his organization rather than the occupation of management that transcends a given organization. This tends to result in a high degree of job immobility among executive personnel. From the point of view of the organization, low turnover may be highly advantageous, provided the manager's performance is judged to contribute to the organization's effectiveness. In the event that his performance is judged to interfere with the organization's attainment of its goals, the organization may transfer him to an innocuous position, induce him to resign, or dismiss him.[20] In the absence of due process of law for junior and middle managers, and we might even add top managers, those who are judged undesirable for whatever reasons—relevant or irrelevant—may be discharged without an opportunity for a fair hearing.

Another consequence of the ideology that is dysfunctional for the organization is the tendency of the organization man to restrict upward communication to material calculated to enhance his self-image and simultaneously not threaten the superordinate in any way. On the basis of studies of experimentally created hierarchies, we would expect that organization men who are upwardly mobile—and this is presumably true of the bulk of junior and middle managers—would be strongly motivated to censor upward communication to ensure positive appraisal and corresponding rewards.[21] Such action, of course, complicates the planning and coordination problems of top management.

Yet another effect of the ideology on the individual executive, related to job insecurity and the pressures for restriction of upward communication, is the tendency for discrepancies to develop between overt and covert behavior. Covert nonconformity occurs provided the probability of the discovery of such action is low. Where covert nonconformity does not occur, we may expect to find covert disbelief in the legitimacy of the authority exercised by the superior together with overt behavioral conformity. The resulting degree of cognitive dissonance, due to the discrepancy between overt conformity and covert disbelief, on the part of the organization man may be considerable. To reduce the resulting dissonance, the organization man can convince himself that his overt behavior is quite satisfactory after all, that is, by changing his cognitions so that they are consonant with his overt behavior.[22]

The effect of the ideology of the organization man on society as a whole is probably more elusive than its effects on the individual manager and on the industrial organization, although nonetheless real. As a result of the premium put on cautious behavior calculated not to offend the preferences and expectations of a superior, the organization man may tend to transfer this behavior pattern and principle of behavior to his community life and engage in only conformist activity. This approach to community life lessens the chances of successfully coming to grips with new and complex social problems requiring innovative rather than conformist behavior. The consequences of this ideology for society as a whole may be especially marked in view of the recent efforts by corporations to encourage management to increase their participation in community affairs.

A related effect of the ideology may be observable in family values and child-rearing patterns of the organization man. The values of seeking approval from superiors, of teamwork, and of "togetherness" may be transplanted from the corporation to the family.[23]

POTENTIAL COUNTERVAILING FORCES TO THE IDEOLOGY OF THE ORGANIZATION MAN

Two potential countervailing forces to the ideology of the organization man are the institutionalization of norms of procedural due process of law for corporate management and the professionalization of management.

As yet it is difficult to discern any evidence for the institutionalization of norms of due process within corporate management. It is possible, however, that such a development may be stimulated by the need for resolving conflicts between staff and line management. The high frequency of such conflicts, in the absence of unionization among staff specialists, may be conducive to the growth of norms of procedural due process. Such a development could pave the way for the extension of this institution to all corporate management.

Another source of influence favoring an extension of procedural due process is external to the corporation. There is a growing awareness of the need for restricting the powers of the corporation. In particular, it is being argued that the courts and the legislatures should extend constitutional guarantees of procedural due process to the corporation or that corporations should develop their own "supplementary constitutional systems.[24]" The venerable doctrine of due process, which dates back at least to the Magna Carta, includes a complex of procedural safeguards against the exercise of arbitrary and unlimited power.[25] These norms seek to ensure that disputes are resolved impartially and fairly. This complex of norms includes the right of all parties to a conflict to be heard, the right to confront witnesses, to cross-examine them, and to introduce evidence in one's behalf. Incorporated in the Bill of Rights in 1791, the Due Process Clause protects the citizen against the arbitrary exercise of power by the federal government. These rights were extended, about 75 years later, by means of the Fourteenth Amendment, to citizens vis-à-vis their state governments. Since then this doctrine has diffused or is in the process of being diffused to other spheres of government; and according to Berle and others it is also likely to diffuse to the realm of private organizations.[26] Thus, it is possible that pressures internal and external to the corporation may develop to institutionalize norms of procedural due process for all employees who come under its jurisdiction.[27]

Another potential countervailing force to the ideology of the organization man is the professionalization of management. In spite of the plethora of discussions for several decades about the professionalization of management, there has been very little progress in this direction.[28] The term "professional manager" at present largely denotes a salaried manager—as distinct from an owner-manager—who pursues his occupation with the aid of a developed and acknowledged body of transmissible knowledge and skills and a code of professional ethics.

Potential pressures for professionalization of management stem largely from ongoing technological changes. In the past, technological changes in industry have "machined out" various manual occupations. However, the age of computer technology and operations research may mean that many jobs now performed by junior and middle executives may in the future likewise be "machined out."[29] The future executive, as has been suggested, will probably require a body of technical knowledge and skills in addition to having an over-all-view of the organization's needs, of being a "generalist", and of having human relations skills.[30] As the knowledge and skills of future management become more complex, training for this occupation will probably become more intensive and prolonged, that is, more professionalized. A set of objective and technical standards for appraising performance may thus develop; appropriate professional organizations may then emerge; methods of colleague control may grow; and in general a code of ethics may come into being to cope with conflicts among managers and to govern their relationships with other occupational and interest groups inside and outside the corporation.

Either of the two potential countervailing forces to the ideology of the organization man may be conducive to the development of the other. As between these two possible developments it appears more likely that professionalization of management will be conducive to the institutionalization of norms of due process than the reverse.

Short of the institutionalization of the norms of procedural due process for junior and middle management, several other mechanisms may upon inquiry prove to have an equivalent function. The first is the institutionalization of the right of job transfer within a company. This would enable a manager, finding himself in an unsatisfactory authority relationship with his superior, to overcome this problem without suffering the consequences of adjustment to an arbitrary superior.

A related mechanism is job rotation. To the extent that this becomes an institutionalized procedure, it affords the executive an opportunity to manifest his abilities to more than one superior and in different organizational situations, which in turn increases the chances of a more objective appraisal of his talents.

A third mechanism that might be a functional substitute for the norms of due process is an increase in the opportunities for intercompany mobility. One of the major impediments to such mobility is the absence of vested pension rights. This discourages job changes because of the financial loss entailed. The vesting of pension rights for executives—such as already exists among university professors—if it should ever develop, would probably betoken a significant measure of progress toward the professionalization of management. Only an occupation with cosmopolitan values would encourage the institutionalization of such a practice.

RESEARCH IMPLICATIONS

The virtual absence of norms of procedural due process of law for corporate management obviously makes field research of an observational or documentary nature difficult. However, the literature of industrial sociology provides at least one significant "deviant case" worthy of intensive investigation. According to Elliot Jaques, the Glacier Metals Company in London has an appeals system that covers all the employees of this organization.[31] An understanding of the structure and functioning of this unique mechanism of due process of law may throw light on various problems, such as the preconditions for the emergence of such an institution in industry as a whole, and the relationship between the ideology of the organization man and due process of law.

In addition to an analysis of this deviant case—and the heuristic potential of deviant case analysis has been established in the masterly study of the International Typographical Union by Lipset, Trow, and Coleman—three other types of research are possible.[32] First, since procedural due process is institutionalized in all federal civil service organizations, a comparison between a government agency similar in function to an industrial organization that lacks due process would be instructive. Possible candidates for such a comparative study are a government research laboratory and an industrial research laboratory.

Second, a field experiment on due process would obviously be of great value. There are enough precedents for field experiments in industrial organizations, such as those conducted by Coch and French, Jackson, Morse and Reimer, and Ross, to make this approach feasible.[33]

Finally, laboratory experimentation is also feasible. Implicit in our analysis is the hypothesis that there is a negative correlation between the degree of objectivity of criteria for evaluating performance and the tendency to conform to a superior's expectations and preferences. Does this hypothesis hold true under an experimentally-induced condition involving a mechanism of procedural due process of law, for example, when subjects are granted the right to appeal the decision of a superior? This hypothesis is now being tested in a laboratory experiment simulating a set of relevant organizational properties.[34]

NOTES

1. For example, such concepts related to reference group theory as "local" versus "cosmopolitan" orientation, in Robert K. Merton, *Social Theory and Social Structure,* rev. ed. (Glencoe, Ill.: The Free Press, 1957), pp. 387–420; "job bureaucrat" versus "functional bureaucrat," in Leonard Reissman, "A study of Role Conceptions in a Bureaucracy." *Social Forces* 27 (March 1949): 305–10; "institution" versus "science" orientation, in Robert C. Davis, Glen Mellinger, Donald C. Pelz, and Howard Baumgartel, *Interpersonal Factors in Research,* Part 1 (Ann Arbor: Institute for Social Research, University of Michigan, 1954), pp. 5 ff; William H. Whyte, *Organization Man* (New York: Simon and Schuster, 1956).

2. Whyte, *Organization Man,* pp. 4–22.

3. *Ibid.,* p. 7.

4. *Ibid.,* p. 6.

5. David Riesman in collaboration with Reuel Denney and Nathan Glazier, *The Lonely Crowd* (New Haven, Conn.: Yale University Press, 1950).

6. Reinhard Bendix, *Work and Authority in Industry* (New York: John Wiley & Sons, 1956); Francis X. Sutton et al., *The American Business Creed* (Cambridge, Mass.: Harvard University Press, 1956).

7. The available evidence for this facet of Whyte's thesis appears to be largely impressionistic and literary.

8. Whyte, *Organization Man,* pp. 10–12.

9. *Ibid.,* p. 13.

10. *Ibid* pp. 13, 217. A similar view is expressed by Crawford H. Greenwalt, *The Uncommon Man: The Individual in the Organization* (New York: McGraw-Hill Book Co., 1959), p. 28, who otherwise appears to take issue with Whyte's thesis.

11. Cf. Bendix, *Work and Authority in Industry,* pp. 226–44.

12. For those in middle management for whom cost accounting yardsticks are applied, objective criteria are available, but whether they are the exclusive or principal bases for evaluation is an empirical question.

13. Paul Kircher, "Measurement and Managerial Decisions," in C. West Churchman and Philburn Ratoosh, eds., *Measurement: Definition and Theories* (New York: John Wiley & Sons, 1959), p. 71.

14. Norman H. Martin and Anselm L. Strauss, "Patterns of Mobility within Industrial Organizations," *Journal of Business* 29 (April 1956): 105–7.

15. Cf. Thomas L. Whisler, "Performance Appraisal and the Organization Man," *Journal of Business 31* (January 1958): 19–27.

16. For a discussion of the distinction between procedural and substantive due process of law, see Morris D. Forkosch, "American Democracy and Procedural Due Process," *Brooklyn Law Review* 24 (April 1958): 183–90. For a further sociological analysis of procedural due process, see William M. Evan, "Conflict and the Emergence of Norms," *Human Organization* 19 (Winter 1960–61): 172–73.

17. "There is no final escape from dependency if the superior is the ultimate authority, with no appeal beyond his interpretation or ruling. Unless there is some outside authority to which the subordinate can appeal, he never can be entirely safe in his dependency or quite able to develop a real independence." Mason Haire, *Psychology in Management* (New York: McGraw-Hill Book Co., 1956), p. 67.

18. Cf. Melville Dalton, *Men Who Manage* (New York: John Wiley & Sons, 1959), pp. 178–81.

19. Muzafer Sherif, "Group Influences upon the Formation of Norms and Attitudes," in Eleanor E. Maccoby, Theodore M. Newcomb, and Eugene L. Hartley, eds., *Readings in Social Psychology* (New York: Henry Holt, 1958), pp. 219–32; Solomon E. Asch, "Effects of Group Pressure upon the Modification and Distortion of Judgements," in Maccoby, Newcomb, and Hartley, *Readings in Social Psychology,* pp. 174–83.

20. Cf. Perrin Stryker, "How to Fire an Executive," *Fortune* 50 (October 1954): 116–17, 178–92.

21. Cf. Harold H. Kelley, "Communication in Experimentally Created Hierarchies," *Human Relations* 4 (February 1951): 39–56; Arthur R. Cohen, "Upward Communication in Experimentally Created Hierarchies," *Human Relations* 11 (February 1958): 41–53.

22. Leon Festinger, *A Theory of Cognitive Dissonance* (Evanston, Ill.: Row, Peterson, 1957), pp. 1–31.

23. Daniel R. Miller and Guy E. Swanson, *The Changing American Parent: A Study in the Detroit Area* (New York: John Wiley & Sons, 1958).

24. Adolph A. Berle, Jr., *The 20th Century Capitalist Revolution* (New York: Harcourt, Brace, 1954), pp. 77 ff.; Benjamin M. Selekman, "Power and Morality in Business," In Dan H. Fenn, Jr., *Management's Mission in a New Society* (New York: McGraw-Hill Book Co., 1959), pp. 317–19.

25. Rodney L. Mott, *Due Process of Law* (Indianapolis, Ind.: Bobbs Merrill, 1926), pp. 1–29.

26. Berle, *20th Century Capitalist Revolution,* pp. 77 ff.; Abram Chayes, "The Modern Corporation and the Rule of Law," in Edward S. Mason, ed., *The Corporation in Modern Society* (Cambridge, Mass.: Harvard University Press, 1960), pp. 25–45; Arthur S. Miller, "Constitutionalizing the Corporation," *PROD* 3 (September 1959): 10–12; also "Private Governments and the Constitution," Fund for the Republic Occasional Paper, 1959; W. H. Ferry et al., *The Corporation and the Economy* (Santa Barbara, Cal.: Center for the Study of Democratic Institutions, 1959), pp. 12–13, 81 ff.

27. At least one spokesman for management has expressed his opposition to any such development. See Greenwalt, *The Uncommon Man,* pp. 24–26.

28. See, for example, Henry C. Metcalf, ed., *Business Management as a Profession* (Chicago: A. W. Shaw Co., 1927); Howard R. Bowen, "Business Management: A Profession?" *The*

Annals of the American Academy of Political and Social Science 297 (January 1955): 112–17.

29. Cf. Russell L. Ackoff, "Automatic Management: A Forecast and Its Educational Implications," *Management Science* 2 (October 1955): 55–60; Harold J. Leavitt and Thomas L. Whisler, "Management in the 1980's," *Harvard Business Review* 36 (November–December 1958): 41–48.

30. Ackoff, "Automatic Management."

31. Elliott Jaques, *The Changing Culture of a Factory* (London: Tavistock Publications, 1951), pp. 51–53, 61–63.

32. S. M. Lipset, Martin A. Trow, and James S. Coleman, *Union Democracy* (Glencoe, Ill.: The Free Press, 1956).

33. Lester Coch and J. R. P. French, Jr., "Overcoming Resistance to Change," *Human Relations* 1 (August 1948): 512–32; J. M. Jackson, "The Effect of Changing the Leadership of Small Work Groups," *Human Relations* 6 (February 1953): 25–44; Nancy C. Morse and Everett Reimer, "The Experimental Change of a Major Organizational Variable," *Journal of Abnormal and Social Psychology* 52 (January 1956): 120–29; Ian C. Ross, *Role Specialization in Supervision,* Unpublished Ph.D. Dissertation, Columbia University, 1957.

34. This type of laboratory experiment, unlike most studies in the literature on small group research, entails the explicit simulation of status relationships and other organizational properties. See, for example, Donald F. Clark and Russell L. Ackoff, "A Report on Some Organizational Experiments," *Operations Research* 7 (May–June 1959): 279–93. For another example of a laboratory simulation of a facet of organizational structure, see William M. Evan and Morris Zelditch, Jr., "A Laboratory Experiment on Bureaucratic Authority," *American Sociological Review* 26 (December 1961): 888–93.

CHAPTER 6

Superior-Subordinate
Conflict in Research
Organizations

Among the various theoretical perspectives in the field of organizational research, the legal or jurisprudential one does not figure prominently, despite the pioneering work of Weber and Ehrlich.[1] By a legal or jurisprudential perspective is meant the analysis of organizational phenomena with the aid of concepts developed for the purpose of analyzing the legal system of a society. This may involve drawing an analogy between the legal system of a society, a relatively macroscopic social system, and the legal system of an organization, a relatively microscopic social system. When this analogy first suggested itself to me, I used the terms "public" and "private" legal system to distinguish between the two levels of analysis.[2]

Sociologically, a legal system consists of at least (1) a body of norms governing the expectations and actions of the members of a given system, and (2) a set of specialized statuses to which are allocated different normative functions. The set of norms of a legal system may differ along various dimensions, as, for example, the extent of knowledge and acceptance of norms on the part of those to whom they apply. The set of specialized statuses of a legal system may also differ in various respects, as, for example, in number and pattern of organization. Regardless of the variations in dimensions, three normative functions are performed by the specialized personnel of any legal system: legislative, judicial, and executive. By a legislative function is meant the authority to innovate norms; by a judicial function, the authority to interpret existing norms in the course of adjudicating disputes; and by an executive function, the authority to enforce norms with the aid of institutionalized sanctions. In combination, the norms and the specialized legal statuses constitute the major components of the structure of a legal system.[3] It is evident that such a conception is applicable to both public and private legal systems. Moreover, it directs attention to the nature of the relationship between public and private legal systems.[4]

This mode of conceptualization suggests several observations. First, the principle of separation of powers underlying the structure of our legal system is rarely observed in designing industrial organizations.[5] Second, executives of various types of organizations are often preoccupied with legislative and executive functions—namely, with what are normally designated as policy-making activities and with the implementation of policies—to the neglect of the judicial function. Third, although management may in fact devote a substantial portion of its time to the settling of interstatus and interunit disputes, the prevailing mode of adjudication is generally on an *ad hoc* basis. Management is neither self-conscious about the judicial function it is performing nor is it inclined to formalize and establish it as an impersonal control mechanism.[6] Fourth, the failure to institutionalize methods of adjudicating conflicts probably leads to the neglect of problems of injustice experienced by personnel of an organization. Finally, a consideration of the judicial function in industrial organizations points to the importance of examining a critical feature of the judicial process of a democratic society, that is, procedural due process of law, which consists of a body of norms protecting the citizens against the arbitrary and capricious exercise of authority.

Thus, the model of a legal system as applied to formal organizations directed my attention to the question of the consequences for organizational behavior of the presence or absence of due-process norms for different categories of personnel. In an earlier publication, interest was focused on the structure of authority relations involving junior and middle executives that appeared to be devoid of due-process norms, and the effect of this authority structure on the ideology and behavior of the "organization man."[7] On theoretical grounds, the absence of due process of law was hypothesized as having dysfunctional consequences for the individual, the organization, and the society. What these consequences are, in fact, requires empirical investigation.

In the course of a theoretical analysis, it was noted that:

Since procedural due process is institutionalized in all federal civil service organizations, a comparison between a government agency similar in function to an industrial organization, which lacks due process, would be instructive. Possible candidates for such a comparative study are a government research laboratory and an industrial research laboratory.[8]

The purpose of this paper is to report some findings of such a comparative study. A research and development organization is a particularly fruitful setting in which to study the effects of differing degrees of institutionalization and internalization of due-process norms because it is precisely in such organizations, that is, in knowledge-producing types of organizations—as distinct from routine- and crisis oriented organizations—where the lack of such norms might have discernible effects.[9]

PROCEDURE

In the course of a comparative study of project-group conflicts in a governmental and an industrial research organization, it seemed relevant to include several questions on whether the respondents perceived that they had a right to appeal the decisions of superiors in case of conflict. The respondents in both organizations were nonsupervisory engineers and scientists, first-line supervisors and second-line supervisors. The source of the data is a self-administered questionnaire. Four questions provided some relevant data. The first question was:

Without divulging any classified information, please describe briefly a problem, difficulty, or conflict which you have had with the supervisor of your project group in the past several months.

This question elicits information on the nature of superior-subordinate conflicts. The second question read: "How was this problem handled?" This question yields information on the mode of conflict resolution. The third question was:

When such a problem arises, does a subordinate have the right to take the matter up with someone at a higher level of management if he is dissatisfied with the way his project supervisor has handled the problem?

This question taps the respondent's perceptions as to the institutionalization of a due-process norm. If the response to this question was "yes," the respondent was asked to indicate whether he thought such a right was beneficial or detrimental. If the respondent's reply was "no," he was asked to indicate whether he thought such a right would be beneficial or detrimental. This question, the fourth and last, is interpreted as a measure of the respondent's internalization of the value of due process.

It should be noted that a self-administered questionnaire may be a strategic way of exploring this delicate problem area because of the anonymity involved. Yet after completing the questionnaire, some of the respondents admitted that they were reluctant to answer these questions fully and candidly for fear that their replies would jeopardize their job. Perhaps an unstructured personal interview that succeeded in conveying to the respondent the nonjudgmental and confidential character of the research effort might induce him to be even more candid than a self-administered questionnaire.

RESULTS

INCIDENCE OF CONFLICT

In view of the delicate nature of the first question, which asks the respondent to describe a conflict with his superior, it is noteworthy that 48 percent of all respondents admitted to having experienced such a conflict.[10] The frequency of such conflicts might be expected to diminish as organizational status increased; that is, from a nonsupervisory engineer or scientist to a first-line and a second-line supervisor, because a measure of authority would afford the status occupant some protection against acts of injustice. Instead, as Table 6.1 shows, there is, surprisingly, a highly significant positive association between incidence of reported conflicts and organizational status in both the governmental and the

Table 6.1   Incidence of Reported Superior-Subordinate Conflicts by Organizational Position

Reported Conflicts	Nonsupervisory Engineers & Scientists %	N	First-Line Supervisors %	N	Second-Line Supervisors %	N
Governmental laboratory[a]						
Yes	37.2	(23)	44.4	(12)	74.0	(20)
No	62.8	(39)	55.6	(15)	26.0	(7)
Industrial laboratory[b]						
Yes	41.0	(53)	47.0	(13)	82.1	(23)
No	59.0	(76)	53.0	(15)	18.9	(5)

[a] $\chi^2 = 10.44$; 2 d.f., p $<$ .005.
[b] $\chi^2 = 15.57$; 2 d.f., p $<$ .0004.

industrial laboratory. In the governmental laboratory, 37 percent of nonsupervisors reported conflicts, 44 percent of the first-line supervisors, and 74 percent of the second-line supervisors; in the industrial laboratory, the proportions for the three statuses are 41 percent, 47 percent, and 82 percent, respectively.

This finding lends itself to two possible interpretations: Either the higher the status, the more superior-subordinate conflicts are actually experienced or else the higher the status, the less reluctant one is to admit to having experienced such conflicts because of the increment of authority that accompanies higher status in the organizational hierarchy. Regardless of which interpretation is valid, the finding suggests the need for the protection of a due process norm for both high-status and low-status occupants.

TYPES OF CONFLICT

As for the substance of superior-subordinate conflicts, three types were anticipated: Technical conflicts, that is, disagreements over means or ends pertaining to the work of the engineer or the scientist; administrative conflicts, that is, disagreements concerning procedures, policies, and allocation of resources; and interpersonal conflicts resulting from personality clashes, barriers to interpersonal communication, and so on. The respondents' descriptions of conflicts were, in fact, coded almost entirely into two categories: technical and administrative. There were so few instances of interpersonal conflicts, as

Table 6.2   Types of Superior-Subordinate Conflict by Organizational Position

Types of Superior-Subordinate Conflict	Nonsupervisory Engineers & Scientists		First-Line Supervisors		Second-Line Supervisors	
	%	N	%	N	%	N
Government laboratory						
Technical	16.1	(10)	11.5	(3)	3.7	(1)
Interpersonal	00.0	(0)	11.5	(3)	7.4	(2)
Administrative	21.0	(13)	19.2	(5)	59.3	(16)
No conflict	62.9	(39)	57.8	(15)	29.6	(8)
Industrial laboratory						
Technical	17.1	(22)	7.4	(2)	10.4	(3)
Interpersonal	6.2	(8)	00.0	(0)	00.0	(0)
Administrative	17.8	(23)	40.7	(11)	72.4	(21)
No conflict	58.9	(76)	51.9	(14)	17.2	(5)

Table 6.3   Perceived Institutionalization of a Due-Process Norm

Perceived Institutionalization of a Due-Process Norm[a]	Governmental Laboratory		Industrial Laboratory	
	%	N	%	N
Yes	96.2	(102)	74.2	(127)
No	3.8	(4)	25.8	(44)

[a] $\chi^2 = 20.52$; 1 d.f.; $p < .001$

Table 6.2 shows, that they are ignored in the discussion. Perhaps this finding is to be expected because interpersonal conflicts are probably generated by technical and administrative conflicts, and, in addition, they are probably more difficult to describe or resolve than either technical or administrative conflicts.

Table 6.2 relates types of superior-subordinate conflict to organizational position in the two laboratories. Although the interstatus differences within each laboratory are not statistically significant, there is a tendency for technical conflicts to decrease with status and administrative conflicts to increase with status. This finding is explainable in terms of the functions performed by the three status groups. If the data in Table 6.1 are related to those in Table 6.2, an explanation suggests itself as to why first-line and second-line supervisors report more conflicts: They are more likely to have administrative conflicts because of the very nature of their jobs.

In the absence of a due-process mechanism, superior-subordinate conflicts are either unilaterally settled or else remain unresolved—if the situation permits this alternative. Where a due-process norm is institutionalized, the parties to a conflict either settle it themselves to their mutual satisfaction or it is adjudicated with the aid of a third party. An examination of the responses to the question on how the conflict was handled indicated that they could be coded as unilaterally resolved, as bilaterally or multilaterally resolved, or as unresolved. The hypothesis that type of conflict resolution is associated with organizational status, that is, that unilateral resolution is negatively associated with status and bilateral or multilateral resolution is positively associated with status, was not confirmed. No consistent or statistically significant findings emerged. Apart from the question of interstatus differences, a higher proportion of personnel in the governmental laboratory report bilateral or multilateral conflict resolutions, whereas a higher proportion of personnel in the industrial laboratory report unresolved conflicts. Although these differences also are not statistically significant, they can be explained by the findings in Table 6.3 on perceived institutionalization of a due-process norm.

PERCEPTION OF INSTITUTIONALIZATION OF A DUE-PROCESS NORM

In response to the question whether a subordinate has a right to appeal the decision of his superior if he is not satisfied, it was expected that a higher proportion of governmental than industrial personnel would acknowledge that they had such a right, because federal civil service agencies have a formal appeal system whereas the industrial laboratory studied did not.

Table 6.3 shows that the respondents' perception of the institutionalization of a due-process norm in the two laboratories was in accord with organizational realities. Although interstatus differences were not statistically significant within either laboratory, a significantly higher proportion of governmental than industrial respondents asserted that they had a right to appeal their superior's decisions. What is indeed surprising about Table 6.3 is the relatively high proportion of industrial laboratory respondents who perceived that a due-process norm was institutionalized. Evidently, an informal appeal system exists as far as these employees are concerned. How such an informal system comes into being and who performs the adjudicative or mediative function are intriguing questions.

Regardless of how formalized or institutionalized a due-process norm is, unless it is internalized, it will have little if any effect on conflict resolution or on behavior in an organization. Because of the difference in the institutionalization of a due-process norm in the two laboratories, a corresponding difference in internalization of a due-process norm was expected. Instead of differences between the two laboratories, however, the data (Table 6.4) showed interstatus

Table 6.4   Internalization of a Due-Process Norm by Organizational Position

Internalization of Due-Process Norm	Nonsupervisory Engineers & Scientists		First-Line Supervisors		Second-Line Supervisors	
	%	N	%	N	%	N
Government laboratory[a]						
Yes	84.4	(49)	61.9	(13)	52.1	(12)
No	15.6	(9)	38.1	(8)	47.9	(11)
Industrial laboratory[b]						
Yes	82.7	(72)	100.0	(18)	40.7	(11)
No	17.3	(15)	00.0	(0)	59.3	(16)

[a] $\chi^2 = 10.14$; 2 d.f.; $p < .006$.
[b] $\chi^2 = 26.64$; 2 d.f.; $p < .00001$.

differences in internalization in both laboratories. That the proportion of respondents in the industrial laboratory manifesting internalization of the value of a due-process norm is as high as it is suggests that the informal appeal system may be quite effective. This interpretation could have been tested had the respondents been asked whether they ever in fact availed themselves of the right to appeal a superior's decision.[11] Such a question would have provided another measure of internalization, possibly even more revealing than whether they regarded the right to appeal helpful or detrimental.

RESOLUTION OF CONFLICTS

The combined differences in institutionalization and internalization of a due process norm in the two laboratories may result in differences in the way conflicts are resolved. In the governmental laboratory, as Table 6.5 shows, there is no statistically significant relationship between type of conflict and mode of conflict resolution; in the industrial laboratory, there is a tendency for technical conflicts to be resolved bilaterally or multilaterally and for administrative conflicts to be resolved unilaterally. Is this difference related to the functioning of a formal versus an informal appeal system?

How a conflict is resolved, particularly whether it is unilaterally resolved, should affect the internalization of a due-process norm. As shown in Table 6.6, a higher proportion of government respondents with multilaterally resolved conflicts manifest internalization of the appeal procedure than do respondents with unilateral or unresolved conflicts. In the industrial laboratory, on the other hand, a higher proportion of respondents with either unilaterally or mul-

Table 6.5   Relationship Between Type of Supervisor-Subordinate Conflicts by Type of Conflict Resolution

Type of Conflict Resolution	Technical Conflict		Administrative Conflict	
	%	N	%	N
Governmental laboratory				
Unilateral	35.3	(6)	41.4	(12)
Multilateral	23.5	(4)	34.5	(10)
Unresolved	41.2	(7)	24.1	(7)
Industrial laboratory				
Unilateral	33.3	(8)	48.9	(23)
Multilateral	50.0	(12)	27.7	(13)
Unresolved	16.7	(4)	23.4	(11)

Table 6.6   Type of Conflict Resolution by Internalization of a Due-Process Norm

Internalization of Due-Process Norm	Unilateral		Multilateral		Unresolved	
	%	N	%	N	%	N
Governmental laboratory						
Yes	89.5	(17)	100.0	(10)	80.0	(8)
No	10.5	(2)	00.0	(0)	20.0	(2)
Industrial laboratory						
Yes	68.4	(13)	66.7	(18)	50.0	(8)
No	31.6	(6)	33.3	(9)	50.0	(8)

tilaterally resolved conflicts have internalized a due-process norm than those who have experienced an unresolved conflict. Although not statistically significant, these differences between the two organizations may also be a function of a formal versus an informal appeal system. Under a formal system, an experience with multilateral conflict resolution may strengthen the internalization of a due-process norm, whereas under an informal appeal system, an experience with either a multilateral or a unilateral conflict resolution may help develop a commitment to the value of a due-process norm.

The data of the present survey do not afford an opportunity to test the hypothesis that the absence of an institutionalized norm of due process has dysfunctional consequences for the individual and for the organization. This is but one of the unanswered problems in this neglected area of research. Another critical question is: Under what conditions is the norm of due process internalized by enough of the employees of an organization so that if a subordinate avails himself of his right of due process, he will not be victimized by his superior?

CONCLUSION

One noteworthy finding of this study is that a very high proportion of the respondents in the industrial laboratory, which does not have a formal appeal system, perceived a due-process norm to be institutionalized and had internalized such a norm. This points to the functioning of an informal appeal system. Such an informal mechanism is probably a response to pressures to constitutionalize the corporation.[12]

Rapidly changing technology, resulting from economic competition and

advances in science, is increasing the need for engineering and scientific personnel in industry. The steady influx of such professionals with values quite different from those of manual and clerical workers confronts management with
the need to reexamine its managerial doctrines. It also probably encourages the
emergence of a new generation of management more attuned to the new
technology and to the values of engineers and scientists. Under these circumstances management may be more receptive to the institutionalization of due-
process mechanisms, whether on grounds of economic rationality or on
ideological principles derived from the ethos of a democratic society.[13]

By studying problems of justice in the corporation with the same thorough-
ness (although not with the same methodology) as legal scholars, social
scientists may discover the conditions favoring the emergence of formal and
informal appeal systems and thus possibly provide guidelines for constitutionalizing industrial and other kinds of organizations. In conducting such
research, social scientists would contribute to the growth of a legal or a jurisprudential theory of organization.

NOTES

1. Max Weber, *Theory of Social and Economic Organizations,* trans. A. M. Anderson and T.
   Parsons (New York: Oxford University Press, 1947); Max Weber, *Law in Economy and
   Society,* trans. Edward Shils and Max Rheinstein (Cambridge, Mass.: Harvard University
   Press, 1954); Eugen Ehrlich, *Fundamental Principles of the Sociology of Law,* trans Walter
   L. Moll (Cambridge, Mass.: Harvard University Press, 1936).

2. William M. Evan, "Public and Private Legal Systems," in William M. Evan, ed., *Law and
   Sociology* (Glencoe, Ill.: The Free Press, 1962), pp. 165–84. See Chapter 12 of the present
   volume.

3. For a further discussion of this point, see *ibid.,* pp. 167 ff.

4. *Ibid.,* pp. 175–80.

5. For a notable exception to this assertion, see Wilfred Brown, *Exploration in Management*
   (New York: John Wiley & Sons, 1960).

6. Peter M. Blau and W. Richard Scott, *Formal Organizations* (San Francisco: Chandler,
   1962), pp. 176–83.

7. William M. Evan, "Organization Man and Due Process of Law," *American Sociological
   Review* 26 (August 1961): 540–47. See Chapter 5 of the present volume.

8. *Ibid.,* p. 546.

9. Cf. Waino W. Suojanen, "Management Theory: Functional and Evolutionary," *Journal of
   the Academy of Management* 6 (March 1963): 12–17.

10. This figure resembles the finding in a nationwide survey of role conflict in Robert L. Kahn
    et al., *Organizational Stress: Studies in Role Conflict and Ambiguity* (New York: John
    Wiley & Sons, 1964), p. 57.

11. For an example of the use of such a question, see William M. Evan, "Due Process of Law

in Military and Industrial Organizations," *Administrative Science Quarterly* 7 (September 1962): 197 ff.

12. Cf. William M. Evan, "Organization Man and Due Process of Law."

13. For two outstanding studies of changes in the ideology of management, see Reinhard Bendix, *Work and Authority in Industry* (New York: John Wiley & Sons, 1956); Francis X. Sutton *et al., The American Business Creed* (Cambridge, Mass: Harvard University Press, 1956).

CHAPTER 7

Power, Conflict and Constitutionalism In Organizations

That power and not property is the source of all manner of conflicts is a proposition more widely accepted now than several decades ago, let alone in the nineteenth century. With the abolition of the propertied classes, Marx believed a new social system would be ushered in, which in turn would pave the way for a new history of man. Weber, on the other hand, perceived a relentless process of rationalization of the Western world, principally by means of the application of rational-legal systems of administration. Notwithstanding their lack of ownership of the instruments of administration, officials of bureaucracies in market economies as well as in centrally-planned economies exercise extensive authority. Weber's thesis, in retrospect, is in harmony with that of Berle and Means concerning the separation of ownership and control in the modern corporation.[1] In an increasing proportion of large corporations, managers wield "power without property." It is also clear that the "iron law of oligarchy" is at least as applicable to the modern corporation as it is to such voluntary associations as trade unions and socialist parties with which Michels was concerned.

It was Dahrendorf, however, who, in rejecting Marx's theory of class conflicts based on property relations, argues for replacing it with one based on authority relations.[2] Following in the footsteps of Weber, Dahrendorf contends

83

that "authority is a universal element of social structure. It is in this sense more general than . . . property. . . ."[3] The differential distribution of authority in all types of organizations gives rise to social conflicts. Although Dahrendorf restricts his analysis to authority, that is, legitimate power, a justifiable reformulation of his position is that power, whether legitimate or illegitimate, is a "universal element of social structure." For if it is true that legitimate power tends to generate conflicts between superordinates and subordinates, then illegitimate power, *a fortiori*, should have a similar effect.[4] Other social scientists have since focused on the relationship between power and conflict, notably Kahn, who asserts that "the exercise of power . . . necessarily creates conflict" and "the existence of conflict (in the sense of disagreement or opposition) gives rise to the exercise of power.[5]

In the context of organizations rather than total societies, when conflicts arise in the course of the exercise of power, the modal response of subordinates is conformity or submission to the dictates of power. There are, however, two other possible responses, "flight" or "fight" or, in Hirschman's more neutral terminology, "exit" or "voice".[6] Although Hirschman, from his vantage point in economic theory, looks upon these options as responses to an organization's deterioration, they may also be relevant—particularly for organization theory—whenever nontrivial conflicts occur, even if unaccompanied by an organization's declining performance. For example, what options are exercised when Roman Catholic priests question the doctrine of celibacy or when students demand participation in the governance of colleges and universities?

Hirschman observes that in many organizations either exit or voice predominates as the mode of reaction of dissatisfied and activist members. In those organizations in which both exit and voice are realistic possibilities he assigns an important role to loyalty in determining the member's response. Except for a small minority of blindly loyal members for whom neither exit nor voice is a likely choice, the greater the loyalty, the higher the probability that members will select voice and defer exit. However, Hirschman is evidently not content to give us a purely positive theory of the option between voice and exit, grounded in a social-psychological concept of loyalty. At several junctures in his essay, he ponders the normative question whether there are institutional mechanisms that would strengthen voice as an option, when it needs strengthening, and enhance the likelihood of exit, when that is a desirable response.

. . . |w|hen an organization arouses but ignores voice while it would be responsive to exit, thought must be given both to making exit more easy and attractive by appropriately redesigned institutions and to making the organization more responsive to voice. The approach to the improvement of institutional designs that is advocated here widens the spectrum of policy choices that are usually considered and it avoids the strong opposite biases in favor of either exit or voice which come almost naturally to the economist and political scientist, respectively. . . . . Corrective policies obviously include efforts to make the organization more responsive to exit, *but also* efforts to have the members of the organization switch from exit to voice. In this fashion, the range of possible remedial measures is broadened.[7]

Assuming that efficient institutional designs were invented or borrowed, an organization would, in effect, approximate Hirschman's "elusive optimal mix of exit and voice.[8]

One proposal for an efficient institutional design is for an organization to borrow a set of norms from the Anglo-Saxon legal system known, somewhat ambiguously, as "due process of law." My purpose in this chapter is to explore some of the structural ramifications of this proposal for institutional redesign, thus in the process specifying the relationship between power and conflict.

DUE PROCESS NORMS

Unlike biological systems, which have homeostatic mechanisms to regulate the internal processes of organisms in relation to their environment, social systems such as organizations generally lack comparable self-regulatory mechanisms, thus suffering from a tendency toward instability. In other words, negative feedback mechanisms are poorly developed or else fail unexpectedly, in which case the system succumbs to positive feedback effects.

An illustration of the inadequacy of existing negative feedback mechanisms in various organizations is the way in which hierarchical conflicts are often dealt with, that is, conflicts between occupants of superordinate and subordinate positions. Although not all organizational conflicts are traceable to one source, a case has been made by Dahrendorf and others for hierarchical differentiation—which in varying degrees underlies the structure of all organizations—as generating one major category of conflicts. As a consequence, power, legitimate as well as illegitimate, is exercised to some degree at each level in the hierarchy, giving rise to dissensus as regards goals, objectives, rewards, and their underlying values. The exercise of power at different levels of an organization, with its attendant conflicts, results in a cycle of conflict that may escalate in intensity unless conflict-regulating mechanisms are activated.[9] Due-process norms, collective bargaining, and third-party intervention in the form of mediation or arbitration are examples of conflict-regulating mechanisms. As Simmel, Coser, and others have observed, conflicts have positive as well as negative consequences for a social system.[10] Among the positive consequences of conflict is the growing awareness on the part of the members of an organization that the available conflict-regulating mechanisms are inadequate.[11] One such mechanism, due-process norms, warrants special consideration.

In the Anglo-Saxon legal system the venerable doctrine of due process, which dates back at least to the Magna Carta, provides a mechanism for a fair and impartial regulation of conflicts. As incorporated in the Fifth and Fourteenth Amendments to the United States Constitution, the due process clause protects the citizen against the arbitrary exercise of power by the federal and state governments. This complex of norms includes the right of all parties to a dispute to a timely notice of the issues or charges, the right to a hearing, the right to counsel, the right to confront witnesses, the right to cross-examination, the right to introduce evidence in one's behalf, and so on. Such procedural safeguards in the handling of conflicts illustrate what Vickers calls a "humanized institution".[12] They serve the indispensable function in a democracy of limiting the exercise of arbitrary power.

Although the courts have generally interpreted the due process clause in a *procedural sense,* they have also developed the concept of *substantive* due process. This concept refers to constitutionally guaranteed rights of "life, liberty, and property" and the multiplicity of rights to which a citizen is entitled by law. He therefore may not be deprived of any of these substantive rights unless he is accorded procedural due process.[13]

A plausible consequence of this evolving doctrine, even for private organizations not subject to the protections of the Fifth and Fourteenth Amendments, is a tendency to circumscribe the exercise of power. As occupants of positions of power in private legal systems become increasingly sensitive to the far-reaching significance of procedural and substantive due process of law, they may decide to wield their power in a restrained and self-conscious manner.[14] Correlatively, the occupants of subordinate positions in private legal systems, upon discovering the potential functions of due-process norms, may individually or collectively assert a rightful claim to them. Rights and duties of members tend to become formalized, thereby augmenting the autonomy of subordinates and reducing the discretionary power of superordinates.

The increasing institutionalization of due-process norms, whether in public or private organizations, brings to the fore an interrelated problem that has hardly received the attention it deserves, to wit: Under what conditions do members of an organization acquire "organizational citizenship"? On the face of it this seems like an odd question to raise. It presupposes that an organization not only has an internal or a private legal system separate from that of the state, as I have argued elsewhere, but that it also constitutes a "sovereignty".[15] Organizations, public, and private, do in fact exercise sovereign powers over their members, including those tantamount to life and death. The power of dismissal or refusal to admit to membership may threaten a member's livelihood, his social status, and his self-esteem. Excommunication from a church or denial of the sacraments because of heretical views illustrate the sanctioning power of a private organization.[16] Confronted with a grievance involving discharge from employment, labor arbitrators are reluctant to sustain the penalty because they regard it as the functional equivalent in industry of capital punishment.[17] Under such circumstances, do members have the status of "citizens"?

ORGANIZATIONAL CITIZENSHIP

Not unlike the concept of due process of law citizenship is an evolving concept referring to a cluster of rights and duties of members of a given polity. In its modern meaning, citizenship has been the focus of an expanding set of rights emphasizing constitutional safeguards and deemphasizing unlimited loyalty. In tracing the evolution of citizenship in England in relation to social class, T. H. Marshall states that:

Citizenship is a status bestowed on those who are full members of a community. All who possess the status are equal with respect to the rights and duties with which the status is endowed.[18]

Marshall distinguishes three dimensions of citizenship: civil, political, and social.

The civil element is composed of the rights necessary for individual freedom—liberty of the person, freedom of speech, thought and faith, the right to own property and to conclude valid contracts, and the right to justice. . . . The institutions most directly associated with civil rights are the courts of justice. By the political element I mean the right to participate in the exercise of political power, as a member of a body invested with political authority or as an elector of the members of such a body. The corresponding institutions are parliament and councils of local government. By the social element I mean the whole range from the right to a modicum of economic welfare and security to the right to share to the full in the social heritage and to live the life of a civilized being according to the standards prevailing in the society. The institutions most closely connected with it are the educational system and the social services.[19]

A reasonable candidate for a fourth dimension of citizenship is "organizational citizenship," by which I mean a complex of procedural and substantive rights accruing to an individual by virtue of membership in any organization less inclusive than the nation-state. Not only are such rights institutionalized but they are accorded to *all* categories of members in *equal* degree. It does not follow, however, that organizational citizenship presupposes equality in *all* respects but only in stipulated rights of a procedural and substantive nature. The substantive rights comprising organizational citizenship may consist of the functional equivalents of Marshall's civil, political and social distinctions at the nation-state level. In organizations in which membership provides a source of livelihood, organizational citizenship may revolve around a congeries of property rights to the job.

Diametrically opposed to membership based on a concept of organizational citizenship is one grounded on an unlimited commitment unaccompanied by any clearly protected rights. Total allegiance and a serf-life fealty are demanded of members in organizations that Coser aptly refers to as "greedy organizations" or "greedy institutions".[20]

...[T]he modern world ... continues to spawn organizations ... which ... make total claims on their members and which attempt to encompass within their circle the whole personality. These might be called "greedy institutions," insofar as they seek exclusive and undivided loyalty and they attempt to reduce the claims of competing roles and status positions on those they wish to encompass within their boundaries. Their demands on the person are omnivorous.

Such organizations may, for example, as does the Catholic Church, require celibacy of their priests, so as effectively to minimize the divisive pull of family obligations. They may, as in the case of Utopian communities, attempt to counteract tendencies toward "singularization" or "particularization" by disapproving of dyadic attachments which have the potential of withdrawing energy and affect from the community. They may, as in monastic and Utopian communities, erect strong boundaries between insiders and outsiders so as to hold the insider in close bonds to the community to which he owes total loyalty.[21]

In between the extremes of greedy organizations, on the one hand, and those providing for organizational citizenship, on the other, is a broad spectrum of organizations making functionally specific and segmental demands of its members with few, if any, clearly specified rights of membership. The relatively small proportion of organizations affording organizational citizenship suggests that it is still a nascent concept in most types of organizations regardless of the type of political and economic system in which they are embedded. As Walzer observes in his analysis of corporate authority, members of various private organizations, even in democratic societies, are "subjects" rather than "citizens".[22] A common justification—which Walzer rejects—for the authoritarian regimes in such organizations is the tacit consent of members and their option to leave if they are displeased. Commenting on Walzer's analysis, Hirschman advances the hypothesis that "the greater the opportunities for exit, the easier it appears to be for organizations to resist, evade, and postpone the introduction of internal democracy even though they function in a democratic environment."[23]

One impetus for the growth of organizational citizenship is the expanding role of the ubiquitous multinational corporation. Although it is incorporated in a particular nation-state and its ownership is usually concentrated in a given country, its operations transcend many a national boundary. In transporting capital, technology, goods, and personnel from one country to another, the multinational corporation has encountered various obstacles stemming from economic and political demands of national sovereignty.[24] Small wonder, then, that some multinational corporations are beginning to speculate about organizational citizenship and a legal status divorced from that of any nation-state. Thus, for example, the president of Nestlé speaks of the desirability of building "Nestlé citizenship" in the framework of an "anational corporation".[25] And the chairman of Dow Chemical Company speculates on the means of implementing his ideal of corporate citizenship:

I have long dreamed of buying an island owned by no nation, and of establishing the World Headquarters of the Dow Company on the truly neutral ground of such an island, beholden to no nation or society.[26]

Assuming that organizational citizenship is not entirely an idealized or utopian construct, what kinds of executives are likely to assume the leadership of organizations exhibiting the institutions of organizational citizenship? Would they have an entrepreneurial or a managerial orientation, that is, a preoccupation with promoting the interests of the owners of the enterprise or of their own self-interests? Or would they have a fiduciary orientation?

FIDUCIARY MANAGEMENT

In their classic study of the *Modern Corporation and Private Property,* Berle and Means consider the legal position of management as the separation of ownership and management becomes even more pronounced. They observe that:

The law holds the management to certain standards of conduct. This is the legal link between ownership and management. . . . The three main rules of conduct which the law has developed are: 1) a decent amount of attention to business; 2) fidelity to the interests of the corporation; 3) at least reasonable business prudence. . . . The law sums up the three rules . . . by saying that the management stands in a "fiduciary" capacity towards the corporation.[27]

The legal concept of a fiduciary imposes duties of loyalty and trust on the part of persons performing this role on behalf of beneficiaries.

One who holds a position of trust, *i.e.,* whose function it is to act for the benefit of another as to matters relevant to the relation between them is deemed in law to be a fiduciary; as such, he is held to the highest standards of conduct—standards which are essentially different from the less demanding obligations imposed upon parties to a transaction which is negotiated at "arm's length," *e.g.,* a buyer-seller relationship.[28]

In short, the fiduciary responsibility involves an ethical commitment of service to beneficiaries that sociologists studying the professions generally associate with the professional-client relationship. Codes of ethics in the various professions impose an ordinance of self-denial to ensure that professionals do not exploit their clients in the face of ample opportunities—and temptations as well—to do so.[29]

The sociological import of the fiduciary role as applied to executives of various types of organizations has yet to be explored. It implies, among other things, that those entrusted with the responsibility for directing the fortunes of an organization will do so with an appreciation of the various "constituencies" whose interests are often incompatible. Instead of making self-serving decisions calculated to protect a self-perpetuating oligarchy or advance the interests of a particular constituency, fiduciary managers seek to reconcile the conflicting interests of the various categories of members comprising the "organization as a coalition", and thus promote the interests of the organization as a corporate entity.[30]

In contrast to the fiduciary manager, the "entrepreneurial" manager governs on behalf of the owners of the corporation, that is, his behavior is guided exclusively by the classical profit-maximization principle of the theory of the firm. A third type of management role, the "discretionary" manager, has been conceptualized by Williamson and others in the course of revising the theory of the firm.[31] Beginning with an assumption of self-interest seeking, Williamson identifies pecuniary as well as nonpecuniary values of discretionary managers, who, he argues, seek to maximize a utility preference function that includes various expense preferences for staff and emoluments.[32] To ensure an opportunity for discretion on the part of managers, Williamson adds a "discretionary profit" component in the firm's preference function, namely, "that amount by which earnings exceed . . . [a] minimum performance constraint" to satisfy the demands of the stockholders.[33]

Thus far no one has succeeded in developing fiduciary management models or corporate welfare algorithms comparable to those Williamson has developed for managerial discretion. Until such models are developed the standards of conduct of fiduciary management will constitute an ideal that can only be approximated but never attained. Fiduciary managers will of necessity fall back on various strategies of conflict resolution, such as mediation and arbitration, to reconcile conflicting interests of members of the corporation in the course of arriving at organizational decisions.[34]

Are managers of corporations as well as of other types of organizations sufficiently professionalized so as to perform their roles as fiduciaries, that is, with fidelity to all of their beneficiaries? Do managers conceive of all categories of members of the organization as their beneficiaries? Are stockholders the exclusive beneficiaries of the corporation or do rank-and-file employees and customers qualify for this status as well? Similar questions can be asked of the managers of other types of organizations, for example, do trustees of a university, together with the president and the provost, have fiduciary obligations to the faculty only or to students and alumni as well?

Such questions in turn point to the need for clarifying the meaning of "membership" in various organizations. Do all categories of members of an organization qualify as beneficiaries of fiduciary managers? In the case of corporations, only stockholders are accorded the status of beneficiaries in common law. Rank-and-file employees, owing to the accomplishments of trade unionism in the twentieth century, probably do not consider themselves as beneficiaries of the corporation but rather as rightful *claimants*—by virtue of collective bargaining contracts—on the resources of the corporation. As for corporate managers, the fiduciary duties are far from crystalized in common law, any more than they are in corporate law or in the decisions of administrative agencies. The impetus for the further articulation of the responsibilities of fiduciary managers will probably come from ongoing conflicts over the social responsibility of the corporation.[35] Although the substantive issues in conflict vary from one type of organization to another, what they seem to have in common are claims to expanding membership rights, namely, growing pressures for organizational citizenship.

If we now combine the three concepts discussed above, namely due-process norms, organizational citizenship, and fiduciary management, we have a composite concept for the design of organizations that I shall designate as "organizational constitutionalism."[36]

SOME HYPOTHESES ABOUT ORGANIZATIONAL CONSTITUTIONALISM

Does the composite concept of organizational constitutionalism and its components have any heuristic value for studying power and conflict in organizations? To justify an affirmative answer—which at this stage is in the nature of an assumption—I shall first consider the interrelationships among the components of constitutionalism.

The concepts comprising organizational constitutionalism are not unrelated. A plausible hypothesis is that they constitute points on a cumulative, Guttman-like scale, with due-process norms being at the lower end of the scale, organizational citizenship at the midpoint, and fiduciary management at the higher end of the scale. Organizations that have institutionalized organizational citizenship will also include in their structure due-process norms; the converse, however, is not likely to be true. And organizations guided by fiduciary management are very likely to have institutionalized both organizational citizenship and due-process norms. If the hypothesis about the components of organizational constitutionalism forming a cumulative scale is borne out empirically, one may in turn raise the related question as to whether the points on the scale constitute stages of organizational evolution. Such an hypothesis is plausible provided the mechanisms accounting for the transition from one stage of evolution of organizational constitutionalism to another can be uncovered.

To be sure, the phenomena of power and conflict can be observed in all organizations, but in all likelihood relatively few organizations reach even the first stage of constitutionalism. Reaching the first stage presupposes an environment conducive to such democratic norms emanating from the legal and political institutions of the society at large and a membership with sufficient leverage on management to institutionalize due-process norms. Another factor that may trigger the process of constitutionalization is a crisis threatening the survival of an organization. By institutionalizing due-process norms, conflicts are regulated with a semblance of fairness that in turn promotes loyalty and internal cohesion of the organization vis-à-vis a turbulent environment.

Once due-process norms are established they are not necessarily applied uniformly or fairly to all conflicts arising in an organization, in part because officials manning the hierarchical structure continue to exercise power, including arbitrary power, and in part because of the timidity of members to avail themselves of their rights. In other words, the obstacles to the effective implementation of due process norms in legal systems are twofold: insufficient degree of *institutionalization* of due process, largely because of excessive discretion exercised by officials, and insufficient *internalization* of due-process norms on the part of the members.[37]

When an organization makes the transition to the next stage of constitutionalism and establishes a framework of membership rights that merits the designation of organizational citizenship, it is reasonable to infer that the due-process norms will be shored up both as regards level of institutionalization and level of internalization. To lay the groundwork for organizational citizenship a high level of articulation is required of procedural and substantive rights that are accorded to all categories of members in an organization.[38]

Organizations that have reached the midpoint of our hypothetical scale of constitutionalism can achieve a relatively steady state without moving further in the direction of fiduciary management. This may be due to one of several factors, such as a relatively transitory membership, a relatively successful level of organizational performance that, in effect, justifies the continuation of the prevailing mode of nonfiduciary management, and social structural support for nonfiduciary modes of organizational leadership. A high level of organizational citizenship plus a crisis in organizational performance are probably at least two prerequisites for the further constitutionalization of an organization in the direction of fiduciary management.

Clearly, the foregoing discussion of the construct of organizational constitutionalism in evolutionary terms is highly speculative in character. It may, however, provide a framework for analysis as we examine some illustrative data from several types of organizations.

ILLUSTRATIVE DATA ON ORGANIZATIONAL CONSTITUTIONALISM

In the interest of exploring the applicability and usefulness of the composite concept of organizational constitutionalism and its components, I shall now consider some data on three different types of organizations: religious, military and academic—in the order of mention since they vary correspondingly in degree of institutionalization of the components of constitutionalism. To the extent that the data permit, Hirschman's theoretical concepts of exit and voice will be employed, largely implicitly, in the analysis of the illustrative data.

RELIGIOUS ORGANIZATIONS

Of the many religious organizations two will be considered from the vantage point of organizational constitutionalism: the Catholic Church and the Protestant Episcopal Church in the United States. Although different in numerous respects both organizationally and doctrinally, these churches have a comparable level of institutionalization of due-process norms. Both churches have been buffeted by the winds of secularism that accompany the industrialization of a society. Whereas the adaptation process in the structure of governance, beliefs, and practices in the Episcopal Church has been slowly occurring for over a century, the pressures for change in the Catholic Church, external and internal, have been largely dammed up until the Ecumenical Vatican Council II in 1962–1965.[39]

A variety of documents and encyclicals have since been promulgated that have provoked a movement for reform, including proposals for increasing the degree of institutionalization of due-process norms.[40] Organizational changes have also been instituted such as synods of bishops to augment their collegial authority, senates or associations of priests at the diocese level to increase their power vis-à-vis bishops, and parish councils that include representatives of the laity. The overall thrust of these changes is to diminish the hierarchical and centralized authority structure and introduce mechanisms of collegial authority at all levels in the Church.

Another potential source of change is the Pontifical Commission for the

Revision of the Code of Canon Law, named by Pope John XXIII in 1962, which has been continuing its efforts since the conclusion of the Ecumenical Council II.[41] As part of this effort the Canon Law Society of America has been active in exploring the unmet needs of due process in the Church. In their 1969 report they state that:

The dignity of the human person, the principles of fundamental fairness, and the universally applicable presumption of freedom require that no member of the Church arbitrarily be deprived of the exercise of any right or office. . . .

The characteristics of a free man are precisely that he has rights, that he is not dependent for the enjoyment of his rights upon the good will of his superiors, and that his rights are effectively protected so as to be legally inviolable. The aim of "due process" is precisely to give such inviolability. For men of our time, the legal protection of inviolable rights in the Church would be an especially persuasive sign of that just freedom proclaimed by the gospel as belonging to all men.[42]

Although canon law provides protection of various rights, they are primarily *de jure,* except for marriage conflicts, because of understaffed and centralized tribunals.[43] In addition, Church law "recognizes no right to judicial review of administrative decisions of ecclesiastical authorities".[44] To correct this glaring deficiency in the legal system of the Church, the Pontifical Commission has formulated in 1972 a proposal for a new canon of administrative procedure.[45]

No such ferment has occurred in the Episcopal Church of the United States in recent years which, of course, does not mean that there are no conflicts that would benefit from the application of due-process norms. According to canon lawyer Rightor, Episcopal priests are not protected from arbitrary dismissal from their parish by a bishop.[46] Nor does the relevant canon on the "dissolution of the pastoral relation" provide for the right of the priest to appeal a bishop's decision. Rightor recommends revision of the relevant canon "to insure that the entire Episcopal Church, as well as the parties involved, develop a clearer under-standing of the Canons, rules, standards, guides and equitable principles which are pertinent to the Bishop's decision in each case".[47]

In view of the contrasts noted in the two Churches, the markedly higher resignation rates of Catholic as compared to Episcopal priests during 1966–1969, for which data were obtainable, is not surprising (see Table 7.1). In a 1969 survey of Catholic priests, it is reported that among the crucial events contributing to the decision to resign from the priesthood are: the encyclical on celibacy (27 percent), arbitrary reassignment by a superior (21 percent), and injustice by a superior (28 percent).[48] Two other researchers on the Catholic Church conclude their studies with gloomy conditional predictions. Struzzo, who studied the relationship between professionalism and authority conflicts of

Table 7.1 Resignation Rates of Catholic and Protestant Episcopal Priests in the United States, 1966–1969

	Catholic (Diocesan) Priests[a]		Protestant Episcopal Priests[b]	
Year	Resignations Total (N)	Resignations %	Resignations Total (N)	Resignations %
1966	142	0.4	28	.0025
1967	306	0.9	30	.0026
1968	548	1.6	27	.0023
1969	753	2.0	24	.0020

[a] *Source:* National Research Center, *American Priests: Prepared for the U.S. Catholic Conference,* Chicago, Ill.: National Opinion Research Center, 1971, pp. 314, 316. The resignation rates are based on a statistical estimate of error due to sampling; the actual rates could very well be higher.
[b] Computed from information provided in *Episcopal Church Annual,* 1967–1971, New York: Morehouse–Barlow.

Catholic priests, ends his report with the statement that:

As long as the existing structures of the church remain in basic contradiction to the professionalization of the clergy, the most likely prospect for the near future is an ever increasing rate of departures from the active ministry of those priests who espouse a professional model for the ministry that is in conflict with hierarchical authority.[49]

And Kotre, who studied the social psychology of Catholics, some of whom defined themselves as *in* and others as *out* of the Church, concluded that:

The Catholic Church is, after all, a voluntary social system; it is an organization that can be left. Indeed, only an act of the mind is necessary to cross the border. . . .
 A voluntary organization that does not change enough to meet the expectations of some . . . can be left. . . .
 The threat caused by loss of members in a voluntary organization, however, is much less obvious, and in an organization like the Catholic Church in which there is little direct data to tell precisely how many are leaving, the threat is vague, slowly communicated, and much less a force for movement. But it is, nevertheless, like violence, a threat to the life of the system.[50]

In short, although efforts at institutionalizing due-process norms are discernible in the Catholic Church as well as in the Protestant Episcopal Church in the

United States, thus far a fairly rudimentary level of institutionalization has been achieved.

MILITARY ORGANIZATIONS

Although military organizations are even more hierarchical and authoritarian than some churches, they have manifested considerable flexibility in adapting their structures and policies in the face of rapid technological changes in weapons systems, new alignments in the international political system, and changing expectations and values of members of society at large. In industrialized societies with democratic political institutions, the armed forces are subordinate to civilian political elites and institutions.[51] There are consequently tendencies to modify the authority structure and ideology of military organizations so that they are more consonant with those of civilian organizations of society.

Whether recruitment of personnel is by means of conscription or enlistment, there is evidently an increasing awareness on the part of the military of the importance of protecting the rights of members of the armed forces. Safeguarding individual rights becomes one of the various inducements to enlistment and retention of personnel as well as a strategy to ensure effective organizational performance. One of the institutions providing due process protection to personnel in the United States Army is the Inspector General (IG) complaint procedure.[52] All Army personnel, enlisted men, officers, and civilian employees have a right to register complaints directly with an Inspector General officer instead of taking them up with their immediate superiors. After inquiring about a complaint—defined in Army regulations as "an allegation of wrong or injustice suffered by the complainant, or of inconvenience, grievance, or injury incurred"—the IG recommends action to the relevant commanding officer.[53] If the complainant is not satisfied with the handling of the grievance, he may appeal to an IG officer at a higher echelon or to the Office of the Inspector General at the Headquarters of the Department of the Army in Washington, D.C.

By examining Army regulations pertaining to the IG complaint procedure during the past two decades, we can ascertain what changes, if any, have occurred and assess their significance. In Table 7.2 the pertinent regulations in 1951, 1960, and 1973 are compared with respect to four criteria: mode of submission of complaints, amount of discretion available to IG officers in processing complaints, requirement to disseminate information concerning the right to voice complaints with the IG, and degree of formalization of regulations.

With respect to all four criteria for comparison, the Army regulations have been changed in the past two decades so as to enhance the protection of the individual's right to due process. As of 1960 all personnel may submit com-

Table 7.2   A Comparison of Army Regulations on the Inspector General Complaint Procedure, 1951, 1960, 1973

Criteria for Comparison	1951[a]	1960[b]	1973[c]
1. Mode of submission of complaints			
Oral	Yes	Yes	Yes
Written	Yes	Yes	Yes
Anonymous	No	Yes	Yes
2. Discretion of IG officers in processing complaints			
Restricted	No	No	Yes
3. Requirement to disseminate information concerning right of personnel to lodge complaints with the IG			
Stipulated	No	Yes	Yes
4. Degree of formalization			
Specificity of detail in regulations	Low	Medium	High
Number of paragraphs and sub-paragraphs in the regulations	15	27	31

[a] Department of the Army, *Army Regulations,* 20-20 (Washington, D. C.: U. S. Government Printing Office, 16 May 1951).
[b] Department of the Army, *Army Regulations,* 20-1 (Washington, D. C.: U. S. Government Printing Office, 2 May 1960).
[c] Department of the Army, *Army Regulations,* 20-1 (Washington, D. C.: U. S. Government Printing Office, 18 April 1973).

plaints orally, in writing, or anonymously; and commanding officers are required to inform all personnel of their right to register a complaint with the IG. As of 1973 the IG officer's discretion in processing complaints has been restricted, with the elimination of the following 1960 discretionary provision: "An inspector general may decline to act upon a matter which he deems to be trivial or inconsequential in nature. . . ."[54] Finally, the regulations have increased in their degree of formalization as reflected in the level of specificity of detail and in the number of paragraphs and subparagraphs in which the regulations are set forth.

Granted that these changes have occurred in the Army regulations, the critical question, of course, is how well they have been implemented. This would require an evaluation study consisting of at least two procedures: (1) an analysis of a sample of complaints lodged with IG officers at a sample of field commands to ascertain how these complaints were processed, what action was recommended, and what action was taken by relevant commanding officers; and (2) a sample survey of Army personnel, such as was undertaken during World War II, to inquire into their experiences of injustice, their perceptions

Table 7.3   Number of Complaints received by the Office of the Inspector General of the Department of the Army, by Category, 1968–1973

Complaint Category[a]	1968	1969	1970	1971	1972	1973
1. Administrative deficiencies	671	594	629	577	615	457
2. Mistreatment	531	573	290	370	364	285
3. Discipline	317	508	458	444	403	279
4. Racial discrimination	199	326	405	406	300	206
5. Assignment or utilization	369	417	297	262	237	182
6. Transfer/Reassignment	347	387	269	281	279	219

Source: Personal communication with Office of the Inspector General, Department of the Army, 29 April 1974.

[a] The categories as defined by the Office of Inspector General are as follows:

1. *Administrative deficiencies.*   Errors in records, except those pertaining to pay; errors in correspondence or other types of administration; excessive delay in completing administration directly affecting an individual's service; excessive delay in replying to correspondence; irregularities in administration; loss of records; nonreceipt of reply to inquiries; inadequate reply to correspondence; and other types [of] administrative deficiencies.

2. *Mistreatment.*   Physical, verbal, or mentally degrading acts adversely affecting individuals, including harassment.

3. *Discipline.*   Appeal of nonjudicial punishment denied; excessive delay in court-martial trial; inequity in punishment; rights denied, unjust punishment; etc.

4. *Racial discrimination.*   Allegations that assignment or utilization, reduction in grade, disciplinary action, duty, promotion, rights denied, unjust punishment, etc.

5. *Assignment or utilization.*   Excessive hours or details; malassignment; improper MOS classification; not assigned duty in MOS; other allegations pertaining to an individual's current assignment or utilization.

6. *Transfer/Reassignment.*   Compassionate request for transfer not processed; unreasonable delay in notification; too many transfers; abuse of assignment policy; reassigned to location incompatible with qualification or requirements.

of the efficiency of the IG to redress wrongs, their fears of being victimized by superiors if they avail themselves of their right to air their grievances, and their degree of internalization of the values of due process.[55]

In lieu of data from either of these procedures a very crude indication of the functions performed by the IG is reflected in the data presented in Table 7.3. For the years 1968–1973 the absolute numbers of complaints are presented in six of the most frequently recorded categories: administrative deficiencies, mistreatment, discipline, racial discrimination, assignment or utilization, and transfer/reassignment (see Table 7.3 for official definitions of these categories). These complaints were submitted directly to the Headquarters of the Inspector

General in Washington, D.C. instead of to officers of the I.G. attached to various field commands. It is obviously impermissible to infer that these data are representative of the population of complaints submitted to the various field commands of the United States Army for the years 1968–1973. Although a cross-tabulation of the number of complaints by rank, function (Military Occupational Specialty), type of field command, age, education, race, and sex would have been illuminating, no such analysis is possible given the simple frequency tabulation provided by the Office of the Inspector General.

It is noteworthy, however, that although the incidence of complaints between 1968–1971 tends to fluctuate, in 1972–1973 there was a noticeable decline in all categories, except for administrative deficiencies. Assuming that these complaint statistics emanate largely from field commands in Vietnam, they may be related to events following the Tet offensive and to the process of American troop withdrawal that was well underway in 1972 and was completed in 1973. The frustrations and agonies experienced in the closing years of America's involvement in the Vietnam war are reflected in the data in Table 7.4 on the rates of AWOL and desertion for the same time period for which the IG complaint statistics are available, that is, 1968–1973. Both the AWOL and desertion rates steadily increase during 1968–1971, and—as in the case of the incidence of IG complaints—markedly decline in 1972–1973.

In summary, due process in the United States Army, as reflected in the functioning of the IG complaint procedure, has been substantially strengthened in the past two decades, in part because of the major transformation of military law that occurred in 1950 with the passage by Congress of the Uniform Code of Military Justice. This trend is likely to continue, judging from the current concern with problems of adapting the United States Army to the realities of a volunteer recruitment system. Two researchers on the Army have proposed

Table 7.4   AWOL and Desertion Rates per 1000 in the United States Army, 1968–1973

Year	AWOL Rate	Desertion Rate
1968	89.7	29.1
1969	112.3	42.4
1970	132.5	52.3
1971	176.9	73.5
1972	166.4	62.0
1973	159.2	52.1

Source: Personal communication with Office of the Chief of Information, Department of the Army, 12 March 1974.

that "some form of improved Inspector General or an Ombudsman channel of complaint could be established" without indicating the direction of improvement.[56] If the ombudsman model were taken seriously as a source of reforms, the IG, for example, would be granted more autonomy in its operations than it currently enjoys as a staff organization. Surely, the experiences of some European countries that have military ombudsman systems—Sweden since 1915, Norway since 1952, and West Germany since 1957—would be instructive inasmuch as their well-developed set of substantive and procedural rights suggest that their armed forces have in effect reached the stage of "organizational citizenship."[57]

ACADEMIC ORGANIZATIONS

The academic organization differs profoundly in its structure and its mission from military, religious, and other types of organizations. In the course of pursuing its two principal goals of teaching and research, the university, if not the junior college or the four-year college, elaborates its organizational structure in terms of departments, schools, committees, research institutes, and the like so that it cumulatively takes on the appearance of a complex bureaucracy with an hierarchical mode of coordination and administration. Yet a university is not predominantly a bureaucracy.[58]

An alternative model of the university is that of a democratic association.[59] The decision-making processes in committees, departments, faculty meetings, and various campus organizations often entail voting and an atmosphere of town-hall democracy in action. Yet, in view of the basic mission of the university and the high degree of inequality of knowledge and competence, it would be misleading to look upon the university as a democratic voluntary association governed by the principle of "one man, one vote".[60]

In its commitment to the principle of freedom of inquiry, to the discovery and dissemination of knowledge, and to rational discourse—namely, to the values of the "cognitive complex"—the university has the attributes of a moral community.[61] Yet, in view of the internal social stratification with its accompanying dissensus, it would be inaccurate to characterize the university as primarily a moral community.

Indeed, if anyone of the foregoing models accurately represented the realities of academia, it is doubtful that the campus disturbances of the 1960s would have escalated to the level of disruption and violence that they did. University administrators, exercising their bureaucratic authority, would have been more effective than they were in managing the conflicts; institutional mechanisms of a democratic polity would have succeeded in bringing the conflicts to a halt when they first erupted; and the moral norms of the community would have been persuasive in transforming the conflict from a "fight" to a "debate."[62]

It is precisely because the university organization is based on an *admixture* of organizational principles, reflecting potentially incompatible interests, that it was so difficult to regulate the conflicts of the 1960s. The rival principles of organization are rooted in the three major internal constituencies of the academic organization: bureaucratic authority on behalf of the administration, collegial authority in support of the faculty, and "participatory democracy" in the interest of the student. Small wonder that the epidemic of campus protests and demonstrations, triggered by the Free Speech Movement at Berkeley in 1964, brought about a crisis in the governance of the university that stimulated various efforts at restructuring and redirecting the organization.

The initial response of many university administrators to campus unrest consisted of disciplinary action, often summary in nature without the benefit of any due-process protections. For example, in the fall of 1964 eight leaders of the Free Speech Movement at Berkeley were summarily suspended for violating a rule, long in abeyance, concerning on-campus solicitation of funds for off-campus political action.[63] And at Columbia University, shortly before the massive sit-in demonstration began in the spring of 1968, leaders of the Students for a Democratic Society submitted to President Grayson Kirk a petition, signed by 1,700 students, requesting that the university sever its relations with the Institute of Defense Analyses. Kirk responded by placing the six leaders of S. D. S. on probation for violating his ban on indoor demonstrations. "The six students thereupon requested an open hearing before a tripartite judicial board, and were refused."[64]

Other responses to campus confrontations included the convening of special meetings of the faculty, the passing of special resolutions, and at some universities, the appointing of "commissions of inquiry." At Berkeley, The Study Commission on University Governance noted that:

The liberalization of the rules governing political activity on the campus, the increased sensitivity of the campus to due process in disciplinary proceedings, the slowly growing receptivity to educational experimentation . . . all of these gains have been due, entirely or in part, to the politics of conflict.[65]

The authors conclude their report by developing a set of "basic regulations governing enactment and enforcement of campus rules."[66]

At Columbia University a Fact-Finding Commission was appointed to inquire into the demonstrations in the spring of 1968.[67] Commenting on President Grayson Kirk's refusal to grant a public hearing to the S. D. S. leaders whom he placed on probation, the report states that:

In a period in which public attention has been focused upon procedural safeguards in criminal proceedings, students have become rightly concerned about procedural safeguards in academic discipline. Their perquisites as students, and, during the current era of selective military service, their status as students, may even attain life-or-death importance.[68]

The Columbia report further observes that:

The governance of the tens of thousands of people who compose Columbia University requires systematization through uniform rules and established organs and agencies. In their absence, arbitrary power flourishes. Power, in turn, encourages recourse to improvisation under pressure.[69]

Such reports have prompted universities to institute two types of reforms designed to reinforce due-process norms. First, to provide a formal mechanism for communicating complaints an office of ombudsman has been established on more than 100 campuses.[70] According to one occupant of this office:

The Ombudsman's job is to be an accessible, objective, and responsive auditor in a setting that is sometimes so impersonal that in his attempt to find relief from frustration an individual may encounter only new frustration. Receiving and examining complaints from members of the university community—students, staff, administrators, faculty—the Ombudsman attempts to secure, where called for, either a satisfactory explanation or expeditious and impartial redress. His door, in short, is open to any member of the community with a grievance against the University or against anyone exercising authority.[71]

Annual reports of ombudsmen from various campuses indicate that a substantial number of individuals are making use of this new grievance procedure.

Second, the judicial systems of many colleges and universities have been reexamined and redesigned in the light of student protest to ensure that students are accorded due-process protections in all disciplinary proceedings.[72] According to a survey in 1969 of 558 colleges and universities conducted by the National Association of Student Personnel Administrators, about three-fourths or more of the institutions included various procedural safeguards in their disciplinary proceedings (see Table 7.5). This finding was confirmed in a 1970 survey by the American Civil Liberties Union of 153 college and university presidents, which found that "the overwhelming majority of the presidents reported that students were entitled to due process in cases that might lead to suspension or expulsion".[73]

These reforms in academic governance are part of a more general trend toward the formalization of policies and procedures to regulate the relationships among administration, faculty, and students, so much so that it has been referred to as the "judicialization" of the campus.[74] One possible function

Table 7.5   Procedures in Student Disciplinary Cases in a Sample of Colleges and Universities, 1969

Procedural safeguards	Percentage of institutions having procedural safeguards	Number of institutions
The accused student is:		
Orally informed of charges	96	542
Given written statement of charges	73	537
Informed of procedures and rights	97	541
Provided with names of witnesses	73	521
Permitted legal counsel	49	515
Allowed other counsel	86	524
Allowed to call witnesses	97	529
Allowed to ask questions of witnesses	98	533
Given explanation for decision	97	544
Permitted right of appeal when decision has been made by:		
a) an administrative officer	96	502
b) a judicial body	89	515

Source: T. Dutton, F. Smith, and T. Zarle, *Institutional approaches to the adjudication of student misconduct,* National Association of Student Personnel Administrators, Monograph No. 2, January, 1969, pp. 6–9; table adapted from the version quoted in Frank Fratoe, *Due process and the student-institution relationship in American higher education,* Philadelphia Pa., University of Pennsylvania, Unpublished Doctoral Dissertation, 1974, pp. 10–11.

of this trend is to protect the academic community from intervention by the courts—by means of judicial review—in its internal affairs.

Over the years the courts' role in the course of judicial review, in either denying or granting due process to students, has been of great significance. According to Van Alstyne, since colonial times three legal models have been developed by the courts in deciding disciplinary cases.[75] *In loco parentis,* a common law doctrine, was the earliest and most durable model that was applied by the courts in cases involving disputes between students and colleges. The rationale of the courts for almost invariably supporting the college was succinctly expressed in a Kentucky Supreme Court decision in 1913:

College authorities stand *in loco parentis* concerning the physical and moral welfare, and mental training of the pupils, and we are unable to see why to that end they may not make any rules or regulations for the government or betterment of their pupils that a parent could for the same purpose. Whether the rules or regulations are wise, or their aims worthy, is a matter left solely to the discretion of the authorities, or parents, as the case may be" (*Gott* v. *Berea College,* 156 Ky. 370 at 379, 161 S.W. 204 at 206).[76]

With the marked growth of institutions of higher education at the turn of the century, it became increasingly difficult for the courts to justify the doctrine that the college was the surrogate parent of the students. Its replacement was the common law of contracts. Upon matriculation a student implicitly agrees to a contract that he will conform to all existing rules of the institution and, in the event of a breach of contract, he will be subject to suspension or expulsion. The transition from *in loco parentis* to a contractual relationship did not enhance the protection of students against summary dismissals, so long as the university could point to a rule in its handbooks, however arbitrary, to justify its decision.

In recent years the third legal model, based on constitutional rights, has emerged in court decisions pertaining to public universities. Beginning with the landmark decision of *Dixon* v. *Alabama State Board of Education* in 1961, in which the court ordered the reinstatement of students dismissed from a college because of the failure to provide them with either a written statement of the charges or with a hearing,[77] the courts have enlarged the scope of procedural due process protections. In addition, they have added other constitutional rights such as freedom of speech, freedom of association, freedom of assembly, and the right to privacy.

If the constitutional rights model becomes more generally accepted by the courts in cases involving the suspension and dismissal of students and if it is extended from public to private universities, it will have the effect of further institutionalizing the student's right to "citizenship" on the campus. In analyzing the protests at Berkeley one social scientist has noted that "the faculty and the administration have 'citizenship' in the university community, while students do not. . . . The very assertion of the students' right to enter into decision-making and policy matters constitutes a quest for citizenship."[78] To the extent that student aspirations are increasingly realized as a result of ongoing reforms in university governance, organizational citizenship will be well on its way to being institutionalized in the academic community.

The progress in recent years toward constitutionalizing the university may in addition pave the way for the emergence of institutions of "fiduciary management." University administrators would self-consciously accept their role as trustees of the organization in its entirety and as guardians of the interests of *all* constituencies who, by definition, constitute their beneficiaries. In the event of conflict among any of the constituencies, they would perform the role of independent and impartial arbiters. Committed to the values of higher education as well as organizational constitutionalism, they would seek to develop policies calculated to advance the welfare of the entire academic community.

In speculating about the future direction of the university, Perkins, a former president of Cornell University, refers to a "new style of management" sensitive to the needs for resolving conflicts and for satisfying the demands for internal and external accountability of performance.[79] Some innovative university administrators are in effect already performing their role in accordance with the concept of fiduciary management. In fact, the academic organization may prove to be a uniquely hospitable environment for the growth and development of the fiduciary style of management.[80]

ORGANIZATIONAL CONSTITUTIONALISM AND HIRSCHMAN'S THEORY

Having presented the concepts of and propositions on organizational constitutionalism and applied them to illustrative data on three types of organizations, I now return to the original question posed by Hirschman: What institutional designs would encourage voice as an option when that is deemed significant and facilitate exit when that is desirable? Rather than rely entirely on loyalty as a mechanism for triggering voice and exit, Hirschman advocates improved "institutional designs."[81] The burden of the foregoing discussion is that the structural redesign of organizations in accordance with organizational constitutionalism would generally strengthen exit and voice, particularly the latter, and thereby promote a better balance between them.

Organizations lacking any appreciable mode or level of constitutionalism would tend to have a high exit rate and a low voice rate. According to Walzer, this is a common phenomenon in many private organizations in democratic societies.[82] Institutionalizing due-process norms as a means of regulating conflicts would have the effect of diminishing abuses of power and generating a sense of fairness among the members of an organization. The resulting organizational climate would promote a strong disposition to exercise the option of voice and a disinclination to have recourse to exit.[83]

Institutionalizing organizational citizenship would likewise have the effect of stimulating voice inasmuch as the members of an organization would be accorded a relatively unambiguous set of procedural and substantive rights. It would also have a positive effect on exit. When the rights associated with organizational citizenship are honored in the breach, members would exercise either the exit or the voice option, whichever they find congenial or expedient. In a sense-organizational citizenship would encourage a movement for the transferability of a set of membership rights from the state as well as from one organization to another within the same class of organizations. This would be analogous to the situation of the college or university faculty member in the United States who decides to accept an offer from another institution of higher

Table 7.6   Hypothesized Relationships Between Hirschman's Concepts and the Components of Organizational Constitutionalism[a]

Constitutionalism Continuum	Hirschman's Concept	
	Exit	Voice
Little or no constitutionalism	+ +	– –
Due-process norms	–	+ +
Organizational citizenship	+	+
Fiduciary management	–	+

[a] A single plus connotes a moderate positive or direct relationship; a minus, a negative or inverse relationship; a double minus or double plus signifies a strong relationship.

education. Among his organizational citizenship rights that are transferable are his pension rights, by virtue of the fact that both institutions are likely to be affiliated with the Teachers Insurance Annuity Association, which provides for complete vesting and transferability of accrued pension benefits. No such organizational citizenship rights have yet been institutionalized in the corporation, either for unionized employees or for the various levels of management, from the first-line supervisor to that of the president.[84]

With the emergence of fiduciary management—initially, in all likelihood, in such organization as colleges and universities, trade unions, and professional associations—members would have the right, of course, to exercise the exit option, but because of the protections afforded by the new system of management the rate of exit would probably decline. On the other hand, the level of voice would probably increase because of the new mode of decision making associated with fiduciary management.

The hypothesized relationships formulated above, with the usual *ceteris paribus* assumption, are summarized in Table 7.6. In other words, by supplementing Hirschman's theory with the concepts of organizational constitutionalism, it is possible to generate new and testable hypotheses. Although Hirschman premises his theory on the condition of a declining organization, clearly the level of organizational performance may be considered one of the parameters along with several others, such as type of organization (economic, religious, political, educational, military, etc.), level of economic development of the society in which the organization is embedded, type of political system of the society, and some attributes of the culture of the environing society.

CONCLUSION

Power as a universal element of organizational structure and functioning often engenders conflicts; and conflicts, whether internally or externally induced, are occasions for the exercise and abuse of power unless institutional restrains are imposed. Organizational constitutionalism, as developed in this chapter, can perform the function of moderating the relationship between power and conflict. To the extent that organizations undergo a process of constitutionalization—involving the postulated evolutionary stages of due-process norms, organizational citizenship, and fiduciary management—abuses of power diminish in frequency, and whatever conflicts arise are subject to consensually-valid methods of regulation. Exit, which according to Hirschman's theory is a common response in organizations suffering from a deterioration in performance, may also be a frequent occurrence in organizations plagued with an excess of illegitimate power. By boosting the level of voice in an organization, organizational constitutionalism can thus counterbalance exit as an attractive alternative.

To test the validity of Hirschman's theory as supplemented by organizational constitutionalism, comparative organizational research would be necessary. This would entail undertaking longitudinal studies of samples of different types of organizations in contrasting political, economic, and cultural settings. In addition, experimental methodology, in the laboratory as well as in the field, might be especially fruitful.[85] Hirschman, in collaboration with others, has designed an intriguing laboratory experiment to test interrelationships of exit, voice, and loyalty in experimentally-created small groups.[86] It is likewise possible to design field experiments in ongoing organizations in an effort to verify Hirschman's theory by itself or in conjunction with organizational constitutionalism. Such research may prove significant for organization theorists in their quest for propositions applicable to all formal organizations regardless of culture and social structure.

NOTES

1. A. A. Berle and G. C. Means, *The Modern Corporation and Private Property,* rev. ed. (New York: Harcourt, Brace and World, 1968).

2. R. Dahrendorf, *Class and Class Conflict in Industrial Society* (Stanford, Cal.: Stanford University Press, 1959).

3. *Ibid.,* p. 168.

4. A justifiable criticism of Dahrendorf's theory of conflict is that without introducing the concept of illegitimate power, it is hard to see how his "quasi-groups" are transformed into "interest groups" and thence into "conflict groups" (Dahrendorf, 1959, pp. 157–205).

5. R. L. Kahn, "Introduction," in R. L. Kahn and E. Boulding, eds., *Power and Conflict in Organizations* (New York: Basic Books, 1964), pp. 2–3.

6. A. O. Hirschman, *Exit, Voice and Loyalty* (Cambridge, Mass.: Harvard University Press, 1970).

7. *Ibid.,* pp. 123–124.

8. *Ibid.,* pp. 120–126.

9. J. V. Baldridge, *Power and Conflict in the University* (New York: John Wiley & Sons, 1971).

10. G. Simmel, *Conflict and the Web of Group Affiliation,* trans. K. H. Wolff and R. Bendix (New York: The Free Press, 1955); L. A. Coser, *The Functions of Social Conflict* (Glencoe, Ill.: The Free Press, 1956.

11. William M. Evan, "Superior-Subordinate Conflict in Research Organizations," *Administrative Science Quarterly* 10 (June 1965): 52–64. See Chapter 6 of the present volume.

12. G. Vickers, "The Management of Conflict," *Futures* 4 (June 1972): 126–141.

13. M. D. Forkosch, "American Democracy and Procedural Due Process," *Brooklyn Law Review* 24 (April 1958): 143–253.

14. William M. Evan, ed., *Law and Sociology* (New York: The Free Press, 1962), pp. 165–84. See Chapter 12 of the present volume.

15. *Ibid.,* pp. 165–84.

16. "When I was a student in the University of Berlin many years ago they showed me the university jail which was separate from the town jail. In this academic hoosegow, distinguished men such as Bismarck had been confined when students. This was a revelation to me, for in my day the school authorities could throw a man out but they could not throw him in." C. E. Merriam, *Public and Private Government* (New Haven, Conn.: Yale University Press, 1944), p. 2, n. 3.

17. R. H. Skilton, *Industrial Discipline and the Arbitration Process* (Philadelphia: University of Pennsylvania Press, 1952), p. 29.

18. T. H. Marshall, *Citizenship and Social Class* (Cambridge: Cambridge University Press, 1950), pp. 28–29.

19. *Ibid.,* pp. 10–11.

20. L. A. Coser, "Greedy Organizations," *European Journal of Sociology* 8, no. 2 (1967): 196–215; Coser, *Greedy Institutions* (New York: The Free Press, 1974).

21. Coser, *Greedy Institutions,* pp. 4–5.

22. M. Walzer, *Obligations: Essays on Disobedience, War and Citizenship* (Cambridge, Mass.: Harvard University Press, 1970.)

23. Hirschman, *Exit, Voice and Loyalty,* p. 84n.

24. R. Vernon, *Sovereignty at Bay: The Multinational Spread of US Enterprise* (New York: Basic Books, 1971).

25. R. J. Barnet and R. Muller, *Global Reach* (New York: Simon and Schuster, 1974).

26. C. A. Gerstacker, "The Structure of the Corporation." Paper presented at a White House Conference on "The Industrial World Ahead," February 7–9, 1972.

27. Berle and Means, *Modern Corporation and Private Property,* pp. 196–97.

28. William M. Evan and E. G. Levin, "Status-set and Role-set Conflicts of the Stockbroker: A Problem in the Sociology of Law," *Social Forces* 45 (September 1966): 73.

29. *Ibid.,* p. 74.

30. R. M. Cyert and J. G. March, *A Behavioral Theory of the Firm* (Englewood Cliffs, N. J.: Prentice-Hall, 1963).

31. O. E. Williamson, *The Economics of Discretionary Behavior: Managerial Objectives in a Theory of the Firm* (Chicago, Ill.: Markham, 1967); *Corporate Control and Business Behavior* (Englewood Cliffs, N.J.: Prentice-Hall, 1970).

32. Williamson, *The Economics of Discretionary Behavior,* pp. 38–60.

33. *Ibid.,* p. 36.

34. "Besides the function that he was trained and picked for—actually managing his business—the CEO [chief executive officer] is being called upon to arbitrate conflicting claims upon his

company by workers, shareholders, consumers, his own government, and often by governments of foreign lands."—Anonymous. "The Top Man Becomes Mr. Outside," *Business Week* 2329 (May 4, 1974): 38.

35. E. M. Epstein, The Historical Enigma of Corporate Legitimacy," *California Law Review* 60 (November 1972): 1701–17.

36. Evan, "Superior-Subordinate Conflict."

37. William M. Evan, "Due Process of Law in Military and Industrial Organizations," *Administrative Science Quarterly* 7 (September 1962): 187–207.

38. The institutionalization of due-process norms and organizational citizenship both entail an increase in the level of formalization of organizational structure which in turn may involve unanticipated costs in performance as well as in adaptability to change.

39. T. P. Ference, F. H. Goldner, and R. R. Ritti, "Priests and Church: The Professionalization of an Organization," in S. A. Lakoff and D. Rich, ed., *Private Government* (Glencoe, Ill., Scott, Foresman, 1973), p. 182.

40. W. M. Abbott, ed., *The Documents of Vatican Council II* (New York: Corpus Books, 1966); E. H. Peters, *De Ecclesia: The Constitution of the Church of Vatican Council II* (Glen Rock, N.J.: Deus Books Paulist Press, 1965); Ad Hoc Committee on Due Process, "Due Process in Canon Law," *Catholic Lawyer* 15 (Autumn 1969): 278–307; J. A. Coriden, *We the People of God . . .* (Huntington, Ind.: Our Sunday Visitor, 1956).

41. Coriden, *We, the People of God . . .* , p. xiii.

42. Ad Hoc Committee on Due Process, "Due Process in Canon Law," pp. 281–86.

43. *Ibid.,* pp. 286–87.

44. *Ibid.,* pp. 287.

45. Pontificia Commissio Codici Iuris Canonici Recognoscendo, *Schema Cononum de Procedura Administrativa* (Vatica: Typis Polyglottis Vaticanis, 1972).

46. H. H. Rightor, "The Need for a Change in the Canon on the Dissolution of the Pastoral Relation," *National Network of Episcopal Clergy Associations* 1 (March 29, 1972): 1–6.

47. *Ibid.,* p. 4.

48. National Opinion Research Center, *American Priests* (Chicago: National Opinion Research Center, 1971), p. 319.

49. J. A. Struzzo, "Professionalism and the Resolution of Authority Conflicts Among the Catholic Clergy," *Sociological Analysis* 30 (Summer 1970): 105.

50. J. N. Kotre, *The View from the Border* (Chicago: Aldine-Atherton, 1971), pp. 195–96.

51. M. Janowitz, "Military Organization," in R. W. Little, ed, *Handbook of Military Institutions* (Beverly Hills, Cal.: Sage Publications, 1971), pp. 24–26; K. Lang, *Military Institutions and the Sociology of War* (Beverly Hills, Cal.: Sage Publications, 1972), pp. 105–31.

52. Evan, "Due Process of Law in Military and Industrial Organizations."

53. Department of the Army, *Army Regulations* (Washington, D.C.: Government Printing Office (May 16, 1951).

54. Department of the Army, *Army Regulations* (Washington, D.C.: Government Printing Office (May 2, 1960), p. 21.

55. Evan, "Due Process of Law in Military and Industrial Organizations," pp. 192–204.

56. Z. B. Bradford and F. J. Brown, *The United States Army in Transition* (Beverly Hills, Cal.: Sage Publications, 1973), p. 180.

57. H. Henkow, "The Ombudsman for Military Affairs," in D. C. Rowat, ed., *The Ombudsman: Citizen's Defender,* 2d ed. (London: Allen and Unwin, 1968), pp. 51–57; A.

Ruud, "The Military Ombudsman and His Board," in *ibid.,* pp. 111–18; E. Lohse, "West Germany's Military Ombudsman," in *ibid.,* pp. 118–26.

58. T. Parsons and G. M. Platt, *The American University* (Cambridge, Mass.: Harvard University Press, 1973), pp. 127–28.

59. *Ibid.,* p. 129.

60. C. Foote *et al., The Culture of the University: Governance and Education* (San Francisco, Calif.: Jossey-Bass Inc., 1968), p. 80.

61. Parsons and Platt. *The American University,* pp. 22–89.

62. A. Rapoport, *Fights, Games, and Debates* (Ann Arbor, Mich.: University of Michigan Press, 1960).

63. S. M. Lipset and S. S. Wolin, *The Berkeley Student Revolt* (New York: Anchor Books, 1965), pp. 109–10; The President's Commission on Campus Unrest, *The Report of the President's Commission on Campus Unrest* (New York: Discus Books, 1971).

64. E. K. Trimberger, "Columbia: The Dynamics of a Student Revolution," in H. S. Becker, ed., *Campus Power Struggle* (New Brunswick, N.J.: Transaction Books, 1973).

65. Foote *et al., The Culture of the University,* p. 19.

66. *Ibid.,* pp. 173–203.

67. The Cox Commission Report, *Crisis at Columbia* (New York: Vintage Books, 1968).

68. *Ibid.,* p. 96.

69. *Ibid.,* p. 36.

70. L. J. Mahoney, *Ombudsman Directory* (San Diego, Cal.: San Diego State University Press, 1974).

71. J. Conarroe, "What's an Ombudsman? The Beginning of an Answer," *Almanac* 18 (September 14, 1971): 3 (University of Pennsylvania).

72. T. F. Lunsford, "Some Suggested Directions for Research," in C. E. Kruytbosch and S. L. Messinger, eds., *The State of the University* (Beverly Hills, Cal.: Sage Publications, 1970), pp. 330–31.

73. M. S. Handler, "Gain by Students on Rights Found," *New York Times* (December 13, 1970).

74. Committee for Economic Development, *The Managing and Financing of Colleges* (New York: Committee for Economic Development, 1973).

75. W. Van Alstyne, "Due Process," *The Encyclopedia of Education,* vol. 2 (New York: Macmillan—The Free Press of Glencoe, 1971), pp. 238–41.

76. *Ibid.,* p. 238.

77. *Ibid.,* p. 240.

78. T. Duster, "Student Interests, Student Power and the Swedish Experience," in C. E. Kruytbosch and S. L. Messinger, eds., *The State of the University* (Beverly Hills, Cal.: Sage Publications, 1970), pp. 198, 200.

79. J. A. Perkins, *The University as an Organization* (New York: McGraw-Hill Book Co., 1973), p. 260.

80. This concept should not be confused with the kindred idea of Parsons and Platt (*The American University,* 18–19) that the university's commitment to the values of cognitive rationality makes it a fiduciary of the culture of the society.

81. Hirschman, *Exit, Voice and Loyalty,* pp. 86, 119, 120, 123.

82. Walzer, *Obligations,* pp. 26–28.

83. William M. Evan, "A Systems Analysis of Organizational Climate," in R. Taguiri and G. Litwin, eds., *Organizational Climate* (Cambridge, Mass.: Harvard University Graduate School of Business Administration, 1969), pp. 107–24. See Chapter 10 of the present volume.

84. William M. Evan, "Portable Pensions and Professionalization of Executives," *Wharton Quarterly* 4 (Winter 1969): 29–32.

85. William M. Evan, ed., *Organizational Experiments* (New York: Harper and Row, 1971).

86. Hirschman, *Exit, Voice and Loyalty,* pp. 146–55.

CHAPTER 8

Organizational Lag

From a theoretical as well as a practical point of view it is important to increase our understanding of recurrent processes in organizations. One such process is innovation, which I take to mean the implementation of a new idea, whether a product of invention or discovery. The relationship between the rate of innovation and the rate of growth is so widely assumed to be positive that a prodigious amount of effort is expended yearly by government, industry, and universities for the production of new ideas. In fact, the research and development laboratory is an organizational embodiment of the commitment to innovation.

That organizations differ in their response to proposals for innovations and to innovations proper is a reasonable assumption. To understand the basis for the differential response of organizations to new ideas, it may be helpful to begin with a distinction between technical and administrative innovations. By a technical innovation, I mean the implementation of an idea for a new product, process, or service; by an administrative innovation, I mean the implementation of an idea for a new policy pertaining to the recruitment of personnel, the allocation of resources, and the structuring of tasks, authority, and rewards. This distinction between technical and administrative innovations relates to a more general distinction between technology and social structure.

Over 40 years ago, Ogburn advanced his well-known hypothesis of "cultural lag," which asserts that technology (material culture) advances at a more rapid

This is a revised version of a paper presented at the Seminar on the Innovative Organization, University of Chicago, April, 1964.

rate than other social institutions (nonmaterial culture).[1] The resulting lag between these two components of culture leads to various social problems. This hypothesis has been criticized on several grounds.[2] First, it presumes that technology is the principal determinant of social change and overlooks the effect of the values built into the culture of a society that may foster or hinder technological change. Second, measuring the rate of technological change relative to the rate of nontechnological change and the resulting amount of lag between the two types of change has proved to be exceedingly difficult. Third, the concept of cultural lag, because of the difficulties of measurement, has tended to be used very loosely. Thus all conceivable social evils have been attributed to cultural lag.

The concept of organizational lag advanced in this chapter need not have the same fate as the concept of cultural lag, possibly because a less aggregate level of analysis is involved. At the organizational as opposed to the institutional or societal level of analysis, it is probably easier to find operational measures of technical and administrative innovations. Following Ogburn's hypothesis of cultural lag, it seems worth exploring the analogous hypothesis that administrative innovations in organizations tend to lag behind technical innovations. The rationale for this hypothesis is that a new technical idea is likely to be viewed by management, especially higher levels of management, as more tangible and more proximately related to the profit goal of an industrial organization than is a new administrative idea. Not only is the potential pay-off of an administrative innovation (e.g., a "dual ladder" system of promotion[3] or an "open project time" policy for research and development personnel),[4] less certain than a technical innovation, but it is also likely to require more time to have any discernible effect. The reverse type of organizational lag, i.e., one in which technical innovations lag behind administrative innovations, may also occur, although probably less frequently.

Both types of lag are subsumed in the definition of the concept of organizational lag—*a discrepancy in the rate at which new technical and administrative ideas are implemented in an organization.* Two hypotheses as to the functioning of the social system of an organization follow from the definition of the two classes of innovation and of the concept of organizational lag. First, the slower moving class of innovations tends in the course of time to retard the faster moving class of innovations. Thus, if the Ogburn-inspired hypothesis is true, then administrative innovations that lag behind technical innovations will in due course retard the rate of technical innovations in an organization. Second, the greater the amount of organizational lag, the lower is the rate of organizational growth.

Members of an organization may adapt themselves to organizational lag by (1) developing a conformist or an apathetic ("ritualist" or "retreatist") orientation to their work, or (2) developing *sub rosa* strategies to circumvent organizational policies. Of the various modes of adaptation to organizational lag, apathy on the part of technical and managerial personnel is probably costlier to the objectives of an organization than unauthorized or rebellious conduct. In fact, out of the gamut of *sub rosa* activity current in organizations (e.g., research and development organizations) very often come significant technical innovations. Arthur K. Watson of IBM provides an excellent example of a "bootleg" project:

The disk memory unit, the heart of today's random access computer, is not the logical outcome of a decision made by IBM management. It was developed in one of our laboratories as a bootleg project—over the stern warning from management that the project had to be dropped because of budget difficulties. A handful of men ignored the warning. They broke the rules. They risked their jobs to work on a project they believed in.[5]

The sources of resistance to technical or administrative innovations are, among others, psychological and social in character. As for psychological sources of resistance, individuals differ in their tolerance threshold for new ideas. Since new ideas frequently involve elements of ambiguity, individuals with a low tolerance for ambiguity are unlikely to espouse new ideas. Scales measuring a traditional versus a modern orientation to new ideas have been constructed in various studies of innovation in farm communities and in social contexts other than a formal organization.[6] With the help of such scales, it is possible to measure the attitudes toward new ideas of personnel at different levels in an organization.

A social source of resistance to organizational innovations is the prevailing system of functional specialization. Each department or division in an organization, with its unique tasks and responsibilities, tends to interpret any new idea, technical or administrative, in terms of its potential impact on the well-being of its members. Since the major functional areas, say, in a research and development organization (and its parent organization) have distinctive perspectives and different vested interests, it is reasonable to expect that they would also differ in their degree of resistance to *technical* innovations. Is the hypothetical rank ordering of functional areas on a continuum of resistance to *technical* innovations, shown in Figure 8.1, borne out in fact? How would the major functional areas be ordered on a continuum of potential resistance to *administrative* innovations? How much overlap in attitudes toward new ideas is there between the various functional areas in an organization? The less the overlap in attitudes toward a new idea among the various functional areas (i.e., the greater the difference in point of view), the lower is the probability of its being implemented. In other words, a new idea has a higher probability of being implemented in an organization if there is a substantial degree of overlap in favorable attitudes in the various functional areas. Moreover, the greater the

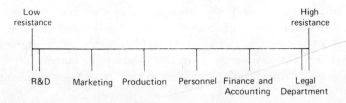

Figure 8.1. Hypothetical ordering of functional areas on a continuum of resistance to technical innovations.

overlap in favorable attitudes toward new ideas among the members of different functional areas (i.e., the more favorable the climate of innovation), the lower is the degree of organizational lag. Another possible indicator of an organization's climate of innovation is the ratio of technical innovations stemming from *sub rosa* activities to technical innovations stemming from authorized activities: The higher this ratio, the less favorable is the climate of innovation and, in turn, the higher is the degree of organizational lag.

Assuming that the concept of organizational lag can be operationalized, several important questions might be raised apart from its consequences for organizational growth. What are the structural features of organizations with a high degree of organizational lag? Do they tend to have a low rate of managerial succession? Are they generally large and centralized in structure? Do they operate on the assumption that new administrative ideas must trickle down the organizational hierarchy, whereas new technical ideas must trickle up the hierarchy?[7]

In the sphere of consumption, particularly as regards women's fashions, a trickle-down theory has been advanced to describe and explain the process of dissemination of new consumption patterns. A new style is developed in or for the upper economic strata and subsequently trickles down to the lower economic strata of a society. In the sphere of formal organizations, management, especially of large organizations, appears to operate with a trickle-down theory of new administrative ideas and a trickle-up theory of new technical ideas. In small organizations approximating the entrepreneurial model, management probably subscribes to a trickle-down theory of both technical and administrative ideas. The other two possible combinations of innovative orientations (i.e., organizations that subscribe to a trickle-down theory of technical ideas but a trickle-up theory of administrative ideas and those guided by a trickle-up theory of both administrative and technical ideas) probably occur very infrequently but are theoretically of considerable interest.

If organizations are to minimize organizational lag—and hence maximize the chances of both administrative and technical innovation—the trickle effect with respect to both administrative and technical ideas would probably have to operate in *both* directions. What structural changes in tasks, occupational differentiation, work flow, information flow, rewards, and authority would encourage a two-directional trickle effect and thus minimize the degree of organizational lag? Only systematic programs of planned changes—introduced as "organizational experiments"—are likely to yield reliable and valid answers to this question.[8]

NOTES

1.   William F. Ogburn, *Social Change* (New York: Viking Press, 1922), pp. 200 ff.

2.   See, for example, James W. Woodward, "A New Classification of Culture and a Restatement of the Cultural Lag Theory," *American Sociological Review* 1 (February 1936): 89–102.

3.   Cf. Herbert A. Shepard, "The Dual Hierarchy in Research," *Research Management* 1 (Autumn 1958): 177–87.

4.   Cf. R. G. Chollar, G. J. Wilson, and B. K. Green, "Creativity Techniques in Action," *Research Management,* 1 (Spring, 1958): 13–14.

5.   Cf. Donald A. Schon, "Champions of Radical New Innovations," *Harvard Business Review* 41 (March–April 1963): 85.

6.   Cf. Everett M. Rogers, *Diffusion of Innovations* (New York: The Free Press, 1962), pp. 62–70.

7.   Lloyd A. Fallers, "A Note on the 'Trickle Effect'," *Public Opinion Quarterly* 18 (Fall 1954): 314–21.

8.   William M. Evan, ed., *Organizational Experiments* (New York: Harper and Row, 1971).

PART THREE

Interorganizational Systems

Since the 1950s an interdisciplinary body of thought known as "systems theory" has emerged. It has its roots in biology, engineering, cybernetics, and information theory.[1] Although several efforts have been made to apply this theoretical framework to organization theory, its impact thus far has been relatively modest.[2] Although a systems perspective has unquestionably penetrated the field of organization theory, it has yet to transform its substance and methodology. Nevertheless, it has already had the salutary effect of sensitizing researchers to the importance of conceptualizing organizations as "open systems" rather than as "closed systems"; it has also contributed to a growing appreciation of the importance of studying organizations in relation to other organizations in their environment.[3]

In the three chapters in Part III an effort is made to break out of the prevailing *intraorganizational*, closed-system paradigm often employed by organizational psychologists as well as organizational sociologists. In Chapter 9, such concepts as the "focal organization" and the input and output "organization-sets" are introduced in order to relate a given organization or a class of organizations to environing organizations. Several dimensions of organization-sets are defined that in turn are used in formulating a number of interrelated hypotheses.

The resulting interorganizational model is partially applied in Chapter 10 in analyzing the climate of an organization.

In Chapter 11, which I wrote as a supplement to Chapter 9, I explicitly reformulate the organization-set model in systems-theoretic terms. Additional dimensions of organization-sets are defined to facilitate an analysis of interorganizational systems. An illustrative application is then presented in an effort to explain the regulatory impact of four federal administrative agencies: the Securities and Exchange Commission, the Interstate Commerce Commission, the Food and Drug Administration, and the Federal Trade Commission.

Clearly, the study of interorganizational relations, which has grown rapidly in the past few years, is still high on the research agenda of organization theory.[4] With the further elaboration and refinement of a systems theory of organization, we can expect substantial progress in the study of interorganizational systems.

NOTES

1. Cf. L. von Bertalanffy, "General System Theory: A New Approach to Unity of Science," *Human Biology* 23 (December 1951): 303–61; Kenneth E. Boulding, "General Systems Theory: The Skeleton of Science," *Management Science* 2 (April 1956): 197–208; Russell L. Ackoff, *Redesigning the Future* (New York: Wiley-Interscience, 1974), pp. 11–17.

2. Cf. Daniel Katz and Robert L. Kahn, *The Social Psychology of Organizations* (New York: John Wiley & Sons, 1966); James G. Miller, "*Living* Systems: The Organization," *Behavioral Science* 17 (January 1972): 1–182; F. E. Emery, ed., *Systems Thinking: Selected Readings* (London: Penguin Books, 1969).

3. F. E. Emery and E. L. Trist, "The Causal Texture of Organizational Environments," *Human Relations* 18 (February 1965): 21–32; Paul R. Lawrence and Jay W. Lorsch, *Organization and Environment* (Boston, Mass.: Harvard University, Graduate School of Business Administration, Division of Research, 1967).

4. Cf. William M. Evan, ed., *Interorganizational Relations: Selected Readings* (London: Penguin Books, 1976).

CHAPTER 9

The Organization-Set

Social science research on organizations has been concerned principally with *intraorganizational* phenomena. Psychologists have studied the individual in an organization; social psychologists, the relations among the members of a group in an organization and the impact of a group on the attitudes and behavior of group members; and sociologists, informal groups, formal subunits, and structural attributes of an organization.[1] With relatively few exceptions social scientists engaged in organizational research have not taken the organization in its environment as a unit of observation and analysis. Selznick's work on the TVA is a notable exception, as are Ridgeway's study of the manufacturer-dealer relationships, Dill's comparative study of two Norwegian firms, Levine and White's research on health and welfare agencies, Elling and Halebsky's study of hospitals, and Litwak and Hylton's study of community chests and social service exchanges.[2]

The relative neglect of *interorganizational* relations is all the more surprising in view of the fact that all formal organizations are embedded in an environment of other organizations as well as in a complex of norms, values, and collectivities of the society at large. Inherent in the relationship between any formal organization and its environment is the fact that it is to some degree dependent upon its environment; in other words, it is a subsystem of the more

This is a revised version of a paper prepared for the Seminar on the Social Science of Organizations, University of Pittsburgh, June 1963. The author developed the concept of organization-set in a proposal entitled, "Law, Formal Organizational, and Social Change," which was submitted to the Russell Sage Foundation in the spring of 1959.

inclusive social system of society. As distinct from a society, which in some respects is relatively self-sufficient in that it runs the gamut of all human institutions, a formal organization is a partial social system inasmuch as it defines only a specific set of goals and statuses as relevant to its functioning.

The phenomena and problems of interorganizational relations are part of the general class of boundary-relations problems confronting all types of social systems, including formal organizations. All such boundary relations tend to be enormously complex. Apart from sheer complexity, problems of interorganizational relations have been neglected by organizational analysts in part because of the concepts and propositions of various theories of organization. For example, the Weberian theory of bureaucracy is concerned largely with internal structural attributes and processes such as specialization of functions, allocation of authority, and formalization of rules. Taylorism and other kindred theories are also oriented toward internal relations among personnel. And the inducement-contribution theory of Barnard and Simon also has an intraorganizational focus.[3] A notable exception to the intraorganizational focus is the theoretical work of Parsons on formal organizations.[4] As a social system theorist, Parsons is concerned with how organizations differing in their primacy of functions solve four system problems: adaptation, goal attainment, pattern maintenance, and integration. Any attempt to investigate how a particular organization solves these problems immediately involves considerations of interorganizational relations.

Notwithstanding the general neglect of interorganizational phenomena by organization theorists, managers are greatly preoccupied with interorganizational relations. Some well-known examples of interorganizational practices are allocation of resources to public relations, cooptation of personnel of environing organizations into leadership positions in order to reduce the threat they might otherwise pose, acquisition of and merging with competitors, use of espionage against competitors, and recourse to litigation, arbitration, and mediation to resolve interorganizational disputes. These and many other interorganizational phenomena and processes await systematic inquiry by organization theorists. Millett's general observation about organization theory is particularly relevant to this problem area: ". . . our practice has far outrun our theory. . . . The art of organization has much more to its credit . . . than has the science of organization."[5] Impeding progress are problems of conceptualizing and measuring interactions among organizations. Prevailing organizational concepts and theories concerned with intraorganizational phenomena are probably not adequate for a study of interorganizational phenomena.

The purpose of this chapter is to explore in a preliminary manner some conceptual and methodological problems of interorganizational relations. In the process we hope to extend the scope of organization theory and to draw attention to the potentialities of comparative research on interorganizational relations.

THE ROLE-SET

One point of departure in the study of interorganizational relations is to examine the utility of the concept of the "role-set," developed by Merton, for analyzing role relationships.[6] A role-set consists of the complex of roles and role relationships that the occupant of a given status has by virtue of occupying that status. A professor, for example, interacts not only with students but also with other professors, with the head of his department, with the dean of his school, and occasionally with the president or with the members of the board of trustees.

In all organizations the occupants of some statuses perform a liaison function with other organizations. Top executives in industrial organizations frequently confer with government officials, with executives of other firms within and without the industry, with members of trade associations, with officials in the local community. As guardians of the "public image" of the organization, they are probably wary of delegating to subordinates contacts with representatives of other organizations that might have critical significance for the welfare of their own organizations.[7]

The difference in orientation and behavior between liaison and nonliaison personnel is clearly brought out in a study by Macaulay.[8] In a study of the use of contract law among business firms, Macaulay found a high incidence of non-contractual relations. Among his other findings was a difference in orientation among the various departments in business firms toward the use of contracts, with the sales department being more negatively disposed to contracts and the comptroller departments being more positively disposed. When interdepartmental conflicts arise about the use of contracts, the house counsel, Macaulay observes, occasionally performs the function of an arbitrator.

A role-set analysis of the sales personnel as compared with the personnel of the comptroller departments suggests a possible explanation for the observed difference in attitudes toward the use of contracts.[9] As the "foreign affairs" personnel of an organization, sales department employees come into recurrent contact with their "role partners" in other organizations, i.e., purchasing agents, with the result that nonorganizational norms develop, making for less recourse to contracts. In contrast, the role-sets of comptroller personnel involve a higher degree of interaction with others within the organization, thus reinforcing organizational norms—including the use of contracts. We may infer from Macaulay's study that systematic inquiry into the role-sets of boundary personnel will shed light on interorganizational relations as it bears on organizational decisions, whether pertaining to the use of contracts or other matters.

THE ORGANIZATION-SET

Analogous to the role-set concept is what I propose to call the "organization-set." Instead of taking a particular status as the unit of analysis, as Merton does in his role-set analysis, I shall take as the unit of analysis an organization or a class of organizations and trace its interactions with the network of organizations in its environment, that is, with elements of its organization-set. In analyzing a particular organization-set I shall refer to the organization that is the point of reference as the "focal organization."[10] To avoid the danger of reifying interorganizational relations, the relations between the focal organization and its organization-set are conceived as mediated by (1) the role-sets of its boundary personnel, (2) the flow of information, (3) the flow of products or services, and (4) the flow of personnel. As in the case of the role-set, conflicting demands by members of the organization-set may be handled by the focal organization with the help of mechanisms analogous to those described by Merton, for example, by preventing observation of behavior and by concerted action to counter the demands of other organizations.[11]

An analysis of the organization-set of a focal organization (or of a class of focal organizations) could help explain: (1) the internal structure of the focal organization; (2) its degree of autonomy in decision making; (3) its degree of effectiveness or goal attainment; (4) its identity (i.e., its public image and self-image); (5) the flow of information from the focal organization to the elements of its organization-set and vice versa; (6) the flow of personnel from the focal organization to the elements of its organization-set and vice versa; and (7) the forces impelling the focal organization to cooperate or compete with elements of its organization-set, to coordinate its activities, to merge with other organizations, or to dissolve. As an example of the possible explanatory utility of the organization-set concept, we shall presently consider the effects of structural variations in the organization-set on the decision-making autonomy of the focal organization.

SOME DIMENSIONS OF ORGANIZATION-SETS

If we are to make any progress in analyzing interorganizational relations, we shall have to identify strategic attributes or dimensions of organization-sets. With the aid of such attributes we can formulate empirically testable propositions about interactions among organizations.

A provisional listing of dimensions of organization-sets follows; its principal value may lie in illustrating a possibly useful direction of conceptual analysis. Whether these dimensions are more heuristic than others that might be abstracted can be determined only by means of empirical research.

1. *Input versus Output Organization-Sets.* The focal organization's environment consists of an input and an output organization-set. As a partial social system, a focal organization depends on input organizations for various types of resources: personnel, matériel, capital, legality, and legitimacy.[12] The focal organization in turn produces a product or a service for a market, an audience, a client system, and so on. For example, a private hospital may have in its input organization-set the community chest from which it obtains financial support, an association of hospitals from which it receives accreditation, and the department of public health of the local or state government from which it receives one or more licenses granting it the right to function. Its output organization-set may include other hospitals with which it cooperates or competes, medical research organizations, government agencies to which it sends data, and the like.

2. *Comparative versus Normative Reference Organizations.* As in the case of an individual, the focal organization may evaluate its performance by using one or more organizations in its set—input or output, more likely the latter—as a standard for comparison, that is, as a "comparative reference organization." On the other hand, if a focal organization incorporates the values and goals of one or more of the elements of its organization-sets, we would refer to it as a "normative reference organization."[13] For example, a firm manufacturing a particular kind of bomber might compare the quality of its product with other firms manufacturing bombers. Such outside firms would then be deemed "comparative reference organizations." Suppose, however, the Department of Defense indicates that the rapid production of a newly developed unmanned decoy bomber is urgently required by the United States. If the firm decided to convert its current bomber production into the production of an unmanned decoy bomber, it will have in effect incorporated as its goal the goal of the government and would be using a representative of the government, the Department of Defense, as a "normative reference organization."

3. *Size of the Organization-Set.* A focal organization may have a relatively large or a relatively small number of elements in its set. Whether it interacts with few or with many organizations presumably has significant consequences for its internal structure and decision making. The size of the organization-set is to be distinguished, of course, from the size of the focal organization, although the two are presumably correlated.

4. *Concentration of Input Organizational Resources.* The focal organization may depend on few or many elements in its input organization-set for its resources. Whether the concentration of input organizational resources is high or low would probably affect the structure and functioning of the focal organization.

5. *Overlap in Membership.* Not infrequently there is an overlap in membership of the focal organization with one of the organizations in its set. This is manifestly the case with (1) employees of an industrial organization who belong to a trade union with which the focal organization has a collective bargaining agreement, (2) scientists or engineers who are affiliated with a professional society from or through which an employing organization recruits its employees, and (3) members of the board of directors of the focal organization who are also directors of organizations in its set.

6. *Overlap in Goals and Values.* The goals and values of the focal organization may overlap with those of the elements in its set. To the extent that this occurs it probably affects the nature of the interorganizational relations that develop. For example, hostility might be engendered between an American military base overseas and a political party in the country in which the base was situated if the party did not share the assessment that the base was performing a protective and deterrent function rather than an offensive and provocative function.

7. *Boundary Personnel.* Classifying the personnel of an organization into those concerned principally with domestic matters and those preoccupied with "foreign affairs" is difficult, although not impossible.[14] In a study of four manufacturing organizations, Haire analyzes the growth of external personnel in relation to internal personnel.[15] Parsons distinguishes among three levels of personnel and functions in a formal organization: institutional, managerial, and technical.[16] The first and third category probably involve a higher proportion of boundary personnel than the second category. In other words, top executives and some staff specialists such as sales, public relations, and house counsel are more likely to be engaged in boundary-maintenance functions than are junior and middle executives.

SOME HYPOTHESES ABOUT ORGANIZATION-SETS

Whether or not our preliminary consideration of some conceptual problems of interorganizational relations will prove useful only empirical research can establish. In the interest of stimulating inquiry in this relatively neglected area, several hypotheses on organization-sets, each assuming a *ceteris paribus* condition, will be formulated with the aid of the attributes enumerated in the foregoing section.

1. *The higher the concentration of input organizational resources, the lower the degree of autonomy in decision making of the focal organization.* A case in point is the difference in degree of independence between a public and a private university. A public university probably has fewer sources of revenue than a private university, and one member in its organization-set, the state legislature, probably accounts for the greatest part of its revenue. Consequently, public universities with a high concentration of input organizational resources probably exercise a lower degree of decision-making autonomy than private universities with a low concentration of input organizational resources.

2. *The greater the size of the organization-set, the lower the decision-making autonomy of the focal organization, provided that some elements in the set form an uncooperative coalition that controls resources essential to the functioning of the focal organization, or provided that an uncooperative single member of the set controls such resources.* Where there is a high degree of conflict among the elements of the organization-set, such conflict may tend to cancel out their effect on the focal organization, thus affording it more autonomy than would otherwise be the case. On the other hand, to the extent that there are coalition formations and to the extent that these coalition formations provide essential resources for or services to the focal organization, this does impose significant constraints on the degree of independence of the focal organization.

A striking example of a coalition formation against a focal organization is the boycott by druggists—organized by their trade association—of the Pepsodent Company when the latter withdrew its California fair-trade contracts.[17] Also impressive is the action of the National Automobile Dealers Association in the courts and in legislatures to curb the power of the three large automobile manufacturers to dictate the terms of contracts and to cancel contracts.[18] By means of concerted action this trade association has become a countervailing power in the automobile industry. But size of organization-set, through an alternative sequence of variations, may produce an increase in the decision-making autonomy of the focal organization as well as the decrease hypothesized above. Quite likely there is a positive association between size of the organization-set and size of the focal organization. The larger the organization, the greater the specialization in liaison functions, the greater the number of boundary personnel, and so the greater the decision-making autonomy of the focal organization. However, some qualifications are necessary. To the extent that the proportion of boundary personnel is indicative of the *actual* rather than the *attempted* impact on the elements of its set, the greater the proportion of such personnel in the focal organization—relative to the proportion of such personnel in the set—the greater is its decision-making autonomy. Thus it may be seen that different mediators of the effects of size of organization-set yield opposite consequences for decision-making autonomy of the focal organization.

3. *The greater the degree of similarity of goals and functions between the organization-set and the focal organization, the greater the amount of competition between them, and hence the lower the degree of decision-making autonomy of the focal organization.* In their study of health and welfare agencies, Levine and White observe that:

... intense competition may occur occasionally between two agencies offering the same services, especially when other agencies have no specific criteria for referring patients to one rather than the other. If both services are operating near capacity, competition between the two tends to be less keen, the choice being governed by the availability of service. If the services are being operated at less than capacity, competition and conflict often occur. Personnel of referring agencies in this case frequently deplore the "duplication of services" in the community.[19]

Another illustration of this hypothesis is the enactment of a law by Congress in 1959 requiring legislative authorization of major weapons programs of the armed forces. The enactment, Section 412 of the Military Construction Authorization Act of Fiscal 1960, substantially affects the process of policy making in military affairs. Previously, major weapons procurement was authorized on a continual basis. Section 412, however, required that procurement of aircraft, missiles, and ships by all the services would require renewed authorization on an annual basis. Section 412 was authorized by the Senate Armed Services Committee, which was seeking to expand Congress' participation in defense policy making. Here it may be seen that the common goal of the Department of Defense and of the Armed Services Committee was the adequate defense of the nation, and that efforts to achieve that goal brought them into conflict, lowering the decision-making autonomy of the Department of Defense.[20]

4. *The greater the overlap in membership between the focal organization and the elements of its set, the lower its degree of decision-making autonomy.* A case in point is the overlapping membership of industrial organizations and trade unions. Overlapping membership, if accompanied by overlapping goals and values, may engender a conflict of loyalties that in turn probably diminishes the autonomy of the focal organization.

In Africa trade unions have become closely associated with nationalist parties, which have almost invariably provided governments of newly independent states with important personnel. Overlapping membership then occurs between a ministry of the central government and a trade union. These union leaders then face a dilemma in the concurrent needs to meet their members' demands for higher living standards and to cooperate with the government in promoting economic development. Their decision-making autonomy is thus reduced relative to the autonomy present when they were only union officials.

5. *Normative reference organizations have a greater constraining effect on the decisions of the focal organization than do comparative reference organizations.* The relations between trade unions of federal civil servants and the government illustrates this hypothesis. In the American public service it has been traditional not to strike; instead public servants have been satisfied to have working conditions determined by legislation or unilateral administrative action. This is probably due in large measure to the fact that the government department for which the civil servant works constitutes a very strong normative reference organization. Civil servants have apparently incorporated the goals of government, one of which is to maintain the continuity of the government in all circumstances. A trade union of office workers outside the government-that threatens to strike will be seen only as a comparative reference organization whose members perform parallel duties with government workers. In the case of the civil servant a normative reference organization clearly determines behavior to a greater extent than a comparative reference organization.[21]

The foregoing hypotheses are but illustrations of the kinds of hypotheses that might be formulated with the help of the properties of organization-sets. These hypotheses revolve around the dependent variable of autonomy in decision making of the focal organization. Clearly, similar hypotheses are needed for various interorganizational processes, for example, coordination, cooperation, competition, conflict, innovation, and amalgamation.[22] Several examples of such hypotheses will be briefly considered:

1. *The greater the size of the organization-set, the greater the degree of centralization of authority in order to prevent the "displacement of goals" generated by subunit loyalties and actions.[23] In turn, an increase in centralization of authority results in an increase in the formalization of rules within the focal organization as a means of guarding against the displacement of goals.*

2. *The greater the similarity of functions between the focal organization and the members of its set, the greater the likelihood that it will compete with them. Overlapping membership, however, probably tends to mitigate competition. If overlapping membership is combined with overlapping goals and values, cooperative action that could lead to amalgamation might ensue.*

3. *The greater the complementarity of functions between the focal organization and the members of its set, the greater the likelihood of cooperative action.*

4. *The greater the capacity of the focal organization to invoke sanctions against the members of its set, the greater the likelihood of coordination and cooperation, provided that memebers of the set do not succeed in uniting in opposition to the focal organization.*

5. *The greater the shortage of input resources on the part of the focal organization, the greater the likelihood that it will cooperate with the input organizations in its set and the more favorable its disposition toward amalgamation with one or more of them.* The academic "common market" or consortium being formed among Midwest universities to pool their resources in graduate education is a case in point.

6. *The greater the competition between the focal organization and the members of the output organizations in its set, the more favorable is its disposition toward amalgamation, provided that the goals and values of the respective organizations are compatible.*

7. *If the members of the organization-set exhibit a high rate of technological change, the focal organization, in order to remain competitive, will be highly receptive to innovations.*

SOME METHODOLOGICAL PROBLEMS

Apart from the conceptual problems awaiting analysis in this area of research, there are measurement problems of considerable difficulty. Describing and measuring networks of interorganizational relations presents a substantial methodological challenge. Some gross behavioral indicators of interorganizational relations are number of contracts, number of clients or customers, volume of sales or services, volume of telephone calls made and received, volume of mail sent and received. Mapping interactions of organizations would require special attention to boundary personnel, as noted above, and to the patterns of interaction of organizational decision makers. Such mapping operations of the behavior of boundary personnel and decision makers could also yield sociometric data on which of the elements in an organization-set are perceived by different categories of members of the focal organization as comparative reference organizations or as normative reference organizations. Two closely related methodological tools that may prove useful in the mapping of interorganizational relations are graph theory and input-output analysis.

GRAPH THEORY

One possible use of graph theory is in the construction of an index measuring the amount of decision-making autonomy of a focal organization or of any of the elements in its set.[24] Let us consider three highly simplified organization-set configurations approximating a "wheel," a "chain," and an "all-channel network."[25] In the three digraphs shown in Figure 9.1, each point represents an organization, each line a type of interaction (a flow of information, of goods, of influence, or of personnel), and an arrow the direction of interaction.

If we take *A* as the focal organization in the three configurations, how do they differ in their degree of decision-making autonomy? Intuitively, we would

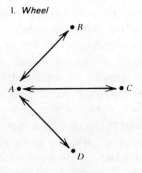

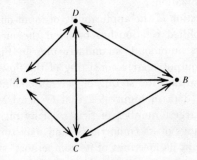

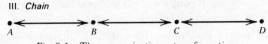

Fig. 9.1   *Three organization-set configurations*

expect that I_A ranks first in autonomy, II_A ranks second, and III_A ranks third. In the automobile industry the supplier-manufacturer-dealer sequence of organizational relationships would suggest that the supplier is in a position comparable to III_A and that the manufacturers are in a position comparable to I_A.[26] Can we construct an index that would yield a "co-efficient of interconnectedness" of elements in an organization-set—and hence decision-making autonomy—that would discriminate not only among the three simplified organization-sets shown in Figure 9.1 but also among other possible configurations?

INPUT-OUTPUT ANALYSIS

One input-output model that may prove useful in the study of interorganizational relations is that developed by Leontief.[27] In the study of the structure of the American economy, Leontief and his associates have, of course, concerned themselves with economic parameters such as prices, investments, and incomes. Is this mode of analysis applicable to noneconomic parameters of interorganizational relationships with which sociologists, social psychologists, and political scientists are concerned? Are the obstacles to an input-output analysis of interorganizational relations insuperable because the data most organizational researchers work with do not take the form of ratio scales, as is true of the data of economists? In most cases the data used by social scientists studying organizations—other than economists—frequently take the form of nominal or ordinal scales and, occasionally, interval scales e.g., flows of information, flows of personnel, or flows of influence. Apart from the level of measurement, do noneconomic data permit the construction of "technical coefficients" of inputs to the outputs of the focal organizations?

One way of raising the question of the applicability of input-output analysis is to consider a highly simplified relationship between the members of an oligopolistic industry, such as automobile manufacturing. In Figure 9.2 we present a hypothetical input-output matrix consisting of the flow of influence on management decisions regarding the styling of new automobiles. It would appear from the hypothetical data in Figure 9.2 that General Motors is the style leader. It receives the largest number of praiseworthy mentions in the minutes of management meetings of its competitors, and it in turn makes the fewest praiseworthy mentions in its meetings of its competitors' styles. Would an input-output analysis of matrices of the type shown in Figure 9.2—possibly in conjunction with additional data, e.g., share of the market—suggest any further operations for analyzing the data or yield any additional insights into the decision-making process concerning automobile styles?

An analogous matrix that might lend itself to an input-output analysis is shown in Figure 9.3. Once again it is clear from the hypothetical data that General Motors enjoys a commanding position: It has the smallest outflux of

Number of praiseworthy mentions received by

		A.M.	Ford	Chrysler	G.M.	Total
Number of praiseworthy mentions made by	A.M.		10	5	15	30
	Ford	2		5	15	22
	Chrysler	3	8		13	24
	G.M.	0	4	6		10
	Total	5	22	16	43	

Fig. 9.2 Hypothetical matrix of flow of influence on styling decisions in the automobile industry (as indexed by frequence of praiseworthy mentions in the minutes of management meetings).

Flow of engineering personnel to

Flow of engineering personnel from	A.M.	Ford	Chrysler	G.M.	Total
A.M.		15	5	40	60
Ford	5		5	25	35
Chrysler	7	8		35	50
G.M.	2	12	6		20
Total	14	35	16	100	

Fig. 9.3   Hypothetical flow of engineering personnel, 1955–1960.

engineering personnel and the largest influx from the other automobile companies. Would an input-output analysis of this matrix, supplemented by data on other characteristics of the organizations, contribute to our understanding of the data?

The matrices shown in Figures 9.2 and 9.3 involve one point in time. Assuming that data are available for two or more time periods, can we apply a Markov chain model to analyze the processes of change in interorganizational relations?

CONCLUSION

The foregoing methodological discussion together with the theoretical analysis may provide guidelines for new research on interorganizational relations. Of particular promise is comparative research on the organization-sets of different classes of organizations. How different are the organization-sets of economic, political, religious, educational, and cultural organizations? And what are the consequences of variations in organization-sets for the internal structure and for the decision-making process of different types of organizations? Do "coercive" organizations have a network of interactions with other organizations different from "utilitarian" and "normative" organizations?[28] How different are the organization-sets of habit, problem-solving, indoctrination, and service types of organizations?[29]

Within the confines of any one class of organizations, how different are the organization-sets of, say, industrial organizations classified by industry? Similarly, what structural variations in organization-sets are observable among therapeutic versus custodial prisons or among hospitals differing in the importance they attach to the goals of treatment, teaching, and research?[30]

Another possible use of organization-set analysis is in the study of intraorganizational dynamics. If each of the major functional areas in a business organization—production, sales, engineering, personnel, and so on—is taken as a unit of inquiry, an organization-set analysis would be applicable in studying interdepartmental relations. Such an approach would probably be especially useful in investigating the problem of innovation in industrial organizations.[31]

As is generally recognized, a formal organization is a particular type of social system. The study of interorganizational relations hence involves an analysis of intersocial system relations. Systematic inquiry into the interactions among various types of organizations may not only unearth new intraorganizational phenomena and processes, but may also provide the wherewithal for bridging the gap between the microscopic *organizational* and the macroscopic *institutional* levels of analysis. The solution of intersystem problems of the most aggregate level, namely, interrelations among societies, presupposes a knowledge of the nature of interorganizational interactions within and between the several institutions of a society.

NOTES

1. See, for example, C. Argyris, *Integrating the Individual and the Organization* (New York: John Wiley & Sons, 1964) and *Personality and Organization* (New York: Harper and Row, 1957). See also T. W. Costello and S. S. Zalkind, *Psychology in Administration: A Research Orientation* (Englewood Cliffs, N.J.: Prentice-Hall, 1963); W. G. Bennis, E. H. Schein, D. E. Berlew, and F. I. Steel, *Interpersonal Dynamics: Essays and Readings on Human Interaction* (Homewood, Ill.: Dorsey, 1964); M. Haire, *Psychology in Management*, 2d ed. (New York: McGraw-Hill Book Co., 1964); R. L. Kahn *et al.*, *Organizational Stress* (New York: John Wiley & Sons, 1964); William M. Evan, "Indices of the Hierarchical Structure of Industrial Organizations," *Management Science* 9 (1963): 468–77; P. M. Blau, *The Dynamics of Bureaucracy* (Chicago: The University of Chicago Press, 1955).

2. P. Selznick, *TVA and the Grass Roots: A Study in the Sociology of Formal Organization* (Berkeley and Los Angeles: The University of California Press, 1949; V. F. Ridgeway, "Administration of Manufacturer-Dealer Systems," *Administrative Science Quarterly* 2 (1957): 464–83; W. R. Dill, "Environment as an Influence on Managerial Autonomy," *Administrative Science Quarterly* 2 (1958): 409–43; S. Levine and P. E. White, "Exchange as a Conceptual Framework for the Study of Interorganizational Relationships," *Administrative Science Quarterly* 5 (1961): 583–601; R. H. Elling and S. Halebsky, "Organizational Differentiation and Support: A Conceptual Framework," *Administrative Science Quarterly* 6 (1961): 185–209; E. Litwak and L. F. Hylton, "Inter-organizational Analysis: A Hypothesis on Coordinating Agencies," *Administrative Science Quarterly* 6 (1962): 395–426.

3. C. I. Barnard, *The Functions of the Executive* (Cambridge, Mass.: Harvard University Press, 1938); H. A. Simon, *Administrative Behavior* (New York: Macmillan, 1945); J. March and H. A. Simon, *Organizations* (New York: John Wiley & Sons, 1958).

4. T. Parsons, "General Theory in Sociology," in R. K. Merton, Leonard Broom, and Leonard S. Cottrell, Jr., eds., *Sociology Today* New York: Basic Books, 1959); T. Parsons, *Structure and Process in Modern Societies* (Glencoe, Ill.: The Free Press, 1960).

5. J. D. Millett, *An Essay on Organization: The Academic Community* (New York: McGraw-Hill Book Co., 1962), p. 3.

6. R. K. Merton, *Social Theory and Social Structure*, rev. ed. (Glencoe, Ill.: The Free Press, 1957), pp. 368–80; see also N. Gross, W. S. Mason, and A. W. McEachern, *Explorations in Role Analysis: Studies of the School Superintendency Role* (New York: John Wiley & Sons, 1958), pp. 48–74.

7. J. W. Riley, Jr. and M. F. Levy, eds., *The Corporation and Its Publics: Essays on the Corporate Image* (New York: John Wiley & Sons, 1963).

8. S. Macaulay, "Non-Contractual Relations in Business: A Preliminary Study," *American Sociological Review* 28 (1963): 55–67.

9. William M. Evan, "Comment on Stewart Macaulay's 'Non-Contractual Relations in Business: A Preliminary Study'," *American Sociological Review* 28 (1963): 67–69.

10. Gross, Mason, and McEachern, *Explorations in Role Analysis*, pp. 50–56.

11. Merton, *Social Theory and Social Structure*, pp. 371–79.

12. William M. Evan and M. A. Schwartz, "Law and the Emergence of Formal Organizations," *Sociology and Social Research* 48 (1964): 276–79.

13. Merton, *Social Theory and Social Structure*, pp. 283–84.

14. J. D. Thompson, "Organizations and Output Transactions," *American Journal of Sociology* 68 (1962): 309–24.

15. M. Haire, "Biological Models and Empirical Histories of the Growth of Organizations," in M. Haire, ed., *Modern Organization Theory* (New York: John Wiley & Sons, 1959).

16. Parsons, "General Theory in Sociology," *op. cit.* pp. 10–16; and *Structure and Process in Modern Societies*, pp. 59–96.

17. J. C. Palamountain, Jr., *The Politics of Distribution* (Cambridge, Mass.: Harvard University Press, 1955), pp. 235–39.

18. *Ibid.*, pp. 107–58; and William M. Evan, "Public and Private Legal Systems," in W. M. Evan, ed., *Law and Sociology* (New York: The Free Press of Glencoe, 1962), pp. 165–84.

19. Levine and White, "Exchange as a Conceptual Framework," p. 598.

20. R. H. Dawson, "Congressional Innovation and Intervention in Defense Policy: Legislative Authorization of Weapons Systems," *American Political Science Review* 56 (1962): 42–57.

21. S. D. Spero, "Collective Bargaining in Public Employment: Form and Scope," *Public Administration Review* 22 (1962): 1–4.

22. J. D. Thompson and W. J. McEwen, "Organizational Goals and Environment: Goal-setting as an Interaction Process," *American Sociological Review* 23 (1958): 23–31.

23. Merton, *Social Theory and Social Structure*, pp. 199–201.

24. D. Cartwright, "The Potential Contribution of Graph Theory to Organization Theory," in M. Haire, ed., *Modern Organizational Theory* (New York: John Wiley & Sons, 1959); F. Harary and R. Z. Norman, *Graph Theory as a mathematical Model in Social Science* (Ann Arbor: University of Michigan Institute for Social Research, 1953); C. Flament, *Application of Graph Theory to Group Structure* (Englewood Cliffs, N.J.: Prentice-Hall, 1963).

25. A. Bavelas, "Communication Patterns in Task-Oriented Groups," in H. Lasswell and D. Lerner, eds., *The Policy Sciences* (Stanford, Cal.: Stanford University Press, 1951); H. J. Leavitt, *Managerial Psychology*, rev. ed. (Chicago: University of Chicago Press, 1964).

26. Ridgeway, "Administration of Manufacturer-Dealer Systems."

27. Wassily W. Leontief et al., *Studies in the Structure of the American Economy* (New York: Oxford University Press, 1953).

28. Amitai Etzioni, *A Comparative Analysis of Complex Organizations* (New York: The Free Press, 1961).

29. W. G. Bennis, "Leadership Theory and Administrative Behavior: The Problem of Authority," *Administrative Science Quarterly* 4 (1959): 259–301.

30. R. A. Cloward, D. R. Cressey, G. N. Grosser, R. McCleery, L. E. Ohlin, G. Sykes, and S. L. Messinger, *Theoretical Studies in Social Organization of the Prison* (New York: Social Science Research Council, 1960); S. Wheeler, "Role Conflict in Correctional Communities," in D. Cressey, ed., *The Prison: Studies in Institutional Organization and Change* (New York: Holt, Rinehart & Winston, 1961), pp. 229–59.

31. William M. Evan, "Organizational Lag," *Human Organization* 25 (Spring 1966): 51–53. See Chapter 8 of this volume.

CHAPTER 10

A Systems Model of
Organizational Climate

In the interdisciplinary field variously known as organization theory, organizational behavior, complex organizations, and formal organizations, the distinction between individual unit data and aggregate unit data is often blurred. It is not surprising that psychologists gather data on an individual unit level and that sociologists, economists, operations researchers, and others gather data on an aggregate unit level.[1] The growing interest in the phenomenon of organizational climate is an example of the intersection of these two levels of analysis.

The utility of a concept such as "organizational climate" may be judged with the aid of at least two standards: (1) Does it help us perceive phenomena hitherto not perceived or identify problems hitherto not identified? (2) Does it link up with other concepts in organizational analysis, thereby generating empirically testable propositions and contributing to the development of theory? Whether the concept of organizational climate is scientifically useful in terms of these two standards may be considered an open question. What is manifestly not an open question is whether the concept is phenomenologically real. People do sense and react to the climate of an organization, whether they belong to it or not.

The use of this concept involves us in an interesting dilemma: From a scientific point of view it appears to be so gross and ambiguous as to be of doubtful

This is a revised version of a paper prepared for a Research Conference on Organizational Climate held at the Harvard University Graduate School of Business Administration in January 1967.

utility; however, from a common-sense point of view, it appears to be useful. Although common sense is scarcely a reliable source of ideas for conceptualization in science, in the case of organizational climate it may prove instructive. The social-psychological reality of this concept is not unrelated to what Merton calls the "Thomas theorem": "If men define situations as real, they are real in their consequences."[2]

The purpose of this chapter is threefold: (1) to propose a tentative definition of organizational climate, (2) to integrate this concept with that of the organization-set in the context of a systems model of organizations, and (3) to develop several potentially testable propositions about the climate of an organization.[3]

A PROVISIONAL DEFINITION OF ORGANIZATIONAL CLIMATE

Among the multitude of concepts used in organizational research, organizational climate is not yet firmly established. Nevertheless, increasingly it is the subject of inquiry, as witness the studies of Michael, Halpin and Croft, Carlin, and Pelz and Andrews.[4] The concept suggests, as noted above, a union between an individual and an aggregate level of analysis.

Among the various kindred concepts that may suggest a definition of organizational climate, several are noteworthy. Argyris in effect equates organizational climate with "organizational culture."[5] This has the advantage of linking the concept with components of culture and with such a related concept as "subculture." However, if we take culture to mean the set of beliefs, values, and norms that constitute blueprints for behavior, then the concept of culture as the basis for a definition of organizational climate seems too broad.

Another cognate concept is "organizational prestige," as used, for example, by Perrow.[6] This concept relates to the public image of the products or services of an organization. "If an organization . . . [is] well regarded, it may more easily attract personnel, influence relevant legislation, wield informal power in the community, and insure adequate numbers of clients, customers, donors, or investors. Organizations may be placed along a continuum from unfavorable to favorable public images. A predominantly favorable image we shall call 'prestige,' and it may range from low to high."[7] Although this concept is suggestive in directing attention to the image that nonmembers have of an organization, it is needlessly restrictive in not including the image members themselves have of the organization; nor does it include the public image of organizational attributes other than products or services.

Yet another conception relevant to organizational climate is Margulies' idea of organizational culture which he defines as the degree to which the organization is capable of adapting to its dynamic environment.[8] This conception is not distinguishable from the concept of "organizational flexibility" advanced a decade ago by Georgopolous and Tannenbaum, nor does it capture the subjective or perceptual dimension conveyed by the term.[9]

To exploit the phenomenological reality of the concept, Halpin and Croft use the metaphor of personality in their study of the organizational climate of schools. Their metaphorical definition guided their construction of the Organizational Climate Description Questionnaire.[10] The impetus for their study was the observation that schools differ in their "feel." Halpin's explanation of his metaphorical definition of organizational climate is as follows:

Anyone who visits more than a few schools notes quickly how schools differ from each other in their "feel." In one school the teachers and the principal are zestful and exude confidence in what they are doing. They find pleasure in working with each other; this pleasure is transmitted to the students, who thus are given at least a fighting chance to discover that school can be a happy experience. In a second school the brooding discontent of the teachers is palpable; the principal tries to hide his incompetence and his lack of a sense of direction behind a cloak of authority, and yet he wears this cloak poorly because the attitude he displays to others vacillates randomly between the obsequious and the officious. And the psychological sickness of such a faculty spills over on the students who, in their own frustration, feed back to the teachers a mood of despair. A third school is marked by neither joy nor despair, but by hollow ritual. Here one gets the feeling of watching an elaborate charade in which teachers, principal, and students alike are acting out parts. The acting is smooth, even glib, but it appears to have little meaning for the participants; in a strange way the show just doesn't seem to be "for real." And so, too, as one moves to other schools, one finds that each appears to have a "personality" of its own. It is this "personality" that we describe here as the "Organizational Climate" of the school. Analogously, personality is to the individual what Organizational Climate is to the organization.[11]

For present purposes, I would like to venture the following definition:

Organizational climate is a multidimensional perception by members as well as non-members of the essential attributes or character of an organizational system.

In this provisional definition I deliberately limit the concept to "multidimensional perceptions" rather than posit some inherent properties such as might be implied in the concept of "organizational culture" or organizational structure. The term "multidimensional" is necessary because the "essential attributes" are not likely to be perceived along one dimension only.

A SYSTEMS MODEL OF ORGANIZATIONS

On the assumption that complex systemic relations give rise to "multidimensional perceptions of the essential attributes" of an organization, a systems model of organizations will now be explored. Such a model may also have the advantage of integrating the concept of organizational climate with other concepts in organization theory. A systems approach to organizational phenomena minimally involves identifying input elements, process elements, output elements, and feedback effects. It also focuses attention on the interrelation of at least three levels of analysis: the subsystems of an organization, the organizational system in its entirety, and the suprasystem. Analyzing the subsystems of an organization entails a study of the interaction patterns of the various subunits; analyzing the organizational system includes an examination of the cultural, structural, and technological components; and analyzing the suprasystem requires, at the very least, an inquiry into the network of interactions of the given organization with the various organizations in its environment. In short, to ascertain the determinants and consequences of organizational climate, as here defined, a model is required of the internal and external relations of an organization.

The model to be explored posits a particular organization or a class of organizations whose behavior is of interest to the investigator, and which is processing various inputs from its environment and generating various outputs. Following Gross, Mason, and McEachern's use of the term "focal position" in their outstanding study of role analysis, I have referred to the organization or class of organizations that is the point of departure of an inquiry as the "focal organization."[12] In the study of roles the "focal role" is viewed in terms of its relation to a set of roles with which it interacts, namely, the "role-set."[13] Similarly, the focal organization interacts with a complement of organizations in its environment, which I refer to as an "organization-set." A systems analysis perspective suggests that we divide the organization-set into an "input organization-set" and an "output organization-set." By an input organization-set, as the term suggests, I mean a complement of organizations that provides various resources to the focal organization. Similarly, by an output organization-set I mean all organizations that receive the goods and services, including organizational decisions, generated by the focal organization. Furthermore, a systems analysis requires that we trace feedback effects—positive and negative, anticipated and unanticipated—from the output organization-set to the focal organization and thence to the input organization-set, or directly from the output to the input organization set. Figure 10.1 summarizes the rudimentary elements of an organization-set model of interorganizational relations.

Thus, if we take as our focal organization a manufacturing company, the input organization set may include a variety of suppliers of raw materials, trade unions, government agencies, courts, universities, research and development organizations, and so forth. The input resources are very heterogeneous indeed, including human, material, financial, legal, etc. These inputs are transformed by the focal organization's social structure and technology into

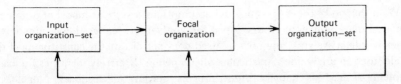

Fig. 10.1 *Some elements of an organization-set model of interorganizational relations.*

products and services that are exported to the members of the output organization-set, which may include wholesale or retail firms. The output organization-set may also include advertising agencies concerned with increasing the sale of its products, trade associations to which information is provided and which may undertake to influence the course of future legislation, and others. The success with which the focal organization manages its multifaceted relations with the members of its output organization-set in turn feeds back into the input organization-set, which again triggers the cycle of systemic relations.

A MODEL OF ORGANIZATIONAL CLIMATE

To relate the systems model of organizations to organizational climate, consider the following assumptions about the latter:

1. Members as well as nonmembers have perceptions of the climate of the focal organization, i.e., the organization or class of organizations which is the object of analysis.
2. Organizational members tend to perceive the climate differently from nonmembers because of the prevalence of different frames of reference and different criteria for evaluating an organization.
3. Perceptions of organizational climate, whether real or unreal, have behavioral consequences for the focal organization as well as for elements of the organization-set, i.e., the complement of organizations with which the focal organization interacts.
4. Organizational members performing different roles tend to have different perceptions of the climate, if only because of (a) a lack of role consensus, (b) a lack of uniformity in role socialization, and (c) a diversity in patterns of role-set interactions.
5. Members of different organizational subunits tend to have different perceptions of the climate because of different role-set configurations, different subgoals, and a differential commitment to the goals of subunits compared to the goals of the organization as a whole.

With the aid of these concepts and assumptions a systems model of organizational climate will now be developed for analyzing organizational climate. In other words, a systems approach by itself does not dictate the constituents of the model used in analyzing a particular phenomenon. It merely identifies the basic elements of analysis, namely, input, process, output, and feedback. Nor does it define which input, process, and output elements to select and which feedback effects to study.

In Figures 10.2 and 10.3 a systems model of organizational climate is presented. Although the cycle of systemic relations can be analyzed from any starting point in the flow chart in Figure 10.2, we shall begin with the focal organization's interface with the input elements in its environment, proceed to the process elements, i.e., the internal processes of the focal organization, then turn to the output elements, and finally consider the feedback effects.

As an open system the focal organization (Figure 10.2A) depends on various resources—human, material, financial, and the like (Figure 10.2G). Whatever its goals, unless the focal organization performs a function vis-à-vis some external organization, client system, or constituency, the demand for its product or service will diminish or disappear (Figure 10.2G).

Yet another input are the legal constraints (Figure 10.2B) in the form of

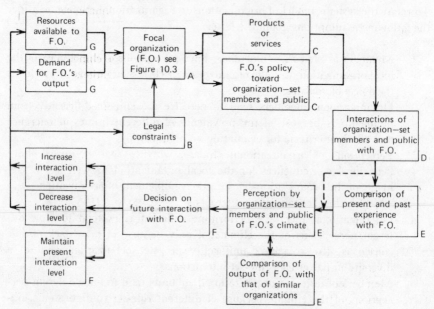

Fig. 10.2   Flow chart of a systems model of organizational climate.

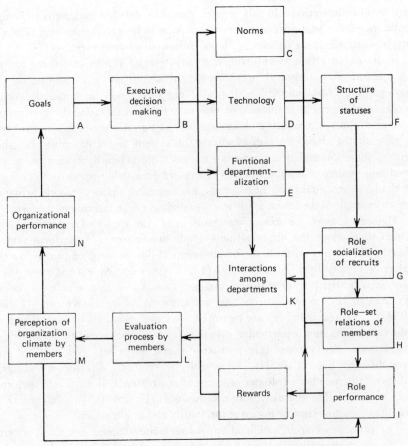

Fig. 10.3   Processes within the focal organization generating an organizational climate.

laws concerning incorporation, taxes, employment, and so on. Implementing these laws are the various courts and administrative agencies of the local, state, and federal government.

The level and quality of the inputs at any particular time activate the complex of intraorganizational processes within the focal organization (Figure 10.3).

The goals of an organization (Figure 10.3A), whether explicitly or implicitly defined, condition the decision-making process of top executives (Figure 10.3B). The decision making of top executives is functionally equivalent to the action of legislators in a governmental context in that it may have system-wide structural ramifications. In this respect, executive decision making is to be distinguished from administrative decision making of lower echelons that officially involves implementing policies or "laws" formulated by top executives.[14]

If the organization is enjoying a steady level of inputs and there are no administrative or technical problems of any significant size looming on the horizon, the "law-making" activities of executives will be minimal. When, however, changes either internal or external to the organization threaten inputs and/or outputs, the policy-making activities of top management are activated, setting off the chain reaction of effects the system model describes. In other words, some internal organizational processes are primarily responsive to the level and quality of inputs, whereas others are primarily responsive to *changes* in the level and quality of those inputs. Management's policy-making activities are an example of the latter, while role socialization is an instance of the former.

The decisions of top executives result in (1) the choice of technology with which to produce the organization's goods or services, (2) the formation of functional subunits, and (3) the development of norms designed to regulate the behavior of members (Figure 10.3C,D,E).[15] As a consequence of these three processes, a structure of statuses emerges, typically of an hierarchical nature (Figure 10.3F), which affects the socialization of new members (Figure 10.3G).[16] As new members are recruited, they are socialized by formal and/or informal means into a particular role that involves the recruit in a network of interactions with various role partners—peers, superiors, and possibly also subordinates (Figure 10.3H). These role-set relations directly or indirectly influence the member's role performance (Figure 10.3I). In turn role performance tends to affect the distribution of rewards (Figure 10.3J), particularly in organizations governed by norms of rationality and universalism.

The processes of role socialization, role-set interactions, and role performance collectively influence the type of interdepartmental relations that develop (Figure 10.3K). In addition, functional specialization among subunits generates not only varying degrees of cooperation but also varying degrees of competition and conflict over the allocation of scarce resources. The rewards received by members for their role performance and their intradepartmental and interdepartmental experiences lead them to evaluate the character of the organization (Figure 10.3L). This evaluation process, influenced in part by the commitment of members to their role, their subunits, and the total organization, results in the formation of a perceived organizational climate (Figure 10.3M). The collective perceptions by members of the organizational climate, possibly because of their feedback effects on role performance (Figure 10.3M-I), influence the organizational performance (Figure 10.3N). And the level and quality of organizational performance in turn influence the degree of goal attainment and future goal-setting behavior (Figure 10.2A), which again triggers the cycle of intraorganizational processes.

The various intraorganizational processes, which give rise to an *internal* organizational climate, are subject to modifications as a result of external relations of the focal organization with various members of its organization-set and the public at large. Initiating these external relations are the outputs of the focal organization and the accompanying policies regarding its outputs (Figure 10.2C). For example, the modes of interaction between the focal organization and members of its organization-set may run the gamut of conflict, competition, coalition formation, and amalgamation (Figure 10.2D).[17] Organizations that are willing to forego formal contractual relations in interactions with members of their organization-set create a different impression from those that uniformly adhere to commercial practices; similarly, organizations that are scrupulously fair and reasonable in their transactions create a quite different impression from organizations that are prone to terminate arbitrarily contracts with members of their organization-set.[18] The impressions created in the course of interactions between the focal organization and organization-set members are evaluated in the light of past experiences (Figure 10.2E). If an organization-set member has had no previous interactions with the focal organization, it bypasses this phase and proceeds directly to evaluating the focal organization's outputs—products or services and policies toward organization-set members—in comparison with those of similar organizations. The outcome of this evaluation process is a perception by organization-set members and the public at large of the focal organization's essential attributes or character, that is, its climate. These collective perceptions constitute the *external* organizational climate.[19]

The focal organization might be disposed to ignore the perceptions of its climate by organization-set members and the public at large if the perceptions were not translated into behavior. However, as in the case of other types of perceptions, we would expect that organization-set members' perceptions of the focal organization's climate would in fact influence their decisions regarding future interactions—whether to increase, decrease, or maintain the present level of interactions (Figure 10.2F).

Whatever the decisions of the organization-set members regarding future interactions, the feedback effects on the input resources of the focal organization are decisive. They partly determine the flow of revenue from products or services, the flow of new personnel, the flow of information, and the flow of other resources (Figure 10.2G). When the changed inputs are fed back to the focal organization, a new cycle of intraorganizational processes is generated that may tend to maintain or alter the internal organizational climate and thereafter affect the state of the external organizational climate.

SOME TESTABLE PROPOSITIONS

The systems model of organizational climate sketched above may prove to be heuristic. As in the case of any theory, the test of a systems model is whether it generates verifiable and significant propositions. Several illustrative propositions, suggested by our systems model, concerning the problem of changing an organizational climate are as follows:

1. The climate of an organization tends to be perpetuated from one generation of members to another unless the structure of inputs and outputs and intraorganizational processes are changed along with the feedback effects. This hypothesis, if true, in effect cautions against the inclination to solve an organizational climate problem by recruiting a new executive. He is not likely to succeed unless he is sufficiently knowledgeable, powerful, and charismatic as to alter the inputs, the intraorganizational processes, the outputs, and the feedback effects.

2. Inertial forces maintaining organizational climate tend to increase with the size of an organization. As the size of an organization increases, differentiation increases both as regards number and type of statuses and number and type of subunits. Accompanying an increase in status and functional differentiation is an increase in the scope of problems of role socialization, role performance, and inter-subunit coordination. In the face of mounting problems associated with an increase in size, the difficulties of deliberately modifying the internal organizational climate are correspondingly greater.

3. If the organizational climate as perceived by members of the focal organization is more favorable than the climate as perceived by members of organizations comprising the organization-set, there will be a lower rate of innovation because of a reduced motivation to change. Conversely, if the climate as perceived by members of the focal organization is less favorable than the climate as perceived by members of organizations comprising the organization-set, there will be a higher rate of innovation.

4. Organizational climate is more susceptible to deliberate efforts to modify it when there is a low degree of consensus regarding it. As between *internal* and *external* organizational climate, it is probably easier to alter the former than the latter because of the greater control that the focal organization can exercise over its members than over the members of organizations comprising its organization-set.

5. As differences in subunit climates of an organization increase, there is a tendency for a greater conflict to arise concerning proposals for innovation and for a discrepancy to occur in the rate of technical and administrative innovations, i.e., for the degree of organizational lag to increase.[20]

6. Technical innovations, because they are manifested in the products or services of an organization, are more likely to generate faster changes in the external organizational climate than administrative innovations.[21]

CONCLUSION

If we are to close the gap between the common-sense meanings of organizational climate and the scientific utility of the concept, systematic research is necessary on the theoretical as well as on the methodological front. Theoretically it is necessary to experiment with more refined concepts of organizational climate, especially with various dimensions of climate, e.g., value climate, interpersonal climate, and task climate. The value climate of an advertising agency, for example, with its emphasis on profit is obviously quite different from that of a social work agency with its emphasis on service.[22] This contrast is probably translated into different interpersonal and task climates. Together, these three dimensions of organizational climate probably have traceable consequences for the internal and external relations of an organization.

Methodologically, it is necessary to explore the utility of various research strategies in studying organizational climate: observational studies, surveys, field experiments, computer simulations, and so on.[23] Whichever strategy is employed, past studies of organizations suggest that a comparative approach would probably maximize the chances of identifying the antecedents and consequences of contrasting organizational climates.[24]

On a quite different methodological plane is the critical problem of developing and testing alternative procedures for assessing climate: adjective check lists, sets of descriptive statements, the semantic differential, and the like.[25] The labor involved in developing research instruments that would prove both reliable and valid is indeed formidable, but unless progress is made in operationalizing the concept of organizational climate, it will remain a common-sense rather than a social science concept.

NOTES

1. P. F. Lazarsfeld and H. Menzel, "On the Relation Between Individual and Collective Properties," in Amitai Etzioni, ed., *Complex Organizations: A Sociological Reader* (New York: Holt, Rinehart and Winston, 1961).

2. R. K. Merton, *Social Theory and Social Structure*, rev. ed. (Glencoe, Ill.: The Free Press, 1957), p. 421.

3. William M. Evan, "The Organization-Set: Toward a Theory of Inter-Organizational Relations," in J. D. Thompson, ed., *Approaches to Organizational Design* (Pittsburgh: University of Pittsburgh Press, 1966). See Chapter 9 of the present volume.

4. J. A. Michael, "High School Climates and Plans for Entering College," *Public Opinion Quarterly* 25 (1961): 585–95; A. W. Halpin and D. B. Croft, *The Organizational Climate of Schools* (Chicago: The University of Chicago, Midwest Administrative Center, 1963); J. E. Carlin, *Lawyers' Ethics* (New York: Russell Sage Foundation, 1966); D. C. Pelz and F. M. Andrews, *Scientists in Organizations: Productive Climates for Research and Development* (New York: John Wiley & Sons, 1966).

5. C. Argyris, "Some Problems in Conceptualizing Organizational Climate: A Case Study of a Bank," *Administrative Science Quarterly* 2 (1958): 501–20.

6. C. Perrow, "Organizational Prestige: Some Functions and Dysfunctions," *American Journal of Sociology* 66 (1961): 335–41.

7. *Ibid.*, p. 335.

8. N. Margulies, "A Study of Organizational Culture and the Self-Actualizing Process." Unpublished doctoral dissertation, University of California, Los Angeles, 1965.

9. B. S. Georgopoulous and A. S. Tannenbaum, "A Study of Organizational Effectiveness," *American Sociological Review* 22 (1957): 534–40.

10. Halpin and Croft, *The Organizational Climate of Schools.*

11. A. W. Halpin, *Theory and Research in Administration* (New York: Macmillan, 1966).

12. N. Gross, W. S. Mason, and A. W. McEachern, *Explorations in Role Analysis: Studies in the School Superintendency Role* (New York: John Wiley & Sons, 1958); Evan, "The Organization-Set."

13. Merton, *Social Theory and Social Structure,* pp. 368–80; Gross, Mason, and McEachern, *Explorations in Role Analysis,* pp. 48–74.

14. For an analysis of legal processes in private organizations compared with those of government, see William M. Evan, "Public and Private Legal Systems," in W. M. Evan, ed., *Law and Sociology* (New York: The Free Press, 1962). See Chapter 12 of this volume.

15. The underlying assumption of its assertion is that the strength and time span of these activities depicted in the flow chart are of the same order of magnitude. This assumption becomes evident when parallel paths (branches) are drawn, for example, from C-D-E to F to G-H-I to J-K to L, and from E to K to L in Figure 10.3. If they are not of the same order of magnitude, the effects of one branch would predominate.

16. William M. Evan, "Indices of the Hierarchical Structure of Industrial Organizations," *Management Science* 9 (1963): 468–77. See Chapter 1 of this volume.

17. William M. Evan, "The Organization-Set," pp. 183–84.

18. Cf. S. Macaulay, "Non-Contractual Relations in Business: A Preliminary Study," *American Sociological Review* 29 (1963): 55–67; V. F. Ridgeway, "Administration of Manufacturer-Dealer Systems," *Administrative Science Quarterly* 2 (1957): 464–83; S. Macaulay, "Changing a Continuing Relationship Between a Large Corporation and Those Who Deal with It: Automobile Manufacturers, Their Dealers, and the Legal System," *Wisconsin Law Review* (Summer 1965): 483–575 and (Fall 1965): 740–858.

19. For an analysis of problems of external organizational climate, see J. W. Riley, Jr., and M. F. Levy, eds., *The Corporation and Its Publics* (New York: John Wiley & Sons, 1963).

20. William M. Evan, "Organizational Lag," *Human Organizations* 25 (1966): 51–53. See Chapter 8 of this volume.

21. For a discussion of the distinction between administrative and technical innovations and an analysis of the concept of organizational lag, see Evan, "Organizational Lag" and William M. Evan and G. Black, "Innovation in Business Organizations: Some Factors Associated with Success or Failure of Staff Proposals," *Journal of Business* 40 (1967)· 519–30.

22. J. Bensman, *Dollars and Sense* (New York: Macmillan, 1967).

23. V. H. Vroom, ed., *Methods of Organizational Research* (Pittsburgh: The University of Pittsburgh Press, 1967).

24. P. M. Blau, "The Comparative Study of Organizations," *Industrial and Labor Relations*

Review 18 (1965): 323–38; T. Burns, "The Comparative Study of Organizations," in V. Vroom, ed., *Methods of Organizational Research* (Pittsburgh: The University of Pittsburgh Press, 1967); S. H. Udy, Jr., "The Comparative Analysis of Organizations," in J. G. March, ed., *Handbook of Organizations* (Chicago: Rand McNally, 1965).

25. Halpin and Croft, *The Organizational Climate of Schools;* Halpin, *Theory and Research in Administration.*

CHAPTER 11

An Organization-Set Model of Interorganizational Relations

The pattern of research in the field of organizational behavior over the past two decades has been the reverse of that in behavioristic psychology. Instead of looking at the stimulus and response, social scientists, with the exception of some economists, have studied what behaviorists refer to as the "black box," that is, the internal structures and processes of an organization.[1] This strategy is justified in view of the complexity and variability of formal organizations, but it is a highly restricted approach to the analysis of organizational phenomena that consist of many external as well as internal interactions. It has nevertheless provided an indispensable prologue to the analysis of the problems of interorganizational relations that some social scientists and practitioners are now attempting to study.[2]

The purpose of this chapter is twofold: (1) to outline a model of interorganizational relations, and (2) to apply the model to some case materials on the interrelation of business and government organizations.

A SYSTEMS MODEL

For several decades social scientists engaged in research on organizations have conceived of formal organizations as social systems. However, they have rarely

This is a revised version of a paper prepared for a Conference on Interorganizational Decision Making at the Graduate School of Management of Northwestern University, February 1969.

pursued the implication of this conceptualization, which is to acknowledge that a systems analysis is required to guide the conduct of research. A systems approach to organizational phenomena begins with the postulate that organizations are "open" systems which, of necessity, engage in various modes of exchange with their environment.[3]

In further postulating the interrelationships of components of a given system, a systems approach identifies input elements, process elements, output elements, and feedback effects. Moreover, it focuses attention on the interrelation of at least three levels of analysis: the subsystems of an organization, the organizational system in its entirety, and the suprasystem. Analyzing the subsystems of an organization entails a study of the interaction patterns of various subunits. Analyzing the organizational system includes an examination of (1) the cultural components, i.e., its values and goals, (2) the structural components, which consist of the various relationships among the subunits, and (3) the technological components. The suprasystem level of analysis of an organization necessitates at the very least an inquiry into the network of interactions or linkages of a given organization with various organizations in its environment.[4]

The particular systems model of interorganizational relations explored here is one I have elsewhere referred to as an organization-set model.[5] The points of departure of this model are several concepts in role theory developed by Merton and Gross *et al.*[6] Instead of selecting a status as the unit of analysis and charting the complex of role relationships in which the status occupant is involved, as Merton does in his analysis of role-sets, let us take as the unit of analysis an organization or a class of organizations and trace its interactions with the various organizations in its environment, namely, its organization-set. Following Gross, Mason, and McEachern's use of the term "focal position" in their analysis of roles, the organization of class or organizations that is the point of reference is referred to as the "focal organization."[7] As in the case of role-set analysis, the focal organization interacts with a complement of organizations in its environment, that is, its organization-set. A systems analysis perspective, however, suggests that we partition the organization-set into an input organization-set and an output organization-set. By an input organization-set I mean a complement of organizations that provides resources to the focal organization; by an output organization-set I mean all organizations that receive the goods and/or services, including organizational decisions, generated by the focal organization. Furthermore, a systems analysis requires that we trace feedback effects from the output organization-set to the focal organization and thence to the input organization-set, or directly from the output to the input organization-set. These feedback effects can, of course, be positive or negative, as well as anticipated or unanticipated, but it is easier to postulate these effects than to operationalize them to facilitate empirical inquiry.

The four components of the model—focal organization, input organization-set, output organization-set, and feedback effects—may be jointly conceived as comprising an "interorganizational system." Figure 11.1 summarizes the structural elements of the model of interorganizational relations.

For purposes of illustration, if we take as a focal organization the Ford Motor Company, the input organization-set may include a variety of suppliers of raw materials, trade unions, government agencies, courts, universities, and research and development organizations. The input resources are very heterogeneous, including human, material, financial, legal, and other resources. These inputs are transformed by the focal organization's social structure and technology into products and services that are exported to the members of the output organization-set, which include principally automobile dealers. The output organization-set may also include advertising agencies concerned with increasing the sale of its products, trade associations to which information is provided and which may undertake to influence the course of future legislation, community chest organizations to which financial contributions are made, and others. The success with which the focal organization, in this case the Ford Motor Company, manages its multifaceted relations with the members of its output organization-set in turn has feedback effects on itself as well as on the input organization-set, which again triggers the cycle of interorganizational systemic relations.

If instead of the Ford Motor Company we take as a focal organization all four automobile manufacturers for the purpose of studying how they "negotiate their environment", the analysis would focus on the "interfirm organization" in a simple oligopolistic market and the members of the output organization-set.[8] Such questions as the following might be asked: How does the focal organization decide on output, prices, policies with respect to automobile dealers, strategy with respect to trade associations, legislatures, and so on? In other words, given the problem formulation, it may not be especially relevant to inquire about the interactions of the focal organization with members of its input organization-set. If the analysis of this particular focal organization were extended to the members of the input organization-set, two potential members would be the Department of Justice and the Federal Trade Commission, one or both of which might inquire into possible violations of antitrust law.

DIMENSIONS OF ORGANIZATION-SETS

It should be clear from the context of this analysis that the phrase "member of an organization-set" refers to an organizational entity with which a focal organization interacts, not an individual member of one of the environing organizations. Apart from distinguishing between input and output organization-sets, various other dimensions of organization-sets need to be explored if we are to

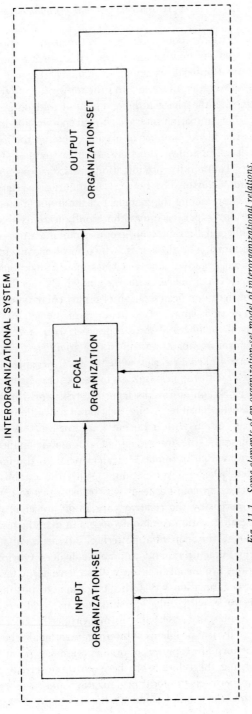

Fig. 11.1 Some elements of an organization-set model of interorganizational relations.

generate some propositions about interorganizational interactions. For present purposes three dimensions may be singled out that, prima facie, have significant consequences for the focal organization, namely, the size and diversity of the input and output organization-sets, and the network configuration.[9] Size of set, of course, refers to the sheer number of input and output organizations with which the focal organization interacts; by diversity of the input and output organization set is meant the number of organizations in the input and output sets differing in gross, manifest functions such as industrial organizations, courts, legislatures, community organizations, prisons, professional associations, hospitals, and so forth. The network configuration refers to the formal properties of interaction among the members of the input and output organization-sets. At least four types of interaction configurations that have loomed large in the experimental literature on group communication network experiments will be mentioned: (1) a *dyad,* in which focal organization *A* interacts with *B,* an individual organization or a class of organizations, in either the input or output set; (2) a *wheel network,* in which the focal organization interacts with more than one organization of a particular type but where there are no mutual interactions among the members of the set; (3) an *all-channel network,* in which all members of the set interact with one another and each interacts with the focal organization; and (4) a *chain network,* in which the members of a set are linked in series with the focal organization, which has only direct interaction with the first link, so to speak, in the chain.

Examples of network configurations from the real world might make these four types appear more plausible. An illustration of a dyadic relationship is the interaction of a trade union with a business organization. A wheel-type configuration would describe the interaction of automobile manufacturers with 30,000 to 40,000 individual automobile dealers prior to the formation of the National Automobile Dealers Association.[10] With the establishment of this association, the interaction configuration was transformed to a modified channel network, thus increasing the relative bargaining power of the automobile dealers. The chain configuration commonly occurs in manufacturing and in distribution processes, e.g., the sequential pattern of interaction of automobile suppliers, automobile manufacturers, and automobile dealers. Obviously these four network configurations are meant to be only illustrative of the formal properties of input and output organization-sets. Other types may be postulated, such as a limited-channel network with only one link to the focal organization. An exploration of the empirically observable formal properties of sets is but one of the many unsolved analytical problems of interorganizational relations.

An analysis of the formal properties of organization-sets points to an intriguing question concerning the relationship between these formal properties and modes of interaction between the focal organization and members of the input and output-sets. Thus, for example, under what conditions in a dyadic linkage between the focal organization and a member of its input set will we observe evidence of cooptation, bargaining, and amalgamation? In a wheel-type configuration, do we find the focal organization dominating the members of the set? If so, under what conditions will pressures emerge to transform the dominance-submission relationship into a bargaining relationship? In an all-channel network or a limited-channel network, would we find a tendency for a coalition to emerge vis-à-vis the focal organization? And, finally, under what conditions would we find in a chain network both cooperation and conflict because of the pressures arising from the constrained pattern of interdependence? Inasmuch as the focal organization will often be involved in diverse network configurations with members of its input and output sets, the question arises as to the relative frequency of different modes of interaction, given the frequency of different network configurations.

Apart from having consequences for modes of interaction between the focal organization and members of its input and output sets, each of the formal properties probably has some reverberations in the internal structure and internal processes of the focal organizations, such as in the formation of new subunits, the formation of new organizational norms, and the articulation of new goals. One hypothetical example will suffice: A state university whose principal source of financial support is derived from the state legislature is an illustration of a dyadic linkage between the focal organization and a member of the input organization-set. In this familiar situation it is difficult to justify substantial budget increases over time for various departments and schools of a university unless new functional units are established. As a consequence, financial constraints encourage subunit differentiation in the focal organization; for example, sociology and anthropology are divided into separate departments; similarly, operations research and statistics, finance and economics, etc. are divided. By establishing new organizational subunits, which may increase student enrollment, it becomes easier to justify substantial increases in the budget of the total university as well as of its components.

ROLE-SETS OF BOUNDARY PERSONNEL

An analysis of modes of interaction between the focal organization and members of its organization-sets, with the aid of the three dimensions discussed above, has one serious limitation. On this level of aggregation there is not only a danger of hypostatizing organizations, i.e., treating them as disembodied entities but also of losing sight of the intervening mechanisms that contribute to the various modes of interaction. It is therefore essential to descend to a lower level of aggregation of social structure and examine the system linkages observ- able in the role-set relations of boundary personnel. It is through the behavior of incumbents of various statuses at the boundary of the focal organization, such as top executives, house counsel, purchasing agents, marketing specialists, personnel officers, and others that various environmental interactions are mediated. Corresponding to the distinction between an input and output organization-set, let us distinguish between input and output boundary roles. As a result of the network of role-set relations of boundary personnel of the focal organization, with their role partners in organizations comprising the input and output organization-sets, various transactions occur involving the flows of people, information, capital, influence, goods, services, and so forth.

Apart from distinguishing between input and output boundary roles, other dimensions need to be identified if we are to generate new propositions about interorganizational relations. The most obvious way of distinguishing between the input and output boundary personnel of one organization compared with another is in sheer number, absolute or relative. One could devise various ratios of boundary to nonboundary personnel of the focal organization's input and output sets. A second dimension is the quality of formal education or the degree of expertise of boundary personnel. It makes a substantial difference whether the house counsel, for example, is a graduate of an Ivy League law school or a night law school.

A third dimension is position in the organizational hierarchy. Whether the boundary person is a shipping clerk, a director of research and development, or a top executive will obviously influence his relationship to his role partners in other organizations. Is the boundary person authorized to engage in organizational decision making, in pre–decision-making activities, such as information gathering, or in non–decision-making activities, such as the internal technical activities of the organization? Parsons's conceptualization of the three levels in the hierarchical structure of organizations is especially suggestive when applied to boundary roles.[11] At the "technical level" in an organization there may be a relatively large number of boundary roles as well as boundary personnel such as foreman, supervisors, purchasing agents, salesmen, clerks, etc. engaged in the primary operations of the organization. Individually, they may have little impact on interorganizational relations, but collectively their effect may be of considerable significance. At the "managerial level" in an organization the number of boundary roles is smaller, but the salience of the managers' behavior, individually and collectively, for interorganizational relations is probably greater than the behavior of boundary personnel at the technical level. Managers also differ from the personnel at the technical level in that they are preoccupied with the tactics of organizational goal formation and decision making. At the "institutional level" in an organization's hierarehy, where the focus is on strategies of goal formation and decision making, there are substantially fewer boundary roles and boundary personnel than at the managerial level, and the decision-making power of such personnel—top executives, members of board of directors, or boards of trustees—in their role-set relations at the interface of the focal organization is appreciably greater.[12]

A fourth dimension of boundary roles is the normative reference group orientation of boundary personnel. Do they orient themselves to the norms and values of their own organization, i.e., of the focal organization, or to those of some other organization? Boundary personnel whose normative reference group is their own organization, i.e., the focal organization, will exhibit greater loyalty in their external role-set relations than those whose normative reference group is an outside organization. Organizations that employ large numbers of professionals, such as universities, hospitals, research and development organizations, bear the brunt of a cosmopolitan normative reference group orientation which may result in behavior impeding organizational goal attainment, including the costs entailed in a high turnover rate.[13]

An analysis of the personnel occupying the boundary roles of a focal organization would be guided by the dimensions identified above as well as by the dimensions of its input and output organization-set. By way of illustrating the heuristic value of our model, we suggest the following hypotheses:

1. As the size of the input organization-set increases, the number of input boundary personnel of the focal organization increases.
2. As the diversity or heterogeneity of the input organization-set increases, the input boundary roles within the focal organization become increasingly differentiated.
3. A similar positive relationship is anticipated between the size and diversity of the output organization-set and the number and role differentiation of output boundary personnel of the focal organization.
4. As the input and output organization-sets become more "turbulent" and uncertain, the input and output boundary roles of the focal organization become more functionally differentiated.[14]
5. If the boundary personnel of the focal organization are not commensurate in number, quality of education, expertise, position in the organizational hierarchy, and normative reference group orientation with the boundary personnel of organizations comprising the input and output organization-sets, the effectiveness of the focal organization will be impaired.

IMPLICATIONS OF THE MODEL FOR A THEORY OF ORGANIZATIONAL CHANGE

The organization-set model outlined above is incomplete in two respects: It needs to be further developed theoretically and also operationalized before it can be put to an empirical test. In its present state it is principally a systems approach to organizational structure and ecology. Upon first consideration the model may suggest a static approach to organizational phenomena. Further examination reveals implications for a positive as well as a normative theory of organizational change. Insofar as it generates explanations for organizational stability as well as predictions concerning organizational change, it qualified as a positive or descriptive theory; and insofar as it suggests guidelines for effecting organizational change, it meets the test of a normative theory. In either case the level of analysis of this model and its implications for a theory of organizational change are principally sociological in nature.

In attending to the internal structure of the focal organization, we are focusing on the structure of roles at the three levels in the hierarchy (technical, managerial, and institutional) and inquiring into (1) the characteristics of the boundary roles and boundary personnel in terms of the four dimensions identified above and (2) the functions performed by boundary personnel in relation to their role partners located in organizations comprising the input and output organization-sets. In examining the input and output sets of the focal organization, such structural dimensions as size, diversity, and network configuration are considered in order to ascertain the sources of support for, opposition to, and constraints on the focal organization.

From the concepts and assumptions of our model it follows that the effectiveness of the focal organization, regardless of its objectives, is a function of (1) internal structure, particularly its role structure, and (2) the characteristics of its input and output sets. We may also infer the following proposition of a positive nature with respect to organizational change: As the input or output organization-set undergoes change as regards size, diversity, network configuration, and so on, the internal structure and level of effectiveness of the focal organization will also change. The direction of causality is in principle reversible; that is, if the focal organization's internal structure (role structure and/or technology) undergoes change, the input and output organization-sets will likewise change. Neither of these propositions, of course, precludes the occurrence of time lags before adaptive responses are triggered.[15] Organizational change, in the sense of growth, occurs when the feedback effects are positive but of a controlled nature. It goes without saying that uncontrolled positive feedback effects can destroy the focal organization; that excessive time lags before adaptive responses occur—especially on the part of boundary personnel at all three hierarchical levels of the focal organization—can undermine organizational effectiveness; and that if no appreciable structural change occurs within a given time interval in the focal organization as well as in its input and output sets, the focal organization can be characterized as stable.

Our model also has implications for a normative theory of organizational change in that it in effect directs change agents—whether internal or external—to intervene at several crucial junctures in organizational functioning. First and foremost, in recruiting personnel for boundary roles at the three hierarchical levels, special attention is warranted in assessing their potential efficacy in interactions with role partners in organizations comprising the input and output sets. Second, to the extent that the socialization of new and old members involves formal and planned activities, particular attention should be devoted to the handling of role-set problems of boundary personnel. In all likelihood, the incidence of role conflicts and role ambiguities is higher among the occupants of boundary roles than nonboundary roles. Hence, if boundary personnel were helped through specially designed training programs to increase their level of competence in managing role-set conflicts and ambiguities, it could noticeably improve their role performance. Third, special efforts are necessary at each of the three levels in the hierarchy of the focal organization for redesigning the interaction network in the input and output organization-sets with a view to increasing organizational effectiveness. Innovative ideas designed to alter the organizational ecology of the focal organization may include proposals for cooperation, cooptation, bargaining, coalition formation, consortia formation, amalgamation, etc. and the like with members of the input and output organization-sets.[16]

Clearly, normative guidelines such as these that are derived from our model differ from but are not incompatible with the psychological and social-psychological propositions of theories of change emerging under the rubric of "organization development."[17] Since few organizational field experiments have thus far been performed, we are not yet in a position to assess the relative merits of different normative theories of organizational change.[18] Much systematic field experimentation will be needed to test the validity of propositions derivable from our model as compared with those derivable from organization development models.

ANALYSIS OF SOME CASES OF INTERORGANIZATIONAL RELATIONS

In the absence of systematic empirical research designed to test some of the propositions derived from the organization-set model and to further develop it, it may prove instructive to make an analysis of four cases of "organizational failure" with the aid of the model.[19] The cases selected are four administrative agencies—the Securities and Exchange Commission, the Interstate Commerce Commission, the Food and Drug Administration, and the Federal Trade Commission—charged with regulating industry in order to protect the "public interest". Our purpose is confined to using our model to throw light on some of the well-known defects of these regulatory bodies. We shall not seek to develop remedies for the organizational failures, which would, of course, far exceed the scope of this chapter.

SECURITIES AND EXCHANGE COMMISSION

Charged with the mission of regulating the securities industry, the SEC's organizational defects, compared with those of the other three regulatory agencies,
are least conspicuous.[20] If we consider the SEC as the focal organization for our
analysis, as is shown in Figure 11.2, the members of its input set at a given time
may include: Congress, which votes on its annual appropriations; the president,
who appoints the commissioners with the confirmation of the Senate; the federal
courts including the Supreme Court, which may accept some of the decisions of
the SEC for judicial review; and other government agencies with which it may
interchange information, people, and so on. The SEC's output set is huge; it
consists of many thousands of public corporations whose securities come under
the scrutiny of the SEC in accordance with the rules of disclosure promulgated in
the Securities Exchange Act of 1934. In addition, the output set includes many
thousands of brokerage firms selling securities to the investing public. In view of
the enormous size and diversity of the SEC's output set, the Securities Exchange
Act provides for self-regulatory bodies, namely, the 14 stock exchanges, which
exercise control over its member firms, and the National Association of Securities
Dealers (NASD), which regulates the conduct of corporations whose securities
are sold in the over-the-counter market and not on the stock exchanges. Any corporation or brokerage firm that is found in violation of the Securities Exchange
Act may be investigated by the SEC. Some of its decisions may in turn be
appealed in the courts, whose decisions in turn affect the SEC's actions. And to
the extent that the securities industry engages in direct lobbying with the SEC or
in indirect lobbying in Congress to protect itself against the enforcement efforts of
the SEC, it becomes a member of the SEC's input set, thus illustrating a positive
feedback effect.

Given the SEC's mandate to regulate the securities industry, the complexity
of its output set poses many problems. The SEC's efforts at regulating the stock

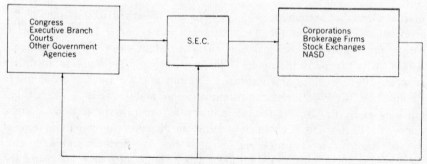

Fig. 11.2   An organization-set analysis of SEC.

exchanges apparently have been more effective than either the NASD's efforts in relation to its members or the efforts of the several stock exchanges in relation to their member brokerage firms. This difference in enforcement effectiveness of the law may be largely a function of the size of the output sets of the different focal organizations. The SEC's regulatory problems in relation to the 14 stock exchanges are considerably fewer than are those of the 14 exchanges vis-à-vis their thousands of brokerage firms, or of the NASD's problems in relation to its thousands of member firms.

Another facet of the pattern of interorganizational relations that may significantly affect the enforcement efficiency of the SEC is the flow of personnel from the regulatory to the self-regulatory agencies and to the regulated organizations. Although the interchange of SEC boundary personnel with members of its output set was not documented in the 1963 study, it is a plausible conjecture that the normative reference group orientation of many of its boundary personnel is the securities industry rather than the SEC.[21] "If the reference group of a substantial proportion of the personnel of the SEC is the brokerage community rather than the regulatory bodies, then the SEC's enforcement efficiency of legal norms is likely to be impaired."[22]

INTERSTATE COMMERCE COMMISSION

The formal composition of the input set of the ICC is similar to that of the SEC. As for the output set, it is probably smaller in size, consisting of approximately 17,000 railway, trucking, shipping, and pipeline companies engaged in interstate commerce; it is probably more diverse; and, unlike the securities industry, there is no provision for self-regulatory agencies. The members of the output set are organized into several influential trade and professional associations: American Association of Railroads, American Trucking Association, Water Carriers Association, Motor Carrier Lawyers Associations, and ICC Practitioners.[23] Conspicuously absent from the output set is any organization representing consumer interests. Compared with the large number of company lawyers and lobbyists representing industry interests, the staff of the ICC, numbering 1,906 in 1969, appears minuscule.

Further hampering effective regulation of the transportation industry is the ICC's extensive informal and formal contacts with industry. Notwithstanding the ICC Canons of Conduct prohibiting employees from engaging in any behavior that could affect their impartiality or adversely affect the confidence of the public in the integrity of the commission, "industry regularly pays for luncheons, hotel rooms . . . , Commissioners and upper staff are commonly transported around at their convenience by corporate jets, private rail cars, and pleasure yachts."[24] There are recurrent conferences between the ICC and 17 organized groups representing the interests of the transportation industry, none of which represents consumers or the "public interest."[25] Through these informal and formal contacts, members of the output set become in the course of time members of the input set, influencing information gathering as well as policy formulation.

Promoting this type of feedback effect is a frequent flow of ICC employees to industry. Of the last eleven commissioners to leave the ICC, six became top executives of companies in the transportation industry, three became ICC practitioners, and two retired.[26]

The manner in which agency officials lay down the regulatory cudgel and pick up the industrial cudgel by changing jobs indicates that they feel an identity between the two roles. . . . Aware that the door to industry employment is open, a Commissioner may keep it ajar by passive regulation that does not step on industry's toes.[27]

Under the circumstances, the boundary personnel of the focal organization and the members of the output set tend to develop a common normative reference group orientation. This factor, together with the absence of an effective countervailing organization representing consumer interests in the input and output sets, encourages passive regulation of ICC statutes.

FOOD AND DRUG ADMINISTRATION

A regulatory agency that is a division of the Department of Health, Education, and Welfare, the FDA, as the name implies, is charged with regulating two mammoth industries. From its annual budget of over $70 million, $23 million is allocated to programs designed to protect the food supply, and the balance to protect the supply of drugs and cosmetics.[28] To enforce the various FDA statutes, this agency employs approximately 5,000 people, including inspectors, scientists, other specialists, and technicians.

The members of FDA's input set, apart from the administration of HEW, are similar to that of the SEC and the ICC. Its output set, however, is larger and more diverse than that of the ICC. It consists of about 50,000 food manufacturing firms, over 1,000 pharmaceutical firms, several trade associations such as the Pharmaceutical Manufacturers Association and the Grocery Manufacturers of America, and professional associations, notably the American Medical Association. Once again we note the absence from the output set of any organized consumer group to exercise countervailing power against other organized interest groups. The coalition between the AMA and the PMA has been especially effective in that it has succeeded in exercising direct influence on FDA decision making as well as indirect influence through Congress by means of political campaign contributions. Since the agency engages in very little original research on food and drugs, it has become increasingly dependent on the research of industry: "Seventy percent of all food standards are initially proposed by the food industry. Nearly all research on food additive safety is conducted by industry, not FDA."[29] Thus, as in the case of the ICC, the "regulatees" have succeeded in the course of time in obtaining access to the input set of the regulators.

Further resembling the ICC, the boundary between the FDA and members of its output set is indeed permeable. Between 1959 and 1963, of the 813 scientific, medical, and technical employees who left the FDA, 83 transferred to companies FDA regulates, 632 were not employed in regulated industries, and information on the remaining 98 was unavailable.[30] Dr. Louis Lasagne, a pharmacologist, commenting on the interchange of personnel noted that the

subtle and potentially most dangerous aspect of the FDA setup [is] the well traveled, two-way street between industry and Washington. Men from the drug industry have gone on to the FDA jobs and—more important—FDA specialists have gone on to lucrative executive jobs in industry. . . . It does not seem desirable to have in decision-making positions, scientists who are consciously or unconsciously always contemplating the possibility that their futures may be determined by their rapport with industry.[31]

Mintz, who has conducted an extensive study of FDA's regulation of the drug industry, points to yet another pattern of interchange of boundary personnel between the FDA and members of its output set:

There has also been a rather more complicated series of movements among the three power centers, the Food and Drug Administration, the Pharmaceutical Manufacturers Association and its member firms, and the American Medical Association—the three components of the FDA–PMA–AMA molecule.

The following are cases in point. Before becoming head of Winthrop Laboratories, Dr. Theodore G. Klumpp had in the late 1930's been chief medical officer of the Drug Division at FDA, subsequently leaving to take a post in the AMA. C. Joseph Stetler, who had been counsel of the AMA and head of its Socioeconomic Division, found it possible to improve his socioeconomic position by becoming executive vice president of the PMA. Dr. Jean K. Weston was with Parke, Davis from 1951 to 1962, when he left his position as head of the firm's Department of Clinical Investigation to join Burroughs Wellcome & Co. In June 1964, Dr. Weston became director of the AMA's Department of Drugs and secretary of its Council on Drugs.[32]

In view of these flows of personnel, it is not surprising that the FDA has opted for a program of voluntary compliance rather than a program of strict enforcement of the law:

Under the FDA's voluntary compliance program, thirty-four thousand representatives of five thousand regulated firms have attended 325 workshops and forty national conferences between 1965 and 1970. The purpose of this massive effort was to help give industry a better understanding of the law and FDA regulations, to make available to industry benefits of FDA research and methodology to help solve contamination and other problems, and to encourage maximum self-regulation.[33]

FEDERAL TRADE COMMISSION

As an independent regulatory agency, the FTC has a dual mission: to counteract monopoly practices (restraints of trade, unfair methods of competition, etc.) and consumer fraud ("deceptive acts and practices"). In 1969 its staff numbered 1,154, of whom 400 were lawyers and 200 were economists and other professionals; its budget was $16,900,000.[34] In investigating compliance with various statutes, FTC lawyers perform a crucial function as boundary personnel. Hence, the questions raised about the quality of the education and the expertise of FTC lawyers touch on an important facet of the enforcement effectiveness of this agency.

In recruiting attorneys the FTC evidently attaches more significance to regional background, old school ties, and political endorsement of applicants than to their ability as reflected in grades or in the quality of the law schools they attended.[35] "As a result, graduates of prestigious law schools such as Harvard and Pennsylvania, which offer outstanding courses in antitrust law, have a poor chance of joining the FTC, compared with graduates of law schools like Kentucky and Tennessee."[36] The author's analysis of data on graduates of classes 1967 and 1968 from five Northern law schools (N.Y.U., Georgetown, George Washington, St. John's, and Brooklyn) and three Southern law schools (Texas, Kentucky, and Tennessee) yielded the following result: 21 percent of applicants from Northern schools were offered appointments compared with 52 percent from Southern schools, a difference statistically significant at the .05 level.[37] Moreover, according to a bureau chief of the FTC,

He preferred to hire older men—who had been out in the world for ten years or so and had come to appreciate that they were not going to make much of a mark—because they tended to be loyal and remain with the FTC. He also reported that he gave less weight to law school grades than to other factors.[38]

To compound the problem of the expertise of its boundary personnel, the FTC lacks medical, scientific, and engineering specialists in its various bureaus that require them:

The FTC's large staff of lawyers also poses a problem of quite a different order—legal competence alone is often not enough for the job. The Division of Food and Drug Advertising in the Bureau of Deceptive Practices is a good case in point. It is responsible, among other things, for detecting and preventing deception in drug-product advertising. Yet it is staffed entirely by lawyers and has no doctors or scientists to advise it. . . . It is then not surprising that the Division of Food and Drug Advertising operates at a low level of energy. . . . It also does nothing at all to enforce the agency's laws on therapeutic devices.[39]

The formal composition of the input set of the FTC is the same as that of any other independent regulatory agency such as the SEC or the ICC. Its output set, however, is both larger and more diverse, consisting of "hundreds of thousands of businesses."[40] Of this enormous population of firms engaged in manufacturing and merchandising activities, the FTC tends to shy away from investigating the compliance of large companies and disproportionately devotes its resources to relatively small firms, especially in textiles and furs.[41] "The FTC's reluctance to go after big companies often lies in its fear of their vast and brilliant legal staffs—particularly if formal action is called for.[42]

Like the FDA, the FTC has deemphasized formal complaint procedures and concentrated on a program of voluntary compliance. Among the informal devices it employs, each of which lacks the force of law, are (1) industry guides, (2) advisory opinions, (3) trade regulation rules, and (4) assurances of voluntary compliance and informal corrective actions.[43]

An analysis of various measures of FTC enforcement activities over a tenyear period has prompted the recent ABA Commission to conclude:

Through lack of effective direction, the FTC has failed to establish goals and priorities, to provide necessary guidance to its staff and to manage the flow of its work in an efficient and expeditious manner. All available statistical measures of FTC activity show a downward trend in virtually all categories of its activities in the face of a rising budget and increased staff. Moreover, present enforcement activity rests heavily on a voluntary compliance program devoid of effective surveillance or sanctions. It thus appears that both the volume and the force of FTC law enforcement have declined during this decade.[44]

This impressive record of organizational failure on the part of the FTC and various other regulatory agencies has stimulated some observers to call for major organizational reforms and others to wonder whether these agencies ought not to be abolished in favor of "greater reliance on market processes and on the system of judicial rights and remedies."[45]

CONCLUSION

Analysis of case materials, however instructive or suggestive it may be, is no substitute for systematic empirical inquiry designed to test and further develop a model. Let us consider, by way of conclusion, some implications of the model for organizational research. This may be regarded as yet another test of the heuristic value of the model. Given a particular substantive problem, the research procedure might be as follows: (1) ascertain the boundary roles and the boundary personnel of the focal organization; (2) ascertain the role-set relations and the transactions mediated by the role-set interactions; (3) map the members of the input and output sets; (4) establish the formal properties and modes of interaction with the input and output sets, especially as they have changed over at least two time intervals; (5) trace feedback effects from the output organization-set to the focal organization and to the input organization-set.

This is indeed a tall order; the methodological imponderables underlying each of these five research procedures should not be minimized. Nevertheless, if a full-scale empirical study of organization-sets were successfully carried out, it might do for interorganizational theory what Gross, Mason, and McEachern, and Kahn and his colleagues have done for role theory.[46] In addition, it would in all likelihood yield various spin-offs for a normative theory of organization-set change, namely, how to modify input and output set interactions in order to increase the effectiveness of the focal organization.

NOTES

1. Oliver E. Williamson, "A Dynamic Theory of Interfirm Behavior," *Quarterly Journal of Economics* 79 (November 1965): 579–607; Almarin Phillips. "A Theory of Interfirm Organization," *Quarterly Journal of Economics* 74 (November 1960): 602–13.

2. Eugene Litwak with the collaboration of Jack Rothman, "Toward the Theory and Practice of Coordination Between Formal Organizations," in William R. Rosengren and Mark Lefton, eds. *Organizations and Clients* (Columbus, Ohio: Charles E. Merrill Publishing Co., 1970); William M. Evan. "A Systems Model of Organizational Climate," in Renato Tagiuri and George H. Litwin, eds. *Organizational Climate* (Boston: Division of Research, Harvard Business School, 1968); Roland L. Warren. "The Interorganizational Field as a Focus for Investigation," *Administrative Science Quarterly* 12 (December 1967): 396–419: Burton R. Clark, "Interorganizational Patterns in Education," *Administrative Science Quarterly*. 10 (November 1966): 224–37: Warren B. Brown, "Systems, Boundaries and Information Flow," *Journal of Academy of Management* 9 (December 1966): 318–27: William M. Evan. "The Organization-Set: Toward a Theory of Interorganizational Relations," in James D. Thompson, ed. *Approaches to Organizational Design* (Pittsburgh: University of Pittsburgh Press, 1966): F. E. Emery and E. L. Trist. "The Causal Texture of Organizational Environments," *Human Relations* 18 (1965): 21–31; and Eugene Litwak and Lydia F. Hylton, "Interorganizational Analysis: An Hypothesis on Coordination between Formal Organizations," *Administrative Science Quarterly* 6 (March 1962): 397–420.

3. Daniel Katz and Robert L. Kahn, *The Social Psychology of Organizations* (New York: John Wiley & Sons, 1966).

4. Evan, "A Systems Model of Organizational Climate."

5. Evan, "The Organization-Set,"

6. R. K. Merton. *Social Theory and Social Structure,* rev. ed. (Glencoe, Ill.: The Free Press, 1957), pp. 368–80; N. Gross, W. S. Mason, and A. W. McEachern. *Explorations in Role Analysis: Studies of the School Superintendency Role* (New York: John Wiley & Sons, 1958), pp. 48–74.

7. Gross, Mason, and McEachern, *Explorations in Role Analysis,* pp. 50–56; Evan, "The Organization-Set," p. 178.

8. Richard M. Cyert and James G. March. *A Behavioral Theory of the Firm* (Englewood Cliffs, N.J.: Prentice-Hall, Inc., 1963), pp. 119–20; Phillips, "A Theory of Interfirm Organization."

9. For other dimensions of organization-sets, see Evan, "The Organization-Set," pp. 178–80.

10. S. Macaulay, "Changing a Continuing Relationship between a Large Corporation and Those Who Deal with it: Automobile Manufacturers, Their Dealers and the Legal Systems" *Wisconsin Law Review* (Summer 1965): 483–575, and (Fall 1965): 740–858; Henry Assael, "Constructive Role of Interorganizational Conflict," *Administrative Science Quarterly* 14 (December 1969): 573–82.

11. Talcott Parsons, *Structure and Process in Modern Societies* (Glencoe, Ill.: The Free Press, 1960), pp. 60–69.

12. Alfred D. Chandler, Jr., *Strategy and Structure* (Cambridge: M.I.T. Press, 1962), pp. 13–21.

13. A. W. Gouldner, "Cosmopolitans and Locals: Toward an Analysis of Latent Social Roles, I," *Administrative Science Quarterly* 2 (December 1957): 281–306; and "Cosmopolitans and Locals: Toward an Analysis of Latent Social Roles, II," *Administrative Science Quarterly* 2 (March 1958): 444–80.

14. Emery and Trist, "The Causal Texture of Organizational Environments."

15. William M. Evan, "Organizational Lag," *Human Organization* 25 (1966): 51–53. See Chapter 8 of the present volume.

16. Evan, "The Organization-Set," pp. 183–84.

17. Richard Beckhard, *Organization Development: Strategies and Models* (Reading, Mass.: Addison-Wesley Publishing Co., 1969): Warren G. Bennis. *Organization Development: Its Nature, Origins, and Prospects* (Reading, Mass.: Addison-Wesley Publishing Co., 1969), and R. R. Blake and J. S. Mouton, *Building a Dynamic Corporation Through Grid Organization Development* (Reading, Mass.: Addison-Wesley Publishing Co., 1969).

18. William M. Evan, ed., *Organizational Experiments* (New York: Harper & Row, 1971).

19. Oliver E. Williamson, *The Vertical Integration of Production: Market Failure Considerations* (University of Pennsylvania, Fels Discussion Paper in Economics and Bureaucracy, #1, 1970 (mimeo).

20. For a report of an extensive inquiry into the SEC, see Report of the Special Study of Securities Markets of the Securities and Exchange Commission H.R. Doc. No. 95, 88th Cong., 1st sess., pts. 1–5 (Washington, D.C.: U.S. Government Printing Office, 1963).

21. *Ibid.*

22. William M. Evan and Ezra G. Levin. "Status-Set and Role-Set Conflicts of the Stockbroker," *Social Forces* 45 (September 1966): 73–83.

23. Robert C. Fellmeth, *The Interstate Commerce Commission* (New York: Grossman Publishers, 1970).

24. *Ibid.,* pp. 16, 19.

25. *Ibid.,* pp. 346–49.

26. *Ibid.*, pp. 20–21.
27. *Ibid.*
28. James S. Turner, *The Chemical Feast* (New York: Grossman Publishers, 1970), pp. 2–3.
29. *Ibid.*, p. 103.
30. Morton Mintz, *The Therapeutic Nightmare* (Boston: Houghton Mifflin Co., 1965), 177.
31. *Ibid.*, pp. 175–76.
32. *Ibid.*, pp. 178.
33. Turner, *The Chemical Feast*, p. 105.
34. Miles W. Kirkpatrick, *Report of the ABA Commission to Study the Federal Trade Commission* (1969), p. 8.
35. E. F. Cox, R. C. Fellmeth, and J. E. Schulz, *Report on the Federal Trade Commission* (New York: Grove Press, 1969), p. 150.
36. *Ibid.*, p. 151.
37. *Ibid.*, p. 228.
38. Kirkpatrick, *Report of the ABA Commission*, p. 33.
39. Cox, Fellmeth, and Schultz, *Report on the Federal Trade Commission*, p. 158.
40. *Ibid.*, p. 57.
41. Kirkpatrick, *Report of the ABA Commission*, p. 27.
42. Cox, Fellmeth, and Schultz, *Report on the Federal Trade Commission*, p. 57.
43. Kirkpatrick, *Report of the ABA Commission*, pp. 8–9.
44. *Ibid.*, p. 1.
45. Richard A. Posner, "Separate Statement," in Kirkpatrick, *Report of the ABA Commission*, pp. 92–119.
46. Gross, Mason, and McEachern, *Explorations in Role Analysis*; R. L. Kahn, et al., *Organizational Stress: Studies in Role Conflict and Ambiguity* (New York: John Wiley & Sons, 1964).

PART FOUR

Trans-Organizational Environments

As we have seen in the chapters of Part III, crossing the boundary of a focal organization to ascertain the effects of environing organizations on internal structures and processes and, in turn, the influences of a focal organization on its organizational environment, is an immensely complex undertaking. Small wonder that the bulk of research in the past two decades has centered on intraorganizational problems that are themselves highly complex. Under the circumstances, if one ventures beyond interorganizational interactions—a realm I designate as "trans-organizational environments" in Part IV—the complexities appear to increase by an order of magnitude. And yet, it is my prediction that organization theory will move in this direction in the future for at least two reasons: A substantial amount of variation in organizational structures and processes would probably be explained by introducing macrolevel variables; and it is important—particularly for organizational sociologists—to forge a link between organization theory and macrosocietal theory, especially since the structures of modern societies are becoming increasingly populated by organizations and organizational networks.

In the chapters of Part IV I have divided trans-organizational environments into two realms: culture and social structure, two baffling and controversial abstractions in sociology and anthropology.[1] The interrelationship of these abstractions, as they bear on interorganizational and organizational systems, are depicted in the concentric circle diagram presented in the Preface. Both abstractions are discussed in some detail in Chapters 15 and 16. By culture, I refer to norms and values that tend to influence the behavior of the members of a society; by social structure, I refer to the patterns of behavior in a society that are manifested in elaborate social networks arising primarily out of the "status profiles" of the population of individuals and out of the "organization-set profiles" of the population of organizations.

A highly visible component of the culture of a society is its legal system. In Chapter 12, a distinction is made between public and private legal systems, that is, between the legal system of the society at large and the microlegal systems—or the governance systems—found in all organizations, even those in the private sector. Some basic attributes of each type of system are discussed, and the various modes of interactions between public and private legal systems are analyzed. Of particular significance to business organizations is the body of administrative law and the plethora of administrative agencies, at all levels of government, whose mandate it is to regulate the activities of such organizations. In Chapter 13, some recent trends in administrative law and organization theory are compared with a view to clarifying the potential value of applying the organization-set model in research on administrative agencies.

In Chapter 15, a general argument is made for including cultural variables in cross-national studies of organizations. After singling out the normative dimension of culture as being most relevant for organizational research, the Kluckhohn-Strodtbeck theory of value orientations is presented. The heuristic value of this schema is illustrated by formulating a set of hypotheses relating dimensions of value orientations to such organizational system variables as recruitment, socialization, communication, and organizational output.

Bridging the analysis of culture and social structure is Chapter 14, which compares two types of transnational organizations, the multinational enterprise and the international professional association. Notwithstanding their rapid rate of growth in the past two decades and their role as mechanisms of change in the international system, these organizations have been largely ignored by social scientists studying organizations and international relations. To throw light on the interactions of these organizations with other components of the international system—nation-states, intergovernmental organizations, and regional organizations—a nonlinear model is developed. With the aid of this model, various system linkages are identified, and the impact of these organizations on the state of the international system is interpreted in terms of four dimensions of integration: normative, economic, organizational, and occupational. A comparative analysis of the structural and motivational problems of these organizations yields five hypotheses concerning their effect on the level of integration of the international system.

In the final chapter of Part IV, a social-structural model of organization is formulated. The constituents of this model are role-sets, status-sets, and status-sequences of organizational members—differentiated by boundary role function and position in the organizational hierarchy—organization-sets, and institutional profiles. In the course of presenting the model eighteen hypotheses are derived. The twin problems of social-structural effects on organizations and organizational effects on social structure are then discussed along with some implications of the model for a new research strategy in organization theory. The chapter concludes with some conjectures about the design of organizations of the future.

The five chapters in Part IV point to an array of unsolved problems in organization theory, the solution of which would give rise to a new paradigm integrating an open systems concept of organization with three supraorganizational systems: the interorganizational system, the cultural system, and the social-structural system. In as much as all these systems are in flux, the new paradigm would have to have the properties of a dynamic model to cope with systems changing over time.

NOTES

1. See, for example, Daniel Bell, *The Coming of Post-Industrial Society* (New York: Basic Books, 1973), pp. 475–80; Talcott Parsons, *Societies: Evolutionary and Comparative Perspectives* (Englewood Cliffs, N.J.: Prentice-Hall, 1966), pp. 1–29, 113–115; *The System of Modern Societies* (Englewood Cliffs, N.J.: Prentice-Hall, 1971), pp. 4–18.

CHAPTER 12

Public and Private
Legal Systems

Virtually all legal scholars and many political scientists view law as being inextricably interwoven with the state, and the state, having a monopoly of coercion, is identified as the sanctioning agent of law. Accordingly, phenomena analytically similar to law that do not fall within the framework of the state have been either largely neglected or else conceptualized in unrelated terms.[1] And the sanctioning power pervasively exercised by organizations less inclusive than the state has been inadequately explored. With its stress on the sovereign state as the source of positive law, analytical jurisprudence has played a dominant role in the articulation of this conception of law.

Certain scholars, however, have departed from the prevailing view of law; two are especially noteworthy. Ehrlich, one of the earliest students of the sociology of law, conceived of law as consisting primarily of rules by which persons in society order their conduct and only secondarily of "norms for decisions" developed by the courts and of legislation enacted by the state. These rules or "facts of the law," as he called them, are developed by various "social associations"—families, clans, religious organizations, corporations, labor unions, employer associations, political parties, social clubs, and so on. It is the "inner order of the [social] associations" that is the "basic form of law."[2] Similarly, Weber's view of law includes a "legal order" that falls outside the province of the state.

We categorically deny that "law" exists only where legal coercion is guaranteed by the political authority. . . . A "legal order" shall rather be said to exist wherever coercive means, of a physical or psychological kind, are available; i.e., wherever they are at the disposal of one or more persons who hold themselves ready to use them for this purpose in the case of certain events; in other words, wherever we find a consociation specifically dedicated to the purpose of "legal coercion."[3]

Ehrlich and Weber, as well as other scholars, acknowledge the efficacy of the sanction at the disposal of nonstate associations such as the church, the corporation, the trade union, and the professional association.[4] A case in point is the reluctance of labor arbitrators confronted with a grievance involving discharge from employment to sustain the penalty because they regard it as the functional equivalent in industry of "capital punishment."[5]

In this chapter I shall consider some implications of a conception of law and legal systems that is not exclusively identified with the state in an effort (1) to reconceptualize law and legal systems in general normative and social-structural terms and (2) to identify some problems and formulate some hypotheses in the sociology of law that are of particular significance for organizational research.

A SOCIOLOGICAL CONCEPTION OF LEGAL SYSTEMS

Sociologically, a legal system consists of at least (1) a body of norms governing the expectations and actions of the members of a given social system and (2) a set of specialized statuses to which are allocated different normative functions.

The set of norms of a legal system may vary with respect to the extent of knowledge on the part of objects (those to whom the norms apply), extent of acceptance by objects, extent of application to objects (whether they apply to all members or to special categories of members of a social system), severity of sanction provided, amount of conformity by objects, and so on.[6] Likewise, the relations among norms comprising the legal system may differ. For instance, they may be logically and substantively independent of one another, contradictory, or reciprocal. A reciprocal relation is one in which the norms, directed to different individuals in interaction, reinforce one another—for example, norms relating to the rights of a member of an association that correlatively set forth the duties of its officers.[7]

The set of specialized statuses of a legal system may also differ in various respects, as in number, distribution of functions, and pattern of organization. Regardless of differences, three normative functions—universal in the type of social system to be discussed—are performed by the occupants of specialized legal statuses: legislative, judicial, and executive. By legislative function is meant the authority to innovate norms; by judicial function, the authority to interpret existing norms; and by executive function, the authority to enforce norms with the aid of institutionalized sanctions. Complementing the set of specialized legal statuses in which is vested authority over the normative processes is the nonspecialized status, the occupants of which constitute the "laity" or the rank-and-file members of a social system.

In combination, the norms and the specialized legal statuses constitute structural elements of a legal system. It is evident that such a legal system has some of the attributes of a formal organization.[8] Hence, unlike Ehrlich, we would not characterize the family, at least of the type common in industrial societies, as a legal system, if only because the statuses are not functionally specific relative to the three analytically distinguishable normative processes. Formal organizations differ in many respects, one being the character of their legal systems, a question I shall presently consider.

A TYPOLOGY OF LEGAL SYSTEMS

Given the structural elements of a legal system set forth above, various typologies might be constructed. For present purposes I shall classify legal systems along two dimensions. Implicit in our discussion is a distinction between legal systems on the basis of jurisdiction, namely, whether they are public or private. A public legal system has its locus in the formal structures of the state such as the judiciary, the legislature, the executive, and the administrative agency. Its jurisdiction extends to all inhabitants of the territory of a society. A private legal system, on the other hand, has its locus in a formal organization relatively independent of the state. Its jurisdiction officially extends only to the organization's members.

The second basis of classification involves a vague, multidimensional but important distinction between democratic and undemocratic types of legal systems. A democratic legal system includes at least three attributes: (1) the separation of powers, (2) procedural due process of law, and (3) the consent of the governed. The first two attributes have the function of delimiting the authority exercised over the members or the laity of the social system. Through the separation of powers, the three normative functions are so distributed as to prevent a concentration of authority in one and the same status.

Procedural due process of law, as distinct from substantive due process, relates to a complex of norms protecting the rights of parties in the prosecution and adjudication of a dispute.[9] Incorporated in the Bill of Rights in 1791, the due process clause protects the citizen against the exercise of arbitrary power by the federal government. These rights were extended after the Civil War by means of the Fourteenth Amendment to citizens vis-à-vis their state governments. Parties to a dispute are assured a fair and impartial trial through such guarantees as the right to notice of hearing, the right to confront witnesses and to cross-examine them, and the right to introduce evidence on one's behalf.[10] The significance of this constitutional doctrine for democracy was underscored by a legal scholar who contends that "due process may almost be said to be a sufficient cause for our democracy."[11] Justice Frankfurter expressed a similar view in asserting that due process is one of the "indispensable conditions for the maintenance and progress of a free society."[12]

Consent of the governed, the third attribute of a democratic legal system, not only affords the laity a veto power through the electoral process, but also implies the right to dissent. Institutionalization of dissent protects the minority among the laity as well as among the officials performing specialized normative functions.[13]

A democratic legal system as defined here—one characterized by the separation of powers, procedural due process, and consent of the governed—maximizes the probability that the institutionalized rights, immunities, and privileges of all members of a social system are protected. On the other hand, an undemocratic legal system, or one lacking these three properties, provides for none of the safeguards against unlimited and arbitrary authority. The occupant of one and the same status in a social system may perform legislative, executive, and judicial functions; there is no institutionalized procedure for impartially adjudicating disputes; and the occupants of statuses that do not have specialized legal functions, the laity, have little or no formal veto power over the officials performing executive, legislative, and judicial functions. Weber's monocratic type of bureaucratic organization is obviously closer to the undemocratic than to the democratic type of legal system.[14]

These two dimensions for classifying legal systems yield four ideal types: (1) public democratic, (2) public undemocratic, (3) private democratic, and (4) private undemocratic. Examples of public legal systems that are formally democratic are the municipal, state, and federal courts, legislatures, and executive branches of government in the United States and other countries with polylithic states. By contrast, the public legal systems of societies with monolithic states are formally undemocratic. Private legal systems that are formally democratic are exemplified by such organizations as trade unions, professional associations, and trade associations. With respect to its employees, the industrial or business organization is an example of a private undemocratic legal system.

This typology of legal systems suggests several general classes of problems for the sociology of law. First, what are some significant structural and functional similarities and dissimilarities among legal systems, public and private? Second, what are the interrelationships between public and private legal systems? Third, what are the interrelationships between public legal systems? Fourth, what are the interrelationships between private legal systems? Fifth, under what conditions do legal systems, whether public or private, undergo transformation from an undemocratic into a democratic type, and vice versa? Sixth, under what conditions do legal systems, democratic or undemocratic, undergo transformation from a public to a private type and vice versa? Although the typology may point to other problems, those enumerated have the merit of dealing with basic problems of normative and structural change about which we have relatively little systematic knowledge.

SOME PROBLEM AREAS IN THE SOCIOLOGY OF LAW

I shall briefly consider four of the classes of problems suggested by our typology because they readily lend themselves to the identification of problems of sociological significance. This discussion is intended merely to illustrate the kinds of problems that a developing sociology of law might embrace.

COMPARATIVE STUDY OF LEGAL SYSTEMS

Comparative studies have been made by legal scholars of public legal systems, either of total systems (judicial, legislative, and executive components) or of subsystems. Thus, for example, Wigmore examines a great variety of public legal systems; Orfield compares the public legal systems of Scandinavian countries; and Hoebel compares the public legal systems of several preliterate societies.[15] An illustration of a comparative study of a subsystem of public legal systems is McRuer's work on judicial process.[16] Since these studies tend to be descriptive in nature, they provide data only for comparative sociological analysis.

Characteristically, Weber developed a classification of analytical categories for his comparative and historical analysis of different public legal systems.[17] His fourfold classification—concerned with law making and law finding, two of the three normative processes—is based on the interrelationship between two dimensions: formal-substantive and rational-irrational.[18] We may infer from Weber's analysis that democratic legal systems may have the attributes of either a formally rational or a substantively rational system, but not of a formally irrational or a substantively irrational type.

The three attributes of a democratic legal system discussed above—separation of powers, procedural due process of law, and consent of the governed—provide the bases for a comparative study of public and private legal systems. In the case of public legal systems we may examine the structural differences and similarities between the democratic and undemocratic types. For example, do democratic legal systems have a higher rate of turnover in key specialized statuses? Is this true of legislative and executive statuses but not of judicial statuses, which may require greater stability of tenure to guarantee the incumbents the necessary autonomy in their role performance? Correlatively, is the status-sequence of occupants of specialized statuses in democratic legal systems characterized by a higher rate of transition to nonlegal or lay statuses than is the case in undemocratic legal systems?[19]

Other differences between these two types of legal systems may be observed in the structure of the legal profession, the judiciary, and the civil service. A legal profession that does not enjoy a high degree of autonomy vis-à-vis the state cannot effectively train recruits to uphold the normative system in a disinterested manner. Similarly, if the court system is organized on the principle of a chain of command, the lower courts are not likely to venture independent interpretations of law for fear that they may be overruled by the higher courts. This hierarchical mode of organization facilitates extralegal control of the judiciary. And if the civil service is not sufficiently professionalized and hence does not administer the law efficiently and in accordance with universalistic standards, it too is susceptible to extralegal control. Are such propositions true?

Related questions may be raised about private legal systems. The high degree of variation among formal organizations of a private character points to a general problem: In what types of private organizations do we find an approximation to a democratic legal system, and in what types an approximation to an undemocratic legal system?

A distinction between administrative organizations and voluntary associations, as advanced by Moore, provides a fruitful preliminary approach to this problem.[20] In administrative or work organizations, in which membership is a direct source of livelihood, the legal system tends to be undemocratic. Authority with respect to normative processes is not limited by any of the three attributes of a democratic legal system. Ruml, for example, in analyzing the structure of corporate management, observes that "the Someone who represents the Company [to potential stockholders] gets his authority from a superior source in the Company's management, a source which *combines legislative, administrative, and judicial powers.*"[21] In voluntary associations, on the other hand, in which membership is generally based on shared norms and values, a democratic legal system tends to predominate. To take but one subclass of voluntary associations, occupational associations are likely to be closer approximations to the democratic type of legal system than are industrial organizations.

A more refined typology of formal organizations than the distinction between administrative organizations and voluntary associations is obviously necessary. A comparison between an industrial organization and a university, both of which are administrative organizations, would show marked differences in their legal systems, with the former resembling an undemocratic legal system and the latter a democratic legal system. This contrast is due to differences in organizational goals—the production of goods versus the creation and dissemination of knowledge—and to a corollary difference in occupational structure. A university generally has a higher proportion of professional personnel than an industrial organization; this is conducive to the growth of an "occupational community" with norms and a social structure consistent with that of a democratic legal system.[22]

Voluntary associations, as in the case of administrative organizations, also differ greatly. Thus a comparison of a professional association with a trade union would probably yield evidence that the former more closely approximates a democratic legal system than the latter, if only because the norms of a professional occupation engender the development of a more cohesive and self-governing occupational community.

A comparative approach to private legal systems might fruitfully inquire into the extent of members' knowledge of norms, the extent of their acceptance of the norms, and the extent of nonconformity. How different are private legal systems in their profiles on these three variables? With respect to knowledge of norms, it may be hypothesized that the laity of an undemocratic legal system is likely to be more informed about the duties pertaining to its status and less informed about its rights, privileges, and immunities, whereas in a democratic legal system no such difference obtains, or the reverse may be true. It may also be hypothesized that in a democratic legal system a higher proportion of the laity approves of and conforms to the norms.

Such comparative inquiry would probably show that the number of persons who perform the functions of legislators, executives, judges, and lawyers in private legal systems is larger than we generally assume; it would probably identify a larger number of litigants, a higher incidence of litigation, and many more sanctions being invoked than we tend to associate with the organs of public legal systems.

INTERRELATIONSHIPS BETWEEN PUBLIC AND PRIVATE LEGAL SYSTEMS

The relationship between public and private legal systems has usually been conceived of and examined in terms of the role of pressure groups in the legislative process, or in terms of the government's regulation of private organizations, especially business organizations. It also has long been observed that public legal systems confer on private legal systems rights, duties, privileges, and immunities through the process of granting a charter of incorporation, license, permit, franchise, and so on.[23] Several modes of interrelationship, however, have been neglected.

First is the increasing tendency for the norms of private legal systems to be judicially recognized, as, for example, in a medical malpractice suit in which the code of ethics of the American Medical Association is invoked, in a suit involving the internal relations of a trade union in which the union's constitutional provisions are accorded legal status by the court, or in a suit by a student against a college or university in which the institution's disciplinary rules are judicially recognized. Such judicial recognition, particularly under a system of common law, results in precedents, that is, in the growth of new legal norms guiding judicial decision making. The adoption, as it were, of the norms of private legal systems by public legal systems is functionally equivalent to the conferral of rights on private legal systems.

A second interrelationship is the diffusion of norms in letter or spirit from private to public legal systems. Although such diffusion is probably less common than judicial recognition of the norms of private legal systems, this is an important source of growth of the norms of public legal systems. An example of such diffusion is the incorporation of the "law merchant" into common law and statutory law.[24] Diffusion of norms should be distinguished from the process associated with the concept of pressure groups. Whereas the concept of pressure groups connotes an "enactive" and intended process of change, diffusion connotes a "crescive" and unintended process. The tempo of the effect of pressure groups on public legal systems may be gradual or rapid. The suffragette movement is an example of a pressure group whose effect was gradual as compared with the right-to-work law pressure groups whose effect, at least in eighteen states, was relatively rapid. By contrast, the diffusion of the "law merchant" to the public legal system was a very gradual and unintended process. Another distinction is that pressure groups are associated primarily with one or two structural components of public legal systems, namely, legislatures and administrative agencies, whereas the diffusion mechanism applies to all structural components of public and private legal systems.

A third form of interrelationship involves the flow of personnel between public and private legal systems. Public legal systems of necessity recruit officials of private legal systems who have the required expertise to administer laws transferred from or modeled after those of private legal systems, as in the case of professionals serving on occupational licensing boards, or business executives serving in such administrative agencies as the Securities Exchange Commission, the Federal Trade Commission, or the Interstate Commerce Commission.[25]

Private legal systems in turn seek to recruit professionals with experience in public legal systems, possibly because of their knowledge of "secrets of the office." Thus, for example, corporations and trade unions may wish to recruit officials of the National Labor Relations Board in the hope that it will help them in their relationships with the agency. Such transfers of personnel may lead to a transfer of norms between public and private legal systems. In other words, the status-sequence of officials of public and private legal systems probably serves as a mechanism for the transmission of norms from one type of system to another.

A fourth interrelationship between public and private legal systems is the emergence of administrative agencies in response to the emergence of private legal systems. In the United States, where this development occurred later than in some European countries, there has been a steadily increasing multiplication of administrative agencies since the establishment of the Interstate Commerce Commission in 1887. Regulation by administrative agencies entails a conferral of both rights and duties on private legal systems.

Private legal systems are obviously not all of equal importance as sources of new legal norms and organs in public legal systems. Those rooted in certain institutional spheres have greater effect on public legal systems than others with different institutional bases. For example, the legal systems of trade associations, professional associations, and trade unions, because of their links with economic institutions, presumably have more effect on public legal systems than the legal systems of, say, educational, familial, or recreational organizations.

The converse of this mode of interrelationship, namely, the impact of the public legal systems on private legal systems, is well known. However, two interrelationships are noteworthy. First is the diffusion of procedural due process of law from public to private legal systems. This process is more readily observable in trade unions than in corporations—for example, in the growth of internal and external appellate review procedures in trade unions such as the Upholsterers International Union and the United Automobile Workers.[26] Berle, however, claims that

[T]here is being generated a quiet translation of constitutional law from the field of political to the field of economic rights. . . . The emerging principle appears to be that the corporation, itself a creation of the state, is as subject to constitutional limitations which limit action as is the state itself.[27]

If in fact this process of institutionalization is under way, we may expect that public legal systems will eventually impose a duty on corporations to conform to procedural due process of law in their internal relations.

The second interrelationship, even less obvious, is the emergence of private legal systems as unanticipated consequences of decisions by public legal systems.[28] Two contrasting examples of this process will suffice: the rise of the League of Women Voters, following the passage of the Nineteenth Amendment, with its functional consequences for the public legal system, and the formation of the White Citizens' Councils, following the desegregation decision of the United States Supreme Court, with their dysfunctional consequences for the public legal system.

INTERRELATIONSHIPS AMONG PRIVATE LEGAL SYSTEMS

The proliferation of private organizations and hence private legal systems, particularly in the United States, has resulted in an increase in the frequency

and types of interorganizational relations.[29] Of the various types of interrelations two will be mentioned because of their effect on public legal systems. One
entails a marked inequality of power in the relationships between two or more
private legal systems; the other, an approximation to a balance of power. In
the former type of relationship, the weaker party may choose one of several
alternatives: submit to the domination of the superordinate power; seek
alliances—as in the case of international relations—to effect a shift in the
balance of power; or have recourse to a unit of the public legal systems to
redress wrongs of the more powerful private legal systems or to augment its
relative power. The latter course of action is illustrated by the National
Automobile Dealers Association's efforts through the courts and legislatures to
curb the power of the three large automobile manufacturers to dictate the terms
of contracts and to cancel contracts.[30] In other words, inequality in power relationships among private legal systems is a major source of pressure on public
legal systems to introduce normative and organizational changes.

Where there is an approximation to a balance of power between two or more
private legal systems, that is, where organizational relationships are of a coordinate rather than a superordinate-subordinate character, one possible consequence is the growth of a degree of consensus regarding goals that eventuates in
a merger or a federation. In the absence of a high degree of consensus regarding
goals, an approximation to a balance of power may lead to the growth of a
partial legal system for the purpose of resolving intersystem conflicts. Private
tribunals for labor and commercial arbitration are notable examples of this
process. The more the parties approach an equality of legal and power status,
the more effective these tribunals are as conflict-resolving mechanisms. It may
be hypothesized that if the formal legal equality of the parties in these tribunals
is not accompanied by equality in economic and political power, the effectiveness of the arbitral process is diminished.[31]

Such mechanisms develop among private legal systems because of the
incompetence of units of public legal systems to cope with the technical problems of private legal systems, the cost and delay of litigation, the lack of legislation or precedents applicable to the novel problems confronting private legal
systems, or because of the importance of maintaining flexible relationships,
which action by components of public legal systems would make difficult.[32]
Bypassing the courts, private arbitration tribunals handle 70 percent—according to one estimate—of all civil litigation in the United States.[33] And in the
case of labor arbitration, the grievance machinery of which it is a part is
administered by a large number of management and union personnel. For
example, approximately half a million shop stewards perform the function of
"counsel" for aggrieved workers.[34] It is small wonder that this private judiciary
with its evolving body of private law is recognized by public legal systems. For
instance, the New York Civil Practice Act takes cognizance of private arbitra-

tion tribunals, specifies procedures, and makes their awards enforceable by the courts.

TRANSFORMATION OF LEGAL SYSTEMS

Reconceptualizing law and legal phenomena in these general normative and social-structural terms generates the insight that the frontier of growth of the law in a modern industrial society such as the United States is not—as is often assumed—only in public legal systems but also in private legal systems. In addition, it suggests several general hypotheses regarding the transformation of legal systems.

First, as private legal systems extend their sphere of jurisdiction beyond their institutional base, the potential for competition and conflict with other private legal systems in the affected institutional sphere increases. Thus, for example, as corporations, trade unions, and churches increase their political activities, their relations with one another and with political parties may become marked with conflict. And conflict, in turn, may continue unresolved; it may elicit efforts at cooptation of the leadership of the threatening organization; or it may call forth the mediating action of other private legal systems or of public legal systems. In the event the public legal system intervenes, new norms arise, whether through legislative enactment, judicial decision, or executive or administrative action. We may also hypothesize that the more each private legal system seeks to extend its sphere of jurisdiction, the more safeguards are thereby erected against the monopolization of power by public legal systems. However, a democratic public legal system can, among other things, protect the rights of the laity of private legal systems against the exercise of arbitrary and autocratic authority.

Second, the progressive differentiation of specialized statuses with respect to the normative processes results in an acceleration of the rate of growth of norms of public and private legal systems. But the multiplication of rules and officials that we associate with the trend toward bureaucratization need not necessarily endanger the rights of the laity if limitations on authority are preserved through the three democratic mechanisms—separation of powers, consent of the governed, and procedural due process.

Third, private legal systems of a democratic type are transformed into undemocratic types under such *exogenous* conditions as the following: (1) if there is a monopolization of power in a given institutional or subinstitutional sphere, or if there is an oligopolization of power in the absence of countervailing private legal systems; (2) if relationships with other private legal systems are principally with those of an undemocratic type of superior economic or political power. Conversely, private legal systems of an undemocratic type are transformed into democratic types under such *exogenous* conditions as the following: (1) if countervailing power in the form of a private legal system develops within a given institutional or subinstitutional sphere to counteract monopolization or oligopolization of power among private legal systems; (2) if relationships with other private legal systems are primarily with those of a democratic type or with those of an undemocratic type of equal or inferior economic or political power.

Fourth, public legal systems of a democratic type are transformed into undemocratic types under such *exogenous* conditions as the following: (1) if the autonomy of private legal systems declines to the point where they cannot challenge the authority of the public legal systems; (2) if there is a monopolization of power among private legal systems in the various institutional or subinstitutional spheres, or if there is an oligopolization of power without the development of countervailing private legal systems; and (3) if most private legal systems are transformed from democratic into undemocratic types.

In the last two hypotheses, with their implicit *ceteris paribus,* we have drastically limited the exogenous conditions of a legal system to relationships with other legal systems in the environment and to the structure of these systems. Obviously other exogenous as well as endogenous factors are operative in the transformation of a legal system from a democratic to an undemocratic type and vice versa.[35]

CONCLUSION

The traditional view of law as an integral part of the state has tended to obscure the fact that law exists in nonstate contexts as well. Taking as the point of departure the legal concepts of Ehrlich and Weber, we have presented a sociological conception and typology of legal systems that bridges the developing field of the sociology of law with that of formal organization. To illustrate the research potentialities of this approach, we have examined four problem areas suggested by our typology: comparative study of legal systems, interrelationships between public and private legal systems, interrelationships among private legal systems, and the transformation of legal systems.

Inquiry into the processes whereby public and private legal systems are transformed will throw light on the general sociological problem of the conditions under which new norms and organizational structures arise and old norms and organizational structures decline. Of particular significance and promise is a comparative study of the structure and functioning of private legal systems and their interrelationships with private and public legal systems. Although these problem areas in the sociology of law may appear new, Ehrlich, one of the earliest students in this field, indirectly suggested them over four decades ago when he asserted that "the center of gravity of legal development . . . from time immemorial has not lain in the activity of the state but in society itself, and must be sought there at the present time."[36] In a sense Ehrlich's perspective combined with the approach outlined in this chapter suggests the need for research on the conditions under which political pluralism—as a type of social system, not as a political philosophy—survives or perishes.

NOTES

1. "Private government is not only a legitimate but a much neglected subject of inquiry by political science." Earl Latham, "The Group Basis of Politics: Notes for a Theory," in Heinz Eulau, Samuel J. Eldersveld, and Morris Janowitz, eds., *Political Behavior: A Reader in Theory and Research* (New York: The Free Press, 1956), p. 235. "Before the rise of the modern state, the existence of a plurality of legal orders was probably too obvious to be remarked on. But even after the claim of the state for the monopoly of lawmaking made itself felt, the existence of nonofficial systems of law was recognized. . . . But an investigation into the real structure of these legal systems, representing, so to speak, as many states within the state, is completely neglected." Alexander Pekelis, *Law and Social Action: Selected Essays*, in Milton R. Konvitz, ed. (Ithaca, N.Y.: Cornell University Press, 1950), p. 68.

2. Eugen Ehrlich, *Fundamental Principles of the Sociology of Law,* trans. Walter L. Moll (Cambridge, Mass.: Harvard University Press, 1936), p. 37.

3. Max Weber, *Law in Economy and Society,* trans. Edward Shils and Max Rheinstein (Cambridge, Mass.: Harvard University Press, 1954), p. 17. See also Introduction by Max Rheinstein, p. lxvii.

4. Ehrlich, *Fundamental Principles,* pp. 61–82; Weber, *Law in Economy and Society;* See, for example, Charles E. Merriam, *Public and Private Government* (New Haven, Conn.: Yale University Press, 1944), p. 9. "The state can throw a man into prison. But an employer can take away his job. As the state can deprive a man of his life, the church can threaten his happiness for the future and make him extremely uneasy and unhappy while he lives. The state may tax, but the monopoly may raise prices and lower standards." Quoted in Robin M. Williams, Jr., *American Society: A Sociological Interpretation* (New York: Alfred A. Knopf, 1951), p. 206, n. 7.

5. Robert H. Skilton, *Industrial Discipline and the Arbitration Process* (Philadelphia: University of Pennsylvania Press, 1952), p. 29.

6. Cf. R. T. Morris, "A Typology of Norms," *American Sociological Review* 21 (1956):610–13.

7. Wesley N. Hohfeld, *Fundamental Legal Conceptions* (New Haven, Conn.: Yale University Press, 1923), pp. 23–114.

8. Cf. Philip Selznick, "The Sociology of Law," in Robert K. Merton, Leonard Broom, and Leonard S. Cottrell, Jr., eds., *Sociology Today* (New York: Basic Books, Inc., 1959), pp. 115–27. "Some of us who have worked in that field [sociology of administration] have discovered that in studying formal organizations we were also studying legal systems," p. 118.

9. Morris D. Forkosch, "American Democracy and Procedural Due Process," *Brooklyn Law Review* 24 (1958): 176–95; Robert L. Hale, *Freedom through Law* (New York: Columbia University Press, 1952), pp. 228–39.

10. Forkosch, "American Democracy and Procedural Due Process," p. 212.

11. *Ibid.,* p. 173.

12. Quoted in Forkosch, *ibid.,* p. 189, no. 43.

13. For a discussion of institutionalization of dissent, see S. M. Lipset, M. Trow, and J. Coleman, *Union Democracy* (New York: The Free Press, 1956), pp. 238–39, 416.

14. Max Weber, *Theory of Social and Economic Organization,* trans. A. M. Henderson and Talcott Parsons (New York: Oxford University Press, 1947), pp. 337–41.

15. John Henry Wigmore, *A Panorama of the World's Legal Systems,* 3 vols. (St. Paul, Minn.: West Publishing Co., 1928); Lester B. Orfield, *The Growth of Scandinavian Law* (Philadelphia: University of Pennsylvania Press, 1953); E. Adamson Hoebel, *The Law of Primitive Man: A Study in Comparative Legal Dynamics* (Cambridge, Mass.: Harvard University Press, 1954).

16. James C. McRuer, *The Evolution of the Judicial Process* (Toronto: Clarke, Irwin, 1957).

17. Weber, *Law in Economy and Society,* pp. 61–64.

18. See Rheinstein's penetrating analysis of Weber's typology, *ibid.,* pp. xlvii–lxiii.

19. Robert K. Merton, *Social Theory and Social Structure,* rev. ed. (New York: The Free Press, 1957), pp. 370, 380–85.

20. Wilbert E. Moore, *"Management and Union Organizations*: An Analytical Comparison," in Conrad M. Arensberg, et al., *Research in Industrial Human Relations* (New York: Harper & Brothers, 1957), pp. 119–30. See also William M. Evan, "Dimensions of Participation in Voluntary Associations," *Social Forces* 36 (1957): 150–52.

21. Beardsley Ruml, "Corporate Management as a Locus of Power, *Social Meaning of Legal Concepts,* no. 3, ed. by Edmond N. Cahn (New York: New York University School of Law, 1950), p. 227. [Italics added—W.M.E.]

22. Cf. Lipset, Trow, and Coleman, *Union Democracy,* pp. 83–140.

23. With respect to the history of the corporation, it should be noted that "it is a matter of dispute . . . whether the British Crown created corporations or found and assumed the control of preexisting collectivities." Adolph A. Berle, Jr., "Historical Inheritance of American Corporations," in Ralph J. Baker and William L. Cary, *Cases and Materials on Corporations,* 3d ed. (Brooklyn: The Foundation Press, 1958), p. 1.

24. Louis L. Jaffee, "Law Making by Private Groups," *Harvard Law Review* 51 (1937): 213.

25. *Ibid.,* p. 231; Walton Hamilton, *The Politics of Industry* (New York: Alfred A. Knopf, 1957), pp. 51–62, 141.

26. See, for example, *First Annual Report of the Public Review Board to the Membership of the UAW,* 1957–1958, no publisher given.

27. Adolph A. Berle, Jr., "Constitutional Limitations on Corporate Activity," *University of Pennsylvania Law Review* 100 (1952): 942–43; also *The 20th Century Capitalist Revolution* (New York: Harcourt, Brace & World, 1954), pp. 77 ff.

28. For an analysis of the impact of public legal systems on private legal systems, see William M. Evan and Mildred A. Schwartz, "Law and the Emergence of Formal Organizations," *Sociology and Social Research* 48(1964): 270–80.

29. Kenneth E. Boulding, *The Organizational Revolution* (New York: Harper & Brothers, 1953).

30. See, for example, Joseph Cornwall Palamountain, Jr., *The Politics of Distribution* (Cambridge, Mass.: Harvard University Press, 1955), pp. 107–58.

31. For a related discussion, see William M. Evan, "Power, Bargaining and Law: A Preliminary Analysis of Labor Arbitration Cases," *Social Problems* 6 (Summer 1959): pp. 4–15.

32. See, for example, Harry Shulman, "Reason, Contract and Law in Labor Relations," *Har-*

vard Law Review 68 (1955): 999–1024; also "The Arbitration Process," in Joseph Shister, *Readings in Labor Economics and Industrial Relations,* 2d ed. (Philadelphia: J. B. Lippincott Co., 1956), p. 249.

33. Soia Mentschikoff, "The Significance of Arbitration—A Preliminary Inquiry," *Law and Contemporary Problems* 17 (1952): 698.

34. Neil W. Chamberlain, *Labor* (New York: McGraw-Hill Book Co., 1958), p. 609.

35. See, for example, the illuminating analysis by Seymour M. Lipset, "Some Social Requisites of Democracy: Economic Development and Political Legitimacy," *American Political Science Review* 53 (1959): 69–106.

36. Ehrlich, *Fundamental Principles,* p. 390.

CHAPTER 13

Administrative Law
and Organization Theory

Each scientific or scholarly discipline or subdiscipline is propelled by forces of an intellectual and extraintellectual nature that tend to develop a momentum of their own. The elite of each discipline perform at least two functions: they create the dominant "paradigm(s)," which nonelite members follow, often much too faithfully, and they stand guard at the frontier to prevent encroachment.[1] Any effort to cross the frontier of a discipline is apt to be hazardous unless the discipline is in the midst of a crisis in its dominant paradigm(s). The sociologist of law has encountered some formidable obstacles in crossing the boundary of law. And any legal scholar who has had the temerity to study behavior with respect to legal phenomena outside the conventional context of judicial decisions may have also experienced his share of frustrations.[2]

It has been more than a decade since a debate was aired in the pages of the *Journal of Legal Education* on behavioral science and administrative law between the political scientist Grundstein and the eminent authority on administrative law, Kenneth Culp Davis.[3] Grundstein argued that administrative law had in effect reached a dead end in its development and was on the verge of being transformed with the help of behavioral science theories and methodologies and, in particular, through systems analysis and simulation.

This is a revised version of a paper prepared for the Eighth World Congress of Sociology in Toronto, August 1974.

Davis countered by pointing out that traditional administrative law was an evolving discipline; that although some contributions in behavioral science were impressive, others were vacuous; and that if "behaviorally-oriented research" produces anything of value "it will be readily and easily absorbed into administrative law research".[4] As a disinterested observer from another discipline, I must confess that I found Davis' arguments more persuasive.

My purpose in this chapter, however, is not to resume this debate but rather to examine (1) some trends in American administrative law, (2) some trends in organization theory, (3) an organization-set model of the administrative process, and (4) several potentially fruitful research strategies. Although the focus will be almost exclusively on American administrative law, my analysis will have implications for comparative research on legal systems.[5] An underlying assumption of this chapter is that the sociology of law can perform the midwife role in the birth of a new style of research linking administrative law with organization theory.

THE EXPANDING ROLE OF GOVERNMENT ADMINISTRATION

Before considering some trends in American administrative law, several brief observations are in order concerning the expanding role of government administration. As Galanter puts it, "[t]hroughout the world, there has been a proliferation of governmental responsibility and a growth of new areas of law. . . ."[6]

Weber's theory of bureaucracy is concerned with characterizing organizations in terms of his ideal type of bureaucracy and with the rise of bureaucracy as an indispensable element in the development of modern Western societies. In the intervening decades since Weber's work appeared, it has become apparent that his analysis may be as relevant for centrally-planned economies as for market economies, and for societies in the process of development as well as for those that are highly developed. In their effort to achieve modernization, developing countries are all too often severely hampered because of their failure to design an effective system of government bureaucracy as an integral component of their legal system. In his analysis of 11 features of a modern legal system, Galanter might have explicitly included the development of a rational-legal system of government administration.

Davis has captured the pervasiveness of government administration in the U.S. with the following observation:

The ordinary person probably regards the judicial process as somewhat remote from his own problems; a large portion of all people go through life without ever being a party to a lawsuit. But the administrative process affects nearly every one in many ways nearly every day. The pervasiveness of the effects of the administrative process on the average person can quickly be appreciated by running over a few samples of what the administrative process protects against: air and water pollution; excessive prices of electricity, gas, telephone, and other utility services, unreasonableness in rates, schedules, and services of airlines, railroads, street cars, and buses; disregard for the public interest in radio and television and chaotic conditions for broadcasting; unwholesome meat and poultry; adulteration in food; fraud or inadequate disclosure in sale of securities; physically unsafe locomotives, ships, airplanes, bridges, elevators; unfair labor practices by either employers or unions; false advertising and other unfair or deceptive practices; inadequate safety appliances. . . .[7]

In terms of the sheer number of administrative agencies at the federal level, in 1949 the Code of Federal Regulation listed 155 agencies; in 1973 the number had virtually doubled—even if allowances are made for multiple listings.[8] At the state and local levels there are undoubtedly many thousands of administrative agencies, and their growth for this period has in all likelihood been similar. Small wonder then that the case load of the federal agencies far outstrips that of the federal courts. For example, in 1963, according to Davis:

The number of civil cases filed in all federal district courts was 63,630 and the number of civil trials was 7,095. In the agencies the number of cases filed is in the millions, but stripping down to the small portion of the cases involving "an oral hearing with a verbatim transcript" and "the determination of private rights, privileges, or obligations," and excluding determinations solely on written applications or on oral presentations in the nature of conference or interview, the number is 81,469 cases disposed of.[9]

Admittedly the 11:1 ratio of administrative to judicial cases is crude. However, even if further refinements were made—as Davis suggests—to make the statistics more nearly comparable, the ratio would still be heavily weighted in the direction of administrative adjudication. This comparison suggests that it might be instructive to develop a cross-national time series for a sample of nation-states, both developed and developing, to test the hypothesis that as the level of economic development increases, the ratio of administrative cases to judicial cases increases. Associated with this hypothesized relationship are such features of modern legal systems as increasing technical complexity and increasing requirements for professional personnel, both of which may be more true of administrative agencies than of courts.[10]

SOME TRENDS IN AMERICAN ADMINISTRATIVE LAW

In his 1970 Supplement to his treatise on American administrative law, Davis states that his original definition of administrative law is still accurate, that is, that it is "the law concerning the powers and procedures of administrative agencies, including especially the law governing judicial review of administrative action."[11] However, he acknowledges that a more comprehensive view of the subject is now required; instead of focusing exclusively on regulatory agencies, particularly those that are independent agencies, it is equally necessary to attend to agencies in the executive branch and, more generally, to *all* administrative agencies, whether federal, state or local.

This major extension in the scope of this field requires a classification of agencies by type of function other than that of regulation. For example, is it sufficient to classify agencies according to whether their primary purpose is to regulate an industry (e.g., the ICC), provide benefits (e.g., the Social Security Administration), render a service (e.g., the U.S. Postal Service), give grants (e.g., the National Science Foundation), or award government contracts (e.g., an office of procurement of the Department of Defense)? Schwartz and Wade, in their comparative analysis of administrative law in Britain and the United States, distinguish between regulatory and benefactory agencies. Britain's agencies are largely of the latter type since their method of economic regulation entails nationalizing industry or establishing special public corporations.[12]

In the course of defining administrative law, Davis also indicates what it is not, to wit:

Apart from judicial review, the manner in which public officers handle business unrelated to adjudication or rule making is not a part of administrative law; this means that much of what political scientists call "public administration" is excluded. Administrative law is also confined to arrangements involving rights of private parties; it does not extend to internal problems affecting only the agencies and their officers and staffs.[13]

These exclusions, as we shall see, unnecessarily constrict the purview of scholars in administrative law.

Another distinctive feature of Davis' 1970 Supplement to his treatise is his delineation of four stages of development of the discipline. The first stage dealt with the constitutional bases of the administrative process; hence the concern with the doctrine of delegation of power from the legislature to the administrative agency and with the separation of powers, in view of the fact that agencies were accorded legislative, judicial, and executive functions. The second stage focused on problems of judicial review, which gave rise to many doctrines pertaining to the reviewability of administrative actions and to the scope of review. The third stage, which characterizes the present state of the field, is concerned with procedures in rule making and adjudication as reflected in the passage in 1946 of the Administrative Procedure Act. During the current stage a plethora of procedural doctrines have been the center of attention, for example, institutional decisions, subdelegation of powers within the agency, separation of functions within the agency, due process requirements, sovereign immunity, and tort liability of public officials. It is the intensive preoccupation with such diverse procedural doctrines that has prompted some political scientists, for example, Grundstein, to complain that "[p]rocedure has been an obsessive concern of American administrative law and research has been subordinated to this concern with procedure."[14]

The fourth stage, to which Davis wishes to direct the field, would be concerned with an understanding of discretionary justice.[15] He admits that his treatise, which is concerned with formal procedure and judicial review, deals with only 10 to 20 percent of the administrative process.

Yet *the strongest need and the greatest promise for improving the quality of justice to individual parties in the entire legal and governmental system are in the areas where decisions necessarily depend more upon discretion than upon rules and principles and where formal hearings and judicial review are mostly irrelevant.* The reason the literature of administrative law, as well as that of jurisprudence and of public administration, has almost completely neglected the vital eighty or ninety percent is that the subject is so exceedingly elusive.[16]

How the transition to the new stage will be made—by means of conventional methods of legal research and legal doctrines or with the help of new methods and theories borrowed from other disciplines—Davis does not say. Judging from his ongoing comparative study of discretionary justice in five countries, Davis is evidently willing to depart from conventional modes of legal research.[17]

A quite different perspective on trends in American administrative law is reflected in the work of Schwartz and his British collaborator, Wade. Schwartz notes that:

Administrative Law until now has been concerned almost entirely with property rights and the extent to and the manner in which they might be regulated by governmental power. The Administrative Law of the future must direct itself to the rights of the person, seeking to ensure a place for the individual vis-à-vis the state in the type of society toward which we are evolving.[18]

Schwartz' formulation is related to the world-wide interest in the Scandinavian Ombudsman concept as an institutional device to protect citizens against administrative injustice.[19]

Wade's transatlantic perspective on changes in administrative law is also noteworthy:

To an English lawyer it is interesting to see how in a few years the emphasis in American administrative law has shifted. Formerly it seemed to be preoccupied, at the federal level at least, with tempering the control of the big regulatory agencies over powerful businesses such as power companies, airlines, broadcasting networks and stockbrokers. The agencies in time became the allies of businesses and there resulted what was called "a welfare state for the wealthy." Today the preoccupation is with social and communal welfare, most of all for the poor. The courts are prodding the administrators into adopting fair rules and fair procedures for enforcing them. The doctrines worked out for the welfare of the wealthy are reaching down the scale into regions where, apparently, arbitrary power used to reign.[20]

Yet another trend in American administrative law is the increasing concern with assessing the performance of administrative agencies, particularly of regulatory bodies. This problem has evoked the interest not only of legal scholars but also of economists, various government commissions and consultants, and consumer advocates.

Economists have conducted an extensive amount of research on the economic effects of regulation and have generally concluded that it either has no impact or that it produces no net benefit relative to costs. Thus, for example, Stigler and Friedland, in their study of electrical utilities found no significant effects either with respect to rates or to rates of return on investment; MacAvoy has observed no net benefits from the regulation of public utilities; and Joskow, in his study of the property insurance industry, also emerged with the negative finding as to the impact of regulation, so much so that he encourages states to eliminate formal rate regulation.[21]

Among the two relatively recent appraisals of regulatory commissions in an effort to "reorganize" and "reform" them so that they will more faithfully fulfill their legislative mandate, those by Landis and the Ash council are especially noteworthy. Deploring the delay in disposition of administrative cases, time-consuming procedures, and the failure to delegate routine problems, Landis made a variety of recommendations principally aimed at augmenting control by the executive branch over the independent agencies.[22] A decade later the Ash council again recommended greater presidential rather than congressional control over the agencies and, in addition, proposed merging transportation agencies (the ICC, the CAB, and the FAA) and subdividing the FTC into two agencies, one dealing with antitrust activity and one with consumer protection.[23]

Consumer advocates, notably Nader and his associates, have exposed the failure of various regulatry agencies to promote the "public interest". They have documented in some detail that some of these agencies, such as the ICC and the FDA, have been "captured" by the regulated industries.[24]

To be sure, administrative law scholars have themselves critically evaluated some of the agencies. In his statistical study of antitrust enforcement of the Department of Justice, Posner charges the department with making little effort to identify monopolistic markets, with not seeing to it that its decrees are compiled with, and with not keeping any useful statistics on its own activities.[25] He concludes his indictment with the telling assertion that it is "inappropriately run as a law firm, where the workload is determined by the wishes of the clients (in this case most unhappy competitors, aggrieved purchasers, and disgruntled employees), and where the social product of the legal services undertaken is not measured."[26]

Jaffe, a distinguished authority on administrative law, criticizes the "broad delegation model" of administrative agencies, that is, that they operate more effectively when the legislative mandate is vague rather than well-defined. In the course of advancing his conception that "the political process . . . provides the milieu and defines the operation of each agency," Jaffe formulates several potentially testable propositions that would gladden the heart of any social scientist reading his article:

Where the ends and means of an agency's role are highly defined, elaborately rationalized—as is the case with tax or social security—the effects of the political process on the agency are marginal though rationalization could never go so far as totally to exclude political choice. . . . Such agencies are to be judged in terms of their fair, uniform, and zealous application of well-articulated law; the very precision of the law may help to reduce pressures from the regulated.

[W]here in form or in substance the legislative design is incomplete, uncertain, or inchoate, a political process will take place in and around the agency, with the likely outcome a function of the usual variables which determine the product of lawmaking institutions.

[A]n agency faced with an uncertain congressional mandate may do no more than it believes Congress expects it to do, which may, in fact, be nothing.[27]

Another recurrent problem in assessing the performance of administrative agencies is the nature of the relationship between the regulatory agency and the client organizations it is charged with regulating. Schwartz and Wade have formulated an intriguing "life cycle" hypothesis concerning this relationship that, as in the case of Jaffe's formulation, is empirically testable:

The influence of regulated upon regulators tends to increase progressively as the regulatory commissions go through what has been seen to be their typical "life cycle." The federal commissions have all gone through periods of youth, maturity, and old age, with their development dominated by what has been termed the progressive law of ossification. It is only during its youthful phase that the commission is vigorous in fighting for the public interest. As time goes on, it loses its early enthusiasm, and administrative aggressiveness is increasingly replaced by apathy. During the phase of maturity, the regulated direct their energies toward taking over the regulators and the commission tends more and more to equate the "public interest" with the interests of the regulated groups. This tendency is carried further in the commission's old age, when it has more or less come to terms with those whom it is ostensibly regulating. Over the years there develops a relationship which can be described only as regulatory symbiosis: regulators

. and regulated have learned to live with each other and have, in fact, grown intimately dependent on each other.[28]

Two other recent developments in American administrative law are noteworthy. In 1964 a new federal administrative agency—the Administrative Conference of the United States—was established for the purpose of studying administrative agencies and for collecting and disseminating information about them.[29] This agency subsequently adopted many recommendations, including one pertaining to the "compilation of statistics on administrative proceedings by federal departments and agencies."[30] To implement this decision the Administrative Conference has recently developed a "caseload accounting system for administrative agency proceedings" which would make it possible to compare various agencies on this dimension of performance.[31] In a recent report in which this system is presented, the author compares the average number of cases disposed of per year by hearing examiners—now upgraded and designated "administrative law judges"—in 16 federal agencies with the average number of cases terminated per year by judges of the U.S. District Courts. According to this study, the performance of federal judges is significantly higher than that of administrative law judges.[32]

Finally, the Board of Governors of the American Bar Association, following the recommendation of its Section of Administrative Law, has recently created a Center for Administrative Justice. The goals of the Center include: "the provision of a central source of information and research materials pertaining to administrative law at all levels of government . . . and [the] conducting of basic research both on its own and on behalf of governmental agencies or private organizations."[33] If these goals are fulfilled in an imaginative manner, we would have another source of data on the functioning of administrative agencies.

From the perspective of the sociologist of law and the organization theorist, the foregoing discussion of trends in American administrative law suggests an increasing sensitivity to problems of administrative law in action. It also suggests that the perennial problems of administrative agencies are unlikely to be solved within the framework of the dominant paradigm in American administrative law. This much is clear from the ongoing work of such administrative law scholars as Davis, Posner, Freedman, and others.[34] Do the recent trends, however, make this field more receptive to the contributions of organization theory?

SOME TRENDS IN ORGANIZATION THEORY

Compared with administrative law, the field of organization theory appears to be highly abstract, diffuse, and even chaotic. In spite of its name there is no *one* commanding theory but a variety of theories differing in scope—some quite narrow, some middle range, and some grand in design. It is in itself an interdisciplinary field on which diverse social sciences, management sciences, and even engineering have converged because of the challenging problems of better understanding and designing complex organizations. It has its roots in the work of the classical school, including Taylor and Fayol in scientific management, and Gulick, Urwick, and others in public administration.[35] Weber, whose theory of bureaucracy has had a pervasive impact on the course of research, has a close kinship with the classical school in his emphasis on the structure of organizations. In fact, in the empirical work of sociologists in the past two decades we encounter the first significant trend in the field, namely, the concern with delineating organizational structure. Instead of using Weber's ideal type of bureaucracy, various dimensions have been conceptualized pertaining to his rational-legal, monocratic system of authority. As a result, such organizational variables as the following have been operationalized: centralization of decision making, administrative intensity (which includes the classical notion of "span of control" and various ratios of managerial to nonmanagerial personnel), the degree of formalization (i.e., the emphasis on written rules governing the conduct of bureaucratic personnel), and the degree of professionalization of personnel because of the bureaucracy's reliance on expertise.

In the work of Blau and his students the concern with structural variables is clearly in evidence.[36] They have established interrelationships among such variables as organizational size, professionalization of personnel, functional and departmental specialization, and administrative intensity. For example, they have found that as organizational size increases, so does functional and departmental specialization.

The Aston group, i.e., Pugh and his colleagues, has similarly focused on structural variables in their study of a sample of organizations in Britain.[37] They have investigated the interrelationships among such variables as functional specialization, formalization, administrative intensity, and centralization of decision making. In short, a dominant trend has emerged involving a *quantitative-structural* analysis of organizations.

In the course of pursuing this style of research, it has become evident that it is important to test hypotheses interrelating structural variables in organizations differing in function, hence the new *comparative* trend in organization theory. Another facet of this trend is the realization of the need for testing whether the structural relationships observed by Blau, Pugh, and their respective colleagues, hold in other countries as well.[38]

In his recent compilation of 30 comparative studies, all involving a quantitative-structural mode of analysis, Heydebrand included only two conducted in government organizations, one dealing with state public personnel agencies of civil service commissions and the other with finance departments of state and local governments as well as with public personnel agencies.[39] By comparison, 11 of the studies pertained to professional and service organizations such as hospitals and colleges, and eight dealt with business organizations. Clearly, sociologists have paid scant attention to the study of administrative agencies, a notable exception being Blau's study of a federal enforcement agency and a state employment agency.[40] The pioneering work of Selznick on the TVA, using the case method to analyze dynamic processes, has not been followed up until the recent work of his student, Nonet, on California's Industrial Accident Commission.[41] In his historical analysis of this agency, Nonet discerns a process of "legalization," i.e., the "growth of the relevance of law in practical problem-solving, as well as to the elaboration of legal rules and doctrines that occurs in this process."[42] This study is perhaps the clearest recent example in the literature of an effort to integrate concepts from organization theory and the sociology of law, on the one hand, with some concepts from administrative law, on the other.

A third trend in organizational research that is in part an outgrowth of the quantitative-structural trend, is a concern with *longitudinal analysis.*[43] Instead of studying relations among structural variables cross-sectionally, it is becoming increasingly clear that a longitudinal mode of analysis is essential. If there is a positive relation between centralization and formalization, does this persist over time or does it change, and if so, in which direction? Only a longitudinally designed study can throw light on such a question.

A fourth trend in organization theory is the increasing attention to *interorganizational relations,* especially since the principal focus of the quantitative-structural research discussed above has been on *intraorganizational relations.* In the work of Litwak, Downs, Evan, and others, we observe this recent emphasis in the field.[44]

In his perceptive study of decision making of government bureaus, Downs starts with the supposition that "every organization's social functions strongly influence its internal structure and behavior, and vice versa. This premise may seem rather obvious, but some organization theorists have in effect contradicted it by focusing their analyses almost exclusively on what happens within an organization."[45] One of the important concepts and variables to emerge from the literature on interorganizational relations is organizational autonomy as it is related to the environmental forces impinging on a given organization.

It is the interorganizational trend in this field *in conjunction with* the quantitative-structural, comparative, and longitudinal trends that can open the way for a new line of research on administrative agencies of potential value to both administrative law and organization theory.

AN ORGANIZATION-SET MODEL OF THE ADMINISTRATIVE PROCESS

In our brief discussion of recent trends in administrative law and organization theory, various concepts have been alluded to. It may now be instructive to juxtapose a "baker's dozen" concepts in each field, as I have done in Table 13.1. In only five of the 13 concepts—those I have asterisked—is there any conceptual correspondence. Thus, for example, institutional decisions presuppose a high degree of centralization in decision making whereas subdelegation of power entails decentralization of decision making. Similarly, rule making is close to the concept of formalization; the concern with the separation of functions—legislative, adjudicative, and executive—involves a process of departmental specialization; administrative discretion reflects in part a pattern of informal organization, namely, one that is not officially prescribed or sanctioned and entails a process of innovation.

To go beyond the mere drawing of interdisciplinary conceptual parallels requires a model in terms of which some of these concepts can be used, thus building a bridge between the two disciplines.[46] A first approximation will be attempted here.

The organization-set model that I have formulated elsewhere has two underly-

Table 13.1. Selected concepts in American administrative law and organization theory.[a]

American Administrative Law	Organization Theory
1. Delegation of powers	1. Organizational size
2. Separation of powers	2. Organizational age
3. Judicial review	3. Complexity of task structure
4. Substantial-evidence rule	4. Technological complexity
5. Primary jurisdiction	5. Organizational effectiveness
6. Sovereign immunity	6. Organizational autonomy
7. Officer tort liability	7. Functional specialization
8. Administrative due process	8. Administrative intensity (bureaucratization)
*9. Institutional decisions	*9. Centralization of decision making
*10. Sub-delegation of power	*10. Decentralization of decision making
*11. Rule making	*11. Formalization
*12. Separation of functions	*12. Departmental specialization
*13. Administrative discretion	*13. Informal organization and innovation

[a] The items asterisked are examples of a degree of interdisciplinary conceptual parallelism.

ing assumptions.[47] First, organizations, in general, and administrative agencies, in particular, are systems of interrelated elements interacting with other systems in their environment; hence an application of a systems perspective is required. This assumption is similar to Downs' premise and to Jaffe's view that "each agency functions in a political milieu."[48] A second assumption is that an organization's performance, however it may be conceptualized and measured, is a function of (1) its goals, (2) its internal organizational structure, (3) the role orientation of its members, and (4) its mode of interaction with its environing organizations.

The point of departure of this model is a consideration of several concepts in role theory developed by Merton and Gross *et al.*[49] Instead of selecting a status as the unit of analysis and charting the complex of role relationships in which the status occupant is involved, as Merton does in his analysis of role-sets, I take as the unit of analysis an organization or a class of organizations and trace its interactions with various organizations in its environment, that is, with elements of its "organization-set". Following Gross, Mason, and McEachern's use of the term "focal position" in their analysis of roles, I have referred to the organization or class of organizations that is the point of reference as the "focal organization."[50] As in the case of role-set analysis, the focal organization interacts with a complement of organizations in its environment, that is, its organization-set. A systems analysis perspective, however, suggests that the organization-set be partitioned into an "input organization-set" and an "output organization-set". By an input organization-set, as the term suggests, I mean a complement of organizations that provides various types of resources to the focal organization. Similarly, by an output organization-set I mean all organizations that are the recipients of the goods and/or services, including organizational decisions, generated by the focal organization. Furthermore, a systems analysis requires that we trace feedback effects from the output organization-set to the focal organization and thence to the input organization-set, or directly from the output to the input organization-set. These feedback effects can, of course, be positive or negative, as well as anticipated or unanticipated.

The four components of the model—focal organization, input organization-set, output organization-set, and feedback effects—may be jointly conceived as comprising an interorganizational system.[51]

For purposes of illustration, if we take as a focal organization an administrative agency such as the FCC (see Figure 13.1), the input organization-set includes: the Congress through its enabling act, the Appropriations Committee, and so on; the Executive Branch, including the president who appoints the chairman and commissioners, and the various executive departments; the courts whose past decisions become guides and constraints on the agency's future actions; and other administrative agencies that may either support, help, or compete with the FCC for scarce resources. The degree to which the FCC is effective in managing the input organization-set, which is very likely plagued

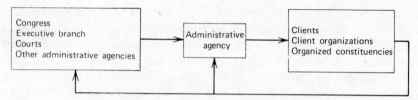

Fig. 13.1   An organization-set analysis of an administrative agency.

with conflict and uncertainty, affects its internal structure and in turn its capacity to perform its regulatory functions.

The output set consists of many thousands of radio and television stations whose licenses and programming are regulated by the FCC's decisions, various trade associations, and a bar association of attorneys in the communications industry.

The success with which the FCC manages its multifaceted relations with the members of its output organization-set in turn has feedback effects on the FCC as well as on the input organization-set, which again triggers the cycle of interorganizational systemic relations.[52]

Managing the boundary relations of the FCC with its input organization-set and its output organization-set are its various boundary personnel, principally attorneys who conduct investigations, administrative law judges, and liaison officers with Congress and the Executive Branch. At least two role attributes, expertise and loyalty, determine the behavior of the boundary personnel and cumulatively affect the performance of the FCC. If the boundary personnel are not high caliber professionals, they will fail to apply the relevant agency rules or legal principles to the problems and facts at hand; and if the norms governing their conduct—their normative reference group—are derived from the regulated industry, rather than from the agency, they will again fail to perform their function with fidelity to the FCC's mandate. Greatly aggravating the dilemmas of the boundary personnel, as Jaffe points out, is the broad delegation of powers in terms of the concept of public interest.[53]

In short, with the help of the organization-set model-supplemented with relevant structural variables, it would be possible to study a sample of administrative agencies differing on such dimensions as type of delegation of power (broad versus narrow), life-cycle position, volume of rule making, scope of jurisdiction (federal, state, or local agency), and so on. Such an inquiry would be able to test propositions of interest to both administrative lawyers and organization theorists. One hypothesis, for example, is as follows:

Administrative agencies with a low degree of organizational autonomy will—all other things being equal—have:

1.   a high degree of centralization of decision making;
2.   a high degree of formalization;

3. a high probability of rendering decisions in favor of organizations that can exercise substantial power over the agency;
4. a low proportion of professionals with a high commitment to the legislative mandate; and
5. a low level of performance, for example, as measured by the case load of its personnel.

To further clarify how the organization-set model would be applied in an empirical study of administrative agencies, 25 variables illustrating the four components of the model are enumerated in Table 13.2. Variables 1 to 6, which are indicators of the input organization-set, include a composite measure of organizational autonomy (Variable 6), namely, of the administrative agency.[54] Variables 7 to 17, which are indicators of the structure of the focal organization, resemble those Blau, Pugh, and their respective colleagues have employed in their studies. The four output organization-set variables (22 to 25) include a composite measure of the degree of regulatory resistance to the focal organization.[55] Finally, the four output variables (18 to 21), which include a composite measure of organizational effectiveness of the agency, would provide a basis for ascertaining negative and positive feedback effects of the interorganizational system.

It should be evident that the list of 25 variables is only a first approximation—particularly those purporting to measure agency effectiveness—to the kind of effort that would be required in any empirical application of the model. With the aid of a carefully selected and operationalized inventory of organization-set variables, it would be possible to test two general hypotheses of interest to administrative lawyers as well as to organization theorists, to wit:

1. The structure of an administrative agency (Variables 7 to 17) is a function of the input organization-set variables (1 to 6) and of the output organization-set variables (22 to 25).
2. The effectiveness of an administrative agency is a function of its organizational structure (Variables 7 to 17), its input organization-set (Variables 1 to 6), and its output organization-set (Variables 22 to 25).[56]

RESEARCH STRATEGIES

To test any facet of the foregoing model would obviously require the most efficient methods available. At least four social science methodologies are clearly relevant. The first is the application of the sample survey method such as Blau and his colleagues as well as the Aston group use in conducting quantitative-structural research. This would involve drawing a sample of administrative agencies, mapping the nature of their interactions with their organizational environment, and measuring the effects of their internal structure and the role orientations of its boundary personnel on its legislative, adjudicative, and executive functions.

A second research strategy is that of the case method as exemplified by the outstanding studies of Selznick and Nonet.[57] Rather than trying to establish quantitative relationships among variables, the focus is on discovering dynamic processes with the help of a given model. Thus, Selznick's use of "cooptation" to throw light on the environmental constraints on the TVA and Nonet's concept of "legalization" illustrate the potential benefits from this mode of research.

A third and least exploited research strategy in this context is that of experimental methodology. Organizational experiments pertaining to intraorganizational and interorganizational phenomena can be conducted with the aid of laboratory as well as field studies.[58] Thibaut, Walker, and Lind, in the course of testing the relative merits of the adversary versus the inquisitorial mode of adjudication, have made a case for the use of laboratory experimentation to simulate decision making in courts as well as in administrative agencies:

> . . . [T]he laboratory method seems best adapted to studies of institutional modes of conflict resolution since these modes embody standardized rules and procedures that can be experimentally replicated in simplified form. In our society the courts and administrative agencies are of course the principal institutional devices for resolution of social disputes. Thus, the obvious application of the suggested laboratory method entails the simulation of a court or administrative process and the introduction of planned variations of substantive or procedural rules in a way that permits exact measurement of the effects attributable to the variations.[59]

As for field experiments, Schwartz, Campbell and Zeisel have advocated the desirability of conducting such research.[60] It does not require a fertile imagination, particularly on the part of some economists who have argued in favor of deregulation of selected industries, either to perform a "quasi-field experiment," such as Campbell has urged, or, more ambitiously, to seek to persuade relevant administrative agencies to modify in a controlled manner their internal structures or policies—to the extent, of course, that this would not violate the law.

Almost as neglected as experimental methodology in the study of legal phenomena is the use of computer simulation, a technique that is slowly attracting the attention of legal scholars.[61] Instead of conducting field experiments—that entail substantial costs and difficulties—to test alternative policies of court administration, law enforcement, administrative adjudication, and the like, it is possible to represent real and hypothetical states of various dimensions of legal systems by means of computer simulation. Although organizational research has thus far made only modest use of simulation models, several studies suggest potentially fruitful applications of this methodology to problems of

Table 13.2. Some illustrative organization-set variables for studying administrative agencies.

Input Organization-Set Variables

1. Type of legislative mandate (broad vs. narrow)
2. Size of input organization-set (i.e., number of organizations)
3. Degree of homogeneity of input organization-set
4. Network configuration of input organization-set (e.g., presence of coalition formation against the focal organization)
5. Degree of adequacy of input resources
6. A composite measure of the degree of organizational autonomy (based on Variables 1 to 5)

Focal Organization Variables

7. Organizational size
8. Organizational age
9. Complexity of task structure
10. Technological complexity
11. a. Functional specialization
    b. Degree of boundary role specialization
12. Degree of professionalization of personnel
13. Type of normative reference group orientation of boundary personnel (i.e., focal organization vs. external organization)
14. Centralization of decision making
15. Formalization
16. Departmental specialization
17. Administrative intensity

Output Variables

18. Cost per administrative action
19. Number of administrative actions per professional employee
20. Percentage of administrative actions reviewed by courts per year
21. A composite measure of the degree of organizational effectiveness of the focal organization (based on Variables 18 to 20)

Output Organization-Set Variables

22. Size of output organization-set
23. Degree of homogeneity of output organization-set
24. Network configuration of output organization-set (e.g., presence of coalition formation against the focal organization)
25. A composite measure of the degree of conflict of the ouput organization-set with the focal organization (i.e., degree of resistance to regulation—based on Variables 22 to 24)

administrative agencies.[62] In fact, the organization-set model outlined above and the 25 illustrative variables operationalizing the model (see Table 13.2) provide the wherewithal for testing an array of functional relationships in a sequence of computer simulation runs.

Although I would obviously not rule out the relevance of conventional legal research, it would be important to select with care a sample of administrative decisions involving *formal adjudication* as well as a sample of decisions involving *informal proceedings,* which, of course, is Davis' principal argument for research on discretionary justice.

CONCLUSION

The burden of this discussion is that the sociology of law can be instrumental in forging a link between administrative law, on the one hand, and organization theory, on the other. If a research partnership were developed between these two disciplines, administrative lawyers would learn how the organizational environments of administrative agencies interact with the internal organizational structures to affect the agencies' legislative, judicial, and executive functions. Organization theorists, on the other hand, in coming to grips with the complex environmental processes impinging on administrative agencies would significantly advance their knowledge of interorganizational relations and in addition contribute to the integration of organization theory and macrosociological theory, inasmuch as the functioning of any administrative agency invariably entails a complex of legal, political, and economic interactions.

In sum, if the arguments advanced in this chapter were taken seriously by researchers in both disciplines, organization theory would make significant strides, particularly in modeling and explaining interorganizational phenomena; and administrative law would probably evolve more rapidly into Davis' fourth stage of discretionary justice, which in turn might usher in a fifth stage of "administrative law in action", informed by concepts, propositions, and models derived from organization theory.[63]

NOTES

1. Thomas S. Kuhn, *The Structure of Scientific Revolutions,* 2nd ed. (Chicago: University of Chicago Press, 1970).

2. For an exceptionally happy and successful venture in interdisciplinary research, however, see Harry Kalven, Jr., "Hans," *University of Chicago Law Review* 41 (Winter 1974): 209–19.

3. Nathan D. Grundstein, "Administrative Law and the Behavioral and Management Sciences," *Journal of Legal Education* 17 (1964): 121–36; Kenneth Culp Davis, "Behavioral Science and Administrative Law," *Journal of Legal Education* 17 (1964): 137–54.

4. Davis, "Behavioral Science and Administrative Law," p. 151.

5. John H. Merryman, "Comparative Law and Scientific Explanation," in J. N. Hazard and W. J. Wagner, eds., *Law in the United States of America in Social and Technological Revolution* (Brussels, Belgium: Establissements Emile Bruylant, 1974), pp. 81–104.

6. Marc Galanter, "The Modernization of Law," in Myron Weiner, ed., *Modernization* (New York: Basic Books, 1966), pp. 153–65.

7. Kenneth Culp Davis, *Administrative Law Text,* 3rd ed. (St. Paul, Minn.: West Publishing Co., 1972).

8. Kenneth Culp Davis, *Administrative Law Treatise,* vols. 1–4 (St. Paul, Minn.: West Publishing Co., 1958); Office of the Federal Register, *Code of Federal Regulations, The President, Appendix, 1972 Compilation* (Washington, D. C.: Government Printing Office, 1973).

9. Kenneth Culp Davis, *Administrative Law Treatise, 1970 Supplement* (St. Paul, Minn.: West Publishing Co., 1971).

10. Galanter, "Modernization of Law," pp. 155–56.

11. Davis, *Administrative Law Treatise, 1970 Supplement;* and *Administrative Law Treatise,* vol. 1, p. 1.

12. Bernard Schwartz and H. W. R. Wade, *Legal Control of Government: Administrative Law in Britain and the United States* (Oxford: Clarendon Press, 1972), pp. 27–37, 37–42.

13. Davis, *Administrative Law Treatise,* vol. 1, pp. 3–4.

14. Grundstein, "Administrative Law and the Behavioral and Management Sciences," p. 122.

15. Kenneth Culp Davis, *Discretionary Justice* (Urbana, Ill.: University of Illinois Press, 1969).

16. Davis, *Administrative Law Treatise, 1970 Supplement,* p. vi.

17. Private communication, 1973.

18. Quoted in B. L. Kass, "We Can, Indeed, Fight City Hall: The Office and Concept of Ombudsman," *Administrative Law Review* 19 (November 1966): 77.

19. Kenneth Culp Davis, "Ombudsman in America: Officer to Criticize Administrative Action," *University of Pennsylvania Law Review* 109 (June 1961): 1057–76; Walter Gellhorn, *When Americans Complain* (Cambridge, Mass.: Harvard University Press, 1965); Walter Gellhorn, *Ombudsman and Others* (Cambridge, Mass.: Harvard University Press, 1968); D. C. Rowat, *The Ombudsman; Citizen's Defender,* 2d ed. (London: George Allen and Unwin, 1968); Roy V. Peel, ed., "The Ombudsman or Citizen's Defender: A Modern Institution," *Annals of American Academy of Political and Social Science* 377 (May 1968): ix–138; William M. Evan, "An Ombudsman for Executives," *New York Times* (August 26, 1973).

20. Schwartz and Wade, *Legal Control of Government,* p. 313.

21. George J. Stigler and Claire Friedland, "What Can Regulators Regulate? The Case of Electricity," *Journal of Law and Economics* 5 (October 1962): 1–16; Paul W. MacAvoy, *The Crisis of the Regulatory Commissions* (New York, Norton, 1970); Paul I. Joskow, "Cartels, Competition and Regulation in the Property-Liability Insurance Industry," *Bell Journal of Economics and Management Science* 4 (Autumn 1973); 426.

22. James M. Landis, *Report on Regulatory Agencies to the President-Elect* (Subcommittee on Administrative Practice and Procedure: Committee on Judiciary of the U.S. Senate) (Washington, D. C.: Government Printing Office, 1960).

23. The President's Advisory Council on Executive Organization, *A New Regulatory Framework: Report on Selected Independent Regulatory Agencies* (Washington, D. C.: Government Printing Office, 1971).

24. Robert C. Fellmeth, *The Interstate Commerce Commission* (New York: Grossman Publishers, 1970), pp. 16, 19; James S. Turner, *The Chemical Feast* (New York: Grossman Publishers, 1970), p. 103.

25. Richard A. Posner, "A Statistical Study of Antitrust Enforcement," *Journal of Law and Economics* 13 (October 1970): 419.

26. *Ibid.*, p. 419.

27. Louis L. Jaffe, "The Illusion of the Ideal Administration," *Harvard Law Review* 86 (May 1973): 1188–90.

28. Schwartz and Wade, *Legal Control of Government*, pp. 32–33.

29. Davis, *Administrative Law Treatise, 1970 Supplement*, pp. 9–11.

30. *Ibid.*, p. 11.

31. Norbert A. Halloran, *Federal Agency Hearings: A Proposed Caseload Accounting System* (Washington, D.C.: Administrative Conference of the United States, 1974).

32. *Ibid.*, p. 8.

33. Frederic B. Davis, "Administrative Law: Today and Tomorrow," *Journal of Public Law* 22 (1973): 335–55.

34. Richard A. Posner, "The Behavior of Administrative Agencies," *Journal of Legal Studies* 1 (1972): 305–47; James O. Freedman, "Summary Action by Administrative Agencies," *University of Chicago Law Review* 40 (Fall 1972): 1–65.

35. J. G. March and H. A. Simon, *Organizations* (New York: John Wiley & Sons, 1958).

36. Cf. Peter M. Blau, *The Organization of Academic Work* (New York: John Wiley & Sons, 1973); Wolf V. Heydebrand, *Hospital Bureaucracy* (New York: Dunellen, 1973); Marshall W. Meyer, *Bureaucratic Structure and Authority* (New York: Harper and Row, 1972); Peter M. Blau and Richard A. Schoenherr, *The Structure of Organizations* (New York: Basic Books, 1971).

37. D. S. Pugh, D. J. Hickson, C. R. Hinings, and C. Turner, "Dimensions of Organization Structure," *Administrative Science Quarterly* 13 (1968): 65–105; D. S. Pugh, D. J. Hickson, C. R. Hinings, C. Turner, "The Context of Organizational Structures," *Administrative Science Quarterly* 14 (March 1969): 91–114; D. J. Hickson, D. S. Pugh, and Diana Pheysey, "Operations, Technology and Organizational Structure: An Empirical Reappraisal," *Administrative Science Quarterly* 14 (September 1969); 378–98.

38. See, for example, Charles J. McMillan, "The Structure of Work Organization Across Societies," *Academy of Management Journal* 16 (1973): 555–69; D. J. Hickson, C. R. Hinings, C. J. McMillan, and J. P. Schwitter, "The Culture Free Context of Organization Structure: A Tri-National Comparison," *Sociology* 8 (January 1974): 59–80; William M. Evan, ed., "Organizational Research Across National and Cultural Boundaries," *International Studies of Management and Organization* (Spring 1975): 3–113.

39. Wolf V. Heydebrand, *Comparative Organization* (Englewood Cliffs, N.J.: Prentice-Hall, 1973), pp. 516–33, 543–59.

40. Peter M. Blau, *The Dynamics of Bureaucracy: A Study of Interpersonal Relations in Two Government Agencies* (Chicago: University of Chicago Press, 1955).

41. Philip Selznick, *TVA and the Grass Roots: A Study in the Sociology of Formal Organizations* (Berkeley: University of California Press, 1949).

42. Philippe Nonet, *Administrative Justice* (New York: Russell Sage Foundation, 1969), p. 2.

43. Edward Holdaway and Thomas A. Blowers, "Administrative Ratios and Organization Size: A Longitudinal Examination," *American Sociological Review* 36 (April 1971): 278–

86; Jerald Hage, "A Longitudinal Test of an Axiomatic Organizational Theory," a paper presented at Eighth World Congress of Sociology, Toronto, August 1974; John R. Kimberly, "Some Issues in Longitudinal Organizational Research," a paper presented at the meetings of the American Sociological Association, August, 1974.

44. Eugene Litwak, "Toward the Theory and Practice of Coordination between Formal Organizations," in William R. Rosengren and Mark Lefton, eds., *Organizations and clients* (Columbus, Ohio: Charles E. Merrill, 1970); Anthony Downs, *Inside Bureaucracy* (Boston: Little, Brown, 1967); William M. Evan, "The Organization-Set: Toward a Theory of Inter-Organizational Relations," in J. D. Thompson, ed., *Approaches to Organizational Design* (Pittsburgh: University of Pittsburgh Press, 1966), pp. 175–90; William M. Evan, "An Organization-Set Model of Interorganizational Relations," in M. F. Tuite, R. K. Chisholm, and M. Radnor, eds., *Interorganizational Decision Making* (Chicago: Aldine, 1972); William M. Evan, ed., *Interorganizational Relations: Selected Readings.* London: Penguin Books, 1976.

45. Downs, *Inside Bureaucracy,* p. 2.

46. See, for example, William M. Evan, ed., *Law and Sociology: Exploratory Essays* (New York: The Free Press, 1962); William M. Evan and Mildred A. Schwartz, "Law and the Emergence of Formal Organizations," *Sociology and Social Research* 48 (April 1964): 270–80.

47. See Chapters 9 and 11 of the present volume.

48. Jaffe, "The Illusion of the Ideal Administration," p. 1189.

49. Robert K. Merton, *Social Theory and Social Structure,* rev. ed. (Glencoe, Ill.: The Free Press, 1957); Neal Gross, Ward S. Mason, and Alexander W. McEachern, *Explorations in Role Analysis: Studies of the School Superintendency Role* (New York: John Wiley & Sons, 1958).

50. Gross, Mason, and McEachern, *Explorations in Role Analysis,* pp. 50–56; Evan, "The Organization-Set," p. 178.

51. See Chapter 11 of the present volume.

52. A much-neglected study in this connection is Sutherland's pioneering inquiry into the decisions of agencies and courts on 70 corporations convicted of violations of the law pertaining to restraints of trade, misrepresentation of advertising, unfair labor practices, rebates, and the like. Sutherland was so preoccupied with using the statistical data on the 70 corporations to demonstrate his thesis of white collar crime that he did not exploit the opportunity of gathering data on the organizational structure of the corporations and their pattern of interaction with the administrative agencies. Edwin H. Sutherland, *White Collar Crime* (New York: Holt, Rinehart and Winston, 1949).

53. Jaffe, "The Illusion of the Ideal Administration."

54. For definitions of some of these variables, see Evan, "The Organization-Set"; "An Organization-Set Model of Interorganizational Relations." See Chapters 9 and 11 of the present volume.

55. For definitions of some of these variables, see Blau and Schoenherr, *Structure of Organizations,* pp. 27–29; Heydebrand, *Hospital Bureaucracy,* pp. 7–11; Pugh *et al.,* "Dimensions of Organization Structure;" Evan, "The Organization-Set."

56. Since this chapter was written, I have developed a model of organizational effectiveness. See "Organization Theory and Organizational Effectiveness," in *Organization and Administrative Sciences* 7 (1976):15–28. The statistical techniques most appropriate for testing the hypotheses are canonical correlation and multiple regression analysis.

57. Selznick, *TVA and the Grass Roots;* Nonet, *Administrative Justice.*

58. William M. Evan, ed. *Organizational Experiments* (New York: Harper and Row, 1971).

59. John Thibaut, Laurens Walker, and E. Allan Lind, "Adversary Presentation and Bias in Legal Decision Making," *Harvard Law Review* 86 (December 1972): 387.

60. R. D. Schwartz, "Field Experimentation in Sociological Research," *Journal of Legal Education* 13 (1961): 401–10; Donald T. Campbell, "Legal Reforms as Experiments," *Journal of Legal Education* 23 (1970): 217–39; Hans Zeisel, "Reflections on Experimental Techniques in the Law," *Journal of Legal Studies* 2 (January 1973): 107–24.

61. See, for example, J. A. Sigler, "A Cybernetic Model of the Judicial System," *Temple Law Quarterly* 41 (Spring 1968): 398–427; Frederick Merrill and Linus Schrage, "Efficient Use of Jurors: A Field Study and Simulation Model of a Court System," *Washington University Law Quarterly* (Spring 1969): 151–83; John N. Drobak, "Computer Simulation and Gaming: An Interdisciplinary Survey with a View Toward Legal Applications," *Stanford Law Review* 24 (April 1972): 712–29.

62. Cf. Charles P. Bonini, *Simulation of Information and Decision Systems in the Firm* (Englewood Cliffs, N. J.: Prentice-Hall, 1963); Kalman J. Cohen and Richard M. Cyert, "Simulation of Organizational Behavior," in James G. March, ed., *Handbook of Organizations* (Chicago: Rand McNally, 1965); W. D. Rowe, "A Model of Bureaucratic Growth Using GPSS," in Arnold Ockene, ed., *Second Conference on Applications of Simulation* (New York: SHARE, ACM, IEEE, SCI, 1968), pp. 173–75.

63. Davis, *Administrative Law Treatise, 1970 Supplement.*

CHAPTER 14

Multinational Corporations and International Professional Associations

Organization theory has for some years been preoccupied with problems of intraorganizational dynamics, principally in the context of industrial organizations. Only recently has a shift occurred in the angle of vision, with some researchers focusing on problems of interorganizational dynamics.[1] Another development, as yet embryonic, is a concern with cross-national comparative research in order to discover the effects of the socio-cultural environment on organizational behavior.[2]

Under the circumstances, it is not surprising that scant research attention has been paid to organizations operating in what political scientists and others call the international system.[3] I refer to two categories of international or multinational organizations: one, a private profit organization that in recent years has come to be designated as the "multinational corporation," and the other, an international professional association, a nonprofit, voluntary association often characterized as an international, nongovernmental organization and abbreviated as INGO.[4] Since World War II both types of organizations have undergone rapid growth.[5] Both organizations also involve participation of

---

This is a revised version of a paper presented at the Seventh World Congress of Sociology, Varna, Bulgaria, September, 1970.

occupational elites—business executives and members of various professions—whose collective efforts could have far-reaching consequences, particularly for the state of the international system.

These two types of organizations pose intricate and challenging problems for organization theory. They raise questions not only of interorganizational dynamices but also of the interaction between organizations and their societal and intersocietal environment. In effect, such questions compel the researcher to shift his focus to a level of analysis more macroscopic than the boundaries of a formal organization.[6]

The purpose of this chapter is to explore some features of multinational corporations and international professional associations as they bear on the degree of integration of the international system.

ALTERNATIVE MODELS OF INTEGRATION
OF THE INTERNATIONAL SYSTEM

It is indeed interesting that the term "international organization," as used by most political scientists and other scholars in the field of international relations, refers to the interaction of nation-states.[7] Haas, acknowledging the ambiguity of the term, states that, "A loose definition of international organization . . . would say that it consists of intergovernmental institutions, members of which perceive each other to be basic units of the world polity."[8] The widespread assumption underlying this usage is that the international system is composed of various relationships among sovereign actors. To improve the prospects for peace between nations, it is necessary to generate normative integration, i.e., a commitment to a common set of values and norms, through the mechanism of a universal intergovernmental organization. With the aid of multilateral agreements, a complex of intergovernmental organizations is created that builds commitment among nation-states to a body of international law designed to increase the forces for international order. With an increase in the level of normative integration, the international system evolves in the direction of a world community of peaceful sovereign states. In effect, the model implicit in this conception of the international system, diagrammed in Figure 14.1, involves a direct, linear process of normative integration increasing as a function of interaction of nation-states within the framework of intergovernmental organizations.

This model guided the formation of the League of Nations and, to some extent, that of the United Nations as well. The failure of the League of Nations to evoke compliance on the part of its sovereign members undermined its authority as well as its capability of generating normative integration. Without abridging national sovereignty, membership in an intergovernmental organiza-

Fig. 14.1   Direct, linear model of integration of the international system.

tion is neither a necessary nor a sufficient condition for the development of normative integration. Nor is normative integration a sufficient condition for significantly transforming the international system. Other modes of integration—notably economic, organizational, and occupational—which create new patterns of interdependence, are essential if the international system is to undergo a major transformation.[9]

The failure of the League of Nations was not lost on some of its former members in Western Europe. After World War II they began to explore problems of economic integration by means of regional organizations that would impose limitations on national sovereignty. The Economic and Steel Community, founded in 1952, was conceived as a supranational organization that paved the way for the more inclusive European Economic Community in 1958.[10] Among the Communist countries of Eastern Europe and the Soviet Union a similar movement toward economic integration was initiated, which gave rise in 1949 to the Council on Mutual Economic Aid (CEMA or COMECON).[11] Similar regional organizations have since emerged in Latin America (the Latin American Free Trade Area and the Central American Common Market), Africa, and elsewhere.[12]

The United Nations Charter recognizes regional organizations and seeks to bring them into closer relations with the United Nations (Articles 32–54). And yet this has thus far not led to any structural changes in the United Nations to foster the growth of regional organizations, to encourage interactions among regional organizations, and to incorporate them within its structure, as has been proposed.[13] In addition, of the 135 nation-states that are members of the United Nations only a small proportion are actively involved in regional organizations. Thus, although the model underlying regionalism, as diagrammed in Figure 14.2, shows much promise of generating economic and normative integration in the international system, it is probably premature to assess its effectiveness in this regard. However, it is doubtful whether in the absence of an infrastructure of multinational, nongovernmental organizations of a profit and nonprofit variety, adequate system linkages can be forged among nation-

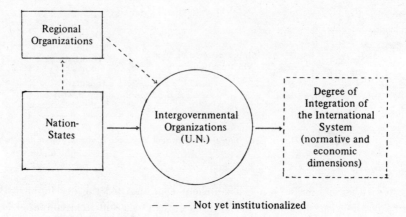

- - - - Not yet institutionalized

Fig. 14.2   Indirect, linear model of integration of the international system.

states, regional organizations, and intergovernmental organizations. This conjecture about the potential role of multinational nongovernmental organizations suggests a complex, nonlinear model of integration of the international system, to which I now turn.

With few exceptions social scientists engaged in the sociology of organizations, the sociology of occupations, and in the study of international relations have ignored the international nongovernmental organization, in general, and the international professional association, in particular.[14] By contrast, researchers in international business and international economics have recently begun to speculate about and inquire into the multinational corporation.[15] Under the circumstances, it should come as no surprise that the functions of these organizations in the international system have not yet been systematically studied, much less clarified. Our basic assumption is that because these types of organizations are simultaneously subnational, cross-national and multinational in character, they already provide or may provide in the future many significant linkages between nation-states, regional organizations, and intergovernmental organizations, thus contributing to the process of *normative, economic, organizational,* and *occupational* integration of the international system.

Instead of conceptualizing the international system with the aid of a direct or an indirect linear model of integration, as shown in Figures 14.1 and 14.2, a complex, nonlinear model with a variety of feedback loops is presented in Figure 14.3. Nation-states, particularly those that are highly industrialized, give rise to multinational corporations, that is, enterprises that develop production, research, and distribution facilities in various countries of the world. Nation-states also spawn a multitude of nongovernmental organizations—a high proportion of which consists of professional associations—that become federated at the international level. Some of these nongovernmental, nonprofit organizations are accorded official consultative status under the United Nations Charter (Article 71).

Each type of organization has mutual interactions with regional organizations. And although there are as yet few linkages between the multinational corporation and the international professional association, they are likely to develop in the future as these organizations discover their intersecting interests in common third parties such as nation-states, regional organizations, and various intergovernmental organizations. Occupations whose activities fall within multinational corporations and those that are organized into international occupational associations are growing in number and diversity. As these types of organizations proliferate, an increasing proportion of members within a growing population of occupations will perform part of their occupational roles in foreign contexts.

Collectively and cumulatively, multinational corporations, international nongovernmental organizations, and regional organizations interact with one another and with nation-states and intergovernmental organizations in such a manner as to increase the degree of integration of the international system along four dimensions: normative, economic, organizational, and occupational.

With the aid of our nonlinear model of integration of the international system (see Figure 14.3), I shall now consider in turn the growth and system linkages of multinational corporations and international professional associations.

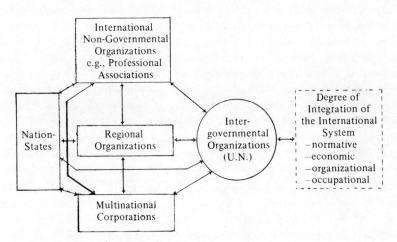

Fig. 14.3   Nonlinear model of integration of the international system.

GROWTH AND SYSTEM LINKAGES

MULTINATIONAL CORPORATIONS

Although the term "multinational corporation" has become current only in the past two decades, the phenomenon of international business operations is, of course, not new. "The first wave of foreign investment by manufacturing companies began in the closing decades of the nineteenth century, and continued, gathering strength, up to 1914. Much of it was American, not only in Canada . . . but also in Europe. . . . A few European companies were also beginning to expand abroad. Lever set up his first soap factory outside Britain in 1899, and Alfred Nobel was establishing armament factories all over Europe."[16] In the interwar years direct foreign investment scarcely grew. It was in the 1950s that the second great wave of business investment began. "Between 1950 and 1967 the United States' capital stake in European manufacturing industry increased more than ten times, to a figure of $9,800,000,000 in the latter year."[17] Other major industrial countries such as Britain, France, West Germany, Canada and Japan have also participated in the burgeoning growth of the multinational corporation. And it is anticipated by some students of international business that the involvement of the Soviet Union and other Communist countries in multinational corporations will increase in the coming decade.

One of the factors that stimulated the exponential growth of multinational corporations in the past decade is the emergence of the European Economic Community.[18] It is now recognized that American corporations have taken more advantage of the economic opportunities created by this regional organization than European corporations themselves, so much so that it has prompted Servan-Schreiber to deplore this trend and exhort his fellow Europeans to ward off the invasion of the American enterprise.[19]

Notwithstanding the rate of growth of multinational corporations, data on this type of firm, particularly of an organizational nature, are hard to come by. For the first time in its history, the Union of International Associations included a section on multinational corporations in the twelfth edition of its *Yearbook on International Organizations.*[20] In a preliminary survey the *Yearbook* reports 7,045 parent companies in 14 European countries and the United States with affiliates in one or more countries. Omitted from this survey are data on Japan, Canada, Communist countries, and others, presumably because they were unobtainable. A subset of these corporations with affiliates in 10 or more countries, totalling 590, is listed by name, which suggested the analysis presented in Table 14.1 of the nationality of the corporate headquarters of these organizations. Of these relatively large multinational corporations, 46 percent are American, 26 percent are British, 7 percent are German, and 7 percent are French, with the remainder distributed among eight European countries.

Table 14.1   Country of Corporate Headquarters of Multinational Firms by Number of Countries in which Affiliates are Located[a]

Country of HQ	Number of Countries in Which Affiliates Located							Total	%
	10–12	13–15	16–20	21–25	26–30	31–40	41+		
Denmark	3	—	—	—	—	—	1	4	1
Netherlands	8	2	4	2	2	—	1	19	3
U.K.	47	31	43	14	10	5	3	153	26
U.S.A.	92	59	40	37	18	14	9	269	46
Germany (FR)	18	10	9	1	2	2	—	42	7
Italy	—	2	2	4	1	1	—	10	7
Sweden	10	4	3	2	5	2	—	26	4
Switzerland	8	3	3	2	—	2	—	18	3
France	19	6	8	5	2	—	—	40	7
Belgium	3	2	1	—	—	—	—	6	1
Norway	—	—	1	—	—	—	—	1	b
Austria	—	2	—	—	—	—	—	2	b

[a] *Source:*   Union of International Associations, *Yearbook of International Organizations,* 12th edition, Brussels, Belgium, 1969, Table 3, p. 1203.
[b] Less than 0.5 per cent.

Underlying this uneven distribution of parent companies among countries is a differential in economic development. This is borne out by a statistically significant rank order correlation coefficient of 0.39 (Kendall tau) between the number of multinational firms in a country and its GNP per capita, shown in Table 14.2.

Although no consensus has yet been reached as to the definition of a multinational corporation, it is evident from the foregoing discussion that we are dealing with a relatively large firm with extensive resources in many countries. "A multinational company does more than import and export from its . . . home plant. It may do research in Germany, engineering design in Japan, and then manufacture in Taiwan, Italy, and Mexico to supply a hundred national markets, including the . . . [home] market in which its headquarters may be located."[21] To perform such highly complex operations in a multitude of differing environments it is necessary to transfer products, capital, managers, and other technical personnel as well as technology. The extensive transfer of the factors of production points to some of the effects—functional as well as dysfunctional—the multinational corporations are having on their host countries.

The most proximate effect is on the host countries in which affiliates are located. By employing nationals in various capacities, from unskilled laborers to professional and managerial personnel, the parent company creates many new employment and career opportunities in the host country. Although no

Table 14.2   Rank Order Correlation of Number of Multinational Firms of a Country and Its GNP per capita[a]

Country of HQ	Number of Multinational Firms	Rank Order	GNP/Capita (000 U.S. Dollars)	Rank Order
U.S.A.	2816	1	8.8	1
United Kingdom	1651	2	1.9	8.5
Germany	801	3	2.0	6.5
France	471	4	2.1	5
Switzerland	349	5	2.5	3
Netherlands	222	6	1.7	10
Sweden	219	7	2.7	2
Belgium	197	8	1.9	8.5
Italy	101	9	1.2	12
Denmark	82	10	2.3	4
Norway	78	11	2.0	6.5
Austria	38	12	1.4	11
Spain	9	13	0.8	13

$\tau = .39$, significant at .03.

[a] *Source:*   Union of International Associations, *Yearbook of International Organizations,* 12th ed., Brussels, Belgium, 1969, p. 1189.

overall figure is available as regards the number of people employed in various countries by the 7,045 multinational corporations reported in the *Yearbook,* one estimate for approximately 3,000 American parent companies is 5,000,000 foreign employees, a staggering number that exceeds the size of the labor force of many countries. And for 1,000 Swedish companies operating in 70 countries, the estimate is 200,000 foreign employees.[22] Invariably, employees in host countries are the recipients of new bodies of knowledge and skills essential to man the technology transferred by the parent company.[23] As one researcher on the transfer of technology observes:

Repeatedly, multinational companies operate training programs for host country nationals on a scale which is equivalent to adding a large technical high school in the country. They train nationals as operators, functional executives, and eventually as top managers. Trained people who leave such companies often seed domestic organizations with competent personnel and so diffuse know-how elsewhere in the economy.[24]

Apart from such beneficial effects on a segment of the host country's labor force and in turn on the standard of living of employees, the inflow of foreign capital potentially stimulates economic development. On the other hand, the outflow of capital from the home country of the parent corporation may have dysfunctions for the labor force of the home country. Trade union officials in the United States point to a net loss of 400,000 jobs over five years due to capital and technology transfers by multinational firms.[25] To counteract the threat posed by the internationalization of the corporation, trade unions are developing strategies for multinational union organization and collective bargaining.[26]

As for reciprocal effects, that is, of the host country on the parent company, several are noteworthy. First, the host country grants the company legal protection of incorporation. Second, it subjects the company to taxation that may be of economic as well as political importance to the host government. And third, as a condition for admission in the first place, particularly in a developing country, the parent company may be required to enter into a joint venture with the host government as a partner.

Less proximate effects of the multinational firm may be discerned in the changing relations between nation-states. By virtue of the fact that these firms operate production facilities in various countries, they stimulate trade among nation-states. And to the extent that they have recourse to vertical integration, international trade includes the transfer of products among affiliates of multinational firms.

... trade is no longer simply the result of national middlemen in one country interacting with importers in another. International firms have taken over, and there is every indication that international business is now the dominant factor in determining changes in the pattern of world exports as well as capital flows. . . . The movement of goods across national boundaries becomes foreign trade and exports even though the goods are only being transferred from one unit of the firm to another unit of the same firm . . . A large and growing share of world exports and changes in them are . . . accounted for by internal product movements of the international company.[27]

Moreover, because such firms often have similar operations in more than one country, there is a tendency over time to standardize technology.[28] There is also a tendency to standardize various policies, including wage scales. At least one international economist has suggested that such companies are exerting an influence in the direction of wage equalization, thus in the long run contributing to a reduction of one source of income inequality between nations.[29]

Yet another impact of these firms on the relationships between nation-states is the recent emergence of what Perlmutter has called the "transideological venture."[30] To modernize their industrial plant, Communist countries have encouraged their state-owned enterprises to enter into co-production contracts with Western firms. Such contracts usually provide for the cooperative manufacture of finished industrial products. A Western firm as a rule contributes a technologically sophisticated component which an Eastern firm uses to produce a finished product salable in highly competitive markets.[31] Several examples of East-West ventures are as follows:

(a) IKEA, a Swedish furniture chain, supplies to associates in Poland machinery and designs under its technical control for the semimanufacture of furniture, which is then shipped to Sweden for finishing by IKEA.

(b) The U.S. based Simmons Machine Tool Corporation has agreed with Czechoslovakia's Skoda to have the latter produce a line of specialized heavy equipment under the Simmons-Skoda trademark. The U.S. firm has exclusive sales rights in the Western Hemisphere, but there are no other territorial limitations for either side.

(c) Krupp of Essen, Germany, and the Csepel machine tool factory of Hungary have jointly developed digitally controlled short lathes based on German designs and drawings, which are to be exported to Germany and other markets.[32]

The benefits derived from such ventures are mutual. According to one scholar:

To the Western firm, they represent an opportunity to expand its market, while reducing to a minimum the drain on the limited hard currency funds of the East European partner. To the state enterprise in the East, a joint venture provides a practical opportunity to broaden its technological horizon, to study advanced management practices and to learn the contemporary marketing techniques of the commercial world.[33]

Whether such co-production contracts will become regularized, whether they will diffuse to such regional organizations as the European Common Market and the Council on Mutual Economic Aid and, in turn, have the effect of attenuating conflicts between Communist and non-Communist countries, only time will tell.

Operating within and between sovereign states exposes the multinational firm to various hazards, chief of which, of course, is nationalization by a host country. Other hazards do not affect all multinational firms alike. If the home government, as in the case of the United States, restricts expansion of enterprises through horizontal integration, such firms can be subject to antitrust law violations. Another restriction on the operations of multinational firms occurs when a home government, in exercising its rights of extraterritoriality, intervenes in the operations of a subsidiary in a host country. A case in point is when the United States, committed to a policy of preventing the proliferation of nuclear weapons, prohibits IBM's subsidiary in France from selling the French government a particular type of computer needed for the production of nuclear bombs.[34]

Such risks and restrictions, stemming from the fact that the multinational company is a citizen of several sovereign states, have prompted some scholars to speculate about a new legal status for this type of organization. Instead of being subject to various sovereignties, they advocate that the multinational firm be chartered, taxed, and controlled by an international organization, perhaps some agency of the United Nations.[35] If such a transformation in legal status were ever wrought, the United Nations and the international system obviously would be the primary beneficiaries. The United Nations would have a greatly expanded source of income from many thousands of companies to finance adequately its own activities as well as the urgent development programs of many poor member states, thus substantially strengthening the economic, organizational, and normative levels of integration of the international system.

An ongoing study, initiated in 1972 by the Economic and Social Council of the United Nations, is considering alternative mechanisms for international regulation of the multinational corporation. Various proposals are being entertained: "a multilaterally negotiated charter and an international organization . . . to administer it"; "a GATT-type of agreement for multinational corporations"; "some general agreement on a code of conduct for multinational corporations"; "an international company law . . . administered by a body of the signatory countries."[36]

In short, the multinationalization of the corporation has brought into being a new "transnational actor" that intentionally or unintentionally affects nation-states and relations among nation-states.[37] As Wells puts it:

Multinational business enterprises are clearly important transnational actors. They move large amounts of resources across international boundaries. Some of them have organizations that centralize decision-making processes so that these resources can be used to fulfil objectives that may be at variance with those of a particular country in which a subsidiary is located. These firms have at their disposal many tools for frustrating governmental policies, but the policies that they frustrate may be those of the host government or those of the home government.

Some multinational enterprises may seem to form alliances with governments. Yet, as they grow and begin to take a more global view, these alliances may prove to be no more lasting than those of nation-states. . . .

The fact that some of these organizations are operating in a coordinated fashion or that they even seem to have the potential for doing so makes them appear to governments as a challenge to their control. The result is a feeling of frustration on the part of governmental officials that results in occasional lashing out at foreign investment. . . . The desire of the government to retain control leads to attacks on enterprises that appear to challenge its sovereignty.[38]

At the level of home and host countries, multinational corporations have dysfunctional as well as functional effects. Issues have been raised in home countries concerning exploitation of cheap labor markets, tampering with national sovereignty, suppression of local entrepreneurial initiative, and promotion of "dependencia" or neocolonialism; in host countries the loss of jobs due to the outflow of capital has aroused protests from trade unions.

At the aggregate level of the international system, the multinational corporation may also have dysfunctional as well as functional effects. Attention has focused on "hot money" movements, effects of intracorporation transactions on international trade, and taxation of the multinational corporations.[39] Nonetheless, the unintended functional effects of the operations of multinational firms in fostering international integration merit equal attention: new patterns of economic interdependence among nation-states, new networks of relationships among enterprises, new roles for occupations, new patterns of transnational relationships among occupations, and new norms or incipient norms governing the transactions of multinational firms with nation-states, regional organizations, intergovernmental organizations, and international nongovernmental organizations.

INTERNATIONAL PROFESSIONAL ASSOCIATIONS

Although it antedates the multinational corporation, the international professional association is also essentially a twentieth century phenomenon. What is more, like the multinational corporation, its growth rate in the past two decades has been impressive.[40] It is by far the most numerous and probably the most influential type of organization in the class usually referred to as international nongovernmental organizations or INGOs. In a study of INGOs, Smoker found that the rate of formation between 1870 and 1960 increased exponentially, except for two slumps associated with World Wars I and II.[41] This finding very likely applies to international professional associations as well.

From the perspective of the sociology of occupations we are dealing with a group of occupations that are either full-fledged professions or in the process of professionalization.[42] In either case, professional associations are formed, in order to contribute to the fund of technical and systematic knowledge underlying an occupation, to promote an orientation of service to society rather than self-interest, and to increase autonomy in professional practice. Some professions, such as medicine, law, the ministry, and teaching, have ancient origins; others have come into being as a result of the emergence of industrialism and the rise of modern science and technology. In the transformation of an occupation in accordance with the two primary characteristics of a profession, i.e., possession of a body of abstract knowledge and commitment to an ideal of service, Wilensky suggests that it entails the following sequence of stages: (1) full-time performance of the occupational function; (2) establishment of a school that is not connected with a university; (3) establishment of a university school; (4) formation of a local professional association; (5) formation of a national professional association; (6) enactment of a licensing law; and (7) development of a formal code of ethics.[43]

Even if this sequence of stages is neither invariant nor exhaustive, we would expect as a rule that international professional associations would emerge following the formation of national professional associations. Thus, in the case of the engineering profession, local professional associations were established in various parts of England and Scotland during the latter part of the eighteenth century. In 1818 the first national professional association, the Institution of Civil Engineers, was established in England. Similar organizations came into existence in the United States in 1852 and in Canada in 1887. Almost a century later, several regional associations of engineering were founded, such as the European Federation of National Associations of Engineers and several highly specialized international associations, such as the World Power Conference. It was not until 1951 that the Union of International Engineering Organizations, an omnibus international association (referred to by Galtung as a super-INGO) was formed under the aegis of UNESCO.[44]

In the development of modern science it is also possible to identify a sequence of stages of professionalization which, however, differs in some respects from that of engineering. Already at the stage of the formation of local professional associations there is an active interest in facilitating the dissemination of knowledge and the collaboration among scientists across national boundaries. With the advent of modern science, learned societies and academies were founded, such as the Royal Society of London in 1662, the Académie des Sciences in 1666, and several decades later, the Berlin Academy of Sciences and the Academy of St. Petersburg. In an address commemorating the three-hundredth anniversary of Isaac Newton, the renowned Russian physicist, Kapitza, referred to Newton's active role in the affairs of the Royal Society. He observed that the Royal Society "in contrast to all academies, has still the character of a non-state society. . . . Since the very beginning of its existence, the Royal Society has maintained contact with many foreign scientists. Sometimes foreigners were elected as Foreign Members of the Society, including our scientists Euler, Kruzenshtern, Struve, Chebyshev, Mechnikov, Pavlov, Timiryazev, Golitsyn. . . . Since Newton's times, the Royal Society has maintained a lively contact with scientific societies the world over."[45]

Until the eighteenth century the scientific community was relatively small and communication was facilitated by the use of common languages—Latin and French—and a common core of knowledge since there were still few fields of specialization. With the growth of the scientific community and the multiplication of specialties in the nineteenth century, national and international associations arose. One of the oldest international scientific organizations, the

International Meteorological Committee, was founded in 1872. Numerous international associations were subsequently founded so that by the end of World War I there was a felt need for a new association to coordinate the multitude of scientific organizations, thus giving rise in 1919 to a super-INGO called the International Council of Scientific Associations.[46]

For a more precise assessment of the growth of different types of international professional associations, we turn again to the invaluable *Yearbook* of the Union of International Associations. Over the years this organization has struggled with the problem of classifying INGOs. In its twelfth edition, nineteen categories of organizations are presented from which I have selected the following six that appear to include a great variety of professional associations: Social Sciences; Law, Administration; Professions, Employers; Economics, Finance; Technology Science; Health, Medicine.[47] Examining various editions of the *Yearbook* yielded data, shown in Table 14.3, on the number of associations reported in each of these seven categories for a 60-year period, from 1909 to 1969.

The first noteworthy finding is that as of 1969 there were 757 international professional associations that constituted 50 percent of the population of 1,515 active INGOs for that year. In all likelihood this percentage underestimates the total number of INGOs that are in fact engaged in professional activities. A reclassification of the population of associations in the *Yearbook* would probably yield a higher percentage. Second, over a 60-year period these associations have increased about tenfold; and during the last 20 years they have increased about 169 percent. The average annual percentage increase in the past two decades is about 9 percent, a striking growth rate that approximates that of the multinational corporation.

The findings in Table 14.3 leave unanswered at least four important questions concerning the growth of international professional associations: (1) How many national professional associations and individual members are involved in these 757 INGOs? (2) How many nation-states indirectly participate in these associations? (3) How widely dispersed is nation-state participation geographically as well as ideologically? (4) What are the annual budgets of these associations?

A partial answer to the third question concerning the distribution of participation in these associations was gleaned from some data reported by the Union of International Associations. In Table 14.4, data on the nationality of the principal officials (viz., the president and secretary general) of the 757 associations are tabulated. Examining the column total of the number of officials for each of the 44 countries listed suggests a rather uneven distribution. France tops the list with 202 officials, and four countries (Guatemala, Peru, Malaysia, and the UAR) have but one official each. Thirteen of the 44 countries with a range of 202 to 11 officials are arrayed in Table 14.5. Also included in Table 14.5 is a

Table 14.3 Growth of International Professional Organizations[a]

Category	1909–1910	1951–1952	1956–1957	1966–1967	1968–1969	% Increase 1909–1969	% Increase 1951–1969	Average Annual % Increase Since: 1909	1951
Social Science	10	35	57	80	90	800	157	13.33	8.26
Law, Administration	13	30	28	48	54	315	80	5.25	4.21
Professions, Employers	2	34	67	93	105	5150	208	85.88	10.99
Economics, Finance	3	14	15	35	40	1238	185	20.55	9.77
Technology	8	35	36	83	102	1175	191	19.58	10.07
Science	21	56	69	137	152	623	171	10.38	9.02
Health, Medicine	16	77	100	173	214	1237	178	20.62	9.26
TOTAL	73	281	372	649	757	939	169	15.61	8.91

[a] Source: Union of International Associations, Yearbook of International Organizations, Brussels, Belgium; 1st, 4th, 6th, 11th and 12th editions.

Table 14.4 *Nationality of Principal Officials of International Professional Associations*

Country	Social Sciences		Law, Administration		Professions, Employers		Economics, Finance		Technology		Science		Health, Medicine		Total by Country	
	No.	%	No.	%	No.	%	No.	%	No.	%	No.	%	No.	%	No.	%
Africa																
Ghana	—		—		—		—		—		2	1	—		2	a
Nigeria	—		1	1	—		—		—		—		1	a	2	a
UAR	—		1	1	—		—		—		—		—		1	a
Others	—		1	1	2	1	—		1	1	2	1	—		6	1
America																
Argentina	3	2	—		—		—		1	1	1	a	3	1	8	1
Brazil	2	1	1	1	—		—		—		1	a	2	1	6	1
Canada	—		1	1	4	3	—		1	1	6	2	6	2	18	2
Chile	—		2	2	—		—		1	1	—		2	1	3	a
Columbia	1	1	—		—		—		1	1	—		—		4	a
Guatemala	—		—		1	1	1	2	—		—		1	a	1	a
Mexico	3	2	—		1	1	1		3	2	—		—		9	1
Peru	—		1	1	—		—		—		—		1	a	1	1
USA	22	16	12	14	7	4	10	19	5	4	36	15	41	14	133	12
Uruguay	—		—		2	1	—		1	1	—		4	1	7	1
Venezuela	—		—		1	1	—		—		—		1	a	2	a
Others	—		1	1	1	1	—		—		—		1	a	3	a

	No.	%	No.	%	No.	%	No.	%	No.	%	No.	%	No.	%	No.	%
Asia																
India	—	—	1	1	1	1	—		3	2	7	3	1	a	13	1
Israel	1	1	—	—	—		—		—		1	a	3	1	5	a
Japan	2	2	2	2	—		—		2	1	5	2	7	2	18	2
Malaysia	—	—	2	2	—		—		—		—		1	a	1	a
Phillipines	—	—	1	1	—		—		—		—		2	1	4	a
Others	—	—	—		—		—		—		2	1	1	a	4	a
Australasia																
Australia	—	—	—		—		—		1	1	2	1	2	1	5	a
New Zealand	1	1	—		—		—		—		1	a	—		2	a
Europe																
Austria	1	1	1	1	3	2	—		1	1	3	1	3	1	12	1
Belgium	16	12	10	12	22	14	11	20	11	8	14	6	22	7	106	9
Czechoslovakia	1	1	—		—		—		—		1	a	—		2	a
Denmark	5	4	—		4	3	—		2	1	8	3	10	3	30	3
Finland	—		15	18	1	1	10	19	—		1	a	—		2	a
France	21	16	—		38	24	—		31	23	31	13	56	19	202	18
Germany	6	4	5	6	6	4	2	4	12	9	9	4	10	3	50	4
Greece	1	1	1	1	1	1	—		—		—		—		3	a

Table 14.4 *(Continued)*

Country	Social Sciences		Law, Administration		Professions, Employers		Economics, Finance		Technology		Science		Health, Medicine		Total by Country	
	No.	%	No.	%	No.	%	No.	%	No.	%	No.	%	No.	%	No.	%
Europe— (continued)																
Hungary	—		—		—		—		1	1	1	a	1	a	3	a
Ireland	2	1	—		—		—		—		—		—		2	a
Italy	9	8	3	4	10	6	1	2	4	3	6	2	20	6	53	5
Luxembourg	—		2	2	—		—		—		—		—		2	a
Netherlands	13	10	2	2	9	6	7	13	9	7	20	8	14	5	74	7
Norway	—		—		1	1	1	2	2	1	5	2	4	1	13	1
Poland	2	1	—		—		—		1	1	1	a	—		4	a
Portugal	—		—		—		1	2	—		—		2	1	3	a
Rumania	1	1	—		—		—		1	1	1	a	1	a	4	a
Spain	1	1	2	1	1	1	—		1	1	1	a	5	2	11	1
Sweden	3	2	1	1	9	6	2	4	3	2	5	2	8	3	31	3
Switzerland	10	7	5	6	13	8	4	7	14	10	31	13	28	9	105	9
U.K.	4	3	13	15	22	14	4	7	22	16	4	2	37	12	138	12
U.S.S.R.	1	1	—		—		—		1	1	2	1	—		6	1
Yugoslavia	1	1	1	1	—		—		—		1	a	—		3	a
Others	1	1	—		1	1	—		—		—		—		4	a

a Less than .5 per cent.

Source: *International Associations,* 19 (May 1967), pp. 354–355.

Table 14.5   Rank Order Correlation of Number of Multinational Firms by Nationality of Corporate Headquarters and Number of Principal Officials of International Professional Associations by Nationality

Country	Number of Multinational Firms	Rank Order	Number of Principal Officials of International Professional Associations	Rank Order
U.S.A.	2816	1	133	3
United Kingdom	1651	2	138	2
Germany (FR)	801	3	50	8
France	471	4	202	1
Switzerland	349	5	105	5
Netherlands	222	6	74	6
Sweden	219	7	31	9
Belgium	197	8	106	4
Italy	101	9	53	7
Denmark	82	10	30	10
Norway	78	11	13	11
Austria	38	12	12	12
Spain	9	13	11	13

$\tau = .69$, significant at .0005

Source: Union of International Associations, *Yearbook of International Organizations,* 12th ed., Brussels, Belgium, 1969, p. 1189; *International Associations,* 19 (May 1967), pp. 354–55.

rank order for the same countries according to the number of multinational firms, which information is reproduced from Table 14.2. The resulting rank-order correlation coefficient of 0.69 (Kendall tau) between the number of multinational firms in a country and the number of principal officials of international professional associations is significant at 0.0005. It suggests that this dimension of participation in international professional associations is in part a function of economic development, since as the development of a country increases, so does the proportion of professionals in the labor force. Some evidence in support of this interpretation is provided by partialling out the effect of economic development (as reflected in GNP/capita), on the rank-order correlation coefficient. When this is done, the original Kendall tau of 0.69 is reduced to 0.55.

Given the number and growth rate of international professional associations, what effect are they having on the process of integration of the international system? In the absence of relevant systematic research, I shall approximate an answer to this question with the aid of the nonlinear model of integration of the international system presented in Figure 14.3. This entails mapping the interaction patterns of these organizations with other components of the international system. To do this, I shall first consider some of the activities of these organizations.

The principal functions of these associations are to convene congresses and other special meetings, publish conference proceedings and research reports, facilitate an exchange of visits, stimulate collaborate research, and the like. In organizing a congress, the international professional association depends upon the cooperation and assistance of its member organizations in various countries. Of the estimated 3,000 to 4,000 international congresses of INGOs held annually, involving at least one million people, probably one-half are convened by international professional associations.[48] It is, therefore, no wonder that the problems of planning and managing congresses have themselves become the subject of international congresses.[49]

On the occasion of the Fifth World Congress of Sociology in 1962, Lazarsfeld and Leeds pointed out that congresses perform three important interrelated functions: They afford an opportunity for personal contacts, stimulate joint research projects, and sensitize participants to theoretical perspectives of members from different countries.[50] That personal contacts, in turn, increase sensitivity to foreign perspectives was recently noted by Marshall, a former president of the International Sociological Association:

When representatives of countries in which the Marxist-Leninist philosophy prevails began to attend international Congresses and meetings in Western Europe, and when, under the auspices of Unesco, similar meetings were held in one or other of the countries of Eastern Europe, there was naturally some tension in the air, and mutual suspicion, tempered by curiosity and a genuine desire to understand. Friendly debate took place in its early stages, more as an exchange of views between two sides than as the free intercourse of independent minds. But by the early 1960's things had changed; the experience of attending fully representative international meetings had become a familiar one, and many of the participants were now old friends. Ideological differences still make themselves felt, of course, and they are sometimes stimulating and sometimes frustrating, but a big step forward has been made towards finding a common ground of scientific discourse on which all can meet without distinction of national origin or political allegiance. It remains to be seen whether, or within what space of time, this idea can be fully realized.[51]

The various functions performed by international professional associations tend to increase the bonds between the parent international organization, as it were, and the affiliated national organizations, that is, the national professional associations in the various nation-states. And by eliciting participation of national professional associations from various nation-states, the international professional association unintentionally creates a network of relationships between nation-states. This is especially true for those associations that are relatively free of ideology. Thus, for example, Kriesberg found that in health and science INGOs, in which consensus is presumably high, participation of professional associations from the United States and the U.S.S.R. is higher than in INGOs in which consensus is low, such as those dealing with international relations, art, and religion.[52]

There are also other links with nation-states, one of which is of considerable moment to the international professional association. The nation-state is the source of incorporation of this type of association. Depending on how liberal its incorporation law is, it affects the legal status of the association and more specifically such rights as owning property, holding funds, entering into contracts, transferring funds from one country to another, and the freedom of its representatives to travel over the world.[53] Another link with the nation-state that is quite different involves rendering expert professional guidance, as in the case of the International Statistical Institute, which has helped nations with their censuses to ensure high professional standards and comparable classifications.[54] In addition, a variety of medical associations such as the International Union Against Tuberculosis have aided nation-states in combatting diseases.[55]

Compared with the links between the international professional association and the nation-state, those with regional organizations are probably fewer. The European Economic Community has accorded consultative status to various INGOs, some of which would fall into the category of professional associations.[56] In all likelihood, *regional* professional associations such as the European Federation of National Associations of Engineers develop closer ties with the European Economic Community than do *international* professional associations. This may also be true in other regional communities such as the Latin American Free Trade Area and their corresponding professional associations, for example, the Pan-American Federation of Engineering Societies.

As regards the bonds between the international professional association and the multinational firm, they seem somewhat tenuous. Several international professional associations such as the international arbitration tribunals of the International Chamber of Commerce and Inter-American Commercial Arbitration Commission perform a direct service to multinational corporations by helping them resolve conflicts outside the framework of judiciaries of nation-states.[57] In view of the fact that there is a high overlap in membership of engineers and scientists in international professional associations and multinational firms and that both organizations struggle with the ambiguities of operating across national boundaries, one would expect a variety of types of interactions to develop among these organizations. It can reasonably be predicted that when each type of organization becomes fully cognizant of the other's existence—and the Union of International Associations already is, witness the addition of a section of multinational corporations in its *Yearbook*—new patterns of interaction will emerge that may significantly increase the level of organizational and possibly also normative integration of the international system.

By far the most highly developed interaction patterns are observable between international professional associations and intergovernmental organizations or IGOs, as they are customarily abbreviated. This is to be expected since some INGOs have for a long time sought to influence the decisions of IGOs. The fact that INGOs are accorded consultative status to the Economic and Social Council of the United Nations and to its many specialized agencies, such as the International Labor Organization, the World Health Organization, and UNESCO, has encouraged the growth of INGOs—so much so that it has been asserted that "Every IGO . . . has at least one counterpart in the INGO world."[58] The reciprocal effects between these two types of organizations have been extensive. Some international professional associations have been instrumental in the formation of some IGOs, and, in turn, some IGOs have created some international professional associations.

According to an official of the International Labor Organization:

. . . medical specialists from different countries gradually formed contacts, and so there came into being the International Committee on Industrial Medicine which before the War Organized International Congresses on Industrial Diseases, the first in Milan in 1908. . . .

The year 1900 saw the foundation at Paris of the International Association for [Labor Legislation], with headquarters at Basle, which represented the first attempt to make an international collection of legislative measures relating to industry, and which arranged for the holding of meetings where problems of hygiene and pathology were discussed resulting in the drawing up of Conventions, such as the Berne Convention relative to the prohibition of the use of phosphorus in the making of matches (1908).

Such tentative suggestions and efforts paved the way for the post-war creation of the International Labour Organization. . . .[59]

The unique role of UNESCO in creating and reorganizing various international associations in the social sciences and in establishing two super-INGOs, namely, the International Social Science Council and the International Committee for Social Science Documentation, is well known.[60] Less well known, and of considerable importance, is the fact that UNESCO provides subventions to various international professional associations to supplement their meager budgets.

In short, there is already in being an elaborate network of relationships between international professional associations and various components of the international system.

SOME HYPOTHESES ON THE INTEGRATION
OF THE INTERNATIONAL SYSTEM

In our discussion of alternative models of the international system, we observed the operation of forces conducive to normative and economic integration. From our analysis of the growth and interaction patterns of multinational corporations and international professional associations, two additional forces appear to be developing—organizational and occupational integration. The many thousands of multinational firms have elaborate relationships with numerous other business organizations in different countries as well as with many host-government agencies and international governmental organizations. Similarly, the hundreds of international professional associations have developed in the past few decades an intricate network of relationships, as we have seen, with various components of the international system.

Each type of organization is generating, wittingly or unwittingly, loyalties—organizational in the case of the multinational firm and occupational in the case of the international professional association—that cut across national boundaries. In effect, both types of organizations are socializing their members into the values of transnationalism, that is, identifying with the objectives of "an organization which transcends national borders, without comprising nations; it is subnational, yet international."[61] Thus, we hypothesize that these emergent loyalties are raising the level of integration of the international system. To test this general hypothesis would require operationalizing the nonlinear model of the international system presented in Figure 14.3 and gathering systematic data—a complex undertaking that would challenge the ingenuity of a team of social scientists. By way of illustrating the potential value of such an endeavor, I shall consider several more specific propositions applicable to both types of organizations.

It is frequently asserted that multiple affiliations breed multiple loyalties, and if the latter transcend national boundaries they can act as a break on international conflict.[62] Human networks "based on cross-cutting professional and other interests, can contribute to the stability and integration of the international system by counteracting tendencies toward polarization along national lines. They create a vested interest in maintaining a pluralistic and peaceful international order."[63] Assuming these are plausible, if not validated, propositions, do they have any implications for the organizational design and functioning of multinational corporations and international professional associations? In Table 14.6, I have identified several structural and motivational variables in terms of which comparative research on both types of organizations could be undertaken that would throw light on their actual or potential impact on the level of economic, organizational, occupational, and normative integration of the international system.[64]

Table 14.6   Within and Between Comparisons of Multinational Corporations and International Professional Associations on Structural and Motivational Dimensions

Dimension	Multinational Corporation	International Professional Association
A. Structural		
1. Nationality of stockholders and/or Principal Officers and HQ staff	One or few vs. many nations	One or few vs. many nations
2. Authority	Centralized vs. Decentralized	Collective vs. individual membership
3. Interface functions of HQ's staff	Low vs. High ratio of boundary/ non-boundary personnel	Low vs. High ratio of boundary/ non-boundary personnel
4. Movement of HQ staff between parent organization and affiliates	Low vs. High rate of rotation of managerial and technical personnel	Low vs. High rate of visits from HQ to member organization and vice versa
B. Motivational		
1. Local vs. Cosmopolitan Orientation	Loyalty to affiliate vs. loyalty to parent company or both	Loyalty to national association vs. loyalty to international association or both
2. Attitude toward legal status of the organization	Preference for incorporation under nation-state vs. under U.N. or other international agency	Preference for incorporation under nation-state vs. under U.N. or other international agency

The first structural variable—nationality of the owners of the firm and of the principal officers and staff of the association's headquarters—is undoubtedly of critical importance. Most multinational corporations—so defined in terms of the nature of their operations in various countries—are owned by stockholders from one or a few nations. "A firm owned and managed multinationally would, almost by definition, be transnational . . ." that is, its "members develop loyalties toward the firm . . . which transcend national identities so that national bias in decision making virtually disappears."[65] Rupert, chairman of Rothmans of Pall Mall Group of Companies, argues in favor of a particular scheme of multinational ownership, according to which "at least 50 per cent of the shares in each separate member company is held locally by the nationals of the host country, and the chairman and majority of Board Members in every country are citizens of that country."[66] Another multinationally owned company, ADELA, invests in Latin America in partnership with local capital.[67] By contrast, General Motors insists on 100 percent ownership "so that the full benefits of central control can be obtained."[68]

A comparison of multinationally owned companies, such as Rupert describes, with those owned uninationally or binationally would presumably disclose important differences in interaction patterns with other organizations in their environments. A comparison could also be made of international professional associations whose officers and staff are drawn predominantly from one or a few nations versus many nations to discover, for example, whether in the latter case the network of interorganizational relations is more developed.

Hypothesis 1. Multinational ownership of corporations and multinational leadership of international professional associations, as contrasted with uninational ownership of corporations and uninational leadership of international professional associations, result in denser networks of interorganizational relationships and, in turn, contribute to a higher level of organizational and economic integration of the international system.

The second structural variable, authority, is frequently discussed in the literature on the multinational firm but rarely, if ever, investigated. Arguments are advanced for the relative merits in a particular industry of a centralized versus a decentralized structure of authority.[69] General Motors, Massey-Ferguson, and Krupp are cited as examples of highly centralized companies.[70] On the other hand, Bata in discussing communication in his shoe manufacturing company—84 companies in eight countries—describes it as a decentralized firm.[71] If a comparative study were undertaken of centralized versus decentralized firms, preferably in the same industry to control for type of products manufactured and technology employed, we could learn the consequences of contrasting authority structures for the network of interorganizational relationships.

A functionally equivalent variable of authority structure in the case of the international professional association is whether the unit of membership is the individual professional or a collectivity, such as a national, regional, or international association. In most international professional associations—in fact, in most INGOs, in general—the unit of membership is the national association.[72] As it happens, the International Sociological Association has recently amended its statutes to provide for individual membership in the interests of democratizing and internationalizing the profession (as well as enlarging its sources of revenue).[73] Clearly, there is sufficient variation among professional associations as regards unit of membership to warrant a study of its effects, for example, on loyalty to the association as well as loyalty to the profession.

Hypothesis 2. Decentralized authority in multinational corporations and individual membership in international professional associations, as contrasted with centralized authority and collective membership, result in a denser network of interorganizational relationships and in a higher degree of organizational and occupational loyalty, thus contributing to a higher level of organizational, occupational, and normative integration of the international system.

The third structural variable deals with a mechanism for handling the interface problems of an organization. Some members of the staffs of corporate and association headquarters specialize in functions pertaining to boundary relations of an organization whereas others specialize in internal functions. This suggests that a ratio of boundary/nonboundary personnel could be constructed for both types of organizations to inquire into, for example, whether there is a positive relationship between this ratio and the size of the organizational network of a given organization.[74]

Hypothesis 3. The higher the ratio of boundary/nonboundary personnel in the headquarters of multinational corporations and international professional associations, the higher the level of coordination among affiliates and, in turn, the higher the level of organizational integration of the international system.

The last structural variable is concerned with the degree of movement of headquarters staff between a parent organization and its affiliates. Do firms with a high rate of rotation of managerial and technical personnel from headquarters to affiliates evidence greater internal coordination of functions and more effective patterns of interaction with other organizations than firms having a low rate of rotation of such personnel? A comparable question might be asked in the case of professional associations but in view of the nonhierarchical relationship between member organizations and international headquarters, it would be important to establish the rates of visits from both directions.

Hypothesis 4. The higher the rate of movement of headquarters personnel from parent organization to affiliates, the greater the degree of coordination in multinational corporations and international professional associations and, in turn, the higher the level of organizational integration of the international system.

The four structural variables briefly reviewed above would in all likelihood be related to the type of motivational orientation of the members of an organization. A structural pattern partaking of transnationalism (i.e., multinational ownership of the firm—principal association officers and staff drawn from many nations; decentralized authority structure of the firm—individual membership in the association; high ratio of boundary/nonboundary personnel in headquarters staff; high rate of movement between headquarters staff of parent organization and affiliates) would engender a motivational orientation of transnationalism.

A "cosmopolitan" as opposed to a "local" orientation in the firm would mean either greater loyalty to the parent company or a dual loyalty to the parent company as well as its affiliate; similarly, it would mean a greater loyalty to the international association than to the national association or a dual loyalty. As regards the second motivational variable—attitude toward the legal status of the organization—a preference for incorporation under the auspices of an international agency rather than a nation-state would reflect a transnational identification.

Hypothesis 5. The higher the level of transnational orientation of the members of multinational corporations and international professional associations, the higher the level of normative, organizational, and occupational integration of the international system.

Clearly, the four structural variables and the two motivational variables listed in Table 14.6 merely illustrate the range of organizational variables that could provide the basis for comparative research on the impact of these types of organizations on the level of economic, organizational, occupational, and normative integration of the international system. The hypotheses presented above indicate some of the relationships between the structural and motivational variables, on the one hand, and the integration variables, on the other, that are in need of systematic empirical testing.

CONCLUSION

Two types of transnational organizations have thus far largely eluded the awareness of researchers in organization theory. This oversight need not continue because the multinational corporation and the international professional association provide strategic sites for coming to grips with two frontier problems in the field: (1) the analysis of interorganizational relations; and (2) the cross-cultural comparison of organizations.

The field of international relations has likewise not done justice to these types of organizations. Many scholars in this field evidently assume that these types of organizations, although operating in the interstices of nation-states, have little consequence for the future development of the international system.[75]

In subscribing to this view they may be overlooking the potential of these organizations for cumulatively and unanticipatedly transforming the international system. This conception of the international system is not unique to international relations specialists. Some futurologists such as Kahn and Wiener, in their broad-gauged analysis of various possible structural modifications of the international system within the next three decades, likewise ignore such nongovernmental international organizations as the multinational firm and the international professional association.[76]

Yet the dynamism of the international system of the future may derive from a force for integration intimated in Durkheim's famous preface to the second edition of *The Division of Labor,* entitled, "Some Notes on Occupational Groups."

. . . as advances are made in history, the organization which has territorial groups as its base steadily becomes effaced. . . . These geographical divisions are, for the most part, artificial and no longer awaken in us profound sentiments. The provincial spirit has disappeared never to return; the patriotism of the parish has become an archaism that cannot be restored at will . . . the State is too remote from individuals; its relations with them too external and intermittent to penetrate deeply into individual consciences and socialize them within. Where the State is the only environment in which men can live communal lives, they inevitably lose contact, become detached. . . . A nation can be maintained only if, between the State and the individual, there is intercalated a whole series of *secondary groups* near enough to the individuals to attract them strongly in their sphere of action and drag them, in this way, into the general torrent of social life. We have just shown how occupational groups are suited to fill this role, and that is their destiny.[77]

Broadly conceived, the multinational corporation and the international professional association may be collectively performing the solidary functions at the international level that Durkheim envisioned for occupational groups within the nation. To those social scientists who discern an intellectual challenge in the study of these organizations, the task that lies ahead is at least fourfold:

1. Developing a model, akin to the nonlinear model of integration diagrammed in Figure 14.3, which copes with the complexity of the linkages among the components of the international system;
2. Operationalizing various dimensions of integration of the international system, such as the four identified in the model presented in Figure 14.3.
3. Designing an information system on various components of the international system—including multinational corporations and international professional associations—of the kind recently described and proposed by Judge;[78]

4. Providing for longitudinal data collection on (a) the various system linkages—such as those postulated in our nonlinear model of integration—and (b) the various dimensions of integration of the international system.

By studying the interaction patterns of these organizations to ascertain whether they are in fact creating networks of people transcending the nation-state and generating new levels of normative, economic, organizational, and occupational integration, social scientists can discover whether Durkheim's anticipations are valid for the international system.

NOTES

1. See, for example, William M. Evan, "An Organization-set Model of Interorganizational Relations," in M. F. Tuite, M. Radnor, and R. K. Chisholm, eds., *Interorganizational Decision Making* (Chicago: Aldine, 1972), pp. 181–200; Paul M. Hirsch, "Processing Fads and Fashions: An Organization-Set Analysis of Cultural Industry Systems," *American Journal of Sociology* 77 (January 1972): 639–59; Gordon B. Baty, William M. Evan, and Terry W. Rothermel, "Personnel Flows as Interorganizational Relations," *Administrative Science Quarterly* 16 (December 1971): 430–43; Herman Turk, "Interorganizational Networks in Urban Society: Initial Perspectives and Comparative Research," *American Sociological Review* 35 (February 1970): 1–19; Eugene Litwak, with the collaboration of Jack Rothman, "Toward the Theory and Practice of Coordination Between Formal Organizations," in William R. Rosengren and Mark Lefton, eds., *Organizations and Clients*, (Columbus, Ohio: Charles E. Merrill, 1970), pp. 137–86; Michael Aiken and Jerald Hage, "Organizational Interdependence and Intra-Organizational Structure," *American Sociological Review* 33 (December 1968): 912–29; James D. Thompson, *Organizations in Action* (New York: McGraw-Hill Book Co., 1967); William M. Evan, "The Organization-Set: Toward a Theory of Inter-organizational Relations," in James D. Thompson, ed., *Approaches to Organizational Design* (Pittsburgh: University of Pittsburgh Press, 1966), pp. 173–91; F. E. Emery and E. L. Trist, "The Causal Texture of Organizational Environments," *Human Relations* 18 (1965): 21–32.

2. J. Boddewyn and R. Nath, "Comparative Management Studies: An Assessment," *Management International Review* 10 (January, 1970): 9–11; William M. Evan ed., "Organizational Research Across National and Cultural Boundaries," *International Studies of Management and Organization* 5 (Spring, 1975): 3–113.

3. Steven J. Brams, "The Search for Structural Order in the International System: Some Models and Preliminary Results," *International Studies Quarterly* 13 (September 1969): 254–80; Edward Miles, "Organizations and Integration in International Systems," *International Studies Quarterly* 12 (June 1968): 196–224; Johan Galtung, "On the Future of the International System," *Journal of Peace Research* 4 (1967): 305–33.

4. Kjell Skjelsbaek, "The Growth of International Nongovernmental Organizations in the Twentieth Century," in Robert O. Keohane and Joseph S. Nye, Jr., eds., *Transnational Relations and World Politics*. (Cambridge, Mass.: Harvard University Press, 1972), pp. 70–92.

5. *Ibid.*; Louis T. Wells, "The Multinational Business Enterprise: What Kind of International Organization?" in Robert O. Keohane and Joseph S. Nye, Jr., eds., *Transnational*

Relations and World Politics. (Cambridge, Mass.: Harvard University Press, 1972), pp. 97–114.

6.   Evan, "The Organization-Set," p. 188.

7.   Michael Haas, "A Functional Approach to International Organization," *Journal of Politics* 27 (August 1965):498–517; Evan Luard, ed., *The Evolution of International Organizations* (New York: Frederick A. Praeger, 1966).

8.   Haas, "A Functional Approach," p. 505.

9.   Johan Galtung, "A Structural Theory of Integration," *Journal of Peace Research* 5 (1968): 375–95.

10.   Ernst B. Haas, *The Uniting of Europe* (Stanford, Cal.: Stanford University Press, 1958); J. J. Schokking, and Nels Anderson, "Observations on the European Integration Process," *Journal of Conflict Resolution* 4 (December 1960):385–410.

11.   Kazimierz Grzybowski, *The Socialist Commonwealth of Nations: Organizations and Institutions* (New Haven: Yale University Press, 1964).

12.   J. S. Nye, Jr., "Comparing Common Markets: A Revised Neo-Functionalist Model," *International Organization 24* (Autumn 1970): 796–835.

13.   William M. Evan, "Transnational Forums for Peace," in Quincy Wright, William M. Evan, and Morton Deutsch, eds., *Preventing World War III: Some Proposals* (New York: Simon and Schuster, 1962), pp. 396–98.

14.   [14] Lyman C. White, *International Non-Governmental Organizations* (New Brunswick, N.J.: Rutgers University Press, 1951); Evan, "Transnational forums"; Paul Smoker, "A Preliminary Empirical Study of an International Integrative Subsystem," *International Association 17* (November 1965): 638–46; Galtung, "A Structural Theory of Integration"; Robert C. Angell, "The Growth of Transnational Participation," in Louis Kriesberg, ed., *Social Processes in International Relations: A Reader* (New York: John Wiley & Sons, 1968), pp. 226–245; Louis Kriesberg, "U.S. and U.S.S.R. Participation in International Non-Governmental Organizations," in Louis Kriesberg, ed., *Social Processes in International Relations: A Reader.* (New York: John Wiley & Sons, 1968), pp. 466–485.

15.   Richard D. Robinson, *International Management* (New York: Holt, Rinehart and Winston, 1967); Richard D. Robinson, "Ownership Across National Frontiers," *Industrial Management Review* 11 (Fall 1969): 41–61; Raymond Vernon, "Multinational Enterprise and National Sovereignty," *Harvard Business Review* 45 (March–April 1967): 156–72; Laurence E. Fouraker and John M. Stopford, "Organizational Structure and the Multinational Strategy," *Administrative Science Quarterly* 13 (June 1968): 47–64; Charles P. Kindleberger, *American Business Abroad* (New Haven: Yale University Press, 1969); Jack N. Behrman, *Some Patterns in the Rise of the Multinational Enterprise* (Chapel Hill: University of North Carolina, Graduate School of Business Administration, 1969); Jack N. Behrman, "Multinational Corporations, Transnational Interest and National Sovereignty," *Columbia Journal of World Business 4* (March–April 1969):15–21; Sidney E. Rolfe, *The International Corporation* (Paris: International Chamber of Commerce, 1969); Howard V. Perlmutter, "The Tortuous Evolution of the Multinational Corporation," *Columbia Journal of World Business 4* (January–February 1969):9–18.

16.   Caroline M. Miles, "The International Corporation," *International Affairs* 45 (April 1969): 259.

17.   *Ibid.,* p. 259.

18.   Rolfe, *The International Corporation,* p. 11; O. Kaufmann, "Diverging Structural Patterns in the Development of American and European Firms," *Management International Review* 10 (January 1970): p. 103.

19. J. J. Servan-Schreiber, *The American Challenge* (New York: Atheneum, 1968).

20. Union of International Associations, *Yearbook of International Organizations* (Brussels: Union of International Associations, 1969), p. 1189–1214.

21. David P. Rutenberg, "Organizational Archetypes of a Multi-National Company," *Management Science* 16 (February 1970): B-337.

22. Kindelberger, *American Business Abroad,* p. 88.

23. Rolfe, *The International Corporation,* pp. 48–60.

24. James Brian Quinn, "Technology Transfer by Multinational Companies," *Harvard Business Review* 47 (November-December 1969):152.

25. György Adam, "New Trends in International Business: Worldwide Sourcing and Dedomiciling," (paper presented at International Conference on Multinational Corporations, May, 1971 at Queen's University of Belfast; Anonymous, "Why Unions Fear the Multinationals," *Business Week* (December 19, 1970): 95–98.

26. Karl Casserini, "The Challenge of Multi-National Corporations and Regional Economic Integration to the Trade Unions, Their Structure and Their International Activities," Hans Gunter, ed., *Transnational Industrial Relations* (London: Macmillan, 1972), pp. 70–96.

27. Stephen H. Robock and Kenneth Simmonds, "International Business: How Big Is It—The Missing Measurements," *Columbia Journal of World Business* 5 (May–June 1970): 6, 7, 13.

28. Behrman, *Some Patterns in the Rise of the Multinational Enterprise,* pp. 74–75; Kindelberger, *American Business Abroad,* pp. 84–86.

29. Kindelberger, *American Business Abroad,* pp. 34–35, 188.

30. Howard V. Perlmutter, "Emerging East-West Ventures: The Transideological Enterprise," *Columbia Journal of World Business* 4 (September–October 1969): 39–50.

31. Leon M. Herman, "COMECON Reform Depends on Trade with World Markets," *Columbia Journal of World Business* 4 (July–August 1969): 51–58.

32. Perlmutter, "Emerging East-West Ventures," pp. 39–40.

33. Herman, "COMECON Reform," p. 53.

34. Kindelberger, *American Business Abroad,* p. 43.

35. Richard D. Robinson, *International Business Policy* (New York: Holt, Rinehart and Winston, 1964), p. 224.

36. United Nations, Department of Economic and Social Affairs, *Multinational Corporations in World Development.* (New York: United Nations, 1973).

37. Raymond Vernon, "Multinational Business and National Economic Goals," in Robert O. Keohane and Joseph S. Nye, Jr., eds. *Transnational Relations and World Politics* (Cambridge, Mass.: Harvard University Press, 1972); Wells, "The Multinational Business Enterprise."

38. Wells, "The Multinational Business Enterprise," p. 113.

39. United Nations, *Multinational Corporations in World Development,* pp. 60–65.

40. Skjelsbaek, "Growth of International Nongovernmental Organizations."

41. Paul Smoker, "A Preliminary Empirical Study of an International Integrative Subsystem," *International Associations* 17 (November 1965): 638–46.

42. William M. Evan, "The Engineering Profession: A Cross-Cultural Analysis," in Robert Perrucci and Joel E. Gerstl, eds., *The Engineers and the Social System* (New York: John Wiley & Sons, 1969), pp. 100–101.

43. Harold L. Wilensky, "The Professionalization of Everyone?" *American Journal of Sociology* 70 (September 1964): 137–58.

44. Galtung, "On the Future of the International System."

45. D. ter Haar, ed., *Collected Papers of P. L. Kapitza,* vol. III (New York: Pergamon Press, 1967), p. 139.

46. Organization for Economic Cooperation and Development, *International Scientific Organizations* (Paris: Organizations for Economic Cooperation and Development, 1964), pp. 11–16.

47. Union of International Associations, *Yearbook,* p. 13.

48. A. J. N. Judge, "Evaluation of International Organizations," *International Associations* 21 (March 1969): p. 144.

49. Union of International Associations, *International Congress Organization: Theory and Practice* (Brussels: Union of International Associations, 1961).

50. Paul F. Lazarsfeld, and Ruth Leeds, "International Sociology as a Sociological Problem," *American Sociological Review* 27 (October 1962): 732–41.

51. UNESCO, International Organizations in the Social Sciences (Paris: UNESCO, 1966), p. 11.

52. Kriesberg, "U.S. and U.S.S.R. Participation," p. 471.

53. Raymond Spencer Rodgers, *Facilitation Problems of International Associations* (Brussels: Union of International Associations, 1960).

54. Nathan Keyfitz, "Government Statistics," *International Encyclopedia of the Social Sciences* (New York: Macmillan Co. and the Free Press, Vol. 6, 1968), p. 235.

55. White, *International Non-Governmental Organizations,* p. 171.

56. Schokking and Anderson, "Observations on the European Integration Process," pp. 392–95.

57. American Management Association, *Resolving Business Disputes* (New York: American Management Association, 1965), pp. 134–78.

58. Rodgers, *Facilitation Problems of International Associations,* p. 8.

59. White, *International Non-Governmental Organizations,* pp. 171–72.

60. UNESCO, *International Organization.*

61. Galtung, "On the Future of the International System," p. 313.

62. Robert A. LeVine, "Socialization, Social Structure and Intersocietal Images," in Herbert C. Kelman, ed., *International Behavior* (New York: Holt, Rinehart and Winston, 1966 pp. 45–69).

63. Herbert C. Kelman, "The Role of the Individual in International Relations: Some Conceptual and Methodological Considerations," *Journal of International Affairs* 24 (1970): 15–16.

64. Paul Smoker, "Nation-State Escalation and International Integration," in Louis Kriesberg, ed., *Social Processes in International Relations: A Reader* (New York: John Wiley & Sons, 1968), p. 501.

65. Richard D. Robinson, "Joint Ventures or Transnational Business?" *Industrial Management Review* 6 (Fall 1964): p. 61.

66. A. Anthony Rupert, "Communicating in a Growing International Organization," in Conseil International pour l'Organisation Scientifique, *Management and Growth* (Rotterdam: Rotterdam University Press, 1967), p. 231.

67. Duncan M. Oppenheim, "Organizational Growth Through International Cooperation," in Conseil International pour l'Organisation Scientifique, *Management and Growth* (Rotterdam: Rotterdam University Press, 1967), p. 116.

68. *Ibid.,* p. 117.

69. *Ibid.*

70. *Ibid.,* Rupert, "Communicating in a Growing International Organization."

71. Thomas Bata, "Communicating in Growing International and Decentralized Organizations," in Conseil International pour l'Organisation Scientifique, *Management and Growth* (Rotterdam: Rotterdam University Press, 1967), pp. 227–30.

72. White, *International Non-Governmental Organizations,* p. 7.

73. William M. Evan, "International Sociological Association and the Internationalization of Sociology," *International Social Science Journal,* 27 (1975): 385–93.

74. Evan, "The Organization-Set"; "An Organization-Set Model"; See Chapters 9 and 11 of the present volume.

75. Judge, "Evaluation of International Organizations," p. 143.

76. Herman Kahn and Anthony J. Wiener, *The Year 2000.* New York: Macmillan Co., 1967), pp. 359–85.

77. Emile Durkheim, *The Division of Labor in Society,* trans. George Simpson (Glencoe, Ill.: The Free Press, 1960), pp. 27–28.

78. Judge, A. J. N. "Information Systems and Inter-organiztional Space," *Annals of the American Academy of Political and Social Science* 393 (January 1971): 47–64.

CHAPTER 15

Culture and
Organizational Systems

Since World War II, two independent developments have occurred which, if they interact in the future, may greatly facilitate the growth of cross-cultural research on organizations.[1] I refer to the internationalization of the firm, on the one hand, and to the internationalization of the social sciences, on the other.[2] With the rapid growth in the number, size, and scope of operations of multinational corporations (MNCs), social scientists in theoretical as well as applied disciplines have turned their attention to this phenomenon. Although the spate of publications on MNCs is still largely conjectural in nature, some exploratory as well as systematic studies have been initiated. It is not unreasonable to view the field of comparative management as a response to the emergence of the modern MNC. For example, the pioneering studies of *Management in the Industrial World* by Harbison and Myers and *Managerial Thinking* by Haire, Ghiselli, and Porter may be read against the background of the marked expansion of MNCs in the postwar period.[3]

The parallel trend of the internationalization of the social sciences, particularly sociology, political science, and psychology, has its roots in the mandate of UNESCO. To promote educational and scientific cooperation among members of the United Nations, UNESCO in the late 1940s and early 1950s was instrumental in establishing international professional associations in the various

---

This is a revised version of a paper prepared for a seminar on "Cross-Cultural Organization Studies" held in the Netherlands and Belgium in April, 1973.

social sciences.[4] Organizations such as the International Sociological Association and the International Political Science Association interrelate the constituent national professional associations, convene world congresses, stimulate formal and informal communication among social scientists, and encourage cross-cultural comparative research. Publications reflecting this development, to name but a few, are: Buchanan and Cantril's *How Nations See Each Other*, Merritt and Rokkan's *Comparing Nations*, and Marsh's *Comparative Sociology*.[5]

In light of these two trends, the efforts among organizational researchers to clarify the relationship between culture and organizational systems has theoretical as well as practical import. Theoretically, it would help explain some of the variation observed or observable in the functioning of organizational systems in different societies; and the accompanying research process would in itself contribute to the internationalization of the social sciences. Practically, such research can be both illuminating and helpful to MNCs that are often handicapped by their failure to grasp the intangible and subtle aspects of the diverse cultural environments in which they operate.

Thus far, the field of organization theory has failed to come to grips with the cultural component of the environments in which organizations are embedded. This is not at all surprising because there are formidable conceptual and methodological obstacles to overcome. The fact that MNCs operate in a multitude of cultural and societal settings not only poses a challenge to executives but also provides an opportunity for organizational researchers to use this world-wide organizational phenomenon as a vehicle for research.

The purpose of this chapter is threefold: (1) to outline an organizationally relevant model of culture; (2) to appraise some research in light of the model; and (3) to consider a paradigm for future research.

TOWARD AN ORGANIZATIONALLY RELEVANT MODEL OF CULTURE

The concept of culture, notwithstanding its ambiguity, is used by laymen and social scientists alike in their efforts to explain behavior. That such explanations are often based on impressions and stereotypes does not deter the layman any more than it does the social scientist from using the concept. Two examples will illustrate the point.

An American executive, interviewed in the Harbison and Myers study in an unnamed foreign country, says:

Somehow or other, we just can't get the local people here to assume any responsibility. They won't make decisions unless you tell them what decisions to make. They hate to take the rap if anything goes wrong. They always want to be in a position to put the blame on someone else if the going gets tough. I think there is some cultural trait in these people which makes them shun responsibility. We will always need Americans here in the key jobs because these local people just don't have what it takes to be a good manager.[6]

In Crozier's study of two French organizations, he states that Frenchmen have a fear of dependence and avoid face-to-face relationships:

Face-to-face dependence relationships are hard to bear in the French cultural setting, because Frenchmen have a very absolute conception of authority. While they cannot bear omnipotent authority, they feel that it is indispensable if any kind of cooperative activity is to succeed.[7]

Such examples by laymen as well as social scientists can be multiplied. Compounding the confusion is the state of the art in the conceptualization of culture.

DEFINITIONS OF CULTURE

Anthropologists have theoretical jurisdiction, so to speak, over the concept of culture. Beginning with Tyler's enumerative definition in 1871, anthropologists have developed in the intervening years innumerable definitions. In their monograph, *Culture: A Critical Review of Concepts and Definitions,* Kroeber and Kluckhohn cite no less than 164 definitions of culture, classified in such categories as descriptive, historical, normative, psychological, structural, and genetic.[8]

A small sample of the types of definitions is as follows:[9]

BENEDICT: . . . that complex whole which includes all the habits acquired by man as a member of society.

BOAS: Culture embraces all the manifestations of social habits in a community, the reactions of the individual as affected by the habits of the group in which he lives, and the products of human activities as determined by these habits.

MALINOWSKI: It [culture] obviously is the integral whole consisting of implements and consumers' goods, of constitutional charters for the various social groupings, of human ideas and crafts, beliefs and customs.

KROEBER: . . . the mass of learned and transmitted motor reactions, habits, techniques, ideas, and values—and the behavior they induce—is what constitutes *culture.*

SAPIR: . . . culture . . . is . . . the socially inherited assemblage of practices and beliefs that determines the texture of our lives.

MEAD: Culture means the whole complex of traditional behavior which has been developed by the human race and is successively learned by each generation.

PARSONS: Culture . . . consists in those patterns relative to behavior and the products of human action which may be inherited, that is, passed on from generation to generation independently of the biological genes.

KLUCKHOHN AND KELLY: By culture we mean all those historically created designs for living, explicit and implicit, rational, irrational, and nonrational, which exist at any given time as potential guides for the behavior of men.

MORRIS: A culture is a scheme for living by which a number of interacting persons favor certain motivations more than others and favor certain ways rather than others for satisfying these motivations. The word to be underlined is 'favor.' For preference is an essential of living things . . . To live at all is to act preferentially—to prefer some goals rather than others and some ways of reaching preferred goals rather than other ways. A culture is such a pattern of preferences held by a group of persons and transmitted in time.

In an effort to reduce the buzzing confusion and bring about a truce between warring anthropologists and sociologists, Kroeber and Parsons set forth a distinction between the concept of culture and the concept of social system:

We suggest that it is useful to define the concept culture for most usages more narrowly than has been generally the case in the American anthropological tradition, restructuring its reference to transmitted and created content and patterns of values, ideas and other symbolic meaningful systems as factors in the shaping of human behavior and in the artifacts produced through behavior. On the other hand, we suggest that the term *society*—or more generally, *social system*—be used to designate the specifically relational system of interaction among individuals and collectivities.[10]

Is it any wonder that Ajiferuke and Boddewyn, in a review of 22 studies of comparative management invoking culture as an explanation, found that only two authors ventured a definition of this much abused concept[11]

THE NORMATIVE DIMENSION

In the interest of facilitating research on the relationship between culture and organizational systems, I shall select what Kroeber and Kluckhohn refer to as the "normative" dimension of culture, namely, that which deals with values and norms—conceptions of what is desirable and prescriptions or proscriptions of conduct—that guide or affect behavior. This dimension of culture has been the focus of research attention by several social scientists in recent years, especially Osgood, Triandis, and Geertz.[12] According to Triandis, "subjective culture" is "a cultural group's characteristic way of perceiving the man-made part of his environment. The perception of rules and the group's norms, roles, and values are aspects of subjective culture."[13] For Geertz,

Cultural patterns—religious, philosophical, aesthetic, scientific, ideological—are "programs"; they provide a template or blueprint for the organization of social and psychological processes, much as genetic systems provide such a template for the organization of organic processes.[14]

A related perspective on culture is the theory of variation in value orientations by Kluckhohn and Strodtbeck, a rather abstract but empirically suggestive framework of ideas. According to Kluckhohn and Strodtbeck:

Value orientations are complex but definitely patterned (rank ordered) principles, resulting from the transactional interplay of three analytically distinguishable elements of the evaluative process—the cognitive, the affective, and the directive elements—which give order and direction to the ever-flowing stream of human acts and thoughts as these relate to the solution of "common human" problems.[15]

Embedded in this definition is a set of assumptions comprising a theory of culture. First, there is a limited number of "common human" problems, five of which have tentatively been singled out by Kluckhohn and Strodtbeck as follows:

1. What is the character of innate human nature (human nature orientation)?
2. What is the relation of man to nature (and super-nature) (man-nature orientation)?
3. What is the temporal focus of human life (time orientation)?
4. What is the modality of human activity (activity orientation)?
5. What is the modality of man's relationship to other men (relational orientation)?[16]

A second underlying assumption is that there is a limited range of variation to the solutions of common human problems. Third, the variation in value orientations in any society results in the co-occurrence of *dominant* and *variant* value orientations. The authors' fivefold classification of value orientations—associated with the five common human problems—and the range of variation postulated for each—is presented in Table 15.1.

It is noteworthy that Parsons and Shils, in their analysis of "cultural systems" as a component of their general theory of action, accord special significance to value orientations. They conceive of value orientations as *"strategically* the most important parts of culture for the organization of systems of action."[17]

To test the differences and similarities in the rank orderings of value orientations in five cultures, Kluckhohn and Strodtbeck constructed a research instrument that consisted of delineating types of life problems and then posing alternatives that are indicators of their theoretically formulated classes of value

Table 15.1   The Five Value Orientations and the Range of Variations Postulated for Each

Orientation	Postulated Range of Variations					
Human Nature	Evil		Neutral	Mixture of Good and Evil	Good	
	Mutable	Immutable	Mutable	Immutable	Mutable	Immutable
Man-nature	Subjugation to nature		Harmony with nature		Mastery over nature	
Time	Past		Present		Future	
Activity	Being		Being in becoming		Doing	
Relational	Lineality		Collaterality		Individualism	

Source: Florence Rockwood Kluckhohn and Fred L. Strodtbeck, *Variations in Value Orientations* (New York: Row, Peterson and Co., 1961), p. 12.

orientations. Unlike most of the contributions to the literature on values, the Kluckhohn-Strodtbeck study is one of the few important theories and research studies that may be of help in advancing our understanding of the relationship between culture and organizational systems. In defining value orientations as "principles" guiding human conduct, they direct our attention to a much-needed research perspective on the relation between culture and organizational phenomena.

From the vantage point of organizational systems, culture is but one of three classes of environmental factors that generate positive and negative inputs to the focal organization, increasing or diminishing uncertainties concerning the mobilization of various resources.[18] The other two environmental components—which I shall mention only in passing in this context—are social-structural and interorganizational in nature. To be sure, these three elements of an organization's environment are only analytically distinguishable.

Culture, in its normative dimension, comprises the "hidden" or "silent", if not "turbulent", component of any organizational environment. It is the most encompassing of the three components in that it influences the role definitions of all members of a society. The social-structural component consists of the status-sets of organizational members in their capacities as role occupants outside the boundaries of the focal organization, that is, in the various institutional spheres of society. The status-set profiles of all organizational members are of crucial import for their role performance within the focal organization. This is especially true of what Parsons calls "institutional" personnel, who are concerned with overall policy making, with the legitimation of the organization, and with the mobilization of resources; and of "managerial" personnel, who mediate between the demands of the "technical" and "institutional" personnel.[19]

The interorganizational component of the organization's environment is the most proximate and most directly affects not only what inputs are obtained but also how the outputs are channeled to various "markets."[20] From a microeconomics-of-the-firm perspective, how competitive the interorganizational environment is and what adaptational strategies are developed to cope with market uncertainties—for example, price collusion, vertical integration of production, interlocking directorates, mergers, and the like—will determine the organizational systems' effectiveness.

How the three environmental components are interrelated is an intricate theoretical and empirical problem. For the present, suffice it to say that they may be conceived as forming three concentric circles around the focal organization, with the first circle being the interorganizational system, the second, the cultural system, and the third, the social-structural system (see the diagram in the Preface).

CULTURE, ORGANIZATIONAL PROCESSES, AND ORGANIZATIONAL SYSTEM OUTPUTS

How can the "cultural circle" be conceptually linked to the organizational system so that the relationship between value orientations and organizational behavior can be investigated? Although the organizational system can be partially broken down into individual behavior, for the purposes of this duscussion I shall consider only the aggregate level at which organizational processes and organizational system outputs are crucial. From a process standpoint there are at least three generic and recurrent activities in all organizations: recruitment of personnel, socialization of personnel, and communication among members in connection with role performance. As regards organizational system outputs, let us assume one or more measures of effectiveness in terms of one or more input-output (O/I) ratios. Now, can we with the aid of Kluckhohn and Strodtbeck's (K–S) theory—or some other value theories, such as Parsons' pattern variables and Hall's proxemics theory—predict organizational-process-behavior profiles and O/I levels of organizational system outputs?[21] My guess is that it is possible. For instance, in terms of the K–S theory, a rank ordering of three of their value orientations—time, relational, and man-nature—might lead to the following hypotheses. A value-orientation profile of:

Future preferred *over* Present preferred *over* Past,
Individualism preferred *over* Collaterality preferred *over* Lineality, and

Mastery-over-nature preferred *over* Harmony-with-nature preferred *over* Subjugation-to-nature,

would be conducive to an organizational recruitment policy based on universalistic rather than particularistic criteria, a formal rather than an informal socialization process, a high frequency of multidirectional instead of unidirectional communication, and finally, high levels of organizational systems outputs. A more detailed formulation of the hypotheses is presented in Table 15.2.

The details of these particular hypotheses are not as important as the concern with explicitly testing for the empirical relationship between dimensions of value orientations on the one hand and dimensions of organizational system behavior on the other. An independent measure of each class of variables avoids the tendency toward tautological explanations: inferring cultural effects from some observed behavior and inferring behavioral effects from some observed cultural attribute. In addition, a test of hypotheses such as these would ideally be undertaken in two contexts: (1) with a representative sample

Table 15.2   Some Hypotheses on the Relationship Between Value Orientations and Organizational System Processes and Outputs

| Value Orientations[a] | Organizational Processes | | | Organizational Outputs |
	Recruitment	Socialization	Communication	Output/Input Ratios (Economic and Noneconomic)
1. Time				
Fu > Pr > Pa	Universalistic	Formal	Multidirectional	High
vs.				
Pa > Pr > Fu	Particularistic	Informal	Unidirectional	Low
2. Relational				
I > C > L	Universalistic	Formal	Multidirectional	High
vs.				
L > C > I	Particularistic	Informal	Unidirectional	Low
3. Man-Nature				
M > H > S	Universalistic	Formal	Multidirectional	High
vs.				
S > H > M	Particularistic	Informal	Unidirectional	Low

[a] See the Kluckhohn-Strodtbeck notation, which uses abbreviations for the types of value orientations (shown in Table 15.1) and the "greater than" symbol to denote "preferred over."

of members of one or more organizations (preferably a sample of organizations) whose rank orderings would be elicited on the K–S value orientation schedule; and (2) with a representative sample of the members of the society as a whole in which the focal organization(s) is(are) located. If a comparison of the organizational with the societal samples were to establish that matched subjects on occupation, education, age, etc., are similar in their value rank orderings, then this would point to the impact of dominant values of the societal culture on the organizational members. However, if the samples differed, it would suggest that the value orientations of the organizational members are reflecting variant values and that there is evidence of what might be called an "organizational subculture."

PROBLEMS OF MEASURING CULTURE

In view of the multidimensional definitions of culture, it is not surprising that relatively few efforts have been made to measure any of its dimensions. Then, too, anthropologists, the principal custodians of this concept, rely almost exclusively on nonparticipant observation and intensive interviewing of informants, and thus have not felt a need for research instruments such as psychologists, sociologists, and other social scientists are accustomed to using. Consequently, there are few research instruments that purport to measure the normative aspects of culture and that can be adapted to cross-cultural research on organizational systems.

A major obstacle to the design of such instruments is to reduce culture-bound assumptions to a minimum—if eliminating such assumptions is impossible. The principle of "functional equivalence" in measuring instruments, developed by Przeworski and Teune in the course of a four-nation study of values in community leadership, will probably prove useful for future designers and redesigners of research instruments measuring cultural variables.[22] According to this principle, it is neither necessary nor advisable to use identical sets of questions in diverse cultural settings if they do not have identical meanings. One can use different items in different cultures provided one has evidence that different indicators refer to functionally equivalent concepts such as norms and values. For example, if one is interested in measuring how people evaluate time in the course of a day's activities, one obviously need not ask whether respondents own watches, look at clocks, or ask others for the time in the course of the day. Functionally equivalent indicators might be questions pertaining to checking a sundial, looking at the position of the sun in the sky, and feelings about lateness in performing a work role or in meeting people.

One of the more promising research instruments for studying the normative aspects of culture is the K–S value orientation schedule designed for a study of five cultures in the Southwestern part of the United States (Navajo, Zuni,

Mormon, Texan, and Spanish-American). This schedule is incomplete in that one of five theoretically postulated value orientations, human nature, was never operationalized. Although it already has been adapted for use in Japan, further cross-cultural applications will probably hve to consider the problem of "functional equivalence."[23] For example, the item in the schedule pertaining to well arrangements is not likely to be perceived as a salient life problem in some urban industrial cultural settings.[24]

Another promising type of instrument is the semantic differential. Selecting concepts as stimuli for analyzing respondents' values may prove more reliable and valid than constructing direct questions or hypothetical situations. The choice of concepts and bipolar scales would require extensive cross-cultural pretesting. The evaluative factor in the semantic differential provides a measure of the ranking of values, as some studies by Osgood, Triandis, and others suggest.[25] Whether it can be used to elicit the rank orderings of value orientations based on the K–S theory is worth exploration.

Another research instrument with some conceptual kinship to the K–S schedule is the Allport-Vernon-Lindzey Values Test.[26] Based on Spranger's theory of psychological types, the instrument measures six value orientations: theoretical, economic, social, political, religious, and aesthetic.[27] Subjects are asked to answer 45 questions with 150 alternative answers, 25 referring to each of six values. The major drawback with this instrument is that from its inception it has been oriented to the captive audiences of college undergraduates. Hence it is so culture-bound in the content of its items as to be wholly unusable with noncollege-educated subjects, let alone with people in relatively exotic cultures such as Rhodesia or Yemen. Clearly, the average members of such societies could not respond to such items in the research instrument as:

13. To what extent do the following famous persons interest you?
   a) Florence Nightingale
   b) Napoleon
   c) Henry Ford
   d) Galileo

21. Are you more interested in reading accounts of the lives and works of men such as (a) Alexander, Julius Caesar, and Charlemagne; (b) Aristotle, Socrates, and Kant?

A similar criticism can be made of Morris's "Ways of Life" questionnaire.[28] Whether such instruments can be redesigned for the purposes of cross-cultural research on organizational systems remains to be seen.

In short, the development and adaptation of instruments measuring value orientations not only presuppose some theoretical framework about cultural variables but also require attention to standard problems of reliability and validity, as well as sensitivity to the especially difficult problems of reducing culture-bound assumptions to a minimum.

AN APPRAISAL OF CROSS-CULTURAL RESEARCH

In light of the organizationally relevant model of culture formulated above, what contributions have past studies made to our understanding of the influence of "cultural variables" on organizations? On the basis of a preliminary study of the literature, I am persuaded by Roberts' conclusion based on her assessment of no less than 526 publications:

Most of the studies . . . are not well thought out. Empirical work . . . is not well guided by theoretical underpinnings, data are often weak, and conclusions are difficult to comprehend.[29]

Comparative studies invoking culture are often implicit rather than explicit in their treatment of the concept and are impressionistic rather than being based on any measuring instrument that has any intersubjective reliability. Virtually no effort is made to distinguish between an independent measure of culture and an independent measure of organizational behavior. Instead, culture—without specifying any dimensions thereof—tends to be inferred from almost any contrast observed among organizations in different countries. Finally, no systematic comparisons are made between the cultural values of a sample of the population of a country and of a sample of employees of one or more organizations in order to ascertain the impact of "societal culture" versus "organizational subculture" on organizational system variables. To provide a basis for these rather sweeping criticisms, I shall briefly consider several self-designated cross-cultural organizational studies.

In his well-known study, *The Bureaucratic Phenomenon,* Crozier observes a dearth of informal relationships and a "general fear of face-to-face relationships" among the employees of the Clerical Agency and the Industrial Monopoly.

These traits . . . appear, to a large extent at least, to be rather well-established French cultural traits. We cannot rely, unfortunately, upon neat comparative tests, since empirical comparative studies remain to be made. . . . The few serious anthropological studies made provide significant and concordant details in the same direction. Lucien Bernot and René Blancard, in their study of a village near Paris, note, for example: "Already among children, one discusses one of the characteristic features of Nouville's life, the absence of groups. One does not find among the children any gang or clique within the village" [30]

Crozier asserts in passing that the French cultural traits he observed: "contrast strongly with the usual picture of the American industrial shop climate as it has been portrayed since the first experiences of the Hawthorne testroom."[31] This assertion illustrates the absence of an explicit cross-cultural comparison, which is also true of other studies in this area, for example, the study by England and Koike of the "personal value systems" of Japanese managers.[32]

By contrast, there are studies comparing two or more countries that purport to be studying a cultural difference when in fact they are not. In a study of perceptions of need satisfaction of blue-collar workers in two glass factories (in the United States and Mexico, belonging to the same parent company), Slocum claims to have isolated culture as an independent variable.[33] The observed differences in perceptions of need satisfaction are attributed to the independent variable of culture which, however, he merely postulates but does not investigate. On the other hand Zurcher, Meadow, and Zurcher did measure a significant dimension of cultural values in Mexico and the United States, namely, Parsons' contrast between a universalistic versus a particularistic value orientation.[34] However, they did not relate the cultural difference they observed to any organizational system variable.

Whitehill and Takezawa, in a study of samples of American and Japanese workers, have observed some significant attitudinal differences regarding authority, work, and identification with the company.[35] They have not, however, ascertained whether the differences are a function of organizational subculture or societal culture, nor whether they are related to any objective role performance measures. Similarly, Whyte and Williams have identified what appears to be a culturally significant contrast between samples of American and Peruvian employees: among Peruvians, a positive correlation between perceived closeness of supervision and general satisfaction with the supervisor, but a negative correlation between these variables among American workers.[36] What difference this alleged cultural difference makes in organizational behavior is not investigated.

National differences were observed by Haire, Ghiselli, and Porter in the attitudes underlying management practices, the managerial role, and need satisfaction of 3,641 managers in 14 countries. Of all the attitude differences observed, 25 percent of the variance was associated with national differences that, after further analysis, prompted the authors to infer that "the cultural influence is present and substantial. It is not overwhelming."[37] However, they did not directly measure cultural values nor did they inquire into any organizational system consequences of the national differences of managers' attitudes. Nor did Sirota and Greenwood, in their study of work goals of employees of subsidiaries of one multinational company in 25 different countries, relate any observed attitudinal differences to organizational behavior. They conclude that there is

. . . considerable similarity . . . in the goals of employees around the world. This finding has an extremely important policy implication: since the goals of employees are similar internationally, corporate policy decisions, to the extent that they are based on assumptions about employee goals, can also be international in scope? . . . In this respect, it would be interesting to determine how much of the difficulty experienced in managing employees in other countries is due not to cultural differences at all but, rather, to the automatic and psychologically self-serving assumption of differences that in reality, may be minor or even non-existent.[38]

The warranty for such a conclusion does not yet exist. The authors evidently overlook the possible impact of the organizational subculture of a multinational corporation in generating a high level of similarly in the attitudes of employees toward work goals. As Hesseling observed:

. . . a dominant pattern of common multinational sub-culture seems to strike many researchers. . . . From multinational headquarters certain values, attitudes and assumptions seem to be disseminated which form a layer upon the national culture and create a new identity for the bearers.[39]

Finally, Graves, in a preliminary report on a study of managerial behavior in an English and a French subsidiary of a multinational firm, seems to be sensitive to the problems of measuring cultural values and organizational behavior.[40] He refers to having used interviews, the diary method, and a business game. Since no statistical results are reported, it is impossible to ascertain whether he has in fact made a contribution to the much-confused problem area of the relation of cultural values to organizational behavior.

A PARADIGM FOR FUTURE RESEARCH

In view of the criticisms leveled at past research purporting to measure "cultural effects", how can an application of the proposed model overcome various deficiencies? The answer admittedly is far from clear; nevertheless, I shall venture to list the desiderata of a research strategy that I think has a high probability of reliably and validly measuring cultural effects. First, a multinational or better still, a multicultural research team is necessary to eliminate as many unconscious cultural assumptions and biases as possible on the part of the researchers themselves. Second, a multidisciplinary team is essential to measure how much of the variance in the structure and performance of organizational systems is attributable to cultural variables, as compared with other variables such as psychological, structural, interorganizational, and societal. Third, one of the principal problems confronting a research team would be to adapt or construct research instruments, such as those mentioned above, that will tap cultural variables with a high level of reliability and validity. Fourth, the research instruments measuring cultural variables would be used on (1) a representative sample of the population of a society and on (2) a representative sample of the members of one or more organizations in order to measure societal culture as well as organizational subculture. Fifth, in designing sample surveys, at least two modes of cross-societal comparisons would be used: (1) intrasystemic comparisons, namely, matching domestic or national firms with those of foreign subsidiaries, distinguishing wholly owned subsidiaries from joint ventures and controlling for various structural and industrial characteristics; and (2) intraorganizational comparisons, namely, subsidiaries of comparable size, function, and technology in different societies.[41] Sixth, in addition to sample surveys, at least two other complementary research methods would be desirable: laboratory and field experiments to test major causal hypotheses suggested or supported by sample surveys, and also to test the impact of cultural variables on organizational behavior and organizational system performance.[42] And finally, Berrien's nine principles, which he labels "A Super-Ego for Cross-Cultural Research," should guide the entire research process. They deserve to be quoted:

The best cross-cultural research is that which: (1) engages the collaborative efforts of two or more investigators of different countries, each of whom is (2) strongly encouraged and supported by institutions in their respective countries to (3) address researchable problems of a common concern not only to . . . science . . . but (4) relevant to the social problems of our times. Such collaborative enterprises would begin with (5) the joint definition of the problems, (6) employ comparable methods, (7) pool data that would be "owned" by collaborators jointly who are free to (8) report their own interpretations to their own constituents but (9) obligated to strive for interpretations acceptable to the world community of scholars.[43]

CONCLUSION

The underlying assumption of our organizationally relevant model of culture is that an "appreciable" amount of the variance in the structure and performance of organizational systems is accountable by cultural variables. However, a significant omission in our discussion thus far is a consideration of the possible influence of time on the hypothesized relationship between culture and organizational systems. In effect, the model and the accompanying research paradigm are cross-sectional in nature. Synchronically it seems justified to view culture as an independent variable or as a constraint on organizational systems. However, if we were to view the relationship over a time-slice, say two decades or roughly a generation, we might discover a feedback loop between organizational systems and culture. In other words, a diachronic research design may identify the influence that organizational systems have on reshaping some elements of culture, notwithstanding its high resistance to change. If such a feedback loop were discovered, it is very likely to be an indirect rather than a direct feedback loop. Mediating between organizational systems and culture are social-structural mechanisms, namely, patterns of interaction comprising the status-sets of employees in the various institutional spheres of society—the family, the economy, the polity, the religious and educational systems, and so on.

From this perspective, it is not wholly farfetched to regard multinational corporations and international professional associations as two significant, albeit unintentional, agents of social-structural and cultural change in the years to come. These organizations not only transcend the boundaries of most nation-states but also have at their helm economic, scientific, educational, and professional elites who in turn have access to political elites. In addition, these organizations have a high commitment to economic, technological, and scientific innovation. In the course of pursuing their respective organizational goals, be it profit, truth, or human welfare, they are unintentionally contributing to the secular process of modernization.

If the convergence theory of modernization is valid, social, political, and cultural differentiation among societies will decrease, in due course, as modernization increases throughout the world.[44] To the extent that the predicted course of change occurs, the amount of cultural variance among societies will diminish, and in turn the impact of culture on organizational systems will decline.

NOTES

1. William M. Evan, ed., "Organizational Research Across National and Cultural Boundaries," *International Studies of Management and Organization* 5 (Spring 1975): 3–113.

2. William M. Evan, "Multinational Corporations and International Professional Associations," *Human Relations* 27 (1974): 587–625. See Chapter 14 of the present volume.; William M. Evan, "International Sociological Association and the Internationalization of Sociology," *International Social Science Journal* 27 (1975): 385–93.

3. Frederick Harbison and Charles A. Myers, *Management in the Industrial World* (New York: McGraw-Hill Book Co., 1959); Mason Haire, Edwin G. Ghiselli, and Lyman W. Porter, *Management Thinking: An International Study* (New York: John Wiley & Sons, 1966).

4. Evan, "International Sociological Association"; see Chapter 14 of the present volume.

5. William Buchanan and Hadley Cantril, *How Nations See Each Other* (Urbana, Ill.: University of Illinois Press, 1953): Richard L. Merritt and Stein Rokkan, eds. Comparing

Nations: *The Use of Quantitative Data in Cross-National Research* (New Haven: Yale University Press, 1966); Robert M. Marsh, *Comparative Sociology* (New York: Harcourt, Brace, and World, 1967).

6. Harbison and Myers, *Management in the Industrial World,* p. 388.

7. Michel Crozier, "The Cultural Determinants of Organizational Behavior," in Anant R. Negandhi, ed., *Environmental Settings in Organizational Functioning* (Kent, Ohio: Comparative Administration Research Institute, Kent State University, 1970), p. 57.

8. A. L. Kroeber and C. Kluckhohn, *Culture: A Critical Review of Concepts and Definitions* (Cambridge, Mass.: Peabody Museum of American Archaeology and Ethnology, Harvard University, 1952)

9. *Ibid.,* pp. 42–56.

10. A. L. Kroeber and Talcott Parsons, "The Concepts of Culture and of Social Systems," *American Sociological Review* 23 (1958): 582–83.

11. Musbau Ajiferuke and J. Boddewyn, "Culture and Other Explanatory Variables in Comparative Management Studies," *Academy of Management Journal* 35 (1970): 153–63.

12. Charles E. Osgood, "Semantic Differential Technique in the Comparative Study of Cultures," *American Anthropologist* 66 (1964): 171–200; and Osgood, "Exploration in Semantic Space: A Personal Diary," *Journal of Social Issues* 27 (1971): 5–64; Harry C. Triandis, *The Analysis of Subjective Culture* (New York: Wiley-Interscience, 1972); Clifford Geertz, "Ideology as a Cultural System," in David E. Apter, ed., *Ideology and Discontent* (New York: The Free Press, 1964).

13. Triandis, *The Analysis of Subjective Culture,* p. 4.

14. Geertz, "Ideology as a Cultural System," p. 62.

15. Florence R. Kluckhohn and Fred L. Strodtbeck, *Variations in Value Orientations* (New York: Row, Peterson, 1961).

16. *Ibid.,* p. 11.

17. Talcott Parsons and Edward A. Shils, "Values, Motives and Systems of Action," in Talcott Parsons and Edward A. Shils, eds., *Toward a General Theory of Action* (Cambridge, Mass.: Harvard University Press, 1951), p. 59.

18. William M. Evan, "The Organization-Set: Towards a Theory of Interorganizational Relations," in James D. Thompson, ed., *Approaches to Organizational Design* (Pittsburgh: University of Pittsburgh Press, 1966), pp. 173–91; and Evan, "An Organization-Set Model of Interorganizational Relations," in Matthew Tuite, Roger Chisholm, and Michael Radnor, eds., *Interorganizational Decision Making* (Chicago: Aldine, 1972). See Chapters 9 and 11 in the present volume.

19. Talcott Parsons, *Structure and Process in Modern Societies* (Glencoe, Ill.: The Free Press, 1960), pp. 59–60.

20. See Chapters 9 and 11 of the present volume.

21. Talcott Parsons, *The Social System* (Glencoe, Ill.: The Free press, 1951); Edward T. Hall, *The Hidden Dimension* (New York: Doubleday, 1966).

22. Adam Przeworski and Henry Teune, *The Logic of Comparative Social Inquiry* (New York: Wiley-Interscience, 1970), pp. 113–31.

23. William Caudill and Harry A. Scarr, "Japanese Value Orientations and Culture Change," *Ethnology* (1962): 53–91.

24. Kluckhohn and Strodtbeck, *Variations in Value Orientations,* pp. 80–81.

25. Osgood, "Semantic Differential Technique"; Triandis, *The Analysis of Subjective Culture.*

26. G. W. Allport, P. E. Vernon, and G. Lindzey, *Study of Values: Text Booklet,* 3rd ed. (Cambridge: Riverside Press, 1960).

27. Edward Spranger, *Types of Men* (Halle, Germany: Max Niemeyer Verlag, 1928).

28. C. Morris, *Varieties of Human Value* (Chicago: University of Chicago Press, 1956), pp. 15–19.

29. Karlene H. Roberts, "On Looking at an Elephant: An Evaluation of Cross-Cultural Research Related to Organizations," *Psychological Bulletin* 74 (1970): 327–50.

30. Michel Crozier, *The Bureaucratic Phenomenon* (Chicago: University of Chicago Press, 1964) p. 216.

31. *Ibid.,* p. 215.

32. George W. England and R. Koike, "Personal Value Systems of Japanese Managers," *Journal of Cross-Cultural Psychology* 1 (1970): 21–40.

33. John W. Slocum, Jr., "A Comparative Study of the Satisfaction of American and Mexican Operatives," *Academy of Management Journal* 14 (1971): 89–96.

34. Louis A. Zurcher, Arnold Meadow, and Susan Lee Zurcher, "Value Orientation, Role Conflict, and Alienation from Work: A Cross-Cultural Study," *American Sociological Review* 30 (1965): 539–48.

35. Arthur M. Whitehill and Shin-ichi Takezawa, *The Other Worker: A Comparative Study of Industrial Relations in the United States and Japan* (Honolulu: East-West Center Press, 1968).

36. William F. Whyte and Lawrence K. Williams, "Supervisory Leadership: An International Comparison," *Proceedings of the Thirteenth International Management Congress* (1963): 481–88.

37. Haire, Ghiselli, and Porter, *Management Thinking,* p. 9.

38. David Sirota and Michael J. Greenwood, "Understand Your Overseas Work Force," *Harvard Business Review* 49 (1971): 60.

39. Pjotr Hesseling, "Organizational Behavior and Culture: The Case of the Multinational Enterprise, *Quarterly Journal of Management Development* 2 (1971): 8.

40. Desmond Graves, "A Cross-Cultural Comparison of Managerial Behavior in England and France," *International Studies of Management and Organization* 2 (1972): 105–16.

41. Anant R. Negandhi and Bernard C. Reimann, "Task Environment and Some Structural Characteristics: A Cross-Cultural Study," *Quarterly Journal of Management Development* 2 (1971): 39–52.

42. William M. Evan, ed., *Organizational Experiments* (New York: Harper and Row, 1971).

43. F. K. Berrien, "A Super-Ego for Cross-Cultural Research," *International Journal of Psychology* 5 (1970): 33–39.

44. Alex Inkeles, "Industrial Man: The Relation of Status to Experience, Perception, and Value," *American Journal of Sociology* 66 (1960): 1–31; Wilbert E. Moore, *Social Change* (Englewood Cliffs, N.J.: Prentice-Hall, 1963).

CHAPTER 16

Social Structure and Organizational Systems

Organizations are of course always part of a larger social structure of the society in which they occur. There is necessarily a certain variability among organizations which is a function of this wider social matrix; an American organization is never quite like a British one, even though they are nearly cognate in function.[1]

Most organizational researchers would probably agree with Parsons' assertion. Yet because of the interdisciplinary nature of organization theory, they would not necessarily agree that studying the relation of social structure to organizations was of either theoretical or practical significance. For one thing, the concept of "social structure" is at least as ambiguous and perplexing as the concept of "culture," which we dealt with in Chapter 15. Small wonder, then, that virtually no systematic empirical research has been undertaken on this subject, notwithstanding the appearance of several suggestive and enlightening theoretical, substantive, and methodological analyses.[2]

Second, a microlevel perspective (i.e., a concern with intraorganizational phenomena involving reliance on individual, interpersonal, group, or subunit levels of analysis) is still common among many organizational researchers. This, in turn, encourages a closed systems orientation to organizational phenomena in spite of the attention paid in recent years to open systems theory. Associated with this view of organizations are two contradictory assumptions that have rarely been articulated: (1) that an organization—indeed, any type of organization—is a *microcosm* of the larger society; and (2) that an organization is a type of social system with a substantial measure of *functional autonomy* from its environment.

The microcosm assumption appears to be persuasive if we consider, for example, such ubiquitous problems as the quality of leadership, the rationality of the decision-making process, and the degree of inequality in reward systems within an organization as compared with the surrounding community or the society as a whole. By studying the internal structure and functioning of an organization, the organizational researcher is in effect studying the larger and more complex phenomena of the environing society.

By contrast, the functional autonomy assumption is conducive to a conception of organizations as having generic properties, for example, hierarchical, formal attributes of structure and a tendency toward internal differentiation for the purpose of securing coordination and control. Whatever their purported objectives and whatever their interrelationships with their surroundings, organizations are conceived as having properties that transcend the culture and the social structure of the society in which they are embedded. Hence, they may be studied *as if* they are functionally autonomous.

Paradoxically, both assumptions, although mutually exclusive, encourage inattention to the encompassing social structure as it relates to organizations. Notwithstanding these assumptions, organization theory has recently witnessed a marked interest in going beyond the boundaries of organizations for the purpose of studying interorganizational relations.[3] If this trend persists and becomes more pervasive in the future—and there is every reason to believe that it will—a prediction I made a decade ago may yet be borne out:

Systematic inquiry into the interactions among various types of organizations may not only unearth new intraorganizational phenomena and processes, but may also provide the wherewithal for bridging the gap between the microscopic *organizational* and the macroscopic *institutional* levels of analysis.[4]

A similar view has recently been expressed by Hirsch:

The emerging subdiscipline of interorganizational relations provides a promising framework for relating the study of organizations to the larger societal setting in which they operate.[5]

It is therefore a propitious time to consider some of the problems of linking organization theory with macrosociological or macrostructural analysis. My purpose in this final chapter is fivefold: (1) to clarify some questions concerning the organization-environment nexus; (2) to examine several alternative conceptions of social structure; (3) to develop an exploratory social-structural model of organizations; (4) to consider the implications of the model for future organizational research; and (5) to entertain some conjectures—in light of the social-structural perspective—about the design of organizations of the future.

THE ORGANIZATION-ENVIRONMENT NEXUS

Much confusion surrounds the concept of "environment" as it relates to organizations. This is due in part to the variety of theories comprising the field of organization theory, each of which is located at a different point on a micro-macro continuum. Theories at the micro end of the continuum, in which the unit of analysis is the individual or the group, are apt to focus on *internal* organizational environments. For example, "work groups are the environment in which individuals act out their roles."[6] Theories closer to the macro end of the continuum, in which the unit of analysis is the total organization, are likely to conceptualize some dimensions of the *external* organizational environment, for example, the state of technology in a society as it influences an organization's functioning.[7] Our discussion will be confined to the *external* organizational environment which, as we shall see, is in need of considerable clarification.

As evidence of the complexities involved, a recently developed typology of 64 organizational environments was based on the following six dichotomized environmental factors: complexity versus non-complexity, routineness versus nonroutineness of "a problem-opportunity state," presence of organized versus unorganized elements, direct versus indirect relationship of environmental elements, high versus low change rate, and stable versus unstable change rate.[8]

The proliferation of terms pertaining to different dimensions of the environment impinging on organizations is a reflection of the growing pains of organization theory as it becomes increasingly macro-oriented. Which of the various concepts will survive the test of time will be determined largely by their heuristic value. To illustrate some of the ambiguities involved, I shall consider in turn the following concepts: context, organizational domain, task environment, social setting, and societal environment.

CONTEXT

The Aston group's well-known study of comparative organizations has identified such *structural* variables as concentration of authority, structuring of activities, and line control of work flow which they have interrelated with what they call "contextual" variables.[9] They have since replicated some of their findings pertaining to the interrelationships of contextual and structural variables in the United States, Canada, and Japan.[10] It is, however, by no means clear what the authors mean by "context," or how this term differs from the external organizational environment. In one publication they report that they scaled "eight salient elements of context": age, size of organization, size of parent organization, operating variability, operating diversity, work flow integration, number of operating sites, and dependence.[11] With the exception of the variable of dependence, which is manifestly an interorganizational variable, all the variables could just as well be conceptualized as *structural* rather than *contextual* in nature. Organizational technology (work flow integration), for example, is clearly distinguishable from the state of knowledge, skill, and resources comprising the technological institutions in the society as a whole; it has, in fact, been conceptualized by other researchers as a *structural* variable.[12] In one passing remark the authors acknowledge that context as "a concept which, though in some respects is narrower than that of environment, is still very wide."[13] Elsewhere some members of the Aston group equate their contextual variables with the "task environment" and then use the expression "contextual 'task environment,'" which is hardly consistent with the usage of Dill or Thompson.[14]

ORGANIZATIONAL DOMAIN

The concept of organizational domain, introduced by Levine and White as part of their exchange framework for studying interorganizational relations, raises some kindred problems.[15] The authors define the domain of an organization as "the specific goals it wishes to pursue and the functions it undertakes in order to implement its goals."[16] In the health agency system Levine and White studied, organizational domain was operationalized "in terms of (1) disease covered, (2) population served, and (3) services rendered."[17] By the same token, a university's domain may be formulated, in general terms, as teaching, research, public service, or, in more specific terms, as teaching and research with a special focus on science, engineering, and public service by contributing to the advancement of the technological capability of the society. Thus formulated, it is hard to differentiate an organization's domain from the primary goal(s) and task structure of organizations; hence, it need not be construed as an environmental variable. However, the authors' related term of "domain consensus," by which they mean the acceptance of the legitimacy of an organization's domain by environing organizations, does qualify as an environmental variable or more specifically as an interorganizational variable. Within the framework of my organization-set model (see Chapters 9 and 11), domain consensus refers to the attitudes of members of the organization-set toward the focal organization.

TASK ENVIRONMENT

The third environmental concept, task environment, was first developed by Dill and was subsequently adopted by Thompson.[18] Although it has acquired other meanings akin to an organizational domain, Dill's definition is as follows: "I have denoted that part of the total environment of management which was potentially relevant to goal setting and goal attainment as the task environment."[19] In his study of two Norwegian firms Dill found that four components of the task environment were of primary significance: "*customers* (both distributors and users), *suppliers* (of materials, labor, equipment, capital and work space), *competitors* (for both markets and resources), and *regulatory groups* (government agencies, unions and interfirm associations)."[20] In other words, the task environment includes all organizations and others (such as consumers) on whom an organization depends for essential resources and with whom it enters into transactions entailing cooperation, competition, and regulation. Except for unorganized customers the task environment is an equivalent concept to the input organization-set and to the output organization-set of the focal organization.

SOCIAL SETTING

Although the task environment has the hallmarks of a useful concept, the question may now be raised as to whether organizational researchers can afford to confine their research to this level of the organizational environment. In the previous chapter, I argued that organizational researchers should include cultural factors in their research because it probably accounts for an appreciable amount of the variance of any major dependent variable such as organizational performance. In effect, I was making a case for the need to go *beyond* the task environment in assessing the impact of environmental variables on organizations. Udy acknowledges this need in formulating his concept of the social setting:

Every organization is located in some society, is subject to its social cultural influence, and in turn can influence the society. In this sense, one thinks of any organization as existing within a *social setting*.[21]

Without further elaborating the dimensions and mechanisms of the "social setting," this concept is too global and too complex to be incorporated in any research design.

SOCIETAL ENVIRONMENT

Negandhi has also recognized the importance of transcending the task environment, which he conceives as but one of three relevant environments for organizational research, the other two being the "organizational environment"— which is equivalent to my use of the term internal organizational environment— and the "societal environment."[22] According to Negandhi, "societal environment" is the "macro-environment . . . in a given nation" and he uses it synonymously with "environmental conditions" which he defines as "social-economic, educational, political, legal and cultural factors which impinge upon the firm's internal operations but are external to the firm."[23] With the help of the Farmer-Richman model of comparative management, Negandhi has included societal environment variables in his cross-national research.[24] The results of Negandhi's ongoing cross-national research will provide a basis for assessing the heuristic value of his approach to conceptualizing the "societal environment."

GENERALIZING CONTINGENCY THEORY

Several conclusions may be drawn from this brief discussion of the organization-environment nexus. First, it is important to delineate different types and levels of the external organizational environment. Second, crucial as the task environment appears to be, it is not sufficient if organizational researchers want to maximize the amount of variance they can account for in their research. Third, transcending the task environment requires that we include the culture and the social structure of a society both of which are combined in Udy's concept of social setting and in Negandhi's concept of societal environment. Unless organizational researchers become more explicit and systematic in identifying and measuring different levels of the environment, including the macrosocial structural level, they will not succeed in explaining cross-societal variations in (1) organizational structure, (2) organizational processes, and (3) organizational effectiveness. Otherwise put, there is a need to *generalize* the contingency theory formulated by Lawrence and Lorsch to include culture and social structure.[25]

ALTERNATIVE CONCEPTIONS OF SOCIAL STRUCTURE

The organizational researcher who turns to the literature on macrotheories in sociology, anthropology, and political science will discover a marked absence of consensus, both within and between disciplines, concerning the concept of social structure.[26] By way of introducing the organizational researcher to some of the vagaries as well as to the potentialities of this concept, I shall begin by quoting ten definitions of this term by anthropologists and sociologists:

RADCLIFFE-BROWN: . . . [H]uman beings are connected by a complex network of social relations. I use the term "social structure" to denote this network of actually existing relations. . . . Social phenomena constitute a distinct class of natural phenomena. They are all, in one way or another, connected with the existence of social structures, either being implied in or resulting from them. Social structures are just as real as our individual organisms. What is meant by social structure is any arrangement of persons in institutionalized relationships.[27]

NADEL: We arrive at the structure of a society through abstracting from the concrete population and its behavior a pattern or network (or "system") of relationships obtaining "between actors in their capacity of playing roles relative to one another." . . . it seems impossible to speak of social structure in the singular. Analysis in terms of structure is incapable of presenting whole societies; nor, which means the same, can any society be said to exhibit an embracing, coherent structure as we understand the term. There are always cleavages, dissociations, enclaves, so that any description alleged to present a single structure will in fact present only a fragmentary or one-sided picture.[28]

FIRTH: The concept of social structure is an analytical tool designed to serve us in understanding how men behave in their social life. The essence of this concept is those social relations which seem to be of critical importance for the behavior of members of the society so that if such relations were not in operation, the society could not be said to exist in that form.[29]

LÉVI-STRAUSS: The term "social structure" has nothing to do with empirical reality but with models which are built up after it. This should help one to clarify the difference between two concepts which are so close to each other that they have often been confused, namely, those of *social structure* and those of *social relations*. It will be enough to state at this time that social relations consist of the raw materials out of which the models making up the social structure are built, while social structure can, by no means, be reduced to the ensemble of the social relations to be described in a given society.[30]

PARSONS: Since a social system is a system of processes of interaction between actors, it is the structure of the *relations* between the actors as involved in the interactive process which is essentially the structure of the social system. . . . A social system is, with respect to its structurally sigificant components, a *differentiated* system . . . it is a system of differentiated roles. The types of which it is composed, how they are distributed within the social system and how integrated with each other must be analyzed. This is what we mean by the social structure in the narrower sense of the term.[31]

SMELSER: At the most general level "social structure" as a construct is used to characterize recurrent and regularized interaction among two or more persons. . . . The basic units of social structure are not persons as such, but selected aspects of interaction among persons. The concepts that are used to characterize this level of analysis are the familiar sociological concepts of "role," "organization," and "institution."[32]

UDY: . . . [W]e shall define "social structure" very broadly as the totality of patterns of collective human phenomena that cannot be explained solely on the basis of human heredity and/or the nonhuman environment.[33]

SHELDON AND MOORE: The uses of the term [social structure] range from the very inclusive concept of any *pattern of action or relationship* . . . to the very restrictive concept of *social differentiation*, particularly with respect to status inequalities. It is also possible to view structures as *social systems*—complete with values and norms and motivated actors playing prescribed roles—or at another extreme, as a set of statistical categories—the age structure of a population, the occupational structure of the labor force.[34]

MERTON: . . . [B]y social structure is meant that organized set of social relationships in which members of the society or group are variously implicated. . . . The patterned arrangements of role-sets, status-sets and status-sequences can be held to comprise the social structure. The concepts remind us . . . that even the seemingly simple social structure is extremely complex. For operating social structures must somehow manage to organize these sets in sequences of statuses and roles so that an appreciable degree of social order obtains, sufficient to enable most of the people most of the time to go about their business of social life without having to improvise adjustments anew in each newly confronted situation.[35]

STINCHCOMBE: I intend to interpret the term "social structure" . . . in a very general sense to include groups, institutions, laws, population characteristics, and sets of social relations that form the environment of the organization. That is, I interpret "social structure" to mean any variables which are stable characteristics of the society outside the organization.[36]

Juxtaposing these definitions highlights the variety of assumptions and types of frameworks currents in macrotheory in sociology and anthropology. Conceptions of social structure differ in scope, unit of analysis, and type of referent: Some are highly abstract and entail a comprehensive model of society, whereas others are substantially lower on the scale of abstraction; some imply a unit of analysis that is the total society in contrast to others that imply subsocietal units; some postulate that a society has a unitary social structure, whereas others assume that society is composed of multiple social structures. These differences, it turns out, are at the root of various controversies on macrotheory in the social sciences.[37]

Radcliffe-Brown, a leader of the British school of social anthropology, subscribed to a concept of social structure that is moderately abstract and empirical in its orientation. On the other hand, Nadel's view was more complex and variegated, particularly in his treatment of role structures.[38] For Parsons as well as Lévi-Strauss social structure is a highly general and abstract concept concerning social systems, for the former, and collective representations, for the latter.[39] In contrast to Parsons and Lévi-Strauss, Merton's approach to social structure is governed by a strategy of middle-range theory construction. Instead of theorizing about social systems or collective representations, Merton concentrates on more circumscribed subjects, such as a theory of status and role structures and a theory of the institutions of science.

From the vantage point of developing linkages between organization theory and macrosocial theory, Merton's conception of social structure and, to some extent, Stinchcombe's as well, offer some highly promising leads. In developing his three social-structural concepts of role-sets, status-sets, and status-sequences, Merton in effect provides us with some of the mechanisms for linking micro- and macrolevels, a problem "of central importance to the development of sociological theory."[40]

Three noteworthy developments in recent years may contribute to an eventual solution to the problem of linking micro- and macrolevels—including organization theory with macrosociological theory. First, since the mid-1960s there has been a rapidly growing field of interest in "social indicators."[41] The impetus for what has become known as the "social indicator movement" in the United States and elsewhere is the growing demand for information systems to monitor social changes and to evaluate public policies, plans, decisions, and programs.[42] Along with the policy-oriented work on social indicators is a concern on the part of some social scientists with constructing analytic indicators for the purpose of modeling social systems.[43] A cognate line of inquiry that is also likely to contribute to operationalizing dimensions of social structure is the comparative analysis of national aggregate data, developed principally by political scientists.[44]

Second, since the early 1950s several British social anthropologists, following the pioneering work of Barnes, have been analyzing "social networks" in urban communities as well as in preliterate societies.[45] They have sought to translate the notion of a social network, on which Radcliffe-Brown, Nadel, and others based their conception of social structure, into more precise terms with the help of graph theory. The common use of the term "network" is "purely metaphorical and is very different from the notion of a social network as a specific set of linkages among a defined set of persons, with the additional property that the characteristics of these linkages as a whole may be used to interpret social behavior of the persons involved."[46] Following Bott's distinction between loose-knit and close-knit social networks, other social anthropologists have sought to develop various measures of formal properties of networks such as reachability, density, range, and connectedness.[47]

Third, still nascent as a trend is the growing recognition of the importance of using the formal organization as a fundamental subsocietal unit in macrosociological research.[48] In his analysis of the impact of the level of literacy, degree of urbanization, the presence of a money economy, the occurrence of political revolution, and the level of past organizational experience on the rate of formation and the likelihood of success of new organizations in a society, Stinchcombe has already demonstrated the potential value to macrosociology "as well as to organization theory" of this mode of analysis.[49] Likewise, Turk has provided some evidence for the utility of using an interorganizational approach in studying urban communities.[50]

Are any of the foregoing ideas useful for developing a provisional social-structural model of organizations?

AN EXPLORATORY SOCIAL-STRUCTURAL MODEL OF ORGANIZATIONS

In presenting the organization-set model (see Chapters 9 and 11), I have already indicated the potential theoretical and empirical value of applying and extending Merton's concept of the role-set. In developing a provisional model linking any formal organization with the social structure of the environing society, I shall explore some implications of Merton's three constituents of social structure in conjunction with several related ideas.

To begin with, the social system of any society may be conceptualized as involving four nested concepts commonly used by sociologists and other social scientists: norms, roles, organizations, and institutions. Norms are prescriptions or proscriptions of conduct; roles consist of regularized (or institutionalized) patterns of behavior associated with various statuses or positions in a social system; organizations, regardless of type or purpose, consist of a structure of roles, whose incumbents tend to behave in accordance with organizational norms and goals; and institutions (or institutional spheres or sectors) consist of an ensemble of roles and organizations whose principal function is to maintain a social system in a steady state. When we observe role behavior and organizational behavior—or their residues—we are dealing with *interactional* phenomena at a relatively microlevel of analysis. When we aggregate role behavior and organizational behavior or clusters of roles and organizations, we are dealing with *institutional* phenomena at a relatively macrolevel of analysis. Merton's three concepts of social structure and my concept of organization-set may be conceptualized as linkage mechanisms between the macro- and the microlevels of analysis. I shall discuss each of these linkage mechanisms before considering the institutional structure of a society as it impinges on organizations.

ROLE-SETS

Merton defines role-sets as the "complement of role relationships which persons have by virtue of occupying a particular social status."[51] Since each member of an organization in the course of performing his role recurrently interacts with a number of "role partners", the resulting social network within an organization, even one the size of only 100 members, can be quite complex. By allocating different amounts of authority to different roles in the organization, the resulting hierarchical structure tends to limit the complexity of the network of role interactions. And by specifying and formalizing the nature of the behavior required of the occupants of various statuses in an organization—particularly one that is bureaucratic in structure—an organization seeks to deactivate the extraorganizational roles of members, namely, the latent social roles, which are deemed irrelevant.[52]

An organization's role structure is further differentiated, according to Parsons, into three hierarchical levels: the "technical" level, the status-occupants of which carry out the primary task of the organization; the "managerial" level, where the function of status-occupants is "mediation between the organization and the external situation, and 'administration' of the organization's internal affairs"; the "institutional" level, the locus of which is the board of directors or trustees, where the status-occupants are concerned with securing legitimacy and support from the environment.[53] Even at the technical level in an organization's hierarchy, some members engage in external relations in the course of performing their roles, as is true of various professionals employed in universities, hospitals, research organizations, industrial organizations, and government agencies who are also active in their professional associations. Hence, at each of the three hierarchical levels we would expect to find boundary personnel, although the ratio of boundary roles to nonboundary roles probably increases from the technical level through the managerial to the institutional level.[54]

If Parsons' three categories of role structure, which appear to be quite general, are combined with the two types of organization-sets, that is, input and output, we have a typology of six boundary roles. Organizations differ, no doubt, in the frequency distributions of boundary personnel according to the six types and, in general, in the role-set profiles of all their members.

Industrial organizations, for example, employ a multitude of specialists in boundary as well as in nonboundary roles.[55] Some specialists in engineering, finance, law, personnel, and industrial relations perform input boundary roles; others in economics and marketing perform output boundary roles; and still other specialists perform a mixture of both types of roles. Since some type of expertise is generally required to mediate between an organization and its environment, the higher the ratio of boundary to nonboundary roles, the higher the proportion of professionally trained members in an organization.

Several hypotheses (H) concerning a number of pivotal variables in organization theory such as organizational structure, processes, and effectiveness[56] follow from these considerations:

H:1. Organizational effectiveness is a function of both the number and the quality (expertise) of personnel distributed in each of the six types of boundary roles.

H:2. If the ratio of boundary to nonboundary roles of the organization's elite is not appreciably higher than that of rank-and-file members, the level of organizational effectiveness is likely to be impaired.

H:3. Since high ratios of boundary to nonboundary roles, particularly at managerial and institutional levels in the hierarchy, are likely to involve employment of a substantial proportion of professionally trained personnel, this will be conducive to the use of "universalistic" rather than "particularistic" criteria for recruitment, and to the reliance on informal rather than formal socialization of members and communication among members.

H:4.   A high ratio of boundary to nonboundary roles is likely to require tasks with a significant discretionary component, and hence will tend to be associated with a low level of formalization of rules and a low level of centralization of decision making.

Clearly, the role-sets of each of the boundary persons in an organization constitute various linkages—principally through the medium of the organization-set—with the environing community and the society at large.

STATUS-SETS

It is the status-set, however, that serves as a direct linkage mechanism between the organization and the wider society. By this term, Merton means "the complex of distinct positions assigned to individuals within and among social systems."[57] Merton's use of the term "social system" in this context can safely be interpreted as "institutions" or "institutional spheres." Each member of a society has one or more statuses with respect to such institutional spheres as the family, the economy, the polity, religion, education, and the law. For example, Mr. X is married, a corporate executive, a Republican, a Protestant, an alumnus of Princeton University, and a law-abiding citizen. Mr. Y is a divorcé, a salesman, a Democrat, a Catholic, a high-school graduate, and a citizen who has been convicted of a crime. These are obviously rather simple, almost impoverished status-sets. Typically, individuals in modern societies have, in each of the six institutional spheres mentioned, several statuses that result in status-sets—and accompanying role-sets—that are far more complex. For instance, as regards the family institution alone, one can, of course, simultaneously have the status of a son, a brother, a father, and an uncle. And with respect to each of these statuses one would have a different role-set. Nevertheless, it is reasonable to assume that individuals vary greatly in their status-sets, some having rather simple ones and others having highly complex status-sets.

Another basis for distinguishing status-sets is the social evaluation or prestige ranking of its various components. Just as the members of various societies assign different prestige rankings—in a fairly uniform manner—to different occupations, so they are also likely to make similar distinctions as to the value of, say, different types of political party affiliations, religious affiliations, levels of education attainment, and the like.[58] Thus, some individuals may have relatively prestigious status-sets whereas others may have relatively nonprestigious status-sets. There are, of course, individuals—perhaps a large proportion of the population in rapidly changing modern societies—whose status-sets do not have consistent prestige rankings. Such individuals are likely to be exposed to multiple role strains and to role-set conflicts in one or more of their social statuses.[59]

Turning now to the status-set profiles of the members of an organization, I hypothesize that:

H:5.   The status-sets of organizational elites, compared to those of rank-and-file-members, are higher in complexity and in level of prestige.

H:6.   The status-occupants of the six boundary roles are all apt to have more complex and more prestigious statuses than members performing nonboundary or internal roles.

In addition, I would expect organizations of a given type that are ranked high in society to have members with status-set profiles higher in degree of complexity and prestige than organizations that are ranked low.[60] The corollary of this hypothesis is an association between the prestige ranking of organizations and the prevalence of cosmopolitan versus local role orientations among members.[61] For example, prestigious universities are likely to have a high proportion of their faculty who have cosmopolitan role orientations—in part because of their complex status-sets—whereas nonprestigious universities are likely to have a predominance of local role orientation among their faculty members.

Another way of formulating some of the organizationally structured differences in status-set profiles is as follows:

H:7.   Members of an organization, particularly at managerial and institutional levels in the hierarchy, tend to become involved in highly complex role-sets in their intraorganizational as well as extraorganizational roles. If their status-sets are relatively prestigious, they are motivated to engage in a great range of interactions in their various statuses which often, directly or indirectly, enhance their organizational role performance and in turn contribute to the organization's level of effectiveness.

A case in point is the corporate executive who is elected to the board of directors of his own company and to the boards of trustees of hospitals, universities, foundations, and so on. As a result of his interlocking directorships, he is likely to become privy to various bodies of "inside information" that may help him perform his role as a corporate executive.[62] That this example is not entirely hypothetical is evident in a recent study of the Du Pont Company.[63] Du Pont executives or family members are directors of major corporations as well as of 90 nonprofit organizations in Delaware, including various types of community organizations, hospitals, social service agencies, colleges and universities, and private foundations.[64]

In short, organizations differ in the status-set profiles of their members. Moreover, the consequences of members' status-sets for such organizational processes as recruitment, socialization, and communication have not eluded organization theorists and practitioners, as Barnard—whose own status set included both of these roles—makes clear:

The general method of maintaining an informal executive organization is so to operate and to select and promote executives that a general condition of compatibility of personnel is maintained. Perhaps often and certainly occasionally men cannot be promoted or selected or even must be relieved because they cannot function, because they "do not fit," where there is no question of formal competence. This question of "fitness" involves such matters as education, experience, age, sex, personal distinctions, prestige, race, nationality, faith; politics, sectional antecedents. . . .[65]

In terms of our dimensions of status-sets, Barnard's assertion suggests that:

H:8.   As the status-sets of organizational elites increase in degree of complexity and prestige, there is a tendency for the recruitment of executives to become more "particularistic" which in turn is conducive to informal rather than formal socialization and communication.

Status-set profiles of members also affect various dimensions of organizational structure as well as the level of organizational effectiveness. Thus:

H:9.   The more complex and more prestigious the status-set profiles of members, especially at the managerial and institutional levels in the hierarchy, the greater the degree of discretion required to perform the role and hence the lower the degree of formalization of rules and the lower the degree of centralization of decision making.

H:10.   As the complexity and prestige of the status-set profiles in an organization increase, there is a higher probability that various types of resources will be mobilized and thereby increase the level of organizational effectiveness.

STATUS-SEQUENCES

Neither role-sets nor status-sets are static, of course; changes occur as individuals move through the life cycle, relinquishing old roles and acquiring new roles and new organizational memberships. This process, designated as "status-sequences," is defined by Merton as the "succession of statuses through which an appreciable proportion of people move."[66] For example, in France, graduates of the École Polytechnique typically fill major administrative posts in government and industry; in England, graduates of Harrow, Eton, Winchester and other prominent public schools "capture most of the places at the pre-eminent universities, Oxford and Cambridge, and, through what is called 'the old boy network' go on to influence and power in government, the armed forces, the church, the diplomatic corps and the major banks and businesses."[67]

And according to a study of the Du Pont Company, "Du Pont Company directors have historically married Du Pont women."[68] Examples can be multiplied of status-sequences that are sufficiently common as to be socially patterned: lawyers embarking on political careers, retired military officers becoming corporate executives, particularly in companies seeking defense contracts, members of major law firms becoming judges, and so on.[69]

From an organizational perspective, status-sequences in the role-set profile and in the status-set profile of the membership can have important consequences for an organization's structure, processes, and effectiveness. The entry and exit of members not only change the role-sets of the membership but may also affect the welfare of an organization. New members, recruited because of special expertise and access to relatively inaccessible channels of information, may be the impetus for significant innovations of a technical or of an administrative nature.[70] An ex-general appointed as a top executive of a corporation may modify the staff-line structure to approximate that of the military; a scientist or an engineer hired by a company may spark a new invention, etc. On the other hand, employees who resign or who are dismissed can be a source of grief to the organization they have left behind because of the "trade secrets" they may possess, which accounts for the contracts some companies require their employees to sign imposing restrictions on an employee's disclosure and use of proprietary information upon termination of employment.[71] Likewise, adherents of religions who become apostates and party members who become renegades or turncoats can be embarrassing or even injurious to their former organizations.

Apart from resignations and dismissals, role-set sequences in an organization are occasioned by promotions, demotions, and lateral re-assignments. In the case of boundary roles, particularly at the managerial and institutional levels, such changes may adversely affect the effectiveness of the focal organization because of the lead time often required to develop new relationships with role partners belonging to organizations comprising the organization-set. To specify the probable consequences of a high rate of status-sequences in the role-set, the following hypotheses are formulated:

H:11.   A high rate of role-set sequences in boundary roles, especially those involving managerial and institutional personnel, is inversely related to organizational effectiveness.

H:12.   Organizations in which role-set sequences of boundary roles are high will tend to respond to the problems of discontinuity that are generated by (1) increasing the centralization of decision making, (2) increasing the formalization of rules, and (3) relying on particularistic criteria for recruitment and formal modes of socialization and communication.

Status-sequences in a member's status-set—and cumulatively in the status-set profile of the membership of an organization—are much less visible and less subject to control by an organization's elite than are the role-set sequences of members. Yet in some societies management does intervene in the status-sets of its members. For example, in Japan, the foreman in an industrial organization often takes an active interest in the family problems of his subordinates; in Communist countries the manager of an enterprise is not unconcerned about the political activities of employees; in the United States, some companies encourage their employees, especially managers, to participate in various community organizations to ensure that the views of the business community are properly represented.

In a well-known participant-observer study of four firms, Dalton found that in one of them, "Masonic membership was usually an unofficial requirement for getting up [the managerial ladder]—and for remaining there"; and membership in the local yacht club "aided a candidate who had other things in his favor."[72] Acquiring an advanced degree often helps an employee obtain a promotion in his company, and joining a prestigious church may have a similar effect. On the other hand, having a serious brush with the law may induce an employer to dismiss an employee for fear that the company will become a target of adverse publicity. In other words, status-set sequences involving charges of a political, familial, educational, religious, or legal nature may affect an individual's position in an organization, although officially such changes in latent social roles may be regarded as irrelevant to an organizational role. The executives of some organizations may, however, unofficially evaluate such changes to ascertain whether they increase or decrease the level of prestige of an individual's status-set and whether they enhance his organizational role performance.

Analogous to the hypotheses concerning role-set sequences, the following hypotheses may be formulated pertaining to status-set sequences:

H:13. Status-set sequences involving an increase in prestige of boundary personnel, especially of those located at the managerial and technical levels of the hierarchy, are positively associated with organizational effectiveness.

H:14. Status-set sequences involving an increase in prestige of boundary personnel, especially of those located at the managerial and technical levels in the hierarchy, tend to be associated with (a) particularistic criteria of recruitment; (b) an informal mode of socialization and communication; (c) a decrease in the centralization of decision making; and (d) a decrease in the formalization of rules.

ORGANIZATION-SETS

Almost as invisible as the status-set sequences of members of an organization are the various properties of organization-sets, a concept I have defined as the complex of environing organizations with which a given organization or class of organizations—referred to as the focal organization—recurrently interacts in the course of pursuing its objectives.[73] This concept is further subdivided into an input set, from which the focal organization obtains its various resources, and an output set through which the·focal organization channels its output, be it goods, services, influence attempts, authoritative decisions, or whatever. Like status-sets, which link individuals to the various institutional spheres of a society, organization-sets link organizations to different institutional spheres. Organization-sets resemble status-sets in yet another respect, namely, they vary greatly in complexity—some are relatively simple and others are immensely complex as regards, for example, the number of elements in the set, the locus of organizational interaction, and the network configuration in its input and output sets.

To illustrate the possible range of variation of organization-sets, let us first consider a feeder plant in the Detroit area that manufactures parts for General Motors. It has a *relatively* simple organization set. Its input organization-set consists of several suppliers of raw materials, one or more banks from which to borrow capital, a trade union with which it enters into a collective bargaining agreement, and some local, state, and federal agencies that enforce regulations affecting the operations of the factory. Its output organization-set consists principally of G.M., to which it sells its products, and the Internal Revenue Service and some local and state agencies to which it pays taxes. The locus of its organizational interactions is primarily in the local area, except for the I.R.S., the state taxing agencies, the regulatory agencies, and possibly the suppliers. Its network configuration is simple not only because of the size of the input and output sets but also because of the type of elements in the sets, namely, organizations each of which directly interacts with the focal organization but none with one another. As a result, the focal organization can concentrate on *first* order, rather than on second or higher order, interactions with elements of its input and output sets.

By contrast, G.M., with which the feeder plant interacts, presents a higher level of interactional complexity by several orders of magnitude. Its input and output sets probably number many thousands of highly diverse organizations; the locus of its organizational interaction is national as well as international—in fact, in several dozens of countries throughout the world—and it is enmeshed in a multiplicity of complex organizational networks with second and higher order interactions with elements of its input and output sets. Clearly, G.M.'s organization-set serves as a major linkage mechanism for innumerable organizations in the United States and in many other countries as well.

Two of the various dimensions of the organization-set exemplify its societal linkage function, on the one hand, and, on the other hand, its consequences for the structure, processes, and effectiveness of the focal organization: (1) the size of the organization-set, and (2) the extent of its institutional interpenetration.

These two dimensions, along with others, may be used as measures of the organization-set profile of the focal organization.

The size of the organization-set is very likely associated with the magnitude of the *resources* at the disposal of the focal organization and with its capacity to *sanction* elements of its organization-set, that is, the power to reward or punish them for their actions. The sanctioning power of an organization is in large measure a function of its resources. These two attributes of the focal organization vis-à-vis its organization-set are also fundamental features, as we shall see presently, of each of the institutions of society. In this respect the organization-set in action resembles the functioning of an institution.

A high concentration of resources and sanctioning capacity on the part of the focal organization tends to enlarge its institutional interpenetration, by which I mean the scope or magnitude of interactions that the focal organization has through its organization set with diverse institutional spheres at the local or national levels of a society. Having multiple linkages through its organization-set with organizations associated, for example, with political, economic, educational, religious, and legal institutions protects the focal organization against threats to its survival. It also protects its claims to autonomy in its decisions with respect to inputs and outputs.

The foregoing considerations suggest several specific hypotheses concerning the relation of the organization-set to the structure, processes, and effectiveness of the focal organization:

H:15. The size of the organization-set is directly related to
    a. centralization of decision making,
    b. formalization of rules,
    c. formal mode of socialization and communication, and
    d. organizational effectiveness.

H:16. The extent of institutional interpenetration of the organization-set is directly associated with
    a. centralization of decision making,
    b. formalization of rules,
    c. formal mode of socialization and communication, and
    d. organizational effectiveness.

To summarize our discussion of the *interactional* components of the social-structural model of organizations, namely, the effects of role-sets, status-sets, status-sequences, and organization-sets, I have presented in Table 16.1 virtually all the hypotheses that have been formulated. Each hypothesis presupposes the usual *ceteris paribus* condition. Cumulatively, the four social-structural components may be thought of as an "organizational environment" profile for which a composite index might be developed based on such variables as I have made use of in discussing each of the components.

Table 16.1 Some Hypotheses on the Relationship Between the Organizational Environment Profile, Organizational Structure, Organizational Processes, and Organizational Effectiveness

Selected Organizational System Dimensions	Role-Set Profile — Boundary Roles (Nonboundary Roles) Low	High	Role-Set Profile — Boundary Roles of Organizational Elites (Boundary Roles of Rank-and-File) Low	High	Status-Set Profile — Complexity of Organizational Elite's Status-Sets Low	High	Status-Set Profile — Prestige of Organizational Elite's Status-Sets Low	High	Status-Sequence Profile — Rate of Role-Set Sequences of Boundary Roles Low	High	Status-Sequence Profile — Status-Set Sequences involving an increase in prestige of Boundary Roles Low	High	Organization-Set Profile — Size Small	Large	Organization-Set Profile — Extent of Institutional Inter-penetration Small	Large
1. Organizational Structure																
Centralization of Decision making																
Low (or decreasing)		×		×		×		×		×		×		×		×
High (or increasing)	×		×		×		×		×		×		×		×	
Formalization of rules																
Low (or decreasing)		×		×		×		×		×		×		×		×
High (or increasing)	×		×		×		×		×		×		×		×	
2. Organizational Processes																
Recruitment																
Particularistic	×		×		×*		×*		×		×		×		×	
Universalistic		×		×		×*		×*		×		×		×		×
Socialization																
Formal	×		×		×		×		×		×		×		×	
Informal		×		×		×		×		×		×		×		×
Communication																
Formal	×		×		×		×		×		×		×		×	
Informal		×		×		×		×		×		×		×		×
3. Organizational Effectiveness																
Low	×		×		×		×		×		×		×		×	
High		×		×		×		×		×		×		×		×

* These hypotheses refer only to the recruitment of executives or organizational elite.

275

INSTITUTIONAL STRUCTURE

We now turn to the *institutional* component of our social-structural model of organizations. This level of analysis involves a process of aggregating the role behavior of a population and the organizational behavior of a population of organizations in a society. This poses a perplexing problem for social scientists for, assuming one can obtain the relevant data for a society such as the United States, how does one aggregate the role behavior of a population of over 200 million people and a population of organizations that includes 1,733,000 corporations, 78,269 governmental units, 329,299 religious organizations, and 17,000 "trade associations, professional societies, labor unions, fraternal and patriotic organizations, and other types of groups consisting of voluntary members"?[74]

Macrotheorists who have analyzed institutions have scarcely concerned themselves with the problem of linking *interactional* data with *institutional* data. Nor have they critically evaluated the relative merits of alternative approaches to classifying institutions.[75] Under the circumstances, I shall fall back on the six institutions I mentioned in connection with the analysis of status-sets (i.e., familial, economic, political, religious, educational, and legal); these institutions have also been referred to in the literature as "subsystems" or "systems" in a society. Other institutions, of course, could be added to this list (e.g., military, technological, and scientific institutions), but these six will suffice for our purpose, which is to delineate the *institutional* components of a social-structural model of organizations.

Two noteworthy contributions toward developing a macrostructural analysis of organizations have been made, one by Farmer and Richman and the other by Stinchcombe.[76] In their research on comparative management, Farmer and Richman have identified four classes of environmental constraints: educational-cultural, sociological-cultural, political-legal, and economic.[77] With respect to each of the four categories, they have developed a list of strategic factors—a total of 29—that are potential measures of their "environmental constraints". Proceeding on the hypothesis that "these constraints tend to have direct and significant influence on managerial and firm performance . . . ," Farmer and Richman then present a "constraint-management process matrix" interrelating 29 constraints with 76 "critical managerial elements."[78] Richman and another collaborator, Copen, acknowledge that this matrix "provides a useful check list for both researchers and practitioners, and it permits the statement of a large number of suggestive relationships in a very small space. What it does not indicate, however, is what quantitative relationships . . ." obtain between the constraints and the managerial elements.[79] Notwithstanding the shortcomings of their model from a conceptual standpoint (e.g., the confusion between cultural and social-structural levels of analysis) and from a methodological perspective (the inadequate operationalization of variables to permit the measurement of relationships), this is a promising approach to developing linkages between *organizational* and *institutional* phenomena.

In a highly suggestive essay Stinchcombe has formulated several propositions concerning the relationship between various societal characteristics and the rate of formation and the rate of success of new organizations. Thus, for example, he hypothesizes that societies differ in the "... *rate* at which special-purpose organizations take over various social functions (economic production, policing, education, political action, military action, etc. . . .);" that the rate of industrialization of a society is "... an indicator of the organization-forming capacity of the population;" and that literacy is related to the "rate of formation of voluntary associations, political party branches, income tax departments, vocational schools, effective police departments, and so on."[80] In addition, Stinchcombe opens up for exploration an intriguing question of the social stratification among organizations, namely, that organizations tend to be differentially ranked according to wealth, power, and prestige. "Organizations as well as individuals have ranks and these ranks are defended with substantial resources."[81]

From the perspective of our social-structural model there is yet another type of stratification system of particular significance not only to the social ranking of organizations but also to their internal structure, processes, and effectiveness. I refer to the stratification of the *institutional* spheres of a society. Societies evidently assign different weights to different institutional spheres or—as Tumin has argued—select *one* of their institutions for special emphasis.

Sometimes religious devotion is stressed; some societies are highly political in ultimate orientation; others emphasize primarily the facts and fictions of kinship; and in still others, the production of goods and services assumes the highest importance. Which institutional complex is emphasized can vary over time within any single society.[82]

Mills, on the other hand, contends that not *one* institution but *three* have a commanding position in the United States:

Within American society, major national power now resides in the economic, the political and the military domains. Other institutions seem off to the side of modern history. . . . Religious, educational and family institutions are not autonomous centers of national power; on the contrary, these decentralized areas are increasingly shaped by the Big Three in which developments of decisive and immediate consequences now occur.[83]

Underlying these propositions about the stratification of institutional spheres is an assumption that each institution controls different amounts of resources and sanctioning power that it uses in regulating the behavior of organizations and individuals associated with it in an effort to maintain its social rank. Thus, it follows that the same type of organization, say, a machine tool company of medium size, one in the United States and one in Spain, is likely to be ranked differently, with the American company probably ranking higher because economic institutions in this country have more power, wealth, and prestige than they have in a society dominated by authoritarian political institutions. In other words, a general proposition may be advanced linking the stratification of institutions with the stratification of organizations:

H:17.   Societies differing in the social ranking of institutions are also likely to differ in the social ranking of organizations associated with the respective institutions.

One way of ascertaining the social ranking of organizations as well as of institutions is to discover which organizational elites from which institutions participate in the making of which critical societal decisions. Whether progress in research on social indicators will yield direct or indirect measures of what might be called the "institutional integration of organizational elites" remains to be seen. Such research would have to take into account salient dimensions for differentiating institutions and, in turn, societies. In Table 16.2 I have indicated how each of the six institutions we have dealt with might be dimensionalized and what social indicators might be used for measuring each of the dimensions. I have also noted the potential utility of such an analysis by formulating six illustrative hypotheses—one for each institutional sphere—each of which links *institutional* variables with *organizational* variables.

Clearly, societies differ in their institutional profiles on such dimensions as are presented in Table 16.2, which thereby define their position on a widely discussed evolutionary scale of traditional, transitional, and modern types of societies.[84] Thus, one type of traditional society might have an institutional profile that includes an extended family system, an agricultural market economy, an authoritarian political system, elitist educational institutions, sacred institutions, and a "formally or substantively irrational" legal system.[85] On the other hand, one variant of a modern society's institutional profile might consist of a nuclear family system, a market economy, democratic political institutions, mass educational institutions, secular institutions, and a formally rational legal system.

By way of summarizing our analysis of the institutional component of the social-structural model of institutions, Figure 16.3 diagrams the potential impact of the prevailing type of institutional structure in a society on (1) the rate of formation of new organizations and the rate of success of new organizations, (2) the social ranking of organizations, and (3) the organizational structure, organizational processes, and, in turn, their joint effect on organizational effectiveness.

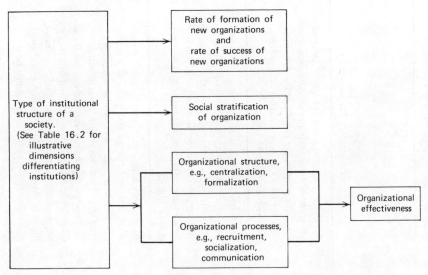

Fig. 16.1   Hypothesized impact of type of institutional structure of a society on its organizational systems.

In other words, a general institutional hypothesis is as follows:

H:18.   As the institutional profile approximates that of a modern society, the rate of formation of new organizations and the rate of success of new organizations tend to increase, a social stratification system of organizations tends to emerge, the structure of organizations tends to become increasingly centralized and formalized, organizational processes tend to involve universalistic recruitment and formal modes of socialization and communication, and these structures and processes in turn affect the level of organizational effectiveness.

EXAMPLES OF SOCIAL-STRUCTURAL EFFECTS ON ORGANIZATIONS

There is no dearth in the literature of organizational research of examples to interpret—with the aid of our model—as manifesting social-structural effects on organizations. Two illustrations will suffice.

In his study of the evolution of the strategy and structure of the 100 largest British manufacturing firms in the period 1950–1970, Channon observes that as the enterprises become increasingly diversified in their products, there is a progressive adoption of the multidivisional structure.[86] In comparing his British firms with the 500 largest American firms, Channon found that 72 percent of

Table 16.2 *Hypotheses Relating Selected Dimensions of Institutional Spheres of Society to Organizational Variables*

Institutional Spheres of a Society	Illustrative Dimensions for Differentiating Institutional Spheres	Illustrative Social Indicators	Illustrative Hypotheses
Familial	Extended family vs. nuclear family	Number of generations residing in a household	Societies that have a nuclear family system, in contrast to those with an extended family system, are freer to use their surplus resources and are likely to have a higher rate of formation of business enterprises.
Economic	Centrally-planned economy vs. market economy	Proportion of all enterprises in a country that are state-owned	In societies with a market economy, as compared to those having a centrally-planned economy, organizational capacities are more widely distributed in the population, and hence the rate of formation of organizations will be higher.
Political	Authoritarian vs. democratic	One-party vs. two-party or multi-party system	In societies with a one-party system, in contrast to those having a two-party or a multi-party system, conflict-resolution capacities tend to be concentrated in government bureaucracies; hence interorganizational conflicts are less likely to be resolved by the organizations directly involved and are more likely to involve the intervention of a third-party government official or government agency.

Educational	Elite system vs. mass system	Mean number of years of formal education in adult population; proportion of 18 to 26 age group attending colleges or universities.	In societies with an elite educational system, in contrast to those having a mass educational system, social distance is greater between organizational elites and rank-and-file members, and hence the rate of organizational innovation—technical and administrative—tends to be lower.
Religious	Secular vs. sacred	Presence of a state religion; presence of religious courts; judicial system influenced by religious law	In societies in which a single religion is dominant, recruitment to organizational leadership tends to be on particularistic criteria—such as a position of prominence in the church—rather than on universalistic criteria. By contrast, in societies in which more than one religion is represented in the population or in which no single religion has a commanding position, recruitment to organizational leadership tends to be on universalistic criteria.
Legal	Formally rational vs. formally or substantively irrational	Degree of emphasis on procedure in court trials; extent of influence of theology in lawmaking and lawfinding; mean number of years of formal training required for lawyers and judges	Societies with a formally rational legal system compared with those whose legal systems are formally or substantively irrational will tend to have a higher level of formalization of rules in organizations not associated with legal institutions.

the British firms had a multidivisional structure compared with 86 percent of the American firms. In his effort to explain this finding Channon refers to the effects of the family and educational institutions in Britain on the British style of management.

An inhibiting factor to the growth of both the strategy of diversification and the adoption of the multidivisional structure appear to have been an initially high percentage of family-controlled companies in the British population. These companies which were slower to diversify and to adopt the multidivisional structure still formed a significant part of the population in 1970. . . . British management tended to come from an upper-class background, to be educated at public schools, and lack higher education, especially training in business techniques other than accounting.[87]

Family-owned enterprises in Britain and elsewhere are constrained to continue in the family tradition, which in this case means pursuing the same product-line rather than adopting the strategy of product diversification; it also encourages maintaining the traditional functional form of organization rather than making the transition to the multidivisional structure.

As regards the educational system, which is still relatively elitist in Britain, "public schools" are held in such high esteem that graduates tend to suspend their formal education rather than continue their education in the professions, in scientific disciplines, or in the humanities. Consequently, British top managers, according to Channon, are technically unqualified to "manage the rapid transition from a non-diversified firm in a non-competitive environment to a diversified company facing intensified competition."[88]

In a related study comparing two multinational chemical companies, Du Pont and Farbwerke Hoechst (Fw H), Staehle analyzed the transformation of these firms from a functionally departmentalized, centralized structure to a decentralized, multidivisional structure.[89] He found that "in decentralizing the functional areas such as manufacturing, sales, purchasing, R and D, Du Pont . . . went much further than Fw H. . . . Consequently, Fw H retains in these areas a high degree of centralization."[90] Staehle concludes his structural comparison of the two firms with the following remark:

Differences in the technical, economic and cultural conditions facing the organizations, as well as differences in the educational background, tradition and philosophy of the top management group, will result in different answers to similar organizational problems.[91]

Two studies of German management provide evidence that throws some light on the different patterns of organizational change in Du Pont as compared with Fw H. Hartmann observes that the "typical" German firm has a highly centralized decision-making structure with three tiers of top management—the supervisory board, the executive committee, and the members of upper management.[92] Ruedi and Lawrence, in their comparison of a German firm in the plastics industry ("Plastik AG") with six American firms in the same industry, also note that "the salient organizational factor in Plastik AG was its hierarchical information and decision structure."[93] Their observation concerning the highly formal mode of communication in their German firm is particularly striking:

The vertical communications network relied heavily on a formal letter-writing and signing procedure. Plastik AG followed the standard German practice of limiting the right to sign letters (the Prokura) to senior middle management, although most of the detailed information was supplied by lower echelons. Since the people who sign letters were responsible for the letters' contents, senior managers spent about one third of their time reading letters prepared by people below them.[94]

In an effort to explain some of these findings as well as the general observation that American firms in the chemical industry are more effective than German firms, Reudi and Lawrence reported differences in values between Germans and Americans, including the fact that Germans have a "stronger desire for explicit and stable relationships, structures and methods" and a lower need for achievement.[95] By way of interpreting some of these differences, Reudi and Lawrence state:

These general tendencies are interwoven with the many institutions of German life and manifest themselves as organizational characteristics. The strong authoritarian relationship of the father, for instance, is transferred to a strong subordinate-superior role-set in the university (where a Ph.D. candidate spends an average of seven years as a particular professor's assistant) and to a similar subordinate-superior role-set in German business. This role-set is quite explicit and manifests itself as a "proper" sense of duty and loyalty to the superior.[96]

Thus an authoritarian family system evidently has a strong impact on organizational role behavior as well as on organizational design. Under the circumstances, it is easier to understand Staehle's finding of the greater reluctance on the part of the management of Fw H as compared with that of Du Pont to decentralize more fully its structure, notwithstanding the pressures of a highly diversified product-line.

EXAMPLES OF ORGANIZATIONAL EFFECTS ON SOCIAL STRUCTURE

Organizational researchers have thus far largely neglected the study of the impact of organizations on social structure. This is understandable in view of the fact that the organizational environment is generally defined in much more circumscribed terms than the approach taken in this chapter. The emphasis in the organizational literature is predominantly on how organizations *adapt* to an uncertain, dynamic, and threatening environment, not on whether and under what conditions they take the initiative to *modify* their environment and thereby further their objectives. Thus the recent increase in research on the functioning of boards of directors is oriented to ascertaining how the size and composition of boards affect the flow of resources and support from the environment and in turn the level of organizational effectiveness.[97] In addition studies of interlocking directorates—which is clearly an important mechanism for integrating the organizational elites in a society—document that they are extensive and enduring, notwithstanding the fact that they are often in violation of the Clayton Act of 1914.[98] Such studies fall short of ascertaining the impact organizations with interlocked directorates have on the social structure. At least one impediment to such research is that organizational effects are difficult to observe. Another is the failure to recognize that organizations capable of modifying their environments engage in what is essentially *political* action. They use their resources and sanctioning power against actual or potential opponents to alter events—role behavior of target individuals, organizational behavior, law, and other institutionalized arrangements. Clearly, organizations capable of engaging in this type of political action are large in size relative to the environing social system, be it a community or a society. Several illustrations of this proposition may be helpful.

The impact of the Du Pont Company and the Du Pont family on Delaware is a case in point. Commanding vast resources and sanctioning power, partly due to the fact that it employs 11 percent of the state's labor force and generates 20 percent of the state's gross product, Du Pont has succeeded in modifying and controlling events in Delaware and beyond.[99] To begin with, the company was instrumental in 1897 in the passage of a corporation law that provided for the maximum of rights for the corporation and its management.[100] Several legislators "prominent in Du Pont affairs" and one family member were active in the legislative deliberations.[101] In the 1967 revisions of the General Corporation Law, Du Pont attorneys appeared before the revision commission, and in 1969 a Du Pont family member, who was in the legislature, introduced the amendments.[102] "Instead of publicly opposing bills that might harm the company, Du Pont first tries to obtain an amendment. . . ."[103] To prepare amendments to bills the company opposes, the company "maintains a large Legislative Affairs Department whose lawyers scan thousands of proposed federal bills."[104] One bill that received the support of "Du Pont-related legislators" and of the governor himself, who was a former executive of Du Pont, provided for a reduction of capital gains taxes.[105]

As impressive as Du Pont's effect is on the social structure of Delaware, its impact—along with that of other multinational enterprises—on the various host countries in which it has subsidiaries is at least as great, if not greater.

When the large MNE [multinational enterprise] enters a local economy, buys out local entrepreneurs, bids up local wages, gets favorable credit and tax treatment, it may rationalize its own organization structure and market control. But for the indigenous economy, it removes at a stroke the scarce resources which can serve the industrial strategy of that country, even if that strategy is not the same as that of the MNE. Once local entrepreneurs are in the service of the MNE, they are not available to pursue local economic goals, but those of the MNE pursuing its own "global" strategy. Once local risk capital is pooled in the service of the MNE, it is not available to foster economic development locally.[106]

This view of how the multinational corporation can modify the institutional structure of the host countries in which it operates has led McMillan to refer to this type of corporation as a "control agent."[107]

A recent United States Senate study documents the resources, if not the sanctioning power, of multinationals by ranking 99 nation-states and world-wide corporations according to GNP or gross annual sales. Of the 99 ranked entities 40 are multinational corporations. In commenting on this rank order, the authors of the Senate report observed that:

If General Motors were a nation, its "economy" would be the 23rd largest in the world, with Standard Oil (New Jersey) and Ford not far behind.[108]

Because of the magnitude of their resources as well as sanctioning power, multinationals have been very effective on the whole in *modifying*—as well as *adapting* to—the multitude of societal and cultural contexts in which they are located.

SOME IMPLICATIONS OF THE SOCIAL-STRUCTURAL MODEL FOR FUTURE ORGANIZATIONAL RESEARCH

If the exploratory social-structural model of organizations outlined above—which is admittedly programmatic in nature—were to become the point of departure for research, it would require a new research strategy, both substantively and methodologically. Instead of treating members of organizations and organizations themselves as though they were isolates, the unit of analysis would be interactions among individuals—as reflected in their role-sets, in status-sets, and in interactions among organizations, as evidenced by their organization-sets. And rather than assume that these interactions are stable, it would also be important to ascertain changes over time in role-sets, status-sets and organization-sets. Moreover, it would be necessary to take account of how specific dimensions of the institutional spheres of a society relate to the interactional components of social structure, namely, role-sets, status-sets, status-sequences, and organization-sets.

With some noteworthy exceptions, the prevailing research strategy in the study of organizations is atomistic and static. This is a function largely of the *organization* of research on organizations and of inadequate resources. Individual researchers or pairs of researchers with modest or minuscule budgets find it more expedient to gather data from isolated, rather than from interacting, individuals and organizations. In addition, as Coleman has pointed out, "survey research methods have often led to the neglect of social structure and of the relations among individuals."[109] In their pioneering study of role conflict and role ambiguity, Kahn and his colleagues traced the role-sets of 53 status-occupants in six industrial organizations.[110] After conducting interviews with each of the 53 individuals, they then interviewed 381 "role senders" or "role partners," an average of about 7 role partners for each of the focal persons or status occupants of the 53 role-sets.[111] The rationale for this kind of survey is clearly different from that of the conventional survey in which the individuals comprising the sample are treated in isolation from one another.

An example of a hypothetical study informed by our social-structural model might clarify some of the issues involved. Starting with the assumption that a general problem in organization theory, as we have seen, is the need to explain variation in structure, processes, and effectiveness, at least two organizations—preferably a sample—markedly different in, say, performance, might be selected in at least two societies. Likely candidates for such a comparison are a chemical firm in the United States matched on size and product-line with a chemical firm in West Germany, in view of the finding by Ruedi and Lawrence that American firms are substantially more effective than German firms.[112] After first measuring the structure of the two firms (with the aid of some of the scales developed by the Aston group or some of the indicators employed by Blau and Schoenherr)[113] and their processes (such as recruitment, socialization, and communication), each organization would then be considered as a focal organization for a social-structural analysis. The role-sets of all boundary personnel would be mapped, along with their status-sets and status-sequences. In the process of gathering such data, the organizations comprising the input and output organization-sets would be identified and the interactions among them ascertained. The institutional ramifications of the status-sets and organization-sets—economic, legal, political, educational, familial, and the like—would then be the focus of inquiry. To deepen their understanding of the relationship between some of the institutional sectors of the society and the organization-sets, the researchers would probably iterate the process of mapping role-sets, status-sets, status-sequences, and organization-sets by selecting the most salient elements in the input and output organization-sets of the two firms and treating them in turn as focal organizations.

In sum, the research strategy based on a social-structural model of organizations has four distinctive features: First, it is *comparative,* not in the sense of a study of a sample of organizations in a given society using multivariate analysis but in the cross-national or cross-societal meaning of the term.[114] Second, it is *longitudinal* because of the importance for the structure and functioning of the focal organization of measuring status-sequences in role-sets and status-sets and changes in organization-sets. Third, it is *interdisciplinary* because of the macrolevel focus that presupposes the need to integrate the knowledge of several disciplines such as sociology, economics, political science, and anthropology. Finally, it is *collaborative* in its *modus operandi.* The academic model of the individual researcher is manifestly inappropriate for the size of the research effort that is required.[115] Not even a team of two or a three researchers would be capable of coordinating such a study. Instead, teams of organizational researchers in several countries would have to be organized to pursue a common research goal. If they were to succeed in integrating the research efforts of widely dispersed team members, all of whom would probably consider themselves professional peers, they would probably discover the need to design a research organization that is *collegial* rather than *hierarchical* in structure.

SOME CONJECTURES ABOUT THE DESIGN OF ORGANIZATIONS OF THE FUTURE

Even if futurology were a more developed field than it is, it would still be hazardous to forecast the design of future organizations. The diversity of forecasts on this subject recently articulated by social scientists is proof of the state of the art.[116] Although few would question the twin assumptions that organizations will continue to exist in the future and to function as primary instruments for achieving a multitude of collective purposes, the question whether they will undergo any basic changes in design is still largely a matter of conjecture. In order not to stray too far from present reality in my conjectures, I shall take two organizations as prototypes of the design of future organizations—the multinational enterprise and the international nongovernmental organization (INGO).[117]

That an entity less inclusive than the nation-state can operate with quite manageable legal and political constraints in a variety of national contexts is itself a surprising development. Equally impressive is the rate of increase during the past two decades in foreign direct investment by American, Canadian, West European, and Japanese multinationals, and the rate of return on their investments. Whatever effects, functional or dysfunctional, multinationals are having on host countries, their financial success is partly a function of their innovative organizational designs. By adopting a divisional structure, multinationals have succeeded simultaneously in decentralizing and maintaining a high degree of headquarters control over geographically dispersed operations. Recent technological developments, particularly computer technology, have made it possible for corporate headquarters staffs to monitor their far-flung subsidiaries. They also systemically scan their external environments for information essential for decision making.

A recent study of the information sources used by executives at the corporate headquarters of United States multinationals found that the overwhelming majority of executives rely on external sources of information. Abroad, however, they rely primarily on sources of information internal to their companies. This finding, according to the author, "explains one of the major strengths of a multinational company—it is a worldwide intelligence gathering and processing system."[118]

By comparison with the multinational enterprise and its vast resources and sanctioning power, the class of nonprofit and nongovernmental organizations (often referred to as INGOs) seems quite feeble. However, they do have at least three significant attributes in common: They are both nongovernmental entities; both types of organizations operate in numerous countries around the world; and both have greatly expanded in the past two decades. The population of INGOs includes a wide spectrum of special-purpose organizations—economic, political, religious, educational, scientific, technological, legal, recreational, and so on. As of 1968 there were approximately 1,900 INGOs, and about one-half of them were international professional associations concerned with contributing to the development of knowledge and facilitating communication among professionals in different countries.[119]

Although membership in INGOs is concentrated in industrialized countries, especially those with democratic political institutions and a pluralistic ideology, the rate of participation is increasing in other countries, particularly in the newly established independent states in Africa.[120] Since the growth of INGOs, according to Skjelsbaek, is largely due to economic and technological developments—and assuming such developments are not interrupted in the future—he predicts a remarkable expansion of INGOs: If the annual growth of 5 percent continues, the population of INGOs by the year 2000 could reach 9,049.[121] In addition, he hypothesizes that interaction among INGOs as well as between INGOs and international governmental organizations will increase. If this hypothesis is confirmed, the influence of INGOs in international decision making will very likely increase substantially.

Given these facts about INGOs and multinational corporations, can these two disparate types of organizations serve as prototypes of the future design of organizations in general? Yes, provided the prognosis of several students of international relations on the progressive development of "transnational interactions" and a "world society" proves to be correct.[122] Nye and Keohane use the term "transnational interactions" to describe "the movement of tangible or intangible items across stable boundaries when at least one actor is not an agent of a government or an intergovernmental organization."[123] Similarly, Burton's concept of a world society characterizes the emergence of a system of interactions transcending the boundaries of nation-states: "The evidence is before us in terms of communications, movements of people, the epidemic spread of ideas and ideologies, transnational corporations, functional institutions that are universal, tourism, migration, sympathies and support across boundaries and other increased transactions associated with the post-1945 era."[124] In terms of this prognosis, INGOs and multinational enterprises are both "transnational actors" on the world scene. Although Gerstacher, the president of Dow Chemical Company, does not use either of the concepts of transnational interactions or world society, he evidently subscribes to the prognosis of Keohane, Nye, and Burton in his assessment of the future of multinational corporations:

We appear to be moving strongly in the direction of what will not be really multinational or international companies as we know them today, but what we might call "anational" companies—companies without any nationality, belonging to all nationalities. We generally conceive of the multinational company as one having a fixed nationality (that of the parent company) but operating in many nations. With the blossoming of a true world economy these multinational bees, whether they are American or British, German or French, Russian or Japanese, will be establishing more hives in the farther fields.[125]

If progress toward a world society and transnational interactions continues in the coming decades, it is a safe conjecture that:

1. A substantial proportion of the millions of organizations throughout the world will tend to become *transnational* in their organizational design and in their scope of operations.
2. As a consequence of what might be conceived as a transnational strategy, organization-sets will tend to become larger in size and more complex in their interactional networks.
3. Rapidly advancing production, transportation, and communication technologies will become increasingly significant determinants of organizational design.
4. With the aid of computer technology, the interaction networks in organization-sets will become more visible to organizational members and nonmembers alike.

5. Organizational members will tend to adopt an increasingly cosmopolitan role orientation that will pose severe problems for the management of organizations.

6. In searching for solutions to recurrent problems of organizational effectiveness, organizations will increasingly experiment with a variety of nonhierarchical designs, including, for example, collegial systems of authority.[126]

If any of these conjectures about the design of organizations of the future are confirmed by events, it hardly follows that organizations will become standardized in their structure and functions. Some organizational researchers who are searching for organizational imperatives would welcome a trend toward uniformity in organizational design. Such a development, if it were to come to pass, would obviously facilitate the discovery of relationships between such variables as size, formalization, specialization, centralization, technological complexity, and so on that are so robust as to be free of the effects of culture and social structure.[127] This admirable goal is likely to be attained only if two events transpire: (1) the decline of the nation-state, and (2) the convergence of the world's economic and political systems. Barring such a global transformation by the year 2000—the current target date for many conjectures—organizational researchers will no doubt continue to wrestle with problems of measuring the impact of social structure on organizations for many years to come. And organizational practitioners will continue to be bedeviled by a multitude of management problems that have their roots in the social structure of society and that impede progress toward achieving organizational goals.

NOTES

1. Talcott Parsons, *Structure and Process in Modern Societies* (Glencoe, Ill.: The Free Press, 1960), p. 44.

2. Arthur L. Stinchcombe, "Social Structure and Organizations," in James G. March, ed., *Handbook of Organizations* (Chicago: Rand McNally, 1965), pp. 142–93; Stanley H. Udy, Jr., "The Comparative Analysis of Organizations," in James G. March, ed., *Handbook of Organizations* (Chicago: Rand McNally, 1965), pp. 678–709; William A. Glaser, "Cross-National Comparisons of the Factory," *Journal of Comparative Administration* 3 (May 1971): 83–117.

3. William M. Evan, ed., *Interorganizational Relations: Selected Readings* (London: Penguin Books, 1976).

4. William M' Evan, "The Organization-Set: Toward a Theory of Interorganizational Relations," in James D. Thompson, ed., *Approaches to Organizational Design* (Pittsburgh: University of Pittsburgh Press, 1966), p. 188.

5. Paul M. Hirsch, "Organizational Analysis and Industrial Sociology in the 1970's: An Instance of Cultural Lag." Paper presented at the annual meeting of the American Sociological Association in New York City, August 1973, p. 24 (mimeo).

6. Peter M. Blau, "The Comparative Study of Organizations," *Industrial and Labor Relations Review* 18 (April 1965): 323–38.

7. *Ibid.*, p. 330.

8. Ray Jurkovich, "A Core Typology of Organizational Environments," *Administrative Science Quarterly* 19 (September 1974): 380–94.

9. D. S. Pugh, D. J. Hickson, C. R. Hinings, and C. Turner, "The Context of Organization Structures," *Administrative Science Quarterly* 14 (March 1969): 91–114.

10. Charles J. McMillan, "The Structure of Work Organizations Across Societies," *Academy of Management Journal* 16 (1973): 555–69; D. J. Hickson, C. R. Hinings, C. J. McMillan, and J. P. Schwitter, "The Culture-Free Context of Organization Structure: A National Comparison," *Sociology* 8 (January 1974): 59–80.

11. Pugh et al., "The Context of Organization Structures."

12. Wolf V. Heydebrand, ed., *Comparative Organizations* (Englewood Cliffs, N.J.: Prentice-Hall, 1973), pp. 21–22.

13. Pugh *et al.*, "The Context of Organization Structures," p. 111.

14. Hickson *et al* "The Culture-Free Context of Organization Structure"; William R. Dill, "Environment as an Influence on Managerial Autonomy," *Administrative Science Quarterly* 2 (March 1958): 409–43; James D. Thompson, *Organizations in Action* (New York: McGraw-Hill Book Co., 1967).

15. Sol Levine and Paul E. White, "Exchange as a Conceptual Framework for the Study of Interorganizational Relationships," *Administrative Science Quarterly* 5 (March 1961): 583–601.

16. *Ibid.*, p. 597.

17. *Ibid.*

18. Dill, "Environment as an Influence on Managerial Autonomy"; Thompson, *Organizations in Action.*

19. Dill, "Environment as an Influence on Managerial Autonomy," p. 410.

20. *Ibid.*, p. 424.

21. Udy, "Comparative Analysis of Organizations," p. 687.

22. Anant R. Negandhi, "A Model for Analyzing Organizations in Cross-Cultural Settings: A Conceptual Scheme and Some Research Findings," in Anant R. Negandhi, ed., *Modern Organizational Theory* (Kent, Ohio: Kent State University Press, 1973), p. 315.

23. *Ibid.*, pp. 287, 315.

24. *Ibid.*, pp. 285–312.

25. Paul R. Lawrence and Jay W. Lorsch, *Organization and Environment* (Boston, Mass.: Division of Research, Graduate School of Business Administration, Harvard University, 1967).

26. Raymond Boudon, *The Uses of Structuralism* (London: Heinemann, 1971), pp. 4–5; Ivan Vallier, "Empirical Comparisons of Social Structure: Leads and Lags," in Ivan Vallier, ed., *Comparative Methods in Sociology* (Berkeley: University of California Press, 1971), p. 227; Eleanor B. Sheldon and Wilbert E. Moore, "Monitoring Social Change in American Society," in Eleanor B. Sheldon and Wilbert E. Moore, eds., *Indicators of Social Change* (New York: Russell Sage Foundation, 1968), p. 5.

27. A. R. Radcliffe-Brown, *Structure and Function in Primitive Society* (New York: The Free Press, 1952), p. 190; "Introduction", in A. R. Radcliffe-Brown and Daryll Forde, eds., *African Systems of Kinship and Marriage* (London: Oxford University Press, 1950), p. 43.

28. S. F. Nadel, *The Theory of Social Structure* (Glencoe, Ill.: The Free Press, 1957), pp. 12, 153.

29. Raymond Firth, *Elements of Social Organization* (London: Watts and Co., 1951), p. 31.

30. Claude Lévi-Strauss, *Structural Anthropology* (New York: Basic Books, 1963), p. 279.

31. Talcott Parsons, *The Social System* (Glencoe, Ill.: The Free Press, 1951), pp. 25, 114.

32. Neil J. Smelser, *Essays in Sociological Explanation* (Englewood Cliffs, N.J.: Prentice-Hall, 1968), pp. 148, 150.

33. Udy, "Comparative Analysis of Organizations," p. 489.

34. Sheldon and Moore, "Monitoring Social Change in American Society," p. 5.

35. Robert K. Merton, *Social Theory and Social Structure,* rev. ed., (Glencoe, Ill.: The Free Press, 1957), pp. 162, 370.

36. Stinchcombe, "Social Structure and Organizations," p. 142.

37. Ithiel de Sola Pool, "Computer Simulations of Total Societies," in Samuel Z. Klausner, ed., *The Study of Total Societies* (Garden City, N.Y.: Doubleday, 1967); Vallier, "Empirical Comparisons of Social Structure"; Boudon, *Uses of Structuralism,* pp. 140–41.

38. Nadel, *Theory of Social Structure.*

39. Guy E. Swanson, "Frameworks for Comparative Research: Structural Anthropology and the Theory of Action," in Ivan Vallier, ed., *Comparative Methods in Sociology* (Berkeley: University of California, 1971).

40. Mark S. Granovetter, "The Strength of Weak Ties," *American Journal of Sociology* 78 (May 1973): 13 60–80.

41. Raymond A. Bauer, ed., *Social Indicators* (Cambridge, Mass.: M.I.T. Press, 1966); Eleanor B. Sheldon and Wilbert E. Moore, eds., *Indicators of Social Change* (New York: Russell Sage Foundation, 1968).

42. Andrew Shonfield and Stella Shaw, eds., *Social Indicators and Social Policy* (London: Heinemann Educational Books, 1972); Helmut Klages, "Assessment of an Attempt at a System of Social Indicators," *Policy Sciences* 4 (September 1973): 249–61; A. Aidenoff and R. Johnston, "International Work on Social Indicators," a paper presented at the annual meeting of the International Studies Association in St. Louis, March 1974 (mimeo).

43. Eleanor B. Sheldon and Kenneth C. Land, "Social Reporting for the 1970's," *Policy Sciences* 3 (July 1972): 137–51; Elaine Carlisle, "The Conceptual Structure of Social Indicators," in Andrew Shonfield and Stella Shaw, eds., *Social Indicators and Social Policy* (London: Heinemann Educational Books, 1972).

44. Richard L. Merritt and Stein Rokkan, *Comparing Nations* (New Haven: Yale University Press, 1966; C. L. Taylor, *Aggregate Data Analysis* (The Hague: Mouton and Co., 1968); C. S. Taylor and M. C. Hudson, *World Handbook of Political and Social Indicators* (New Haven: Yale University Press, 1972).

45. J. A. Barnes, "Class and Committees in the Norwegian Island Parish," *Human Relations* 7 (February 1954): 39–58; J. Clyde Mitchell, ed., *Social Networks in Urban Situations* (Manchester: Manchester University Press, 1969); Jeremy Boissevain and J. Clyde Mitchell, eds., *Network Analysis Studies in Human Interaction* (The Hague: Mouton and Co., 1973).

46. Mitchell, *Social Networks in Urban Situations,* pp. 1–2.

47. Elizabeth Jane Bott, *Family and Social Networks* (London: Tavistock Publications, 1957); Mitchell, *Social Networks in Urban Situations,* pp. 12–20; J. A. Barnes, "Graph Theory and Social Networks: A Technical Comment on Connectedness and Connectivity," *Sociology* 3 (May 1969): 215–32.

48. Vallier, "Empirical Comparisons of Social Structure," pp. 213–16.

49. Stinchcombe, "Social Structure and Organizations," pp. 145–69.

50. Herman Turk, "Interorganizational Networks in Urban Society: Initial Perspectives and Comparative Research," *American Sociological Review* 35 (February 1970): 1–19; *Interorganizational Activation in Urban Communities* (Washington, D.C.: American Sociological Association, 1973).

51. Merton, *Social Theory and Social Structure,* p. 369.

52. Alvin W. Gouldner, "Cosmopolitans and Locals: Toward an Analysis of Latent Social Roles—I, II," *Administration Science Quarterly* 1 and 2 (December 1957 and March 1958): 281–306; 440–80.

53. Talcott Parsons, *Structure and Process in Modern Societies* (Glencoe, Ill.: The Free Press, 1960), pp. 59–62.

54. Evan, "The Organization-Set," p. 180; Evan, "An Organization-Set Model of Interorganizational Relations" in M. F. Tuite, M. Radnor and R. K. Chisholm, eds., *Interorganizational Decision Making* (Chicago: Aldine Publishing Co.), pp. 188–90.

55. J. Boddewyn and A. Kapoor, "The External Relations of American Enterprises," *International Studies Quarterly* 16 (December 1972): 433–53.

56. For purposes of the present discussion, organizational structure is used in a manner analogous to that of the Aston Group, D. S. Pugh, D. J. Hickson, C. R. Hinings, and C. Turner, "Dimensions of Organization Structure," *Administrative Science Quarterly* 13 (June 1968): 65–106; Peter M. Blau and Richard A. Schoenherr, *The Structure of Organizations* (New York: Basic Books, 1971). The same three organizational processes—recruitment, socialization, and communication—have been selected as were used in Chapter 15 of the present volume. The concept of organizational effectiveness is employed in a multidimensional sense of productivity, profitability, performance, and so on. For a systematic treatment of this concept, see my paper, "Organization Theory and Organizational Effectiveness," *Organization and Administrative Sciences* 7 (1976): 15–28.

57. Merton, *Social Theory and Social Structure,* p. 380.

58. Alex Inkeles and P. H. Rossi, "National Comparisons of Occupational Prestige," *American Journal of Sociology* 61 (January 1956): 329–39.

59. William J. Goode, "A Theory of Role Strain," *American Sociological Review* 25 (August 1960): 483–96; Merton, *Social Theory and Social Structure,* pp. 371–80.

60. Stinchcombe, "Social Structure and Organizations," pp. 171–176.

61. Gouldner, "Cosmopolitans and Locals."

62. William M. Evan and Ezra G. Levin, "Status-Set and Role-Set Conflicts of the Stockbroker: A Problem in the Sociology of Law," *Social Forces* 45 (September 1966): 73–83.

63. James Phelan and Robert Pozen, *The Company State* (New York: Grossman Publishers, 1973).

64. *Ibid.,* pp. 9–13.

65. Chester I. Barnard, *The Functions of the Executive* (Cambridge, Mass.: Harvard University Press, 1938), p. 224.

66. Merton, *Social Theory and Social Structure,* p. 382.

67. Michael Stern, "British Labor's Abolition Plan Scraping Raw Nerve of Class," *New York Times* (December 19, 1973), p. 41.

68. Phelan and Pozen, *The Company State,* p. 113.

69. Albert D. Biderman, "The Retired Military," in Roger W. Little, ed., *Handbook of*

Military Institutions (Beverly Hills, Cal.: Sage Publications, 1971), pp. 153–157; Phelan and Pozen, *The Company State,* pp. 154–55.

70. Gordon B. Baty, William M. Evan, and Terry W. Rothermel, "Personnel Flows as Interorganizational Relations," *Administrative Science Quarterly* 16 (December 1971): 430–43.

71. Phelan and Pozen, *The Company State,* pp. 427–28.

72. Melville Dalton, *Men Who Manage* (John Wiley & Sons, 1959), pp. 181, 185.

73. See Chapters 9 and 11 of the present volume.

74. U.S. Bureau of the Census, *Statistical Abstract of the United States,* 95th ed. (Washington, D.C.: Government Printing Office, 1974, pp. 46, 477; U.S. Census of Governments, *Governmental Organization,* vol. 1.(Washington, D.C.: U.S. Government Printing Office, 1973); Margaret Fisk, ed., *Encyclopedia of Associations National Organizations of the U.S.,* vol. 1 (Detroit, Mich.: Gale Research Co., 1973).

75. Karl Marx, *A Contribution to the Critique of Political Economy* (Chicago: Charles H. Kerr, 1904), pp. 11–13; J. O. Hertzler, *Social Institutions* (Lincoln, Nebr.: University of Nebraska Press, 1946); Talcott Parsons and Neil J. Smelser, *Economy and Society* (Glencoe, Ill.: The Free Press, 1956), pp. 18–28; S. N. Eisenstadt, *The Political Systems of Empires* (New York: The Free Press, 1963), pp. 376–78.

76. Richard N. Farmer and Barry M. Richman, *Comparative Management and Economic Progress* (Homewood, Ill.: Richard D. Irwin, Inc., 1965), pp. 15–45; Stinchcombe, "Social Structure and Organizations."

77. Farmer and Richman, *Comparative Management and Economic Progress,* pp. 29–30.

78. *Ibid.*

79. Barry Richman and Melvyn Copen, *International Management and Economic Development* (New York: McGraw-Hill Book Co., 1972), p. 43.

80. Stinchcombe, "Social Structure and Organizations, pp. 143, 151.

81. *Ibid.,* p. 169.

82. Melvin Tumin, "Some Disfunctions of Institutional Imbalances," *Behavioral Science* 1 (July 1956): 218–23.

83. C. Wright Mills, *The Power Elite* (New York: Oxford University Press, 1956), p. 6.

84. Talcott Parsons, *Societies: Evolutionary and Comparative Perspectives* (Englewood Cliffs, N.J.: Prentice-Hall, 1966); and Parsons, *The System of Modern Societies* (Englewood Cliffs, N.J.: Prentice-Hall, 1971).

85. Max Weber, *Max Weber on Law in Economy and Society,* ed. Max Rheinstein (Cambridge, Mass.: Harvard University Press, 1954), pp. 61–64.

86. Alfred D. Chandler, Jr., *Strategy and Structure* (Cambridge, Mass.: M.I.T. Press, 1962); Derek F. Channon, *The Strategy and Structure of British Enterprise* (Boston, Mass.: Division of Research, Graduate School of Business Administration, 1973).

87. Channon, *Strategy and Structure of British Enterprise,* pp. 88, 216–17.

88. *Ibid.,* p. 217.

89. W. H. Staehle, "A Comparison of Organization Building at Du Pont and Farbwerke Hoechst," *Management International Review* 10, no. 6 (1970): 33–44.

90. *Ibid.,* p. 40.

91. *Ibid.,* p. 44.

92. Heinz Hartmann, *Authority and Organization in German Management* (Princeton, N.J.: Princeton University Press, 1959).

93. André Ruedi and Paul R. Lawrence, "Organizations in Two Cultures," in Jay W. Lorsch and Paul R. Lawrence, eds., *Studies in Organization Design* (Homewood, Ill.: Richard D. Irwin and the Dorsey Press, 1970).

94. *Ibid.*, p. 58.

95. *Ibid.*, p. 70.

96. *Ibid.*, p. 71.

97. Jeffrey Pfeffer, "Size and Composition of Corporate Boards of Directors: The Organization and Its Environment," *Administrative Science Quarterly* 17 (June 1972): 218–28; and "Size, Composition and Function of Hospital Boards of Directors: A Study of Organization-Environment Linkage," *Administrative Science Quarterly* 18 (September 1973): 349–64.

98. Peter C. Dooley, "The Interlocking Directorate," *American Economic Review* 59 (June 1969): 314–23; Joel H. Levine, "The Sphere of Influence," *American Sociological Review* 59 (February 1972): 14–27; Thomas R. Dye, E. R. Declercq, and J. W. Pickering, "Concentration, Specialization, and Interlocking Among Institutional Elites," *Social Science Quarterly* 54 (June 1973): 8–28.

99. Phelan and Pozen, *The Company State*, p. 1.

100. *Ibid.*, p. 163.

101. *Ibid.*

102. *Ibid.*, p. 317.

103. *Ibid.*, p. 318.

104. *Ibid.*

105. *Ibid.*, p. 344.

106. Charles J. McMillan, "Social and Political Implications of the Multinational Enterprise," in The Open University, *The Problem of Organizations* (Walton Hall, Milton Keynes: The Open University Press, 1974).

107. *Ibid.*, p. 40.

108. U.S. Senate Committee on Finance, *The Multinational Corporation and the World Economy* (Washington, D.C.: Government Printing Office, 1973).

109. James S. Coleman, "Relational Analysis: The Study of Social Organizations with Survey Methods," in Amitai Etzioni, ed., *Complex Organizations* (New York: Holt, Rinehart and Winston, 1961), pp. 441–64.

110. Robert L, Kahn, Donald M. Wolf, Robert P. Quinn, J. D. Snoek, and Robert B. Rosenthal, *Organizational Stress: Studies in Role Conflict and Ambiguity* (New York: John Wiley & Sons, 1964).

111. *Ibid.*, p. 41.

112. Ruedi and Lawrence, "Organizations in Two Cultures."

113. Pugh *et al.*, "Dimensions of Organization Structure;" Blau and Schoenherr, *The Structure of Organizations*, p. 28.

114. Blau and Schoenherr, *Structure of Organizations*, pp. 6–7; Wolf V. Heydebrand, "The Study of Organizations," in Wolf V. Heydebrand, ed., *Comparative Organizations* (Englewood Cliffs, N.J.: Prentice-Hall, 1973), pp. 31–56; Glaser, "Cross-National Comparisons of the Factory"; William M. Evan, ed., "Organizational Research Across National and Cultural Boundaries," *International Studies of Management and Organization* 5 (Spring, 1975): 3–113.

115. W. O. Hagstrom, "Traditional and Modern Forms of Scientific Teamwork," *Administrative Science Quarterly* 9 (December 1964): 241–63.

116. Warren G. Bennis, "A Funny Thing Happened on the Way to the Future," in Harold J. Leavitt and Louis R. Pondy, eds., *Readings in Managerial Psychology* (Chicago: University of Chicago Press, 1973), pp. 760–87; Bertram M. Gross, "An Organized Society?" *Public Administration Review* 33 (July–August 1973): 323–27; James D. Thompson, "Society's Frontiers for Organizing Activities," *Public Administration Review* 33 (July–August 1973): 327–35.

117. See Chapter 14 of the present volume.

118. Warren J. Keegan, "Multinational Scanning: A Study of the Information Sources Utilized by Headquarters Executives in Multinational Companies," *Administrative Science Quarterly* 19 (September 1974): 411–21.

119. Kjell Skjelsbaek, "The Growth of International Nongovernmental Organizations in the Twentieth Century," in Robert O. Keohane and Joseph S. Nye, Jr., eds., *Transnational Relations and World Politics* (Cambridge, Mass.: Harvard University Press, 1972), p. 75; William M. Evan, "International Sociological Association and the Internationalization of Sociology," *International Social Science Journal* 27 (1975): 385–93.

120. Skjelsbaek, "Growth of International Nongovernmental Organizations," pp. 82–83.

121. *Ibid.,* p. 84.

122. Joseph S. Nye, Jr., and Robert O. Keohane, "Transnational Relations and World Politics, in Robert O. Keohane and Joseph S. Nye, Jr., eds., *Transnational Relations and World Politics* (Cambridge, Mass.: Harvard University Press, 1972); John Burton, "International Relations or World Society," in J. W. Burton, A. J. R. Groom, C. R. Mitchell, A. V. S. Dereuck, *The Study of World Society: A London Perspective* (Pittsburgh: University of Pittsburgh, International Studies Association, 1974), p. 3–29.

123. Nye and Keohane, "Transnational Relations and World Politics," p. vii.

124. Burton *et al., The Study of World Society,* pp. 6–7.

125. Carl A. Gerstacker, "'Rebalancing' the Corporation," in White House Conference on the Industrial World Ahead, *A Look at Business in 1990* (Washington, D.C., Government Printing Office, 1972), p. 275.

126. William M. Evan, ed., *Organizational Experiments* (New York: Harper & Row, 1971).

127. D. J. Hickson *et al.,* "The Culture-Free Context of Organization Structure: A Tri-National Comparison," *Sociology* 8 (January, 1974): 59–80.

Author Index

297

Subject Index

305

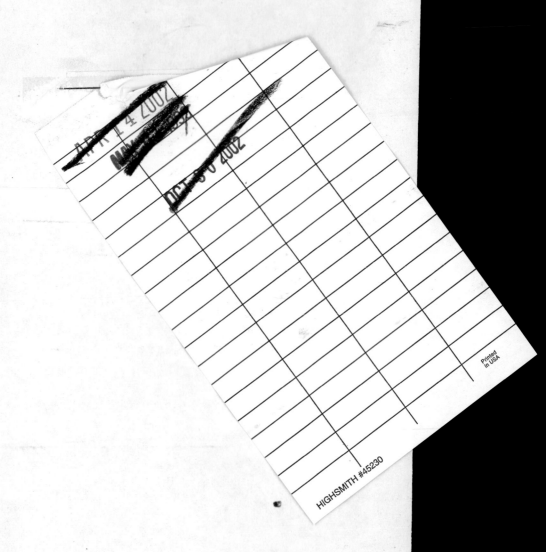